Praise for *The Voice Dialogue Facilitator's Handbook…*

"Miriam Dyak has gifted us with a heartfelt, beautifully written guide. I have facilitated for ten years, yet this Handbook elevated my sessions to exciting new levels of energetic sophistication. Every facilitator needs this book!"

Judith Hendin, NMT, Counselor, and Voice Dialogue Facilitator, Pennsylvania.

"I encourage all beginning or advanced facilitators to study this manual because it thoroughly covers the facilitation process. The Handbook describes in accurate detail the essential elements of Voice Dialogue work as well as many nuances of guiding a person in their Aware Ego process. Nothing is left out here, and especially important is the emphasis on the facilitator's own personal work. Over the years it has become clear to me that the strongest facilitators are those who are facilitated regularly and actively work with and develop the Aware Ego in their own lives. This manual is valuable for all of us in reflecting on our personal and professional use of the Stones' powerful perspectives and techniques."

Martha-Lou Wolff, Ph.D., International Teacher.

"Miriam Dyak has a gift for putting into clear, concise words Voice Dialogue's very energetic and subtle process. She has presented the work on a moment to moment perceptive level that I feel is so important for new facilitators to experience. I am excited to have a tool like this available for my own Voice Dialogue students!"

J'aime ona Pangaia, Voice Dialogue facilitator and teacher, Portland, Oregon.

"Miriam Dyak's Voice Dialogue Facilitator's Handbook fills a real need for those involved in serious exploration of the Voice Dialogue Method. Building on the work of Hal and Sidra Stone, it offers clear guidelines for those wishing to facilitate the process. Her approach honours the flexibility of the work while helping beginning and advanced trainees in the method towards mastery of the work. Miriam's combination of question and answer, sample facilitations, and clear exposition of the theory makes this one of the most useful handbooks I have read on any topic. Above all, the book is underpinned by Miriam's profound understanding of the Aware Ego process, the heart of this work."

Paul Gale Baker, B.A., Dip. Ed., principal of Victorian Voice Dialogue and Latona Consulting in Australia

"Thank you Miriam Dyak, for fulfilling a collective need for our progressively evolving Voice Dialogue Community by creating 'The Voice Dialogue Facilitator's Handbook.' The Handbook reflects The Voice Dialogue Process in its balanced expression and honoring of the Selves, in relationship to the essential and continual strengthening of The Aware Ego. I am grateful to you for gifting us with a living tool for furthering the work of my father, Hal Stone, and Sidra Stone."

Judith Tamar Stone M.A. C.H.T., Executive Director of Voice Dialogue Connection International, Creator of "The Body Dialogue Process," Los Angeles, California

"My selves were delighted with the keen insights and practical tools Miriam has set forth in this exciting handbook. She unfolds Voice Dialogue with a rare ability to help readers access and integrate this multifaceted work. It is a must for every facilitator."

Sindona Casteel, MFCC and Director of Mountains and Rivers Voice Dialogue Center, California.

"This Handbook is an excellent addition to the Voice Dialogue Library. It provides a strong introduction to the specifics of Voice Dialogue, while being gently supportive of the learning process. I am profoundly impressed with Miriam's work on energetics, which is a cornerstone of all Voice Dialogue work. Miriam has explained energetics in an imaginative, yet concrete fashion. In addition, she has given us many new concepts to utilize in our facilitations, and in our teaching sessions: these include the facilitator as an energy coach, the energy journal, and energy field exercises."

Dassie Hoffman, Dance Therapist, Voice Dialogue facilitator and teacher, MA, ADTR, AMHC in New York City

"Miriam has designed a facilitation handbook that not only embodies the essence of the development of the Aware Ego, but also offers us a practical guide for working with clients in an easy and thorough manner."

Karinna James, Change Management Consultant, Vancouver, B.C.

"This Handbook presents a clear, comprehensive and practical guide to the Voice Dialogue Method for both experienced and new facilitators. It provides the facilitator with in-depth examples of alternative ways to handle a Voice Dialogue session. Most importantly, it skillfully weaves the 'how-to' and 'step-by-step' approach to Voice Dialogue facilitation with an understanding of the Psychology of Selves, the application of energetics, and the development of the Aware Ego process. This is a 'must-read and use' handbook for both the seasoned and new facilitator."

Francine Pinto, Voice Dialogue teacher and facilitator, B.A., J.D., Northern Virginia and Washington, D.C.

"This book is a joy! Miriam is a magical and intuitive Voice Dialogue facilitator herself and she brings the essence of this work to life in her clear and practical guide for other facilitators. Reading it is like attending a marvellous workshop in book form and she communicates so well the wonderful teachings of Hal and Sidra Stone. It is a 'must' for anyone interested in facilitating the process of psychospiritual growth and transformation. It will intrigue the newcomer and be a welcome companion for the experienced Voice Dialogue facilitator. Thanks Miriam!"

Mary Langley, Organizational Effectiveness Consultant and Personal Growth Counsellor, Calgary, Alberta

The Voice Dialogue

Facilitator's Handbook

Part I

By

Miriam Dyak

With illustrations by Suzanne Perot

L.I.F.E. Energy Press
Living In Full Expression
Seattle, Washington

Copyright © 1999 Miriam Dyak

Published by L.I.F.E. Energy Press, 6523 California Ave. SW #193, Seattle, WA 98136

Editorial collaborator: Richard Berger
Copy editor: Jamie Streichler
Cover Design and Illustrations: Suzanne Perot
Page Layout and Graphics Tuning: Karl Bettinger

This entire publication was created on Apple Macintosh computers. Writing was done using Filemaker Pro 3.0 and Microsoft Word 5.1 on a Powerbook 180c. Page layout was done on a Power Macintosh G3 computer, using Adobe Pagemaker 6.5. Illustrations were scanned on a Linotype-Hell scanner at 300dpi. Graphics and illustrations were tuned in Adobe Photoshop 4.01. Section and chapter graphic titles were created in Aldus TypeTwister 1.0. Body type is set in 10.5 pt. Palatino. Zaph Dingbats is used for bullets. All products are trademarks of their respective companies, and acknowledgment is hereby given. Our printer is Gilliland Printing in Arkansas City, Kansas. *The Handbook* text was printed on a Miehle/Roland RZK 2-color, 40 inch press, the cover was printed on a Komori 6-color, 40 inch press, and the full-color Map of Personia was printed on a Miehle/ Roland RZK 2-color, 40 inch press. *The Handbook* is printed on recycled 62# Halopaque Antique and cover stock is 12 point Carolina, coated one side.

FIRST EDITION

Printed in the USA

Library of Congress Cataloging-in-Publication Data
Dyak, Miriam.

The voice dialogue facilitator's handbook, part I: a step by step guide to working with the aware ego/ Miriam Dyak. – 1st ed.

1. Human potential movement – Study and teaching.   2. Choice (Psychology) – Study and teaching.   3. Self-actualization (Psychology) – Study and teaching.   4. Individuation (Psychology) – Study and teaching. I. Title.

BF637.H85   158.1/071   98-94077
                                        Publisher-supplied CIP

ISBN 0-9668390-0-5

Important Information

The physical, emotional, and spiritual health of you, your loved ones, and those in your care is important. Treat this *Handbook* as an educational tool that will enable you to better understand, assess, apply, and teach Voice Dialogue techniques, strategies, and exercises. If you use the Voice Dialogue method to treat others make sure you are doing so in conformance with the business and licensing laws of your city, county, and state or province, as well as the laws of your country. If you are not sure, consult an attorney knowledgeable on the subject.

The Voice Dialogue method is a new, experimental, and by definition unconventional method to achieve personal growth. Neither the Voice Dialogue method nor this book should be used as a substitute for treatment by licensed health care or medical professionals. The author and publisher must, and do, disclaim any responsibility for your well-being and for how you apply the information herein. We believe *The Handbook* is a source of extraordinary and valuable information, but ultimately you, the reader, must take responsibility for your health and well-being, and for the health and well-being of those in your care.

We would also like the reader to know that the examples of facilitations in this book are purely fictional, and that any resemblance of any facilitators or subjects in these examples to any persons living or dead is coincidental and unintended.

This book is dedicated to you, the facilitators,
and to the people you facilitate.
May you find in working with the Voice Dialogue method
a vehicle for your creative spirit and a path to
an empowered and balanced way of life.

for
Gladys and Saul Weinberg
in gratitude for a childhood rich in cultural contrasts, travel, and experience –
all the things that have made it possible for me to accept so many parts of myself
and relate comfortably to an extraordinary diversity of human expression.

Table of Contents

Acknowledgments

I would first of all like to thank Hal and Sidra Stone for creating the Voice Dialogue method and for their pioneering work in the Psychology of the Aware Ego as this is the foundation for all that I have written in *The Voice Dialogue Facilitator's Handbook.* I deeply appreciate their personal encouragement and advice to me on this project. To whatever degree this book supports the development of their work, I will have succeeded in achieving my own goals.

In addition to the Stones, there are other teachers and facilitators who have given me tremendous encouragement and support through their enthusiasm for this project, letting me know that a facilitator's handbook is something we all really need and can put into immediate practical use. I especially want to thank Joseph Heller for convincing me to divide *The Handbook* into two parts. I think what he actually said was, "Stop! You have a book already and we need it now." I am grateful to Robert Stamboliev for his clarifying work on Voice Dialogue and energetics and his personal enthusiasm for this project back when it was only a pile of notes in a data base. Thanks also to Paul Gale Baker for his helpful comments in the margins of the manuscript and for leading the Australian cheering section for *The Handbook.* So many teachers and facilitators have been remarkably supportive – in particular I would like to mention Judith Hendin, Dassie Hoffman, Judith Stone, Sindona Casteel, Carolyn Conger, J'aime ona Pangaia, Francine Pinto, Lora O'Connor, and Mary Langley.

Just as the Psychology of the Aware Ego is in its initial exploration phase, so too is Voice Dialogue facilitation. It is something that we are continually creating and learning from each other as the work evolves. I owe a great debt to my first full-time facilitator, Anna Ivara. Several years of sessions and classes with Anna in New York City colored everything I know about facilitation. Dr. Betty Bosdell is an ongoing inspiration – her work with imagery taught me to use my imagination, trust my intuition, and dive to a deeper level in this work. Lydia Duncan opened up new ways of working with dreams. In trading sessions with Catherine Keir I learned a number of now favorite questions to ask when interviewing selves and have passed many of these treasures on to you. I thank Dr. Martha Lou Wolff for her generosity in sharing her way of channeling energies through the Aware Ego.

My clients, students, and the participants of Delos trainings where I have been on staff, have all contributed enormously to my own development in this work and to my understanding of what it is that facilitators need to know. Working with all of you has trained me to be a better facilitator, and supervising sessions of those learning to do Voice Dialogue work has given me essential information about which elements of facilitation are the easiest and which are the most difficult to learn. Many of you have to come me with specific topics of discussion to include in *The Handbook* and I hope that many more of you will continue to participate in this project, contributing to *Part II* and to future editions of *The Handbook* through the facilitator's forum on the website. (A special thanks to Lorna Knox for the quote at the top of p. 243.)

I have grown to realize that learning how to facilitate is one thing and being able to write a book about it is quite another! I could not have created this *Handbook* on my own, and I want to thank and celebrate my team, without whose creativity, perseverance, and devotion, this book would not have come into being. I am in awe of Suzanne Perot's magical ability to take my ideas and turn them into energy-filled illustrations. With her background as an artist and lots of experience being facilitated and facilitating, I am convinced she was and is the perfect person for the job of illustrating *The Handbook.* Karl Bettinger is responsible for both book and website design, and for coming to the rescue cheerfully every time a computer glitched or crashed. Without Karl's initiating me into computer mysteries and several years of coaching me through an amazing jungle of hardware and software, I would never have had the courage to embark on such a large and comprehensive project. And, a special thanks to James Baker for expert computer consulting and for resurrecting my powerbook when anyone else would have given it up for lost.

So many people have put time and effort into making this *Handbook* an easy-to-read, easy-to-use guide for the facilitator. A team of proof readers have spent long hours going over the manuscript – my gratitude to Ann McMillen, Lynn Pruzan, Cathrine Fox, Robin Rose, and Peg Giffels. I have been doubly blessed with two editors who have different and complimentary skills. Jamie Streichler has patiently hunted down every errant comma, every run-on sentence, every bit of mismatched formatting. At the same time, she has brought the gift of beginner's mind to the work itself, asking me penetrating questions about the nature of energetics, the Aware Ego, the selves, facilitation, etc., so that my explanations have had to become clearer and more understandable for those readers who do not have an extensive background in this work. Richard Berger, my husband, brings fifteen years of experience with Voice Dialogue facilitation as well as a wealth of training and information in the fields of consciousness and energetics. He has read, and re-read, and re-read *The Handbook,* editing out passages that were written by primary selves and bringing in over and over again the neutral, balanced voice of the Aware Ego. In many places his contribution has gone beyond the scope of editing and moved into the realm of co-authorship. Richard has also been the business mastermind and financial expert behind publishing *The Handbook,* and he has patiently and quite cheerfully weathered three years of marriage to a wife who refuses to leave her computer. I simply would not have been able to write and publish this book without his guidance and support.

Foreword

The Voice Dialogue method blossomed in our relationship and grew out of our desire to learn more about one another. This gives it a special quality; it is a non-judgmental exploration of psychospiritual reality. Voice Dialogue enables us to look at the psyche to see what "is" rather than looking at the psyche to discover what is dysfunctional, pathological, or wrong and therefore needs fixing.

Over the past twenty-five years Voice Dialogue has continued to evolve. It is now a powerful tool, used by both professionals and nonprofessionals, for the subtle exploration of the psyche and the creation of an Aware Ego, a method that combines focus and mental alertness with a sensitivity to the nuances of energetic realities. For many years we have wished for an in-depth guide to the complexities of this seemingly simple and straightforward method.

Miriam Dyak studied with us for many years and has staffed many of our workshops. Her two volume *Voice Dialogue Facilitator's Handbook* captures the soul of Voice Dialogue facilitation and gives us a readable and clear handbook for facilitators. In it, she keeps alive the original excitement of this work, reminding us always of the surprises that are in store for both facilitator and subject. She emphasizes the non-judgmental quality of facilitation and shows the reader how to stay open to each self and the gifts it brings to the total psyche.

Voice Dialogue is an instrument which can be played in many different ways. Its tone varies depending upon the skill and background of the facilitator. For those who have studied directly with us, we have emphasized the relationship of Voice Dialogue to the separation from Primary Selves and the creation and enhancement of an Aware Ego. Others use Voice Dialogue as an adjunct to their own approach to the psyche and personal growth or healing.

Whatever one brings to this work determines what one can take from it. With this in mind, this manual gives guidance not only in the actual conduct of Voice Dialogue sessions, but also gives suggestions on ways in which the facilitator might wish to deepen and enrich her/his own background in order to bring more to these sessions.

This manual presents Voice Dialogue, as a method, within the framework of the Psychology of the Aware Ego in much the same way that we teach facilitation at our training intensives. It shows the role of the selves (both primary and disowned,) the role of Awareness, and the role of the Aware Ego. It gives the facilitator an appreciation of the importance of the Voice Dialogue method in the development of the Aware Ego which is, for us, the ultimate aim of this work. It demonstrates how to help birth an Aware Ego and how to encourage its subsequent growth.

It is always difficult to translate work with energies into words, but Miriam is a writer and a poet and she is able to speak of energetics directly and clearly. Her touch is deft. She combines guidelines for conducting Voice Dialogue sessions with anecdotal examples taken from her own and others' experiences. She enhances her writing with illustrations that give a visual "feel" to the material. She brings in a great deal of information about energetics, showing how to work with the energies of the selves, how to teach energetic linkage, and how to develop and strengthen an Aware Ego using Voice Dialogue facilitation as the basic tool.

For us, the aim of the Voice Dialogue method is the creation of an Aware Ego. For you, it may be the enhancement of your own way of working with yourself or others. Whichever your aim, we welcome you to this marvelous adventure, the exploration of the complex and ever-fascinating world within!

Hal & Sidra Stone

Introduction

I'm writing this book because I love facilitating Voice Dialogue sessions. Facilitating is my professional work, and for me it is also a great pleasure and a form of creative expression. With every person who picks up this *Handbook* and finds that any part of it makes learning and doing facilitation easier and more rewarding for them, my effort will be complete. I want to acknowledge that there already is an excellent body of literature by Drs. Hal and Sidra Stone and others on the theory of the Psychology of the Aware Ego and the experience of using the Voice Dialogue method, but up until now no one has written a comprehensive manual that explores the myriad, nitty gritty situations and choices a facilitator faces in the course of doing Voice Dialogue work. I have spent three years writing this book in an attempt to fill that gap.

In the last fifteen to twenty years thousands of people have attended Voice Dialogue lectures, workshops, trainings, courses, and Summerkamps around the world. Almost all of us have gone home wishing we had more explicit information about facilitation to refer to as we began to experiment with doing this work on our own. This is especially true for those who don't have other facilitators close by for mutual feedback and support, and it is even more pertinent for those who have become acquainted with the Voice Dialogue method through books and tapes alone. With or without the advantage of hands-on training, we can all benefit from more specific and detailed guidance in the art of facilitation. In addition, there is a growing group of Voice Dialogue teachers who are training others to be facilitators and could put a manual on basic facilitation skills to immediate use in their classes. It is for all of these individuals and groups that I have written this *Handbook*. My hope is that it will facilitate facilitation – i.e. *make it easy!*

The Handbook is intended as a tool for professional and non-professional alike. As Voice Dialogue work has evolved over the years and as the Stones have deepened their exploration of the Psychology of the Aware Ego, more and more people, on an individual as well as a professional basis, have begun to integrate the Voice Dialogue method with other related approaches to personal growth. *The Handbook* can be used by those working with Voice Dialogue as a vehicle for personal growth and communication in relationship, as well as by those in practice as therapists, business consultants, body workers, movement therapists, or in any other profession that might incorporate Voice Dialogue facilitation in its approach. (To acknowledge that not all facilitators are working with Voice Dialogue professionally, I have chosen throughout The Handbook to use the word "subject" rather than "client" to refer to the person being facilitated.)

As long as you have had some prior experience with Voice Dialogue – perhaps having been facilitated in a private session or having participated in a workshop or training, or even having read books and/or listened to tapes – you will find *The Handbook* an informative and practical guide to begin learning how to be a Voice Dialogue facilitator. If you have already begun to work with the Voice Dialogue method, then *The Handbook* can be used as a coach to help you improve your facilitation skills. And for those who have had formal training, *The Handbook* should serve both as a refresher course and, hopefully, as a source of new ideas, providing answers to at least some of those questions that never seem to come up until after the workshop is over and we're on our own. I began writing *The Handbook* after twelve years experience as a facilitator, and I can quite clearly say that the process of writing this book has improved my own facilitation skills, made me more conscious of energetics, and helped me to be a more accurate observer. This is exactly what I hope will happen for those who use *The Handbook* as a guide for their own work, whether they are new to Voice Dialogue or have been facilitators for a long time.

This is *Part I* of *The Voice Dialogue Facilitator's Handbook*. The first two sections include a brief background on Voice Dialogue and the Psychology of the Aware Ego, information on how to become a facilitator, ground rules for facilitation, and an exploration of energetics. The third section provides a step by step journey through a Voice Dialogue session with an emphasis on working with primary selves and initiating the Aware Ego process. In addition, the fourth section explores working with body language, silence, dreams and learning to channel the energies of the selves through the Aware Ego.

The Handbook, Part II will continue with discussions of various ways to deepen the work including further facilitation of primary selves, how to facilitate disowned and vulnerable selves, how to work with bonding patterns in relationship (including the bonding patterns we call transference and counter transference that occur between facilitator and client), and how to work with transpersonal energies, body voices, images, and dream selves. In *Part II* we will also discuss support for the facilitator and creating an effective work space, how to structure a Voice Dialogue practice and/or work with peer partnerships and self-facilitation, as well as additional directions for the work in combination with other modalities.

Last but not least, this *Handbook* along with our new website at <http://www.life-energy.net> holds the potential to be a place of sharing and communication among facilitators from around the world. *The Handbook, Part II* will include contributions from several long-time facilitators, sharing ideas and experience in their particular areas of focus, and my hope is that readers will want to send in stories and wisdom gained in facilitating so that we can all continue to learn from each other. "How you can contribute to *The Handbook*," on p. 312, details how you can take part in "writing the next chapter" of *The Voice Dialogue Facilitator's Handbook*.

November, 1998
Seattle, Washington

How to get the most out of this book...

This is an interactive *Handbook* with lots of opportunities for you, the facilitator, to structure your own learning program in a way that works best for you. Please feel free to participate in whichever way most supports *your* work and *your* intention. If you are completely new to Voice Dialogue facilitation you may want to read through *The Handbook* and just let the information absorb *before* you begin focusing on any particular exercises or try to apply specific suggestions. If you are already facilitating and want to get some assistance with an aspect of the work that has been challenging for you, you may want to dive right in to a chapter that deals with your questions so that you can focus on information that will be immediately helpful to you. As you become more and more involved in the work, you may find that *The Handbook* provides a valuable "classroom" where you can participate by using the exercises and thinking through the questions and discussions, taking time to talk out or write down answers of your own.

However you chose to work with Th*e Handbook,* I invite you to *put yourself in the story.* All the facilitators in the examples have been left nameless on purpose to create an opening for you to step into their role and think through each example as if it were your own session – every time you read the word, "facilitator," you are welcome to put yourself in that place and see how your unique perspective may change the session. Just as scientists have discovered that we cannot be completely outside the phenomena we observe and that our presence changes what we are observing, so too there is no such thing as a Voice Dialogue facilitation separate from the unique energy of the person facilitating it. *Voice Dialogue facilitation changes each and every time with each and every facilitator and subject, and no two sessions are ever alike.* If you and any one of your colleagues or facilitation partners were to facilitate the same person in the same place about the same issues, your sessions could be remarkably different from each other. This is an aspect of Voice Dialogue that has kept me challenged and inspired for many years, and I hope it will be the same for you.

In keeping with this individual approach to the facilitation process, the questions throughout *The Handbook* are followed by discussion rather than answers. The intent is to stimulate creative exploration rather than to test the reader on the ideas that have been introduced. In many instances there may be several "right" answers, and, even more importantly, responding to these questions involves adding your own experience, skills, and perspective into the mix. Ideas that are put forth in the discussions are offered as additional information to stimulate your imagination, and many of the questions are left for you to explore on your own. The only "wrong" answers to these questions would be ones that run counter to the ground rules for the work. I am hoping both the questions and discussion of them will provide a basis for much inquiry and improvisation.

This *Handbook* is based on experience and experimentation, both my own and that of many other Voice Dialogue facilitators. Much of this experience defies definitive analysis and, when it comes to energetics, almost escapes description. If this were a cookbook, more important than precise measurements of ingredients for making a pie, would be descriptions of the way pie dough feels in your hand when just the right amount of ice water has been added. Voice Dialogue works with intuition, energy, feeling, as well as mental understanding. Energetics which is key in Voice Dialogue work, is as poetic and elusive as a cook's touch, so I encourage you to intuit the feel of the work in addition to "following the recipe." To support this way of working, the structure of The *Handbook* is designed to accommodate both linear and nonlinear approaches to learning. The structure, illustrations, and design of your *Handbook* are here to help you shift from a more traditionally mental, book-reading mode to a depth of comprehension and participation that hopefully reaches many levels of your perception.

Please keep in mind that it is far *more* complex to take the Voice Dialogue facilitation process apart and examine the pieces than it is to actually work with a person, once you have acquired some experience and a "feel" for the work. Certainly it is not intended that you, the reader, will go through the cumbersome process of memorizing each of these pieces and then function as a walking Voice Dialogue facilitation encyclopedia, but rather that here and there these examples and insights will begin to absorb into your consciousness and integrate with your own way of doing things so that you will be more and more at ease with the facilitation process and more able to allow your own creativity to come to the fore. Every Voice Dialogue session is an unknown quantity – so many variables come into play, unexpected selves pop up, and the details cannot be imagined or anticipated ahead of time. Your *Handbook* can only give you ideas of what to look for, suggestions of useful ways in which to hold your own energy and consciousness, information about things that definitely have and haven't worked for other others. How you use this information is up to you and the way you'll put it together in your own facilitation will be unique, so there is no need or pressure to recreate exactly what you read in this book. Each facilitation is a one-time event, and probably the most important instruction you can remember is to relax with the process and have fun!

A word about grammar...

How we perceive our world is woven invisibly and powerfully into the way we structure our language – how we choose to speak about our perceptions and experience. I have made some specific grammatical choices in this *Handbook* that depart from the accepted literary norm. These choices are to help provide clarity and an alternative to our habitual ways of thinking.

To focus our attention on the most important part of Voice Dialogue work, I have chosen to capitalize "Aware Ego" all through *The Handbook*. You may read other Voice Dialogue literature where aware ego is not capitalized and this is also correct.

The *facilitator* is referred to sometimes as "he" and sometimes as "she." Since there are many female and male facilitators it seems easiest to me to use both pronouns randomly rather than the popular but tedious process of saying "he or she," or the inaccurate and often offensive use of one gender to imply both.

I have also chosen to refer to each *person* being facilitated (i.e. the "subject") with the plural pronouns "they," "them," "their." I know that this isn't "good grammar," but it really helps to simplify your reading of *The Handbook*. Without this option, and with so many facilitators, subjects and selves to refer to, the pages of your *Handbook* would be filled with "he's" and "she's" to the point where it would be almost impossible to untangle who is who.

To further minimize confusion, I have also chosen to refer to all *selves* with the neuter pronoun "it." Of course, selves are most often definitely quite masculine or feminine, but along with our first challenge of distinguishing facilitators from subjects, it's far too complex on the page to add selves into the equation without some easy way to keep the pronouns separate. *In an actual session, gesture, expression, and voice tone all serve to clearly indicate which "he" or "she" the facilitator is referring to.* (And, yes, I've opted most often to end sentences with prepositions because, fortunately or unfortunately, people speak that way these days, and I want this *Handbook* to feel more like a conversation than a textbook.)

So to repeat: all subjects are "they," all facilitators are "he's" or "she's," and all selves are "it." In the interest of clarity and understanding, please forgive what some primary selves may perceive to be serious lapses in grammar.

Introduction to Section One

In this first section of your *Handbook* we will talk about what Voice Dialogue is, how it's used and who uses it, and how you can learn to be a Voice Dialogue facilitator.

Voice Dialogue facilitation is a method developed by Drs. Hal and Sidra Stone for working with subpersonalities and the Psychology of the Aware Ego. Voice Dialogue is designed to help create greater choice, consciousness and flexibility in our lives. In their books, the Stones discuss in great detail the theory of the Psychology of the Aware Ego and the use of the Voice Dialogue approach for individual personal growth and in relationships. *It is not the intent of this Handbook to repeat the Stones' work, but rather to supplement it with specific and clear guidelines for the Voice Dialogue facilitator.* If this book is your first introduction to the Psychology of the Aware Ego and/or the Voice Dialogue method, you may want to read any one of the Stones' excellent books or listen to their audio tapes (listed in the bibliography) as well as continuing with *The Handbook*.

What is Voice Dialogue?

Voice Dialogue is a tool for conscious transformation. It offers us a path into a new dimension of being human, beyond dualistic thinking, where we stand in balance between the powerful opposites that have given us no peace since our first "either/or" experience in the proverbial Garden of Eden. Voice Dialogue work allows us to transform the unconscious struggle of opposites that we carry within us into a conscious acceptance of all of our humanness. It makes it possible for us to disengage from old, automatic, reactive patterns and become more fully alive in the present.

Voice Dialogue work is based on the theory of a multi-faceted human personality made up of numerous (perhaps innumerable) selves. These selves, which are also called "voices" "subpersonalities," "complexes," "parts," and "energies" or "energy patterns," are real live autonomous "people" in their own right. They have their own feelings, desires, memories, opinions, world views – they are not merely concepts and this is not therapeutic role playing. Many of these selves have grown up with us our whole lives, taking care of our early survival, our identification as individuals, and our success in the world. These are the "primary" selves which form the core of our personality – in fact we think of them as who we are. Other "disowned" selves have experienced a lifetime of repression, becoming evident only when we lose control and act contrary to character, or more commonly when we project these disowned qualities out onto others, usually those we either overvalue or deeply dislike. Still other selves remain dormant within us and may not be born until later in our lives.

How do our "selves" come into being?

Human beings are unique among all creatures on earth. Not only are we born more vulnerable than other mammals, but it takes us years to develop the level of independence a fawn or a foal or a lion cub or newborn dolphin achieves in days. It may not be essential for a lamb or a wolf cub to be endearing to its biological parents in order to receive food and protection, but human babies have to develop a personality that "both protects us and makes us attractive to others"* in order to ensure that we will be cared for and survive.

Drs. Hal and Sidra Stone, the originators of Voice Dialogue, describe an "inner family" of selves that evolves in each person. These selves are patterned after "family members, friends, teachers, or anyone who has had any kind of influence over us." Or, they may develop as the exact opposite of the models we have had in our lives. The Stones talk about the selves and the importance of understanding their role in our lives:

> Learning about this inner family is a very important part of personal growth and abso-
> lutely necessary for the understanding of our relationships since the members of this
> inner family, or "selves," as we like to call them, are often in control of our behavior. If we
> do not understand the pressures they exert, then we are really not in charge of our lives.

*Stone & Stone, *Embracing Your Inner Critic*, p. 13.

How does this inner family develop? As we grow in a particular family and culture, each of us is indoctrinated with certain ideas about the kind of person we should be. Since we are very vulnerable as infants and children, it is important that we be the "kind of person we should be," and we behave in a way that keeps us safe and loved and cared for. The need to protect our basic vulnerability results in the development of our personality – the development of the primary "selves" that define us to ourselves and to the world.*

The Stones explain that the energy of the vulnerable child, which is where we begin in life, remains at our core and holds our essential nature, our "psychic fingerprint." The primary selves come into being in order to protect this core vulnerability. Very often by the time we reach adulthood they have become very over-protective, guarding us against dangers that may no longer even exist in our lives or at least are not now the enormous threats they once were. *The primary selves are often so vigilant in hiding our vulnerability away from all harm that we lose touch with it ourselves – we lose touch with the way to connect with our own soul.* One of the goals of Voice Dialogue facilitation is to enable us to once again be connected to our essence and still have the protection we need to function in the world.

> *"The primary selves are often so vigilant in hiding away our vulnerability that we lose touch with it ourselves – we lose touch with the way to connect with our own soul."*

What are the disowned selves?

The primary selves are intent on protecting us from outside harm, and they are also determined to inhibit any behavior on our part that might elicit negative reactions from the world around us. In *Embracing Each Other,* the Stones state that *"each of the primary selves has a complementary disowned self that is equal and opposite in content and power."* These disowned selves hold all the qualities we have been taught to either under- or over-value. This includes what we despise, or are ashamed of, as well as what we think is far better than anything we could ever be. Our primary selves have a full-time job keeping a reasonably safe distance from the positive disowned selves (the ones we admire in others) and at the same time making sure that the negative disowned selves never (or hardly ever) see the light of day.

The primary selves not only dislike people who act out the disowned parts of our personalities, they are actually frightened that other people's personalities will be contagious. The primary selves worry that just being around other people who carry our negative disowned energies will cause us to lose control and long-repressed parts of us will start to "run wild in the streets." Primary selves are like over-anxious parents who are terrified we'll start going with the wrong crowd and get into serious trouble; they become very agitated around people who hold the qualities they think are dangerous for us. Popular phrases such as "that person pushes my buttons," "she gets under my skin," or "I can't stand it when he does that, it just gets to me" are all indications of alarms going off in the primary self system. For example, if my primary selves are invested in my always being inconspicuous and restrained, never allowing me to "show off," then a person who is loud and colorful and very full of themselves may trigger judgment, anger, even fear in my primary self system.

*Stone & Stone, *Embracing Each Other,* p. 4.

4

Attraction is just as much an indication of disowned selves as repulsion. For example, if I am deeply attracted to qualities in someone else that I can't conceive of having in myself ("They're sooo wonderful! I *can't imagine* being so talented..."), this is also an indication of disowned selves. Whether it's a matter of annoyance or falling in love, repulsion or attraction, we all encounter people who carry our disowned selves. If we can get beyond our primary selves' reactivity, we'll find that the people who disturb us also bring us powerful gifts – energies we need to accept in ourselves in order to achieve balance and wholeness. To receive these gifts we have to become conscious of our inner family of selves and come to understand where we are out of balance and where we are heavily charged, i.e. polarized in one direction or its opposite.

Voice Dialogue facilitation gives us direct access to the selves and their experience. It also enables us to separate from the selves and become aware of them. Out of this separation and awareness is created the space to birth a new aspect of personality, an Aware Ego,* and it is this Aware Ego that can stand in balance between opposite selves, honoring both of them, perceiving their sometimes mutually exclusive needs, and taking action based on *wholeness and integration* rather than on duality, control, and repression.

What is an Aware Ego and how is it different from an ordinary ego?

The Stones, originators of the Voice Dialogue method, describe the ego in Western psychological terms as the "executive function of the psyche" and also as the "CEO of the entire personality." Most people, however, don't have an ego that can function and make choices independent of the dictates of their inner selves. Instead of an ego, there is actually a group of dominant selves that have taken over "running the company" in the ego's place.

> *Thus, what is functioning as the ego, may, in fact, be a combination of the protector/ controller, pusher, pleaser, perfectionist, and inner critic. This unique combination of subpersonalities, or energy systems, perceives the world in which we live, processes this information, and then directs our lives.***

"Operating ego" is the term the Stones have given this group of primary selves that act in place of an ego. Even though the operating ego is a group, it functions more or less as one person, and usually the person doesn't realize that a group of selves is actually running their life. They also do not realize to what degree this unconscious take-over by the primary selves – which originally was essential for survival – may now be costing them precious life energy and limiting both their freedom and their choices. An operating ego, however, *is* to some degree aware that there are

"Understanding the reality of the operating ego explains the mystery of why so many of us sabotage our efforts at success. From the perspective of the operating ego, success is safety, comfort, and the status quo."

different parts. For example it's quite normal for people to say "a part of me really wants to leave this job," or "one part of me will always be connected to this place."

---

*As the central focus of Voice Dialogue facilitation, "Aware Ego" is capitalized throughout *The Handbook*.
**Stone & Stone, *Embracing Our Selves*, p. 21

One simple way to tell the difference between an operating ego and an Aware Ego, is that the primary selves that comprise the operating ego are very attached to the way they have already arranged our lives and are very fearful of change. *Understanding the reality of the operating ego explains the mystery of why so many of us sabotage our efforts at success. From the perspective of the operating ego, success is safety, comfort, and the status quo.* Taking on a bigger project, becoming more accountable, getting out there in the world, being more visible, leaving a relationship, etc., all threaten the security of this group of primary selves – to them success is making as few waves as possible. The Aware Ego on the other hand has no investment in our being any particular way because it can hold both polarities and is attached to neither. Unlike the individual selves, it has no allegiance to the past and puts no limitations on the future. The Aware Ego is capable of perceiving both sides of the story and can make choices that honor the concerns of the primary selves while allowing us to evolve beyond their constraints.

The operating ego does its best to keep life smooth even if that means denying the existence of problems or pain. Let's take the example of Jim, who when something angers him, his operating ego usually wants to calm him down and keep him out of trouble. If the primary selves that make up the operating ego are really good at steering clear of conflict and emotional discomfort, he may not even be aware that he's angry at all – he may have a drink or get a headache or become involved in a lot of analytical thinking instead. His primary selves may succeed in internalizing his anger so deeply that he becomes ill. Or, they may become exhausted, and one day, when he's too tired and too upset, he'll finally "lose it" and explode.

An Aware Ego, however, gives us more choice. If Jim develops an Aware Ego in relation to these two opposite parts of himself, his anger and his internal control, he won't have to either bury his feelings or explode – he will be able to chose an altogether different option that honors his own needs *and* the outer reality of the particular situation. In fact, the Aware Ego is capable of drawing on the energy of both the unconstrained angry self and the controlled self, perhaps creating a unique blend of the two that yields a contained empowered energy, both polite and assertive, capable of expressing his needs while holding strong boundaries. The Aware Ego is able to do this by *harmonizing these energies within itself.* It neither manipulates nor overpowers the opposite selves or tries to make them reconcile their differences. The Aware Ego can stand between the opposites and is able to say "I *have* a very conservative part of me that doesn't like conflict" which is a big change from "I *am* the kind of person who can't stand conflict." At the same time the Aware Ego acknowledges that "there is a part of me that feels really angry" and honors this part as well.

"The Aware Ego experiences and manages the energy of the selves consciously – it isn't compelled to repress or disown them."

Does having an Aware Ego protect us from conflict or pain? As we'll see when we begin to work with Voice Dialogue facilitation, the selves have no choice but to react to each other and to other people unconsciously, often with destructive consequences. *However, the Aware Ego experiences and manages the energy of the selves consciously – it isn't compelled to repress or disown them.* The development of the Aware Ego frees up a tremendous amount of energy which allows for the emergence of new and creative solutions in our lives. While life still includes conflict and pain, because we're separated from the selves and are aware of them, we don't suffer in the same old way. Even better, we don't suffer the often dire consequences of denying and burying pain until it turns into physical illness or uncontrollable upheaval in our lives. There's no telling exactly what will happen for Jim when he begins to have an Aware Ego in relation to his controlled and angry selves, but it won't be the same tug-of-war he has experienced in the past.

It's important to understand that the "operating ego" doesn't disappear as soon as an Aware Ego begins to develop. The operating ego keeps on operating and it seems to be in inverse proportion to the Aware Ego – the more the Aware Ego is able to be present, the less the primary selves are compelled to run the show. *The primary selves don't decrease their vigilance unless they know that their concerns are being recognized, honored, and "handled" by the Aware Ego.* No

> *"The primary selves don't decrease their vigilance unless they know that their concerns are being recognized, honored, and "handled" by the Aware Ego."*

matter how much we work with Voice Dialogue or other ways of developing our consciousness, we can expect to function from the operating ego much, if not most, of the time.

How does the Aware Ego come into being?

The Aware Ego comes into being a little bit at a time as we separate from each specific primary self and its opposite disowned self. When we are unconsciously living in the primary selves, we literally can't see the forest for the trees – in fact we *are* the trees! In order for an Aware Ego to come into being we have to disidentify with the trees and step back where we can see the forest. This means we must achieve separation from the selves and gain an awareness of them. Separating from one pair of opposites, however, only helps us to develop an Aware Ego process in relation to that particular pair of opposites. Other selves may remain practically unknown to us until we create space in our consciousness to be aware of them. This is one of the major reasons why the development of an Aware Ego is a gradual and on-going process.

The Voice Dialogue method is uniquely designed to facilitate the birth of the Aware Ego. For example, for me to have an Aware Ego in relation to the self that won't let me rest until I finish writing this book, I have to get enough distance from that self to be able to see that it's not all of who I am. In a Voice Dialogue session my facilitator would have me physically move over and be the "driven self," have a conversation with that part, hear its concerns about this book and other sources of its anxiety in my life. At the end of that conversation, when I returned to the place I had started, *it would actually be a different me coming back.* When I started out I was completely entangled with that driven, highly motivated, and rather anxious energy, but now I'm quite literally separated from it. Now I have an Aware Ego in relation to the part of me that pushes to get the book done. It helps even more if the facilitator also has me find and separate from the part of me that wants to take it easy, spend time on the beach or in the garden. The likelihood is that without an Aware Ego in relation to these opposites, the first self would simply push me nonstop until I "took it easy" by "spacing out" and not being able to write any more, or by getting sick – a pattern that I've experienced in the past.

After exploring and separating from my "driven self" and my "take-it-easy self," my Voice Dialogue facilitator would guide me to the awareness level, a place of pure witness outside the system of selves, where I could simply observe the energies of these parts without any judgment, analysis, emphasis on change, or any effort to take action in relation to them – very much like the dispassionate observation achieved through meditation. The act of witnessing the selves from the neutral perspective of the awareness level helps me to separate from these opposites even more. When I return again to the Aware Ego I'll be able to draw on the observation of awareness, and I'll be able to feel the experience of the selves without being taken over by their energy. As a result, I'll have information from both sides available to support me in making an informed "executive" decision on how to act/respond in a balanced way.

The process of separating from selves, becoming aware of them, and birthing an Aware Ego in relation to them is ongoing; it happens over and over again, and in the process the Aware Ego grows and strengthens. *As long as we have parts of ourselves of which we are not aware, we have no Aware Ego in relation to those parts.* One Voice Dialogue session probably won't be enough to effectively separate from the most dominant selves, the ones that have always run our lives. These primary selves already have a lifetime of habit and control, and the Aware Ego

"The Aware Ego doesn't ever try to get rid of the primary selves but only to utilize their energy in a more balanced and appropriate way."

is the upstart on the block. The Aware Ego starts out small and has to prove to the primary selves that it can take care of us at least as well as they can. In fact the primary selves can be compared to worried, over-protective, anxious, critical, very powerful, yet exhausted parents. Once the Aware Ego develops into a real presence in our lives, it gradually begins to take care of these primary selves, offering them a well-deserved break. This changing of the guard, from operating ego to Aware Ego, develops organically over time, and the primary selves are always available and ready to jump in when needed. In her book, *The Shadow King*, Sidra Stone explains that *"the Aware Ego is not a destination that can be reached, but rather a process that must be lived."** The process is one of gradually becoming more conscious of and independent of our many selves.

As the Aware Ego develops, the operating ego continues to run our lives in every area and every moment where there is no Aware Ego functioning. The operating ego will continue to function as long as we have selves we're not aware of, and even when we have separated from our primary selves, we may often need their intervention. *The Aware Ego doesn't ever try to get rid of these primary selves but only to utilize their energy in a more balanced and appropriate way.* Think of a long-lost prince (or princess) coming back at last to rule the kingdom. In the old stories he (or she) banished or imprisoned all the officials who usurped the kingdom in his/her absence. In our new story, the Aware Ego is the wise prince or princess who keeps these officials as part of his or her court, uses their talents to best serve the entire kingdom, while also implementing new policies these old rulers never even dreamed of. This is what living beyond either/or, and beyond win/lose, is all about.

The Voice Dialogue model of consciousness

Voice Dialogue makes the assumption that consciousness is not a state to be achieved but a process that continues to unfold throughout our entire lifetime. The elements of human experience we have been discussing comprise a dynamic model of consciousness *in which ordinary life is the vehicle for our evolution rather than an obstacle to it.* In Voice Dialogue we

*Sidra Stone, *The Shadow King*, p. 176.

see human consciousness as made up of three interactive, interdependent parts:

① **the awareness level** which stands outside of us observing the selves and does not take action.

② **the selves** which are immersed in living, the level on which we experience life.

③ **the Aware Ego** which stands between opposites, makes choices based on information from the awareness level, and calls in the appropriate selves or energies in each situation. (The Stones compare the Aware Ego to a symphony orchestra conductor who knows all the parts and calls on each instrument to play at the appropriate moment in the performance.)

Awareness is an essential ingredient in our three-part model of consciousness because it allows us to step back and see what is going on in our lives without any attachment to the outcome. Awareness is not a self. It occupies a vantage point located *outside the system of the selves*, outside the personality, and even outside the Aware Ego. Being in awareness is like being able to hover over the map of the psyche in a helicopter or balloon and observe the selves and the Aware Ego from a different perspective. Awareness frees us from rigid attachments to people, places, things, ideas, even to our own self image. It has no goals, intentions, or preferences. It simply observes without judgment or reaction. Historically, the concept of the awareness position in Voice Dialogue is based on the witness state familiar to many through meditative practices, or in "traditional psychological systems, this awareness would be related to the concept of pure insight."*

Unlike the detachment and neutrality of the awareness level, the selves are polarities, highly charged, and passionately attached to their needs, to other people, to feelings and opinions. In our model of consciousness there is no need to try to change or get rid of these selves – we don't have to try to "stop the world and get off!" Many traditional schools of spiritual development direct us to try to give up an active life in the world and retreat into awareness in order to "become conscious," but the Stones point out that "you can't 'aware life,' you have to live it."** In fact, through the experience of the selves, we will undoubtedly continue to do all the "dysfunctional" stuff we've always done – get into arguments with

> *"The Aware Ego's ability to embrace all with attachment to none is a profoundly conscious act with radical implications for the evolution of human consciousness."*

people, repeat old patterns, become sick, etc. – *and this will all still be a part of the consciousness process.* This is because, the Stones say, "consciousness is simply experiencing the selves, witnessing our experience through awareness, and holding the tension of the opposites in the Aware Ego." This concept of consciousness while sounding very simple, draws on the vast range of energies (selves) that comprise the totality of human experience.

It's truly the concept of the Aware Ego that makes our Voice Dialogue model of consciousness both entirely new and uniquely powerful. Where awareness sees the opposites, the Aware Ego *holds the tension of opposite selves*, embracing them equally, and then balancing their energies appropriately in the moment. This is the potential we talked about earlier in our example of helping Jim to balance his anger *and* internal control and bring them into a harmony

*Stone & Stone, *Embracing Our Selves*, p. 19.
**Quotes from the Stones without book or tape references are from lecture notes.

of assertiveness and containment. *The Aware Ego's ability to embrace all with attachment to none, and then take appropriate action based on awareness and acceptance, is a profoundly conscious act with radical implications for the evolution of human consciousness.* It means we don't have to be perfect or even appear spiritual in order to be conscious human beings. We don't have to stay trapped in irreconcilable dualities, or give up our essence and our vitality in a bid for safety, comfort, and acceptance. Instead, we can simply go on living life, becoming more and more aware of our selves, continuing to develop an Aware Ego in relation to the many energies that live inside of us. *We begin to live consciously by developing an Aware Ego that can hold our conflicting desires, that makes choices which create new ways for us to express rather than deny our humanness.*

How is the Voice Dialogue model of consciousness different?

In the past, more traditional models of consciousness have seen the achievement of awareness (the ability to be outside yourself and witness without attachment what is going on in your life), as all that was needed to become conscious. However, there are drawbacks to perceiving consciousness as becoming aware and nothing more. Life has to be *lived*, and striving only for awareness can cause us to withdraw from active living and from the experience of life, since awareness is uninvolved in actual living. Awareness does not and cannot choose, make decisions, or take action – it is not in its nature to do so. It is also important to realize that many of the old models of consciousness direct us to do away with our unacceptable selves and replace them with new spiritual, "conscious" selves. This just puts us in the same old struggle between opposite selves we've always experienced, often leading to ironies such as spiritual selves harshly judging other selves (and other people) for being "too judgmental." It's not surprising that it's a rare few who have ever become "enlightened" following this dualistic approach.

In the Voice Dialogue model of consciousness no part of life has to be given up or rejected in order for us to realize our fullness as human beings – there is no need to withdraw from our attitudes, from our feelings, or even from the "dark side" of ourselves. It's also not necessary to abandon our defenses, strategies the primary selves have used to insure our safety and survival. *This does not mean indiscriminately acting out negative or destructive parts of ourselves.* Instead, our challenge on the consciousness journey is one of learning to dance gracefully with opposing energies and express them *through the Aware Ego* rather than either running amok or engaging in an endless struggle to achieve some static state of imagined perfection.

A very positive consequence of this approach is that everything that happens in our lives is useful in the process of evolving consciousness. Voice Dialogue allows for all our energetic patterns or selves and leaves nothing out. You can imagine it would be difficult to leave pieces of who you are out of your own story and still expect to become whole, and yet that is what many practices and teachings require. In contrast, working with the Psychology of the Aware Ego, it doesn't matter what "mistakes" we make along the way because these "negative" aspects provide just as essential ingredients for the development of the Aware Ego as anything that might be traditionally seen as more positive. In the Stones' words, "the consequence of this view is we don't have to be perfect – it's really okay having a life."

Picturing the Process

Understanding the selves, awareness, and the Aware Ego

(This section is available in ready-to-copy format for use as a teaching tool for your clients and students. See p. 312 for ordering information.)

The interrelationship of the selves, awareness, and the Aware Ego: Here is a set of illustrations to help you understand your inner family of selves and how Voice Dialogue work affects your energy and your consciousness. To make the concepts of primary and disowned selves more real and alive for you, we have pictured these selves as an actual family living inside of a person we'll call Andie.

In our first drawing of Andie we see what a normal operating ego looks like. Andie has a whole family of selves that live inside her, but she is hardly conscious of these parts, even the primary ones that manage her life. Andie's decisions and actions in her life will be based on how these selves want her to be, especially the selves that are primary and have the most power and authority in her personality. These primary selves live on the ground floor, the part of the house that you would get to see if you came over to visit. Down in the basement, out of view of "polite company," are the disowned parts of Andie, selves that she is ashamed of, or that are too volatile or too vulnerable to let out. (Of course, this metaphor is true for *Andie's* inner family and probably for a lot of people, but for others the basement may not house the disowned selves. What is disowned territory for one person may be the home of someone else's primary selves. For example, a person who came from a tough biker background might have primary selves that are pretty earthy and that live in the basement with the bikes and the tools. This person might have a disowned accountant locked away upstairs!)

Our second drawing is a close-up of the family of selves. As you can see, these inner selves are drawn somewhat simplistically without the dimensionality that we see in Andie. This is because each self *is* one-dimensional in the sense of being only a narrow band on the entire spectrum of energy that is possible for Andie – a subpersonality can be very rich, but it's still only one "color" in our whole rainbow of possible human expression. Only when we add all these selves together do they make up the multi-dimensionality that is Andie.

There are undoubtedly more primary selves in Andie's personality than we could picture here, and the family members we do see may each represent more than one inner self. For example, on the couch we have an internalized, stern-looking father who represents all the parts of Andie that take after her father. Andie has quite a strong Inner Critic, and her Controller, Protector, Conservative, Rational Mind and Inner Patriarch are also represented in this figure. Standing next to the couch, busy on the telephone and absent-mindedly patting the head of the Cute Child, is a mother who represents the selves in Andie that take after her mother. Because Andie's mother was a "super mom," juggling career and home, Andie has a big Pusher, a strong Responsible Self, and a self that is focused on contributing to the community.

Turning her back on her irritated father is a Rebellious Teenage Daughter, the spunky part that helped Andie leave home and strike out in a direction of her own – the Rebellious Teenager and the Stern Father are in conflict with each other. Andie works with disadvantaged teenagers as part of her job as a counselor, and her teenage self has helped her to create great rapport with "her kids." Lastly, holding out cookies and cocoa to the teenager, is a Caretaker, a part of Andie who learned very young to get on everyone's good side by pleasing people and taking care of them. This part endears Andie to other people by being dependable and devoted.

Downstairs is a very different story. Here we have the disowned selves, energies that the primary selves try to repress or keep hidden. An Angry Male energy is trying to blast through into the living room above – his uncontrolled anger and overt physicality is quite a disowned opposite to the very controlled and intellectual father upstairs. A needy, Neglected Child is an opposite to the Caretaker and also to the sunny Cute Child. The frightened Withdrawn Self hiding in the corner is the last thing Andie's very together and out-going mother would want to be, though she would also be pretty disgusted and frightened by the down-and-out Bag Person knocking at the door. In addition there are very deeply disowned Instinctual Selves down here in the basement (we can only see their animal eyes glowing in the dark).

If the ground floor represents the parts of herself Andie presents to the public, the basement is definitely what she keeps not only hidden from others, *but also locked away in her own unconscious mind, hidden from herself.* There's a lot of clutter down here, all the stuff Andie's primary selves don't want her to look at, though probably

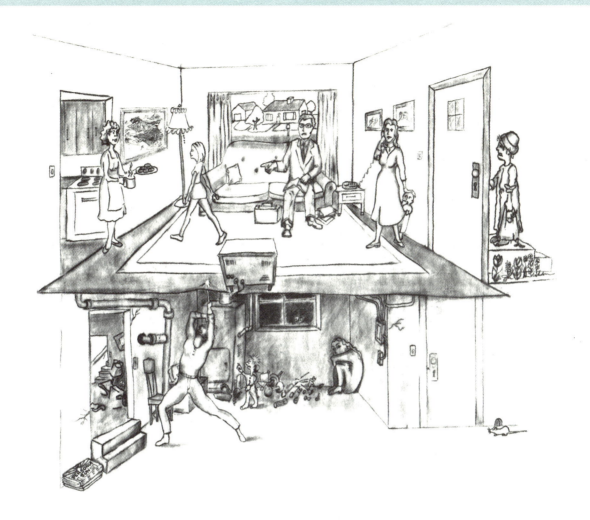

basement scenes and characters come up at night into her dreams or leak out in her relationships. Andie's disowned selves will also very likely show up in the personalities of her boss, her co-workers, mate(s), children (her own and/or the ones she counsels), and even strangers; and when they do, Andie may find these people particularly difficult or irritating. If Andie is at all like most people, she will automatically react to and unconsciously judge or blame people for expressing energies that she represses in herself. Even so, some of these disowned selves in Andie will inevitably spill out around the edges of her personality. Just like the guy busting through the basement ceiling into the living room, Andie will occasionally lose her temper and be amazed ("I don't know what came over me!"), or she may find some days that the "bottom drops out" of her life, that she's withdrawn and depressed, and nothing works to pull her up out of the corner of her internal basement.

Thinking further about the metaphor of the house and family, we can also think of the house as the physical body that houses our selves. The basement would be the place where we store and manage our energy (in the furnace, the fuse box, the plumbing) and where we have our structural foundation. When we shut ourselves off from our power sources, neglect maintenance, and use too much energy to force our disowned selves to stay hidden, our physical and emotional health begin to suffer. As we'll see in our next drawings, the Psychology of the Aware Ego and the Voice Dialogue method give us a way to separate from this internal "upstairs/downstairs" struggle (so we don't get "floored" by opposing energies inside of us). By working to separate from our selves and develop an Aware Ego process, we begin to evolve a new consciousness that allows us to embrace all of who we are.

Our third drawing illustrates what happens when awareness enters into the picture. Andie is reading a book that talks about the inner family of selves, and by the proverbial light bulb going off in her mind we can tell that she now has an awareness of two of her most prominent inner selves, the father and the teenage daughter. The awareness is on the level of mental understanding. Andie can see something about herself – she can see the internal struggle and perhaps understand that it evolved out of her experience growing up. Andie may even start to notice that she gets irritated with her boss because interacting with him reminds her of her old conflicts with her father, but this awareness doesn't actually give her the ability to change anything in her life as awareness is essentially a choiceless form of perception.

Awareness doesn't take action in our lives, it just witnesses what is going on. And, *since it is Andie's operating ego (a group of primary selves) that is actually reading the book*, these primary selves will most likely use the information in the book to back up their already firmly entrenched opinions about how Andie should behave in life. The Father/Critic/Controller will most likely tell Andie that she "should" work this struggle out and the fact that she hasn't yet is a sign of failure. The Mother/Pusher/Responsible Self will tell Andie to read as much as possible and work on herself as hard as she can. The Rebellious Daughter probably won't read the book at all; or if she does, she'll use it to reinforce her own attitudes about what a hard time Dad gives her. Awareness alone doesn't give us the ability to change the energetic patterns in our inner system or family of selves. Awareness helps us to see, but it doesn't by itself give us choice. It also doesn't necessarily help us to take action or change direction – that's the job of the Aware Ego. *Without a functioning Aware Ego, the information that awareness brings into the system is readily co-opted by various selves to support their own purposes.*

In our fourth picture Andie has separated from these two opposite selves and is now standing in balance between them in the Aware Ego. Andie has had the opportunity in a Voice Dialogue session to separate both from her Conservative/Controlling Father Self on the one side and her opposite Rebellious Teenage Daughter. You can see that the father is still his stern and grumpy self, and the daughter still has a smirk on her face – the Voice Dialogue facilitation hasn't in any way tried to change them. Andie, however, now has a very different relationship with these two parts of herself. *As long as she remains in the Aware Ego* (which probably won't be for a very long time at the beginning of the process), she is aware of these two sides of herself from a centered place. Her hands on their shoulders indicate that she is willing and able to be with both these energies in herself, conscious of who they are and what they think and want, without being taken over or pushed around by them. Inside her we can see that even though other selves in the house are still at odds, the struggle between father and daughter has eased for the moment. The father has gone back to reading his book and the daughter has settled down to watch TV. There is a sense of spaciousness and internal calm that comes with separating from the selves and initiating an Aware Ego process in relation to them.

What is Voice Dialogue Facilitation?

The Voice Dialogue method is designed to bring about the birth and growth of the Aware Ego, and the Voice Dialogue facilitator is a midwife and model in this process. Of course it's possible to get acquainted with one's inner selves on one's own, and certainly there are many meditative practices that lead one into a state of awareness, *however creating the necessary separation from the primary selves to initiate an Aware Ego process is most easily accomplished through Voice Dialogue facilitation.*

After all, we think we *are* our primary selves, so it's unlikely for most of us that we'd be able to disengage from our basic personality without some help. A person who is very identified with the mind, for example, might be terrifically *interested* in the theory of the Psychology of the Aware Ego and might have all kinds of *ideas* of what different selves they might explore. But the last thing this person would probably ever think of would be to move over and allow the mind to speak as a separate self, initiating an Aware Ego process in relation to the intellect. It's not like the mind to think of separating from itself! And though the mind might have learned about the importance of developing its opposite, i.e. developing feeling and intuition, it's one of those stories where "you can't get there from here." The mind just won't be able to take this person into a non-mental, feeling state. A Voice Dialogue facilitator, however, will be able to help the person she is facilitating separate from the mind and experience the energetic reality of its opposite. Once the initial separation occurs through Voice Dialogue facilitation, this person will begin to have both their thinking and feeling capacities available to them and will be able to experience both more easily on their own.

The goal of facilitation is to learn to stand in balance between opposites – first with the help of a facilitator and eventually on our own. The Stones comment in their lectures that, *"In the early stages of the work, when one is separating from the primary self system, it's like going against gravity. The Aware Ego is like a spaceship literally leaving the orbit of a master planet, and you need a facilitator to boost away from the gravitational field. The hard work is leaving the planet; once you're free* [of the pull of the primary selves] *it becomes easier and easier to hold the energy of the opposites."* Voice Dialogue is a tool for gaining freedom of choice and freedom of

> *"Creating the necessary separation from the primary selves to initiate an Aware Ego process is most easily accomplished through Voice Dialogue facilitation."*

expression, enabling the Aware Ego not only to come into being but to function on its own. I always feel I have succeeded as a facilitator when a person reports back to me that they are able to notice when they have been stuck in a particular self and then can facilitate themselves, separating from the energy and returning on their own to the Aware Ego.

Voice Dialogue facilitation empowers us to literally expand the range of human expression and awareness. For thousands of years we humans have been caught in a struggle between seemingly irreconcilable opposites. Almost every religion and philosophy around the world holds certain aspects of life to be good and others bad. Human society reflects this in innumerable divisions between white and black, mind and body, spiritual and sexual, mascu-

"Working with Voice Dialogue facilitation to develop the Aware Ego makes it possible to center ourselves between opposites and choose what is appropriate and useful in each of them."

line and feminine, good and evil, business and art, city and country, rational and intuitive, caring and selfish. I could go on and on! We're asked to pledge allegiance to one side or the other not only in war and politics, but also in our neighborhoods, our families, *and inside ourselves.* As we have already discussed, holding back part of our humanness is exhausting and ultimately futile because even if we manage to keep certain selves disowned, they inevitably show up in our more challenging relationships, at our jobs, in our dreams, in our enemies, and perhaps worst of all, in our physical bodies where they manifest as illness and even death. Working with Voice Dialogue facilitation to develop an Aware Ego offers a real way out of this ancient tug-of-war because it is at last possible to center ourselves between these opposites and choose what is appropriate and useful in each of them.

Of course this does take work. Separating from the selves, doesn't mean the Aware Ego is protected from what they are feeling. The Aware Ego feels what is going on inside us, including things we have been trying to avoid feeling for a long time. And the Aware Ego has the pressure of having to decide how to act in life. But even though this may be difficult, *it takes a lot less energy than disowning parts of ourselves and is much easier than being perpetually "jerked around" from one voice inside ourselves to another.* Best of all, the energy that is freed up is now available to explore more of our potential. Each of the primary selves and their opposites, regardless of how small or large they loom in our lives, has a rather narrow outlook and perspective on life. When we separate from these selves new options magically appear and our capacity for life expands. As more and more people enter this non-dualistic reality together, there is no telling how "human beingness" itself may change and expand.

Voice Dialogue facilitation:

- ♦ initiates the Aware Ego process.
- ♦ gives us direct access to our primary and disowned selves, as well as to still unknown and undiscovered aspects of our psyches.
- ♦ takes the person being facilitated through all three levels of the consciousness model.*
- ♦ is a tool for gaining freedom, choice, inner balance, and enhanced communication.
- ♦ is a vehicle for bringing the Aware Ego into being and enabling it to function on its own.
- ♦ helps us to expand the range of human expression and awareness.

Who uses Voice Dialogue and why?

Voice Dialogue facilitation is a companion for the "journey home" to oneself. It is best used in adulthood by people who have developed and stabilized their primary self system, and now find it's time to turn inward and reclaim their essential self. The context for this journey home, however, can be as varied as the people who follow it. For many, therapy pro-

*See description of consciousness model on page 8.

vides the framework for their journey, and if the form of therapy is one that is fundamentally non-pathologizing *and* encourages a deepening awareness of self, it will most likely be very compatible with Voice Dialogue facilitation. The Stones comment,

> *Voice Dialogue is compatible with any system of psychotherapy or growth. It can be integrated into any way of working with consciousness. That's a very exciting idea to us. It's true also with the theory of selves. The theory of selves is basically not incompatible with any way of working. So it's important to realize for anybody with a Gestalt background, Jungian background, psychoanalytic background, body work background… this is the kind of work that can be integrated into your own system.**

Voice Dialogue facilitation is definitely a creative tool. It can be very useful to people working in every art form because it naturally helps people achieve a more lively and aware expression of themselves. For example, one ideal use for Voice Dialogue work is in the theater. (I first encountered Voice Dialogue in a class taught by an acting teacher who used it to help develop psychological flexibility and authenticity of expression.) Business is another area where there is a tremendous need for an Aware Ego and separation from the primary selves. Body work and health care are also natural partners for Voice Dialogue work because so many people first discover the need to bring the opposites in their personalities into greater balance through imbalances they experience in their physical bodies.

Voice Dialogue tends to appeal to people who are active seekers of self-knowledge and are involved in what has come be known as "personal growth." Some people are drawn to Voice Dialogue directly; they read the Stones' books or listen to their tapes and seek out a Voice Dialogue facilitator or training to help them become more involved in the process. Others discover Voice Dialogue facilitation inadvertently. They may work with a therapist who includes it in his therapy work, attend a professional training or workshop which incorporates Voice Dialogue exercises, or the word may get out that a particular facilitator does "something wonderful."

One of the most valuable applications for Voice Dialogue facilitation is for people in relationship because separating from our interlocking primary selves in relationship can free us from the enchantment of both positive and negative bonding patterns** and help us to create an entirely new form of intimacy with each other. So often we come into a relationship with a lover, a child, a friend, a co-worker, bringing "gifts," i.e. qualities the other person lacks; and they, of course, come bringing similar "gifts" to us. Voice Dialogue work enables us to separate from the selves that judge and resist other people in our lives. It helps us to actually receive the valuable but sometimes difficult offerings we bring to each other. Voice Dialogue work itself is a gift of Hal and Sidra Stone's relationship. The Stones comment that *"everybody says it's such a beautiful and gentle way of working with people,"* and believe this is because Voice Dialogue grew out of exploring their relationship together.

> *"Separating from our interlocking primary selves in relationship can help us to create an entirely new intimacy with each other."*

Most importantly, Voice Dialogue facilitation is best used by facilitators and subjects who truly enjoy it! If this work stops being fun and creative, then that may be an indication to let go and use some other, more appropriate approach. Voice Dialogue facilitation

---

* Stone & Stone, "Introducing Voice Dialogue," an audio tape in *The Mendocino Series.*
** For an explanation of "bonding patterns" read *"Embracing Each Other"* by the Stones.

is definitely not for everyone, and in the chapter on Ground Rules in Section Two we'll discuss the contra-indications for facilitation. Voice Dialogue is, and I'm sure will continue to be, experimental. We're still at the beginning of discovering all the uses for this way of working with consciousness, and because it changes us as we use it, there's no telling who will be using it and how we'll be applying it in the future.

Who benefits from Voice Dialogue facilitation? In the same way that Voice Dialogue facilitation is a creative and open process with very few hard and fast rules or restrictions, so also the uses for Voice Dialogue whether in therapy, business, the arts, spiritual growth, etc., are many and limited only by our own imagination. In general, one can say the people who benefit most from facilitation are:

♦ people who feel caught, immobilized, or torn between opposites in themselves.
♦ people seeking balance, wholeness, and creative expression.
♦ people who want more choice and freedom in how they live their lives and in being who they are.
♦ people who enjoy the work and find it to be a fun and inspiring way to evolve and grow.
♦ facilitators who benefit doubly from being facilitated, gaining self awareness, and training in how to facilitate others.

What does it take to become a Voice Dialogue facilitator?

Voice Dialogue is primarily experiential, and to facilitate effectively the facilitator has to be involved in her own on-going Voice Dialogue process. This is definitely not a "spectator sport," not the sort of work you can instruct someone else in if you've never done any of it yourself. Even though there are excellent books to read and trainings to attend, *the first and last requirement to be a Voice Dialogue facilitator is to be facilitated.* Because Voice Dialogue work is essentially intuitive and energetic, the facilitator may find that presence, ease, natural talent, and enjoyment are all just as important as conceptual knowledge.

The facilitator must have an attitude of openness and a willingness to collaborate with the subject. Voice Dialogue is a joint (ad)venture in the exploration of consciousness; the facilitator is the guide but the person being facilitated (especially their primary selves) decides in what direction it's okay to be guided. Facilitator and subject are exploring the map of the psyche together with the goal of enhancing the subject's Aware Ego process. Voice Dialogue isn't really therapy even though it's used by therapists, and the facilitator is not looking for problems to solve, selves to take care of, or disturbances to label. Rather than attempting to change the selves or the subject in any way, the facilitator is an interested, non-judgmental, well-mannered interviewer, asking the selves straightforward respectful questions while always honoring their limits.

"The first and last requirement to be a Voice Dialogue facilitator is to be facilitated."

Voice Dialogue facilitators are fluent in the language of energy and enjoy the surprise of working with the unknown. You never know exactly who will show up when you ask a self to move over, and when a self does arrive on the scene, the facilitator has to be able to recognize its energy pattern and match it with her own. For some facilitators this comes naturally and others have to work at it. In either case there is an understanding that both working with energetics and an ability to be flexible and improvise are essential to the process.

Facilitators come from many different backgrounds and bring a wide variety of skills and talents to the work. As a facilitator you may find your life experience and training in other fields to be just as valuable as what you specifically learn about the Voice Dialogue method. The Stones comment on "Introducing Voice Dialogue," an audio tape in *The Mendocino Series*:

> *We have noticed that the broader a person's background and the deeper their insights, the more powerful the tool [Voice Dialogue] will be. We see Voice Dialogue somewhat like a musical instrument. The instrument is the same for everybody, but the music that you get from it is going to depend a lot upon who you are, your own maturity, and your own skill.*

Becoming a skilled facilitator is a gradual evolutionary process, very similar to the development of the Aware Ego itself. My own experience is that as I've become more comfortable with facilitation and more familiar with the territory of the psyche, the selves of the people I work with have become more and more comfortable with me as a facilitator. The facilitator really does come across after a while as an "old hand," a guide who is at ease expecting the unexpected, and the selves (especially the primary ones) feel it's safe to relax and be facilitated.

The facilitator is someone who:

- ♦ has begun the on-going process of separating from his own primary selves.
- ♦ balances intuition and intellect in his work.
- ♦ is respectful of all the selves and genuinely interested in them.
- ♦ is non-judgmental and never takes sides for or against a self.
- ♦ can recognize a particular self when he "sees" it and can distinguish the different energies of the primary and disowned selves.
- ♦ is fluent in energetics and can match the subject's energy.
- ♦ is comfortable with the unknown and enjoys work that is full of surprises.
- ♦ can help the subject separate from the selves and be in the Aware Ego.
- ♦ guides the subject in channeling the energies of the selves through the Aware Ego.
- ♦ models the Aware Ego and the Aware Ego's ability to manage and balance energetic involvement.
- ♦ honors the sovereignty of the person being facilitated.

How do I train to be a Voice Dialogue facilitator?

Your training as a facilitator begins when you first experience the energetic reality of your own selves and start to separate from them, initiating an Aware Ego process. This could happen through being facilitated in a private Voice Dialogue session, through participation in a workshop, from doing one of the exercises suggested in some of the books written on Voice Dialogue, and even, interestingly enough, through observing someone else's Voice Dialogue session and experiencing the energy of their work in yourself. *One way or another it is essential to have an energetic experience of the work and to have the beginning of an Aware Ego in relation to at least one of your primary selves (and its opposite), before attempting to facilitate.* If you don't, you can count on it that your operating ego will "manage" Voice Dialogue for you in the same way it takes care of everything else in your life. The facilitation will most likely be one set of primary selves (yours) trying to facilitate another set of primary selves (the subject's), and then the work will be vulnerable to all the usual entanglements that occur between selves when there is no Aware Ego present. *This is why being facilitated is the core of any training to be a Voice Dialogue facilitator.*

When you have been facilitated even once or twice, everything you read and hear about Voice Dialogue facilitation becomes 100% more clear to you. I'm doing the best I can in this *Handbook* to describe in words elements of Voice Dialogue work that are energetic and non-verbal, and the Stones and others have also attempted with considerable success to convey energetics in books and on tapes. Still, everything that has been written is far easier to understand and use if you have had some real life experience with the work.

As you may have already discovered, there is no official certification for Voice Dialogue, no degree, and certainly no one way to learn the work. This means that facilitation remains available as a tool for all kinds of creative uses in many different fields. The lack of "Voice Dialogue orthodoxy" leaves the work open to creative input from all the people who become involved in it.

The open availability of Voice Dialogue means that facilitation can be used by professional and nonprofessional alike. Even though the Stones had been practicing psychologists for many years, Voice Dialogue facilitation was something they discovered in the context of their own personal relationship and not as part of clinical research. Many people around the world learn to use facilitation in this same way, as a tool for enriching communication in relationship. Others find "facilitation partners" to work with on a regular basis in an arrangement similar to co-counseling. In contrast to those who use Voice Dialogue in this very personal way are a variety of teachers and professional facilitators in private

> *"Being facilitated is the core of any training to be a Voice Dialogue facilitator."*

practice. In addition to Voice Dialogue facilitators and teachers, these professionals include clinical therapists, business consultants, acting teachers, movement and massage therapists, and many others who incorporate Voice Dialogue facilitation into their work.

While it's not necessary to be a therapist or to be licensed in any way to *begin* using Voice Dialogue facilitation, it is essential to recognize when the work starts to cross the line into therapy (usually in any long-term work with private clients) and make sure that you are either equipped with the advanced training and skills in Voice Dialogue needed for deeper long-term work, *or* can refer people in need of a therapist for professional help. *If you receive payment from clients for Voice Dialogue facilitation, then you must be sure to follow the laws of your state and/or country that govern professional counseling, consulting, therapy, etc.*

> *"If you receive payment from clients for Voice Dialogue facilitation, then you must be sure to follow the laws that govern professional counseling, consulting, therapy, etc. in your area."*

If you are not a licensed therapist and are not charging a fee for your time, then you would simply need to use your own discretion in doing any ongoing Voice Dialogue work. Many individuals, for example, form successful peer facilitation partnerships. In *The Voice Dialogue Facilitator's Handbook, Part II,* there will be many ideas and suggestions for how to structure your work as a facilitator and how to deal with some of the challenges you may encounter.

One of the best aspects of becoming a facilitator is that there are so many excellent options for learning Voice Dialogue work. It's quite amazing to realize that just two very dedicated and creative people, Hal and Sidra Stone, have in such a short time traveled the world teaching Voice Dialogue, training people in facilitation and seeding training centers, while also leading intermediate and advanced workshops at their own home in California. As a result there are to date facilitators and/or facilitation teachers in many parts of the US and Canada, in England, Australia, Israel, Holland, France, Italy, Germany, Norway, Sweden, Switzerland, Luxembourg and South Africa. In addition, other prominent teachers such as Shakti Gawain and Joseph Heller have incorporated Voice Dialogue work and training into their own programs. Robert Stamboliev of Amsterdam has created the Institute for Transformational Psychology (ITP) in the Netherlands which gives the equivalent of a Masters degree in Voice Dialogue and related work. The options for learning Voice Dialogue facilitation, from weekend workshops to three-year trainings, are many. You will find a brief listing of (mostly English language) training opportunities on page 308, and the Stones keep an updated listing on their website at <http://www.delos-inc.com>.

It is up to each facilitator to decide her own optimal level of involvement in the work and tailor a training program to her individual needs. One person may start in by attending a class or workshop in her area and then follow that training with ongoing private sessions. In addition she may use the Stones' books and tapes as excellent self-education tools as well as employing this *Handbook* as a "personal trainer." Someone else will begin their exploration differently, perhaps by first reading *Embracing Our Selves* by the Stones, the basic book on the theory and practice of Voice Dialogue, then finding a facilitator in his area to initiate his own Voice Dialogue work. What started out as a purely personal pursuit may evolve into an interest in facilitating, and then this person may go on to take a local workshop or class. One of the most enjoyable aspects of the work is finding your own organic way into it.

Beyond the introductory level, those who determine that they want to make a career of Voice Dialogue facilitation and working with the Psychology of the Aware Ego, will want to pursue advanced training with the Stones and/or other senior level facilitation teachers. They will also most likely go into a deeper personal process with the work, being facilitated regularly over a period of several years. And again, those who wish to pursue facilitation as a professional career will need to complete any education and requirements for being a counselor, therapist, or consultant in their own country or state.

Therapists and other professionals wanting to incorporate Voice Dialogue into an existing career in consulting or therapy might begin familiarizing themselves with the work by teaming up with colleagues to facilitate each other while using tapes, videos, and books for guides. This is a good starting place if there are no workshops in your area and it's too costly to travel. It helps enormously if at least one person on the team has been facilitated by an experienced Voice Dialogue facilitator, and *it is essential that each professional (regardless of how extensive his expertise is in other areas) experience a clear separation from a few of his primary selves and their opposites before attempting to do the work with clients.*

There are many Voice Dialogue teachers who will travel to teach workshops. (The Stones keep an up-to-date list on their website at <http://www.delos-inc.com>.) If a group of therapists or consultants brings in a Voice Dialogue teacher, the teacher can both give you, as professionals, feedback on your facilitation skills *and* give a workshop that will introduce your clients to the Psychology of the Aware Ego. For advanced training there are a number of training programs around the world (check the resource list at the back of *The Handbook* as well as the website). Currently week-long intermediate and advanced programs are available at Delos, the Stones' home and training center in Albion, California, although these opportunities are becoming somewhat limited.

If you are already highly skilled in other therapeutic methods, it is particularly important to come to Voice Dialogue with a "beginner's mind." To the uninitiated (or I should say "unfacilitated"), Voice Dialogue often *appears* similar to other well-known modalities, and the tendency for many people is to think from reading or hearing about Voice Dialogue work that they already know what it is and that they can start right in facilitating without ever experiencing or at least observing a facilitation. This isn't workable, in part because Voice Dialogue is so deeply energetic and experiential that a lot gets "lost in the translation" in books or even tapes. More importantly, *until the facilitator separates from her primary selves, it will be primary selves (the operating ego) and not the Aware Ego doing the work.* If you are already a therapist, counselor, consultant, or teacher, you can use Voice Dialogue facilitation to help you discover the primary selves

> *"Until the facilitator separates from her primary selves, it will be primary selves (the operating ego) and not the Aware Ego doing the work."*

involved in your professional life. You might want to begin your own facilitation by having your facilitator talk with your "professional therapist self." Separating from the "professional therapist" or "professional consultant" self will not only make it much easier to facilitate Voice Dialogue, but it will also help you to more deeply appreciate this important part of you and use its skills more consciously. You will then be able to conduct your sessions more from an Aware Ego place rather than from several primary selves which may have been in the habit of doing the work for you.

Even though it's essential to "begin at the beginning" with facilitation, be sure to bring all your talents and gifts with you. You may very well find that skills you thought were completely unrelated to Voice Dialogue are invaluable in learning to be a facilitator. I realize in retrospect that many of the different things I've learned and done in my life have helped me in facilitating. Learning to be a shiatsu (acupressure) therapist taught me to connect energetically with people and trained me to have my attention totally on my client, to forget about me, how I'm doing. Meditating made the idea of awareness or witness very familiar to me. Being a workshop leader and public speaker helped me gain experience with observing and understanding group dynamics – now I work with inner groups, and groups of inner groups.

Many people have found that training in the martial arts, especially Aikido, has been very helpful to them in becoming a successful facilitator – in everything from learning to follow and read the flow of energy to developing more ability to be impersonal. Visual artists, theater art-

In all likelihood, any facilitator you might interview would have a completely different account of how they went about developing their facilitation skills. I certainly can't suggest that anybody try to do the same things I did, because for one, it may not be optimal for them and also some of the programs I attended no longer exist in their original form. Instead, by sharing my particular story, I hope to communicate how totally individual the process of learning Voice Dialogue facilitation is and encourage each reader to use all the resources available to them.

How I became a Voice Dialogue facilitator

I became involved in Voice Dialogue in 1983 in New York City when my husband invited me to take a weekend workshop. After the workshop (I was totally inspired after one weekend!), I took an ongoing class where I practiced facilitating with different partners. Also, for the next three years, my husband and I (either jointly or separately) had two private Voice Dialogue sessions a week with our Voice Dialogue teacher, and we began the difficult but very rewarding process of learning to facilitate each other as well. During this time I had the good fortune to attend several of Hal and Sidra Stone's workshops when they came to the area. This entire process meant I had the opportunity to be facilitated by many teachers and staff assistants, as well as by the other people learning along with me. I was also able to observe other people's sessions and learn a great deal from a variety of facilitation styles.

Over time I became more skilled and began to assist at workshops. I was already a teacher and counselor before I learned Voice Dialogue, and I began to incorporate facilitation into my professional work. By 1986, having moved to the west coast, I began to teach some small introductory classes and workshops in Voice Dialogue. I attended Voice Dialogue "Sum-

ists, musicians, and photographers are all trained to see and hear subtle differences and changes in people and in the environment. Anyone who works with the body, from healers to dancers, has the skill needed to "read" the non-verbal "language" through which the body and the emotions express themselves. These are just a few examples of life experience and areas of expertise that can contribute to facilitation.

There's no need, though, to run out and learn any of the particular disciplines mentioned here in order to improve your facilitation! *What is useful is to start noticing what you already know or have experienced that can strengthen your work with Voice Dialogue.* It is the uniqueness of each facilitator's background, the gifts he brings to the work, that make Voice Dialogue so rich, creative and exciting.

merkamp" and "Winter Institute" in California (two programs that are no longer available in the United States) and was on staff for the last US Summerkamp in 1994. Since that time I have been a senior staff teacher at the Delos training intensives in California with the Stones, while continuing a private Voice Dialogue facilitation practice in Seattle. In 1995, realizing that there has never been any kind of written guide specifically for the facilitator, I began working on this book.

That outlines my "official" training and experience in Voice Dialogue, but as I look back, I realize that there were many other influences that contributed just as much to my skill as a facilitator. Being raised bi-culturally and growing up in both Europe and America in a variety of greatly contrasting socioeconomic situations made me quite comfortable relating to a wide range of people and/or selves. Years of training in shiatsu taught me how to pay attention to people on an energetic level, and years of experience with meditation and visualization helped me to be in touch with my own intuition and imagination when facilitating. And, perhaps most importantly, working consciously with the dynamics of my primary relationships provided a superb (if often uncomfortable) classroom for learning about the "dance of the selves," the challenge of managing my energy, and the nature of developing an Aware Ego process. Probably, if I really think about it, there isn't a whole lot in my life experience to date that hasn't been useful in Voice Dialogue facilitation. I'm convinced that the best facilitators all draw on a wealth of life experience in addition to their training. This makes facilitation alive and creative and results in no two facilitation styles ever really being alike.

Becoming a Voice Dialogue Facilitator - the best training is a combination of learning opportunities that suits your personal needs and style of comprehension.

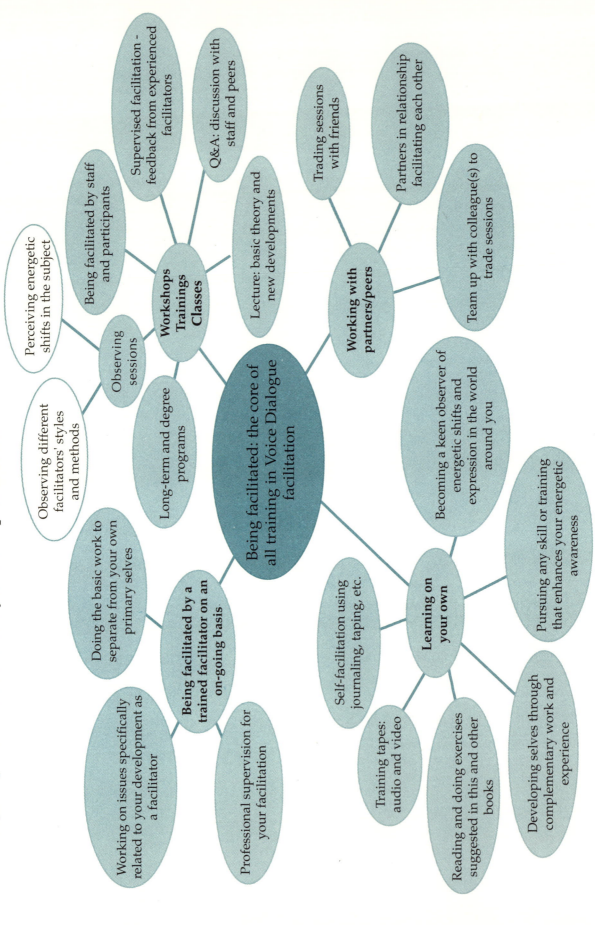

- Perceiving energetic shifts in the subject
- Observing different facilitators' styles and methods
- Observing sessions
- Being facilitated by staff and participants
- Supervised facilitation - feedback from experienced facilitators
- Q&A: discussion with staff and peers
- Lecture: basic theory and new developments
- **Workshops Trainings Classes**
- Long-term and degree programs
- Trading sessions with friends
- Partners in relationship facilitating each other
- Team up with colleague(s) to trade sessions
- **Working with partners/peers**
- Becoming a keen observer of energetic shifts and expression in the world around you
- Pursuing any skill or training that enhances your energetic awareness
- **Being facilitated: the core of all training in Voice Dialogue facilitation**
- Doing the basic work to separate from your own primary selves
- Working on issues specifically related to your development as a facilitator
- **Being facilitated by a trained facilitator on an on-going basis**
- Professional supervision for your facilitation
- Self-facilitation using journaling, taping, etc.
- **Learning on your own**
- Training tapes: audio and video
- Reading and doing exercises suggested in this and other books
- Developing selves through complementary work and experience

Introduction to Section Two

The second section of your *Handbook* builds the foundation for your work as a facilitator. We begin with the *ground rules,* which will give you and the people you facilitate a solid, safe footing as you explore working with the selves. After the "ground is prepared," it is the understanding of the nature of *energy* and working directly with energetics that enables the facilitator and subject to develop the Aware Ego process and thereby initiate profound levels of insight and change. *A central goal of Voice Dialogue is to develop the ability to manage our energy consciously in our daily lives.*

Once you have a clear understanding of the basic requirements of facilitating and have learned to pay attention to energy both in yourself and in others, you are ready to begin working with Voice Dialogue facilitation.

Ground rules
support the vitality and safety
of facilitation

Ground rules simplify facilitation, making it easy and safe. Just as the soil holds the structure that supports growth and life, the ground rules in Voice Dialogue hold a structure that supports the organic, natural flow of the work. Following the ground rules enables the facilitator to relax about facilitating because as long as she follows these few requirements it's very unlikely that a session will go seriously off track. The facilitator can also feel free to improvise and try out new ideas without worrying about the consequences – the new idea may or may not work out, but as long as she adheres to these ground rules no harm will be done.

My colleague, Shelly DeGroot, a therapist in Seattle, uses an image that is perfect for explaining the importance of ground rules. Imagine you are driving across a two lane bridge high over a rushing river. The bridge is well-built, has solid guard rails on the sides, and you drive over it enjoying the scenery with hardly a thought about the height or any potential danger. Now imagine going across the same bridge without the guard rails. The bridge is still just as strong and the pavement is the same width, the scenery is still beautiful, your driving skills are as excellent as always, but of course it doesn't feel the same at all! It's a rare person who will even venture onto such a bridge and if they do it will probably be at a very slow speed straddling the center line. We suddenly realize that guard rails don't just stop the occasional crash off the side of the bridge, they also provide an emotional and energetic safety net, a containment and protection from our own fears.

Like guard rails on a bridge, the ground rules in Voice Dialogue provide a container for facilitation, insuring a safe and comfortable passage for both facilitator and subject. In this way, it's easy to understand that these rules provide support rather than restriction. There are ground rules for both the work itself and for the facilitator's behavior and preparation. The rest of this chapter will go over these rules, explaining what they are and how they support the work.

Ground rules for Voice Dialogue work

Voice Dialogue is a dynamic process that is still being invented – very literally we are only at the beginning of this work and can expect new and creative approaches and applications to unfold in the years to come. As a facilitator, your ideas and experience will contribute to the evolution of the work as well. During the first 20 years of doing Voice Dialogue work Drs. Hal and Sidra Stone, along with many facilitators worldwide, learned through trial and success as well as trial and error that there are certain fundamentals of Voice Dialogue facilitation which insure the integrity, safety, and right outcome of the work. One can do other kinds of personal growth work and not adhere to these fundamental requirements, but then one could not call the process Voice Dialogue. These ground rules are so basic to Voice Dialogue that they essentially define it.

1) The purpose of facilitation is the development of an Aware Ego

The goal of the work is always the birth and enhancement of an Aware Ego. As facilitators we are midwives for the birthing of the Aware Ego – our own and that of the people we facilitate – over and over again. As interesting as the different selves may be, experiencing them is not an end in itself. Neither is learning to work with energy an end in itself. Rather, *each element of the work, each part of a session whether it is having a conversation, facilitating a self, observing from awareness, etc., is geared toward the support and development of the Aware Ego process.* Keeping

"When in doubt about what direction to take in facilitation, simply answer the question, 'Will this help the Aware Ego to become stronger and more functional in this person's life?'"

this fundamental rule in mind will help the facilitator every step of the way to make the best choices in facilitation. It can be tempting to use up most if not all of the time in the session talking with individual selves, continuing to go deeper and deeper into exploring their energies, as this is often a fascinating journey. However, this conversation is only useful to the degree that it increases awareness and enhances the Aware Ego's ability to separate from the self. Once there is an awareness of and separation from the selves, then time needs to be spent training the Aware Ego to manage the selves' energy. *When in doubt about what direction to take in facilitation, simply answer the question, "Will this help the Aware Ego to become stronger and more functional in this person's life?"* Knowing the answer to this question will give the facilitator the best guidance for where to go next in any Voice Dialogue session.

2) Always honor the primary self system

In Voice Dialogue we honor the primary selves as the gate keepers to the psyche and as the lifesavers and protectors they have been for our vulnerability. We don't trespass on the territory of the primary selves without their permission and we don't attempt to push past them in order to seek out vulnerable or disowned selves. In the facilitation process this means first working with *only* the primary selves until the subject has begun to separate from these selves and they are comfortable with allowing the work to move into the disowned selves as well. If a disowned self appears suddenly, it's best to return to the Aware Ego (operating ego) place and work with the energy of the disowned self from that central position, rather than running the risk of upsetting a primary self(ves). This is also why *The Handbook, Part I,* only has examples of facilitating primary selves, and we will not be working directly with any of the disowned selves until *Part II.*

It's the facilitator's job to support the primary selves in their protection of the subject's vulnerability. At the beginning of working with a particular subject (for as many sessions as it takes), *stay with the primary selves until a solid relationship with, and separation from, the primary self system has been established.* Once this has occurred, the work will naturally progress to facilitating vulnerable and disowned selves, and these selves may indeed experience profound emotional release. This will then happen with the permission of the primary selves and not by either defying or disregarding them. It is especially important to refrain from going to the vulnerable selves too soon. This means that even if the subject walks in weeping, the facilitator would have them* stay in the operating ego and work with the vulnerability from center, from the ego place. No matter how experienced a subject is in doing Voice Dialogue work, the facilitator is always safe in starting each session, at least briefly, with a primary self.

Honoring the primary selves is especially important to keep in mind when combining Voice Dialogue with other forms of therapy and personal growth work. Voice Dialogue takes a very different approach from many popular therapies which tend to be anti-control (i.e. anti primary selves). The Voice Dialogue facilitator always honors the primary selves – the selves that are conservative, that have built up defenses, that worry about what other people think and how to please them, that manipulate situations for safety, that protect the person's vulnerability, that avoid emotional outbursts, etc. Instead of encouraging emotional release or attempting to help the person "let go" of their perfectionist, or pleaser, or overly responsible caretaker, etc., Voice Dialogue works to *separate* from these energies and to develop an Aware Ego in relation to them. The Stones comment:

> *The profession of therapy has been seen by society to encourage the sensual, rebellious, anti-establishment, laid-back and self-centered parts of people. It's no wonder that the primary selves of the world want to cut funding available for therapy!*

If we don't honor the primary selves, the likelihood is that we will experience a primary self system backlash. The backlash may come on an external level when society's funding gets cut for public programs that are too liberal, or on an internal level when we lose private emotional or energetic "funding" for new ventures that go beyond the comfort zone of our own personal primary selves. Always honoring the primary selves provides protection against this backlash and insures that the results of facilitation will be long-lasting

"We don't trespass on the territory of the primary selves without their permission and we don't attempt to push past them in order to seek out vulnerable or disowned selves."

and organic. Furthermore, as the Aware Ego begins to function more consistently in a person's life, the primary selves are able to take it easier, maybe even go into semi-retirement or evolve into a more relaxed and benign version of themselves. *This is a natural rather than a forced process.*

3) Energetics are more important than words

For a self to be present, its energy has to be present. A vulnerable child, for example, is not an *idea* of vulnerability – it is a real live child energy and it is truly vulnerable. If the subject moves over to a self that talks about vulnerability for the child and feels and sounds like a grown-up, then that's not the child, but a different self altogether. This self has the energy of a protective, interpretive adult, not a child. *When in doubt in any facilitation situation it will always be the energy that tells you where you are and where you need to go, regardless of what any of the selves have to say.*

---

*See "A word about grammar" on p. xix at the beginning of your *Handbook* for an explanation of why plural pronouns are used here to refer to singular subjects.

Becoming fluent in the language of energy is an essential aspect of facilitating and being facilitated. Most facilitators have had the amusing and sometimes frustrating experience of trying to explain Voice Dialogue work, only to find that explanations are useless until the person experiences at least a little of the energy of the work. It is the energetics that brings this work to life, and the conscious exploration of energetics that makes it uniquely effective. Separating from the primary selves allows an Aware Ego to be born, and then *working with energy in the Aware Ego* is what enables us to take the power of Voice Dialogue out of the session and into our everyday lives. Training the Aware Ego to manage energy is a practical and revolutionary goal of Voice Dialogue work, and the unfoldment of an Aware Ego process through working with energetics gives us the unique opportunity to *choose* which energies/selves we want to express in our lives and when. This is very different from being *taken over* by those same energies and living out old patterns from habit. The more the Aware Ego evolves, the more it becomes a true master of energy.

"When in doubt in any facilitation situation it will always be the energy that tells you where you are and where you need to go, regardless of what any of the selves have to say."

4) The subject physically moves into the selves and back to the Aware Ego

As we have already noted, the selves are *real* energies, not mental concepts, and physical movement is an essential part of accessing their energy. It is through physically moving over into a self and then back to the Aware Ego that a very literal separation from the self occurs, and this separation in turn enhances the development of the Aware Ego process in the person's life. Of course, we shift in and out of different selves all day long, and anyone who has ever tried to sit and meditate knows how easy it is to do this without moving at all. However, most of our shifting in and out of selves in our daily lives is unconscious and therefore does not enhance the Aware Ego process. The purpose of Voice Dialogue facilitation is to separate from the selves (i.e. disidentify from them) and bring an awareness of that separation to the ego, to create an *Aware* Ego. The act of physically moving into the selves and back to the Aware Ego takes this process out of the realm of visualization or fantasy and grounds it in physical reality.

The facilitator stays in one place to anchor the energy of the session. The facilitator would not arbitrarily get up and move to another chair, as it is the facilitator's job to maintain a solid, stabilizing presence in relation to the subject and the selves. This is not to say that the facilitator must sit in the same spot for every session. What is important, however, is that once the session is underway the facilitator maintains a clear physical reference point for the subject's Aware Ego and for the selves that are being facilitated. *Under no circumstance is the facilitator to move out of the way and give her own place over to a self that is being facilitated – this can be an invitation for confusion and chaos.*

Facilitators who are very experienced in the work and skilled in energetics may on occasion change their position in a session, perhaps getting down on the floor with a child self or even moving with a very expansive self into another room, but this has to be done with consciousness and a clear awareness of energetic shifts so that the facilitator maintains her *energetic* position as an anchor for the subject. It is easier, especially when first learning to facilitate, to simply stay in one place, remembering that as facilitator you are standing in as the Aware Ego for the subject, while the subject's own Aware Ego is evolving.

5) Never try to change or get rid of a self

In Voice Dialogue we honor all the selves. A self may change and evolve naturally, but nowhere in the work does the facilitator or the subject try to force that change. It's not unusual for a subject to come back to center after being facilitated in a self and exclaim that they don't like the part of themselves that was just out – they can't stand being in that energy or wish that part would go away. That's *not* the Aware Ego talking! Instead it's another self, usually a primary self, that has emerged in reaction to the facilitation. The natural direction for a facilitator to go in this session is to have the subject move out of the Aware Ego place and talk with the part that wants to force a change or eliminate another part of the personality. Whenever a person wants to control or eliminate a particular self, it is clear that it isn't the Aware Ego expressing this desire.

> *"Whenever a person wants to control or eliminate a particular self, it is clear that it isn't the Aware Ego expressing this desire."*

Through the development of the Aware Ego we learn to step out of the age old tug-of-war inherent in "either/or" thinking and stand in balance between opposites. This is the beauty of the Voice Dialogue approach. At long last we don't have to give up one side of our personality to have the other. The Aware Ego is literally able to play on both sides of the field, and developing this ability to stand in balance between opposites is nothing less than a paradigm shift out of dualistic thinking and into what the Stones call "trinity."

> *The Aware Ego provides a way to move out of duality into trinity. The Aware Ego becomes the third point to any pair of opposites, and in this way we don't have to get rid of any of the bad guys to find God* [i.e. we don't have to eliminate some presumed negative aspect of ourselves in order to become good, spiritual, positive].

The facilitator is the model for this new way of being with our inner selves. *The role of the facilitator, like the Aware Ego, is to embrace all the selves.*

6) The selves do not interact with each other

Selves do not talk or relate to each other and no attempt is made to get them to like each other or "make nice." This rule avoids internal manipulative behavior within the system of selves and supports the development of the Aware Ego as "command central" for the personality. The essential lesson is that consciousness does not mean resolving the tension between the opposites in ourselves. It is not only not possible, but not even desirable, as such "resolution" usually means the repression of some part of our humanness. The *consciousness* we are working toward in Voice Dialogue is the ability to be in the Aware Ego and simply hold the tension of opposites, embrace them, and create an on-going dynamic balance in the center, expressing our full range of energies as appropriate in the moment.

It is the Aware Ego that must learn to interact with the selves and manage their energy. We have already experienced a lifetime of our selves interacting with each other. Stronger selves either protect or overwhelm weaker selves. Inner patriarchs and matriarchs try to keep independent selves in line according to the demands of the society. Critics, controllers, pleasers, pushers disown the parts of us that focus on our own needs or simply want to rest and be, or want to enjoy our sensuality and sexuality. Some relationships between the selves are naturally positive and supportive, but others can be vindictive and manipulative. If the selves are allowed to relate to each other within the context of a Voice Dialogue session, there is definitely the danger that some will be overwhelmed by others that have a lifelong habit of taking over. *Remember that the purpose of the session is to support the enhancement of the Aware Ego, to create the space for it to function and then train it to take over the job of managing all these different selves from a place of balance and acceptance.* This is very different from the unconscious rivalry, judgment, manipulation and coercion that *can* go on between some selves without benefit of the Aware Ego's impartial and supportive management.

> *"Remember that the purpose of the session is to support the enhancement of the Aware Ego and train it to take over the job of managing all these different selves from a place of balance and acceptance."*

7) The subject retains sovereignty

The person being facilitated remains in charge of their own process and does not go beyond their safety limits. This means that the primary selves are in charge of how fast and deep the work goes. Following this rule leads to empowerment. The opposite situation, where the subject gives up their safety and power to the facilitator, leads to dependence and violation of the primary self system. *The primary selves are like parents waiting for signs that the Aware Ego is capable of taking care of their "baby," and they're not going to let some facilitator push them into letting go too soon.* The primary selves, or operating ego, will gradually and organically give way to the Aware Ego as they begin to trust that the Aware Ego can handle difficult situations in the subject's life. Forcing someone to give up their sovereignty and go beyond their safety limits may seem to work in the moment, but it will in the long term inevitably entrench the primary selves more deeply in their defenses and create a distrust of the Voice Dialogue process. And, it will inhibit the growth of the Aware Ego. You simply cannot get to an Aware Ego from an unconscious place of disempowerment. The process of developing an Aware Ego is a process of evolving into greater consciousness and sovereignty in one's life. *To whatever degree I can access my Aware Ego is the degree to which I can be fully aware of my energy and can manage it on my own – I can choose how and when to express the different aspects of myself.* Enhancing sovereignty, empowerment, and consciousness is what Voice Dialogue work is all about.

> *"The primary selves are like parents waiting for signs that the Aware Ego is capable of taking care of their 'baby,' and they're not going to let some facilitator push them into letting go too soon."*

The more you work with Voice Dialogue (either as facilitator or as subject), the more you will realize that this process is a collaboration in which both facilitator and subject create, direct, and share responsibility. Since the purpose of the work is to support the development of an Aware Ego that can make clear choices, then it is important for the subject to have the final say about what does and doesn't work for them. The facilitator has to honor the subject's feedback and encourage them to be proactive in the session. This means inviting the subject to express any discomfort about the way the work is going, to put out their own ideas for what to explore next, to state their needs, etc. In *Embracing Our Selves*, the Stones speak about the subject's responsibility:

> *Because Voice Dialogue is a joint exploration, it is the subject's responsibility to react to the facilitator. The aim here is the expansion of consciousness, not the validation of the facilitator's view of life. Thus if anything feels wrong or uncomfortable, the subject is responsible for stopping the facilitation, returning to the ego, and discussing the interaction. It is not always possible to do this; sometimes a dialogue must be completed first. But once back in the ego state, by all means react! The facilitator is striving to become conscious, too, and [the subject's] reactions will only help matters.**

Ground rules for the facilitator

In addition to the ground rules that form the foundation of the work itself, there are also several basic requirements specifically for the facilitator. *Following these rules protects the vulnerability of both facilitator and subject and gives the facilitator essential support in doing Voice Dialogue work with grace, flair, ease, and enjoyment.* Whether you are new to Voice Dialogue or have been facilitating for some time, reminding yourself of these facilitation essentials can make your work more effective. If you run into a problem facilitating, it is time to read through this list again. The likelihood is that the problem is the result of forgetting one of these requirements and will most likely be solved easily by remembering and fulfilling it.

1) Do your own on-going Voice Dialogue work

The facilitator must initiate and develop her own Aware Ego process. As we discussed in our earlier chapters on Voice Dialogue facilitation and on training to be a facilitator, *without being facilitated on a regular basis*, the facilitator will most probably be functioning from certain primary selves and will be unable to effectively model for her subjects how to manage the energy of the selves from an Aware Ego. Also, if the facilitator doesn't do the work to separate from her own primary self system, she will be much more likely to get caught in positive and negative bonding patterns with the people she facilitates, and she

> *"The more the facilitator is involved in her own personal ongoing Voice Dialogue work, the more adept she will become at facilitating others – this is practically a guarantee."*

won't have the experience and the tools to disengage herself from these patterns.** On the other hand, *the more the facilitator is involved in her own personal ongoing Voice Dialogue work, the more adept she will become at facilitating others – this is practically a guarantee.* Although there are many other kinds of personal growth work and life experiences which contribute to developing skill in Voice Dialogue facilitation, *there is nothing that replaces being facilitated.*

---

*Stone & Stone, *Embracing Our Selves*, p. 77.
**For an explanation of positive and negative bonding patterns in relationship, read *Embracing Each Other* by Drs. Hal and Sidra Stone. *The Handbook, Part II,* will also explore the challenge of bonding patterns in the facilitator/subject relationship.

Another very important reason for doing as much of your own Voice Dialogue work as you can, is that it is often very difficult (sometimes impossible) to facilitate energies/selves that you have not embraced in yourself. It can be like trying to talk with someone with whom you have nothing in common, and if you're uncomfortable or a bit afraid that makes it even worse. "A Voice Dialogue work list for the facilitator" on p. 301 at the back of *The Handbook* gives suggestions for selves to work with in your own Voice Dialogue sessions. In addition to supporting the natural unfoldment of your own process, working with these particular selves can be very helpful in building your capabilities as a facilitator.

2) Be aware of energy and work with it throughout the whole session

The entire process of Voice Dialogue facilitation is one of working with energy, from the time the subject first walks in the door to the time they leave. This is such a key point in learning to be a skillful facilitator that we'll be talking about it again and again all through this *Handbook*. First of all, *the facilitator's ability to notice which energies are present and to match those energies with his own is what enables him to induct the selves – to help them be more fully present.* Without this energetic component, the work can become more a mental exercise than a transformative process. Facilitating a Voice Dialogue session can seem quite complex at first,

"The facilitator's ability to notice which energies are present and to match those energies with his own is what enables him to induct the selves – to help them be more fully present."

and for some people it's difficult to remember to pay attention to energy. Or, a novice facilitator may remember about energy when they are talking with one of the selves, but then forget energy altogether when the subject returns to the Aware Ego or goes to the awareness position. However, once you grow accustomed to focusing on energy and energetic connection, you'll find that this is what holds the real "juice" and power of the session, and you won't forget to stay energetically connected. In a very real sense disconnecting energetically would feel like leaving your subject and walking out the door! *This is especially important because inducting energy is only half of the facilitator's job; the other half is energy education.* Experiencing the different selves and separating from them is the beginning of the work. Then it's the facilitator's job to teach each person she facilitates to become aware of and manage their energies from an Aware Ego. This is why learning to master your own energy field and being energetically present all through the session are essential aspects of becoming an effective Voice Dialogue facilitator.

3) Honor all the selves – never judge a self or take sides

The facilitator models the Aware Ego's capacity to stand between opposites, embracing all and favoring none. This doesn't mean the facilitator condones any and all actions by the selves, but rather that she fully accepts without judgment the *energy* of each self and honors its role in the subject's life. This is another reason doing your own Voice Dialogue work is so supportive. *Having the capacity to be truly open to another person's selves without being triggered into a reactive pattern is a direct result of separating from your own primary and disowned selves.*

Remember that a self can only be itself. It can't bring in a different more protective energy if it feels attacked or judged during a session. A self's only choices are (depending on its nature) to become aggressive or to withdraw/disappear. If a self feels you are judging it, it won't open up in the session. Then both you and your subject will miss getting to hear its perspective. If you become a focus for a self's reaction, you won't be able to get behind the scenes and discover how it functions in the subject's life. Not surprisingly, when a self or selves do feel that a facilitator is criticizing them or is

> *"This doesn't mean the facilitator condones any and all actions by the selves, but rather that he fully accepts without judgment the energy of each self and honors its role in the subject's life."*

taking sides against them, the subject often terminates the work. This is not unlike what often happens in social situations. If I meet someone and they think I really don't like them or that I disapprove of them in some way, it's quite rare that they will come out and talk directly to me about it. Instead, they will most likely form a matching opinion of me as an unpleasant, judgmental person and try to avoid running into me again.

It's also important that the facilitator not become involved in the subject's internal conflict. As we have discussed earlier, it is quite typical for people to project their disowned selves on to the people they encounter in life and then try to resolve what is really an internal struggle through external conflict. If a facilitator and subject (or one of the subject's selves) get caught up in reaction with each other, this reactive pattern is likely to mirror and intensify the internal conflict already going on between the subject's selves, and it can make it much harder (if not impossible) for the subject to separate from those selves. For example, if I'm your facilitator, any judgment I have of you or of one of your selves will simply add fuel to your own inner critic or to some other judgmental primary self. The same is true if I have an overly positive reaction and become entranced by one of your disowned selves – the primary selves will feel rejected and betrayed. *I will have entered your internal struggle and now my reactions will be in the way of your being able to separate from these selves and develop an Aware Ego in relation to them.* For the work to succeed, the facilitator must hold a clear acceptance of all the selves so that they will feel safe and open to communicating.

Non-judgmental also means non-pathologizing. Voice Dialogue is compatible with many forms of therapy and personal growth work, *but diagnoses or attitudes that label people as dysfunctional, disordered, disturbed, deranged, etc. are not compatible with the non-judgmental Voice Dialogue approach.* Clinical therapists are often taught to categorize the behavior of their clients (many of whom are ordinary people with everyday problems) using terminology that can feel quite pejorative. This may automatically activate unconscious judgments in the facilitator toward the selves which is antithetical to the nature of Voice Dialogue work. In contrast, in Voice Dialogue facilitation, it is a delight to discover that it's *a particular self* and not the whole person

> *"For the work to succeed, the facilitator must hold a clear acceptance of all the selves so that they will feel safe and open to communicating."*

who "acts out" or "dissociates" or is "narcissistic," etc., and that the self has a long history of good reasons why it developed as it did and why it does what it does. Rather than judging or labeling this self, we can respect its motives, *separate from it*, and begin to activate an Aware Ego process in relation to it (and to its opposite). With the new balance we find between such opposites, it becomes possible to free ourselves of the compulsion to act out these parts that are labeled

A valuable note to therapists...

It is important to understand that the transformational or therapeutic value of Voice Dialogue does not occur through any attempt to therapeutically treat or change the *individual selves* in any way. The therapeutic changes in Voice Dialogue work occur by helping the person to develop an *entirely new relationship* with their inner selves, grounded in awareness and managed by the Aware Ego.

In the Voice Dialogue process no effort is ever made to correct any disturbance or "pathology" that a self may present. The selves are always honored as they are. The extraordinary changes that do occur through working with the Voice Dialogue method are generated not by correcting the selves, but by the actual separation from the selves and the Aware Ego's growing ability to stand between opposites and manage their energy consciously. The inner dynamics of the personality begin to shift remarkably – from an operating ego or primary self system functioning entirely "on automatic" – to an ongoing Aware Ego process where there are gradually increasing levels of conscious choice. This occurs without ever having to label any part of the personality as dysfunctional.

The work evolves through the facilitator being present with the selves and supporting the development of the Aware Ego process. There is no need to attempt any solutions or cures. This non-pathologizing aspect of Voice Dialogue work can pose a problem for those therapists who have the difficult challenge of having to diagnose and label clients in order to meet insurance and health management organization requirements. In such situations it would be important to create a very clear separation between judgments that have to be made to satisfy the system and the non-judgmental attitude required of the therapist/facilitator in order to do effective Voice Dialogue work.

dysfunctional. Of course, there are also situations that require therapy and medical treatment, and that are beyond the scope of Voice Dialogue work. *It is very important to remember that Voice Dialogue is not a substitute for medical treatment.* At the end of this chapter there is a discussion of when Voice Dialogue work is inappropriate.

4) Return to the Aware Ego if *you* become destabilized

The best of facilitators will occasionally lose his center and get "plugged in" to a self. The moment you notice that you have lost your neutrality and have become so caught up in an emotional or judgmental reaction to the self that you can't regain your own centeredness, *bring the subject back to the Aware Ego place at once.* This applies when you have an *overly positive* reaction to a self as well as a negative one. Because the subject is in an altered state of consciousness when they are in a self, it is your responsibility as the facilitator to see that you both return *at least* to the operating ego, and to the Aware Ego if you can get there. Remember that a self can only be what it is and won't be able to shift energy and defend itself against your reactivity, so it's up to you as facilitator to stay alert to the situation and bring the subject back to "home base."

"Your vulnerability in acknowledging how you became destabilized, and your responsibility in returning the subject to the ego place, will provide a valuable and lasting lesson in how to work with consciousness."

Once you are back in the ego place, you can talk together about what happened. *Ironically, what started out as a "mistake" on the facilitator's part can turn into a very empowering experience for both facilitator and subject.* As facilitator, you are trying to teach the subject how to manage their energy and become aware of when they project their disowned selves onto other people. What better way to teach this than by modeling the process yourself? *Your vulnerability in acknowledging how you became destabilized, and your responsibility in returning the subject to the ego place, will provide a valuable and lasting lesson in how to work with consciousness.**

Please note: The above requirement does not apply if the facilitator merely has a passing judgmental thought about a self or feels a tear in the corner of his eye. It's natural and unavoidable to have thoughts and feelings move through you. It's when these thoughts and feelings take over, and you can't let them go and refocus, that you need to give up trying to work with this particular self and return to the Aware Ego.

5) Never walk out on a self or let your subject leave the session "in voice"

Voice Dialogue work creates an altered state of consciousness when the person being facilitated moves into the various selves. The state of being "in a self" is a little like experiencing a waking dream, or a guided meditation, or being under hypnosis. In this state the subject experiences the singular reality of one self at a time and doesn't really have access to the various reality filters the other selves could provide. This makes it hard for the subject to shift from one energetic expression to another if the facilitation is interrupted, and they are therefore quite vulnerable to distractions and disturbances. So it's very important that the facilitator avoid interruptions altogether if possible or at least keep these to a minimum.

As facilitator, you always want to keep your full attention on your subject, but if some interruption does come about, it's essential that you bring the person you are facilitating back to the ego place *before* responding to the interruption. Also, if the subject wants to go to the restroom or go get something outside of the room, always bring them back to the ego first, so you don't have a sub-personality wandering around loose. When facilitating a self, it is essential that *the facilitator not leave the room* for any reason until the subject is back in the ego place. Not

"The facilitator is responsible for seeing that the subject gets back 'home' to the Aware Ego (or at least to the operating ego) before going out on the street."

only do you want to return them physically to the ego place, but you also want to take the time to tell them what is happening and check their energetic response to make sure that they really have come solidly back into the operating ego/Aware Ego before you leave.

*You may want to review "The Voice Dialogue model of consciousness" on p. 8.

The same rule applies at the end of a Voice Dialogue session. The facilitator is responsible for seeing that the subject gets back "home" to the Aware Ego (or at least the operating ego) before going out on the street. This does not mean that issues will be resolved or loose ends in the person's life will be all neatly tied up. Nor does it mean that some of the selves that have been out in the session won't come back in and take over again. It does mean, though, that the subject will be energetically grounded and enough in control of their emotions to safely negotiate ordinary reality. To make sure this happens, the facilitator has to allow enough time for the subject to come out of deep work. It also helps to come back to the primary self at the end of the session and then spend more time in the Aware Ego place as well.

6) Keep the work non-directive and refrain from offering solutions

The job of the facilitator is to support the growth of the Aware Ego, and it is the Aware Ego that will take action and make decisions. If the facilitator attempts to resolve the tension between the opposites in the subject's life, then their whole process of learning to separate from the opposite selves and stay in balance between them can be undermined. This does not mean, of course, that the facilitator can't offer an opinion based on what she observes in the subject's process, but it's best to clearly qualify such an observation as only her opinion while reinforcing the understanding that the subject's Aware Ego is the real expert and will have the responsibility for decision and action.

"If the facilitator attempts to resolve the tension between the opposites in the subject's life, then their whole process of learning to separate from the opposite selves and stay in balance between them can be undermined."

This rule not only applies in talking with the subject in the Aware Ego but is even more important in talking with the individual selves. It is natural, especially for people trained in other therapeutic methods, to listen to the concerns of the various selves and want to help them, but it is essential to remember that regardless of whatever problems the *subject* is working with, *the selves are not people in need of therapy or solutions.* It is much more productive to think of selves as individuals with interesting lives, concerns, and agendas of their own, and the facilitator's job is to interview rather than fix or even try to help them. This approach will lead to the desired outcome of developing an Aware Ego that can recognize and manage the diverse energies of these many different selves. It also makes the facilitator's job simpler and more enjoyable.

7) No physical contact

There are too many selves that will just shut up and withdraw when there is physical contact because someone in the primary self system has decided it is not safe. Some touch can feel very threatening and holding a person to comfort them can be infantalizing. Touch can keep the person in their vulnerability and limit the development of the Aware Ego process. Voice Dialogue is all about learning to be there for yourself from the Aware Ego place and physical contact can inhibit this process.

If the facilitator moves to physically touch the person she is facilitating, she may usurp the space that needs to be held open for the subject's Aware Ego to step into. Plus, if the facilitator moves to physically connect with a self, she will abandon her own center space and won't be able to clearly model the Aware Ego and the Aware Ego's separation from the selves. There are, of course, many kinds of therapy work where the therapist or coach does touch the client and body work is all about touch. In general, though, even when combining Voice Dialogue facilitation with body work or other methods which involve physical contact, it is better to give the selves more space and refrain from any physical connection *during* the actual Voice Dialogue work.

When *not* to do Voice Dialogue

Please keep in mind that Voice Dialogue work isn't for everyone or for all situations. In addition to following the ground rules to make facilitation effective and safe, it is also important to recognize when not to do any facilitation at all. Certainly, if the subject is going to retain sovereignty, it is essential that they participate willingly in the session. *Don't ever push it – even if you are completely enthusiastic about the work and truly feel it would be perfect for this particular person.* Here are some indications of when facilitation is inappropriate. Can you think of others?

➡ **If the subject isn't ready, able or willing to accept the reality of selves** – some people simply can't accept this concept.

➡ **When a strong primary self(ves) refuses to acknowledge the existence of any other parts of the personality,** the person can end up fighting the work, making it unpleasant and unproductive.

➡ **If the person has no operating ego,** there is no one at center who can identify the different selves. This is particularly true of people who suffer from multiple personality disorder and who would only become further split by doing Voice Dialogue facilitation. Remember that the Aware Ego develops *out of the operating ego* – there has to be an operating ego functioning as the organizing principle in the subject's personality in order to begin Voice Dialogue work. To review our definitions, this means there is a group of primary selves which comprise my "operating ego" and this operating ego is who I "know" myself to be. It is the operating ego that answers to my name, can account for my actions, whereabouts, etc. However, in a person experiencing a multiple personality disorder this central identification and accountability are often missing.

➡ **When the subject is immersed in grief or rage, or is in a very vulnerable state** and needs to do other kinds of therapeutic work to release and/or stabilize their emotions before they are ready to work with any of the selves. Staying in the operating ego while the emotions are running high honors the primary selves and their protection of the subject's vulnerability.

➡ **If a person is in severe depression or in the process of a full-blown psychotic episode,** Voice Dialogue is not the healing method of choice in these situations or for most crisis intervention situations. It is essential that the facilitator acknowledge immediately if the situation is more than she can handle and refer people to a qualified professional who can help prescribe medication or other forms of treatment needed in extreme situations. As the situation comes under control, facilitation may again become an appropriate part of this person's healing process.

One excellent guideline: If you are uncomfortable doing Voice Dialogue facilitation with a particular person, chances are that this person is also uncomfortable with the work. Have a conversation about it from the ego place. The Stones remind us *"that there is a big difference between Voice Dialogue as a method and the Psychology of the Aware Ego as a theory - the theory leads to thousands of applications of which Voice Dialogue is only one."* Following your intuition in addition to following the ground rules will help you as a facilitator to be of service to those you facilitate and to truly enjoy your work.

Are there people who shouldn't be Voice Dialogue facilitators? If a person doesn't want to do the fundamental work of exploring and separating from their own selves and developing their own Aware Ego, it will be essentially impossible for them to facilitate others in this process. Voice Dialogue facilitation, for example, is definitely not a method for the professional who prefers to examine someone else's vulnerability while ignoring or avoiding his own. However, the fact that Voice Dialogue facilitation may at first seem a bit awkward or unfamiliar should not discourage you from pursuing it at a pace that is enjoyable and rewarding for you. *As long as you appreciate working with energy, respect the selves, and are willing to follow the ground rules, chances are you will be able to use the Voice Dialogue method with success.*

Summary

Voice Dialogue is creative and improvisational, and the facilitator's freedom to follow his intuition and imagination is grounded in seven basic rules which shape the character of the work and ensure both its safety and success. These ground rules provide a supportive framework for the novice facilitator and allow the advanced facilitator to feel confident in experimenting with new ideas. New ideas may not always fly, but so long as the ground rules are honored no harm will be done, and it will be easy to get back on track. For quick reference, the seven ground rules for Voice Dialogue work are:

☆ *The purpose of facilitation is the development of an Aware Ego.*

☆ *Always honor the primary self system.*

☆ *Energetics are more important than words.*

☆ *The subject physically moves into the selves and back to the Aware Ego.*

☆ *Never try to change or get rid of a self.*

☆ *The selves do not interact with each other.*

☆ *The subject retains sovereignty.*

The more experience you have in facilitating, the more you will appreciate the support of these ground rules "under your feet" as you work. In addition to our basic ground rules, following the requirements for the facilitator will make your work even easier. In fact, adhering to these rules and requirements can make facilitation so smooth and easy, you may have a hard time calling it "work." Keep referring to this checklist till you know it as well as your own name.

☆ *Do your own on-going Voice Dialogue work.*

☆ *Be aware of energy and work with it throughout the whole session.*

☆ *Honor all the selves – never judge a self or take sides between selves.*

☆ *Return to the Aware Ego if you become destabilized.*

☆ *Never walk out on a self or let your subject leave the session "in voice."*

☆ *Keep the work non-directive and refrain from offering solutions.*

☆ *No physical contact.*

Energy
our hidden language

It's impossible to say anything about Voice Dialogue without talking about energy. Just in going over the ground rules, the word "energy" or "energetics" has come up at least 50 times, and yet because energy is essentially intangible and unquantifiable, each reader may interpret these terms quite differently. Before we begin the actual work of facilitating, let's take some time to explore what we mean by energy and how it relates to Voice Dialogue facilitation.

Energy – the way we feel, the tone we set, the "vibration" we send out – is at the heart of all communication and connection between people. Energy is also at the center of our internal shifts and changes from one part of our personality to another. I don't just *have* different things to say at the office than what I talk about at home, *I literally become a different person,* i.e. another subpersonality is present in my work mode than when I am taking care of children or vacationing with my sweetheart or going to a dance class. Each of my different selves has its own energy signature and its own way of interacting with the world. In fact, each subpersonality can be seen as a specific and unique energy pattern within the whole energetic expression of my personality.

Even though we may not think about energy or ever talk about it, by the time we grow up we have learned to express the appropriate energy – or its opposite – in each life situation. Reading energy is essential to our survival because if our energy is "off," if it doesn't fit the social norm, we may run into real trouble in making our way in the world. Here are just a few of the things our (usually unconscious) energetic programming determines:

- ♦ **whether we are successful at getting our needs met** as an infant, child, and adult.
- ♦ **our acceptance** in our family, culture and/or subculture.
- ♦ **whether we can send and receive the right signals** for attracting relationships.
- ♦ **whether people take us seriously** and believe we mean what we say.
- ♦ **the strength of our boundaries** and the respect we receive.
- ♦ **our ability to lead.**
- ♦ **whether people trust us,** perceive our words and energy as congruent.
- ♦ **whether we receive a positive or negative response** to our creative efforts in the world.

All of us receive a constant stream of very unconscious, yet specific, energetic training designed to shape us to our culture, class, gender, and anything and everything that determines our place in life. Women typically are conditioned to be energetically open to everyone. Of course, nobody ever tells a little girl to "keep her energy open" – instead she is told to smile, and is rewarded when she is sweet, personal, receptive, generous. And, she is chastised when she is grumpy, willful, selfish, or withdrawn. Men have their own energetic conditioning. They are taught to pull their energy in and to put up a tough front regardless of what they might feel inside. *Fulfilling the energetic expectations people have of us is often more important than anything we say or do.* Many women, for example, have discovered that they can "get away" with behavior that is radical "for a woman" as long as they don't step out of a conventional feminine energy pattern. They may run a big corporation or venture into other male territory, but they are careful not to adopt a non-female energetic expression. As a result, the men they encounter are disarmed. "Looks like a woman, feels like a woman... How threatening can she be?"

What are your "energy" memories?

Was there a specific way that you were expected to behave in your family?

How were the expectations different for boys than for girls?

Can you remember particular times when you were being quiet, wild, spirited, serious, playful, conformist, rebellious, loud, adventurous, timid, sickly, sensual? Which of these was rewarded and which met with disapproval?

Do you remember anyone from your childhood, a peer or an adult, who seemed to have irresistible energy? Were there things they could get away with that you or others couldn't? Were they admired, envied, shunned, punished, or all of the above?

Did you learn how to contain your energy, tone it down? at home? at church? at school?

How did your energy change at puberty?

How do you react now when you meet someone who doesn't meet your behavioral (energetic) expectations?

Primary selves are the energies we feel safe expressing in the world. They are the parts of us that have crafted our basic personality and the way we see and identify ourselves, while disowned selves are natural parts of our energy that we are socialized – energetically conditioned – to keep hidden from others (and often even from ourselves). The process of learning to divide our energy in this way is guided by usually unspoken but well-understood family and community cues and rules. In thousands of little, unnoticed ways we are trained how to use our own energy and we're taught what kind of energy to expect from others. If everyone had the same primary and disowned selves, these distinctions would remain unconscious and irrelevant. We would all behave according to pattern and the few unlikely aberrations would meet a quick demise. The human dynamic, however, doesn't work that way. In every group of people, no matter how large or small, there is usually at least one person who behaves counter to the energetic norm. This person may be a black sheep, a radical, someone who holds the disowned energy for all the rest of the group. They may be scapegoated for their inability or unwillingness to conform or they might turn the tables and take advantage of others who aren't as adept as they are in manipulating energy. Such a person might turn out to be a con-artist, a showman, a politician, or a corporate raider. It's also possible, though, that our energetic maverick could be an inspirational leader. A traditional (or one could say tribal) way of looking at people who are outside the energetic norm is that they cause trouble for themselves and for everyone else. In the new understanding of developing consciousness, we could say that *such people bring the opposites to our awareness* and energetically confront individuals and groups to integrate the energies that are missing so that they may reclaim their projections and grow toward wholeness.

When we begin to understand the vast communications that are continuously going on beyond our words, we become conscious of our energy habits and expectations, and a whole new world begins to open up. It then becomes possible to separate not only from our own primary and disowned selves, but also from generations of traditional energetic behavior. Then we can *begin through the Aware Ego to use energy in an entirely new way, by choice rather than automatically following in the "energetic footsteps" of everyone who has come before us.* Society is changing, and one of the ways human beings are evolving is that we are becoming more conscious of, and speaking about, phenomena such as energy that used to be purely unconscious and never mentioned. Nowhere is this happening more than in the United States and other parts of the western world where there is a dissolution of social structures and radical changes in family and community. We leave home, move far away, meet and partner with people who have expectations quite the opposite of our own, and we can no longer count on our social system to keep our lives under control. Instead we are left muddling through on our own, struggling with relationships, but also inspired to gain a deeper understanding of ourselves.

> "We begin through the Aware Ego to use energy in an entirely new way, by choice rather than automatically following in the 'energetic footsteps' of everyone who has come before us."

Working with energetics is at the heart of Voice Dialogue facilitation

The beginning of Voice Dialogue work is about experiencing the different energetic realities of the various selves. This is often an astonishment for people first encountering Voice Dialogue. They are amazed at how distinct and real each self feels; or if they observe someone else being facilitated, how different each part looks from the outside. Voice Dialogue facilitation gives us a direct experience of energetic change – same person, same body, but an entirely different energetic presence. However, this is only the beginning of the work. Our intention is first to experience these diverse energies *and then to be able to manage them consciously in our daily lives.* The first step is becoming aware of our energies or selves, and outside of a Voice Dialogue session we are most often alerted to their presence by other people's reactions to them.

It's not what you say but "who" says it – which energy/subpersonality is expressing itself – that determines how your words are received. Everything we say and do is accompanied by invisible but nonetheless obvious energetic packaging. We are capable of delivering what appears to be even a very simple statement such as "I think I'll go to the movies," in an amazing variety of "energy packages" depending on which self or subpersonality delivers the message. Maybe it's a rebellious son who is trying to prove his independence by going off to the movies. Maybe a spontaneous adventurous self just suddenly got the idea to up and go. Maybe there's a part that wants to be alone and have more space – and the *energy* of this "simple" statement feels like a cold front coming in.

The energy sent out determines the energy that comes back. Depending on which self is talking, our friend who wants to go to the movies will evoke responses ranging from hurt and anger to "Great, I'd love to come too!" If he receives a negative response, from your experience what do you think he will say? One possibility is: "What's wrong with you? All I said was I wanted to go to the movies!" The other person may know something didn't feel very good in the way our movie-goer stated his intention, but they're at a loss to explain it. Because our attention is locked into the words and content of our communications, we are often entirely unconscious of the *energy* we are transmitting as well as of the energetic content of communications we receive from others.

We don't have an accepted language to explain how we feel about the "invisible" part of our communication. We are reduced instead to bickering about "he said, she said," *when the argument is not really with the words but with the energy.* For many people this is confusing and disappointing. "What do you mean you don't like my tone of voice?" "Why do you always take things the wrong way?" Often it is actually our disowned selves that slip into the conversation

"The number one job of the facilitator is to help the people she facilitates achieve conscious choice in their energetic expression through the Aware Ego."

and cause a great deal of trouble. These disowned parts of us are not allowed a voice of their own, they're not permitted to come out and speak directly, so instead, in their attempt to be heard they insert themselves *energetically* into our conversation and we end up sending out a mixed message. *Until we realize that we are communicating energetically as well as verbally and learn to pay attention to the energy message we're sending out, it's very likely that our communication will not feel "clean" no matter how carefully we try to word our statements.* The words we say frame the communication, but it's the energy inside that word frame that holds the real life of what we are saying. If we only pay attention to the frame, we'll definitely miss the "picture," and we'll miss what others are "seeing" in us. *The number one job of the facilitator is to help the people she facilitates achieve conscious choice in their energetic expression through the Aware Ego.*

Learning energy management

The selves, primary and disowned, really have no choice. Each self is a specific energetic configuration, and when we're in that self, we're caught in its particular pattern. Only when we separate from the self and from its opposite do we begin to be free of these patterns and

Catch the energy at the moment of change...

One of the easiest ways to become sensitive to energy is by noticing when it shifts because like most things in life, energy is more noticeable at the point when change occurs. There are shifts you can observe with your eyes and ears, and then there are changes that everyone can *feel* even if we can't see or hear them. Let's start with the simple and familiar:

Think about when one person starts laughing and it becomes infectious – everybody begins laughing along. You can hear the laughter but it's the energy that makes it contagious.

What about when someone in your family is in a bad mood and it follows them like a "black cloud" all over the house, casting a pall on everyone else's good time. Or, you've had a great day, but you just can't hold on to your cheerful mood and buoyant feeling when your down-in-the-dumps partner walks in the door. Of course, you don't see a literal black cloud and your partner didn't overtly say or do anything, but you can definitely feel the change "in the air."

If you're a parent, you are very aware that it is easy to get the playful energy of small children revved up to a fever pitch and you are probably quite adept at toning your own energy down, getting energetically "quiet," to help shift them into a calmer mode.

These are all examples of shifts in the energy that may occur quite independently of anything being said in words. One person can (most often unintentionally) change the whole energetic atmosphere of the space around them. Novels, in fact, are full of melodramatic descriptions of just such changes:

When he strode into the hall, the air felt electrically charged and you could hear a pin drop...

Wherever she went heads turned and everyone caught their breath. A long sigh subsided like a wave as she went out of sight...

These subtle, and not so subtle, energetic changes are very much the stuff of romance. It is this level of sensing the energy, beyond the facts, that turns prose into poetry and makes, for example, an historical novel seem so much more alive than factual history. And these same changes, perhaps a bit difficult to describe at times, but nonetheless familiar and real, are what we're talking about when we look at energetics. Every facilitator encounters some quite dramatic energy shifts as the people they facilitate move in and out of energetically opposite selves. Actually, Voice Dialogue work is designed to make it easy to notice energetic shifts – having the subject get up and move to the different selves really accentuates the changes in energy. Once your awareness becomes attuned to these shifts, it will be easy to catch on to more subtle changes when the person you are facilitating is in the ego place as well. In fact, you'll begin to notice energetic shifts in your co-workers, your mate, your friends, your children, your dog or cat, characters in the movies and in random encounters at the grocery store and on the street! Have fun watching for energy changes in people *and in yourself* throughout the day and you'll become a sharper facilitator as a result.

to have conscious choice about the use of our energy. To understand this better, let's return to the story of our movie-goer and assume that his motivation for going to the movies is to be alone. Unfortunately, his loner self has a hard time getting away from people because on the other side is a self that wants to please people and hates to ever come out and say "I want some time for myself." The movie-goer is unconsciously caught between these opposites. The pleaser self will probably get to *talk* more, but while that self is busy trying to be pleasing, the *energy* of the one that wants to be alone may come out and push other people away. As long as no one pays any conscious attention to energy, this works just fine. The movie-goer is only held accountable for his words, not his energy, and his words are of course always blameless. When he gets a negative reaction to his energy, he can self-righteously protest, "What's wrong with *you?* All I said was I want to go to the movies!" Now the other person is the "bad guy" and our movie-goer never has to upset his primary pleasing self by making any direct demands. Of course, he gets snarled up in a negative bonding pattern (you can read more about those in the Stones' *Embracing Each Other* and in *The Handbook, Part II),* but it's certainly "not his fault," "he didn't do anything." The energetic expression from the self that wanted to be alone started it, *but that energy is invisible to him,* and so far as he's concerned, if it isn't seen it doesn't count.

According to the Stones, the Aware Ego "has an arm around both opposites," and it is able to respect both sides without capitulating to either or ping-ponging between the two. If our movie-goer could separate from his opposite selves and develop an Aware Ego in relation to them, he would become aware of both the part that wants to be alone and the one who wants to please. Then he could find a balance that honors both of these energies instead of unconsciously pushing someone else away or breaching his own boundaries. As this process happens over and over again with each pair of opposites, we gradually find that we can actually learn to manage our energy rather than being unconsciously run by it.

It's amazing, but even though energetic expression is central to all human experience, most western European cultures don't teach energy management, and, in fact, don't even have a concept of needing to do this. There is, however, in popular psychology, in the recovery movement, and in the women's movement a concern with the ability to create boundaries and the ability to say "no" effectively. These are just two recognized energetic skills that become far easier to master when we are conscious of and able to manage energy from an Aware Ego place. Accessing the different energies inside us, separating from them, and learning to manage these energies with ease, wit, and grace is what Voice Dialogue work is all about.

The facilitator as an energy coach

As we discussed in the chapter, "What is Voice Dialogue?" there are three parts to our concept of how consciousness works: (1) the selves live life, (2) there's an awareness of what the selves feel and do, and then (3) there has to be an Aware Ego capable of taking action (or not taking action) based on both awareness and experience. Back to our movie-goer again. Didn't you get the feeling this is an old pattern for him? He knows he wants to get away, and he knows he hates to come out and say anything someone else might not like, so there you have experience and the awareness of it. Experience and awareness by themselves don't really offer him the level of choice one would expect. It isn't until he actually separates from the part that pleases and the part that wants to get away that he really can do anything differently, and he's probably going to need to repeat the separation process over and over again until the Aware Ego grows big enough and strong enough to begin to manage these aspects of his life.

The facilitator is an "energy coach" who helps build the strength and presence of the Aware Ego. The facilitator:

♦ **helps induct or bring out the energies** of the different selves.
♦ **provides an energetic safety zone** of acceptance and containment.
♦ **models the Aware Ego's ability to stand in balance** between opposites.
♦ **demonstrates from the Aware Ego** how to safely encounter both primary and disowned energies without being taken over by them.

With the help of a sensitive facilitator in a Voice Dialogue session, our movie-goer will probably feel it's safe to move over and let the pleaser speak without having to worry about being judged for being indirect or manipulative. The pleaser, in turn, once it has been listened to, will probably feel it's safe to let the part that wants to be alone speak as well. Maybe they'll find out that going to the movies is the only place this loner self gets to come out. From a place of awareness the movie-goer will be able to notice the very different energy patterns of these two selves, and back in the Aware Ego place the facilitator will begin to help him separate from these opposite parts of himself and learn to manage and balance their energies.

Facilitating the selves brings the energy patterns to consciousness, *but it's not enough to simply have consciousness,* **one has to apply it in order to make choices and interact with the world.** The first part of Voice Dialogue work involves separating from the selves and becoming aware of them. If we stop there, the Aware Ego will be aware of the selves but really won't be able to do much more than observe them. *The second and more significant part of the work is training the Aware Ego to work with energy. The Aware Ego doesn't just do this automatically, it has to practice.* The facilitator needs to help educate the Aware Ego about energy – how to work with it and balance it. One can compare the Aware Ego to a director of a play. Without the director, we would have a bunch of actors (selves/energies) taking over the stage and acting out "the play" of the person's life based on old directions left from the family or from school or from various life experiences. When the Aware Ego first appears on the scene, it is more observer/audience than actual director, but gradually with practice over time the Aware Ego gains authority and presence and is able more and more to be a real director, making sure that the appropriate self is selected for each part that needs to be lived.

> *"The second and more significant part of the work is training the Aware Ego to work with energy. The Aware Ego doesn't just do this automatically, it has to practice."*

I'm not even sure my Aware Ego knows how to manage my own energy yet. How can I teach someone else? Ah, now you are beginning to sense why the number one requirement for facilitators is to be facilitated and to keep doing on-going work throughout your facilitation career. This is *not* because you need to be perfectly aware of your own energy before you can work with another person. Rather, the key idea is for the experience you are facilitating – separating from the self, bringing in awareness, and moving into an Aware Ego – *to be familiar and real to you,* even if you are (and we *all* are) still at the beginning of developing your energetic awareness. Remember that Voice Dialogue is evolving, and that, in fact, the Aware Ego itself is an on-going process and not an endpoint of perfection. For myself, and for most of the facilitators I know, it's been a process of learning and then teaching what I just learned, and learning some more and teaching that, and so on. This is the nature of doing experimental work, and there's no better classroom than your personal Voice Dialogue sessions.

The basics of working with energetics

The first step toward working with energetics is becoming aware of what you already know and have already learned in your life. Every reader/facilitator who uses *The Handbook* is encouraged to utilize her imagination and develop her own direction with the work. Even though there are very advanced and sophisticated ways of working with energetics, your *Handbook* will, I hope, demystify "energy" and help you to realize that *most of what you'll need to*

We talk about energy all the time...

☞ **We say a person is:**

available, up front, clinging, stand-offish, pushy, contained, like a big teddy bear, remote, threatening, reserved, draining, exuberant, cold, warm, a real spitfire, focused, aloof, invasive, scattered, intense, flaky, bouncy, cerebral, etc. ...

More likely than not, each one of these epithets really tells us about the person's energetic expression, about the way they carry themselves, their tone, their posture, their movement, etc. The cues we're getting about the person don't really come to us from the words they say.

☞ **Think about common expressions you use and hear** that have to do with energy:

If looks could kill...
I feel like he has a wall around him and I can't get near him.
Wherever she goes, she takes up the whole space.
I don't like this place, it feels creepy.
He looks like he's walking around in a fog.
She's dug her heels in on this issue; you can't budge her.
I don't care what you say, I just don't feel good around those people.
She walked in and the whole room lit up.

Each one of these terms or phrases or situations gives us an "energy picture." We actually know a lot more about energy than we think we do. For example, we know perfectly well what it *feels* like to be in a room with someone before they even say a word (or even if they never say a word). There are hundreds more colloquial expressions like the ones I've listed above, and once you take the time to notice them in conversation and in reading, you'll see that we talk about energetics all the time in our culture whether we're conscious of it or not.

become an excellent Voice Dialogue facilitator is based on experiences you've already had and uses what you already know. The basics for working with energy consist of:

➡ **assuming there is an energetic component** to all communication and desiring to understand it.

➡ **paying attention to body language** and other forms of non-verbal communication.

➡ **learning the ways energy connects us** to each other.

➡ **beginning to study and understand** the human energetic system.

All communication has an energetic content and as we've already seen, it's often the energy that holds the deeper message of the communication. Energetic communication can't really be seen or heard directly, but it moves *through* easy-to-observe expressions such as gesture, posture, movement, voice tone, facial expressions, changes in the eyes, breath speed, making sighs and sounds. Basically, everything you observe about a person (or self) beyond what they are saying will give you clues as to what energies are present.

It is very common for people to pay attention to the verbal content of their communication and allow all these other forms of expression to "run on automatic." We may or may not consciously pick up on energetic expression in others or in ourselves as we converse with each other, but we feel the energy and respond to it with remarkable accuracy. Some research indicates that perhaps as much as 90% of all communication is actually accomplished non-verbally. *A big part of becoming a good Voice Dialogue facilitator is learning to bring these non-verbal forms of communication to consciousness by paying at least as much attention to them as we do to the content of what is being said.* In all the facilitation examples in your *Handbook* you will find descriptions of energetic communication – the "silent" conversation that accompanies the spoken one. In the chapter called "Locating the self in the body" in Section Four, we'll pay special attention to refining the facilitator's ability to pick up on energetic information.

"A big part of becoming a good Voice Dialogue facilitator is learning to bring these non-verbal forms of communication to consciousness by paying at least as much attention to them as we do to the content of what is being said."

Beyond simply being observant, there are really only a few basic concepts we need to understand in order to begin to work effectively with energetics. In his excellent book, *The Energetics of Voice Dialogue*, Robert Stamboliev outlines three simple and essential principles of working with energy:

> *"Energy follows thought"*
> *"Energy is both inductive and resonant"*
> *"Energy is neutral"*

"Energy follows thought. " This literally means that my intention shapes the energy through which I will communicate. If I'm not conscious of what I'm thinking (or of which part of me is thinking), I may send out all kinds of energy without being aware of it, but as I start to become more conscious of my selves and have clear intentions about my energy, it's much easier to begin directing it. *Knowing that energy naturally follows focused thought or intention takes a lot of worry and effort out of facilitating.* If you ask a person to move over and be a particular part of

themselves, most of the time this will happen easily just because you suggested it. If they move over and an opposite energy shows up, you still have a self to work with without your having to go through any involved process to get it there. The person you are facilitating may express worry that they "won't be able to find a self," and you can assure them that if they are willing to move over and just *intend* to be a particular self (maybe the one who is worried about being able to do the Voice Dialogue process), the self will in all likelihood simply appear because they want it to. Then the facilitator's job is to think about and sense into a matching energy that he wants to bring out in himself and it will surface as well.

"Knowing that energy naturally follows focused thought or intention takes a lot of worry and effort out of facilitating."

"Energy is both inductive and resonant." One person expressing a strong energy will most often bring that same energy out in other people – or, a reaction against it. The energy of each self is like a tuning fork that vibrates one particular tone. If you "strike the note" of your playful self, for example, somewhere inside of me a similar vibration will begin to hum in resonance with yours. If my primary selves are comfortable being playful at this particular time, then my playful part will come out too – you will have "inducted" it in me. However, if my primary selves are embarrassed by what they see as inappropriate behavior, they will stop me from playing with you and probably either think you should "grow up" or actually tell you to. The resonance will still be there but because I am unaware of suppressing my playful energy, the opposite energy is inducted.

Being able to induct the energy of a self and resonate with it is what makes Voice Dialogue work effective and alive. If you ask me to move into my inner patriarch, for example, my inner patriarch will feel much more comfortable talking with you if your energy is very similar to his, if you have the same upright, conservative, masculine air. If I'm having a bit of trouble getting into my inner patriarch, your bringing in the solid energy of *your own inner patriarch* will make mine feel comfortable, at home, as if he's walking into the men's club. If you were to stop "holding the energy of the inner patriarch" while you were facilitating me, I might not be able to hold on to that energy myself. Your ability to induct the energy and resonate with it really supports that part of me being present in the session. Matching energy in this way is a key dynamic in Voice Dialogue facilitation. *The facilitator needs to both support the selves in being fully present by resonating with their energy and also has to be careful not to induct an energy so strongly that it creates discomfort and activates an opposite primary self.*

"The facilitator needs to be careful not to induct an energy so strongly that it creates discomfort and activates an opposite primary self."

"Energy is neutral. " The energy that we carry in our many selves is fundamentally neither positive nor negative. However, it's hard for us to understand that energy is basically neutral when we feel so "charged" about the issues in our lives. This is really because we experience energy *through our selves* and most of our selves, primary and disowned, tend to be polarized for or against everything they encounter. As the Aware Ego begins to develop, we begin to free ourselves from our reactivity and discover that energy is indeed neutral and the charge was in our *selves*. One analogy would be to think of money as a form of energy that is neutral in and of itself but can be used very negatively or positively depending on who has it and how they choose to spend it. One person can use money to help build a better world and another might actually destroy people's lives with it – neither choice changes the quality of the energy of the money itself which remains neutral. Who uses any form of energy, to what extremes they go with it, and their choice of when and where to use it, is what gives the energy its positive or negative aspect.

A central part of your work as a Voice Dialogue facilitator is helping people to become aware of different energies in themselves and to develop the consciousness needed to express these energies appropriately. Let's look at a subject named Brian as an example of how one might express energy *inappropriately*. Brian adheres rigidly to one way of behaving, quiet and controlled, and then occasionally he "loses it" and flips over to an opposite aggressive energy. More often, instead of becoming aggressive himself, Brian finds that he magnetizes aggressive people who make his life miserable. A facilitator working with Brian can help him to express the opposite energies inside himself much more appropriately by enabling him to separate from the primary control side and learn to access just enough of that aggressive energy to become a bit more assertive and outgoing in his life. His primary quiet and controlled selves will still be predominant, but he won't be at the mercy of internal or external "hostile takeovers."

> *"The facilitator's role is to help the subject separate from the positively charged primary self so that they can also begin to let go of the negative charge they have attached to the opposite disowned self."*

In the process of doing this work it becomes obvious that each energy in itself is neutral – it's just how *much* of it a person uses and *when*, that makes it seem to have a positive or negative charge. As with a medicine that can be either toxic or healing depending on how much is taken, we have to figure out the right "dose" of a particular energy to use in our lives. The facilitator's role is to help the subject separate from the positively charged primary self so that they can also begin to let go of the negative charge they have attached to their opposite disowned self. Each time this separation occurs, the Aware Ego is strengthened, and *it is the Aware Ego that can experience the true neutrality of the energy.* Letting go of our charge on things and discovering that energy is neutral brings balance, discretion, and compassion, and eliminates blame. With these principles in mind, let's look further at how energy manifests in ordinary human interaction and how we can use this awareness of energy in facilitating Voice Dialogue sessions.

Linkage – energetic connection and communication

What do we mean by linkage? The Stones define linkage as "a generic term that refers to any energetic connection from any self, group of selves, or through the Aware Ego." In a sense, people can be placed along a linkage continuum: on one end are the ones who love and want linkage and can't get enough of it, and on the other end people who don't link with anyone at all and can't imagine what we might mean by "energetic connection." Of course, these opposites are often paired up with each other – a quintessential example being the energetically "warm" feeling woman, who wants and needs connection, married to an energetically "cold" intellectual man who wishes she'd stop bugging him about love and feelings. Certainly this sounds familiar. If you are already used to thinking in terms of primary and disowned selves, you would realize, "Aha! That woman is *identified* with feeling and with energetic linkage and her husband is *identified* with the opposite, with a rational, non-feeling, non-linkage way of being."

Whether we are identified with our personal or impersonal (linkage or non-linkage) sides, until we can separate from our primary selves, we're locked into carrying one kind of energy and reacting to people who carry the opposite. We could say about the husband and wife in the above example that *they are each carrying the other's disowned energy.* This is, in fact, the traditional idea of a marriage where each spouse carried only their half of the energy spectrum and relied heavily if not entirely on the other to carry for them the energies that they had disowned. In a sense, only together did they complete themselves and feel like a whole person. People even used to speak jokingly of their "better half." Though this example may seem outdated and extreme, these same dynamics are very much alive *on an energetic level* today. However strongly each of us is identified with either the linkage or non-linkage sides of our personalities, we will magnetize to the same degree the opposite energies in our relationships.

The "linkage side" of the personality includes among others the feeling, empathetic, personal, nurturing, pleasing selves. These selves carry a lot of sensitivity and sweetness, but someone who is overly identified with this side may be so hypersensitive to every little shift in energy that they worry constantly about how others are responding to them. Being overly identified on the linkage side often results in very weak energetic boundaries with the consequence that the person either invades other people's space by being needy or feels victimized and abandoned by people when energy is withdrawn. It is such a relief for this kind of person to experience linkage through the Aware Ego, to have an energetic connection *with* boundaries instead of the total fusion they are used to. All of a sudden they are able to contain their own energy in a healthy balanced way and still feel warmth and intimacy with others. In fact, ironically, beginning to experience the Aware Ego process often allows the person who has been identified with personal feeling selves to actually enjoy their connection with people *more,* since it's not so compulsive and anxiety-driven.

On the "non-linkage" side we find the selves that are very intellectual and rational or that have to do with power and control. Obviously, it's important to have a good intellect and the ability to take control of one's life, to focus on goals, to be independent and strong. However, people who are overly identified with the mind may be completely "in their heads,"

"Learning to become conscious of our energy and link energetically through an Aware Ego is perhaps the most freeing and empowering aspect of the work."

oblivious to their own and others' energy. For this kind of person, the initial separation from the rational non-linkage side, and their first taste of energetic connection with another person through the Aware Ego, is a life-changing experience – it is quite literally "mind-blowing." As a facilitator, you may find that you have to first help some subjects separate from a very strong non-linkage primary self before you can create any energetic connection with them. After all, people who are "very mental" are used to sitting down and batting ideas around for hours without any energetic linkage. The mind "doesn't mind" this lack of connection, but without linking energetically, other more feeling selves will be left out in the cold.

Only the Aware Ego is in touch with and can balance both the linkage and non-linkage sides of the personality. The Stones explain that through facilitation we can give people an "awareness and experience of linkage as they have been using it, and show them how it is possible to use linkage with choice through the Aware Ego." Suddenly becoming aware of where we've been on the "linkage continuum" and being able to make choices about this previously unconscious part of life can feel like being given access to a magical tool. Imagine having walked through a room in the dark for years always stubbing your toe on invisible obstacles. Suddenly the light goes on and it's so much easier to chart a graceful course.

As exciting as it is to discover the many parts of ourselves in Voice Dialogue, *learning to become conscious of our energy and link energetically through an Aware Ego is perhaps the most freeing and empowering aspect of the work.* For those people who have been "in their heads" (stuck on the rational, power side of their personality), a whole new universe of feeling and beauty opens up to them. For people who are so energetically open that they link everywhere and have no boundaries, a wonderful experience of independence and

"The facilitator pays attention to linkage in the context of facilitation, helping her subjects become aware of their own energy and aware of their energetic exchange with her."

energetic containment begins to build so they can have the pleasure and empowerment of connecting without giving themselves away. For both, learning to link through the Aware Ego means having access to more of themselves. The Aware Ego by its nature is open to the linkage and non-linkage sides of our personality and this offers us an entirely new kind of intimacy with others. It is an intimacy that is both deeply connected and has strong and viable boundaries.

The Voice Dialogue session is a wonderfully creative and safe place to practice working with energy. As a Voice Dialogue facilitator, you are in the unique position of being an energy coach for the people you facilitate. The facilitator pays attention to linkage in the context of facilitation, helping her subjects become aware of their own energy and aware of their energetic exchange with her. The Voice Dialogue session is a supportive place where the subject can experience different kinds of energy inside themselves and practice managing energy through the Aware Ego. The more conscious the facilitator is of her own energy, the easier it will be to coach someone else. Sample facilitations in each part of this Handbook will help you to build on your understanding of energetics and learn how to work with energy in your facilitations. To strengthen your general ability to work with energy, let's next look at developing more energy awareness in all aspects of your life.

Deepening your energy awareness and skills

One can easily make a lifelong study of energetics. As a Voice Dialogue facilitator, you may become more and more intrigued by energy and decide to pursue some discipline or course of study that will teach you more about it. Please keep in mind, however, that your first and perhaps most productive source of understanding energy will be your own life experience and your Voice Dialogue sessions (both when you are facilitating or being facilitated). We've already seen that whether we realize it or not, everyday life is full of energetic communication. Just identifying shifts in energy and noticing that they are happening all the time gives the facilitator a perspective and awareness that most people don't have. Paying attention to simple things such as body posture and gesture, breathing pattern, etc., in his subject and noticing how these things echo in his own body and energy field, gives the Voice Dialogue facilitator a key to opening a

Monday — I was not looking forward to seeing Sue today because I usually get hooked right in to her energy. She's so! loud and I don't think she has any sense of boundaries, mine or hers. But I surprised myself! I tried "turning the dial down" on my own energy and was actually amused instead of irritated. We got along fine.

Wednesday — I was just relaxing after dinner, when I overheard Jules talking on the phone and I could tell by the tone of his voice that something wasn't going well. It felt the way it does when I'm going down stairs and miss the bottom step and there's nothing solid supporting me. My energy is really tied to his — I "go down the tubes" with him, a lot.

Friday — Last day of the week and last day of our project at work. I love the feeling of everybody's energy coming together. There's just this moment when everything starts to feel in sync, like it's going to gel and from then on I know it will be fine.

Sunday — Went out dancing tonight! It was as if I'd pulled out an old energy that used to be me, but I realize I haven't allowed that dancing part of myself out in a long time. It was fun, but I felt sort of pleased and embarrassed at the same time.

Tuesday — Liz commented that my new phone message really sounds different, more relaxed and welcoming, and my voice is deeper. Maybe this energy stuff is starting to have an effect after all.

whole new world of meaning and communication. Then, over time he can work with it more consciously and intentionally as this new awareness of energy builds.

Each self is an energy within the personality. If you pay attention to energy, you'll be able to perceive which selves are being expressed. And the converse is true as well – if you discern the different selves, you will by definition be noticing different energy patterns. No matter which way you approach it, the process becomes more natural and easy, and in surprisingly little time you may find that you're quite a pro at reading the energetics within a group of selves or a group of people.

Besides facilitation, how can I easily improve my ability to work with energy? There are lots of ways to work with energetics, and many of them are deeply life-enhancing, furthering one's personal and spiritual growth. The following suggestions by no means cover all the possibilities, but they offer a good start. (And, as facilitators we can also share with each other our favorite ways of working with energetics – see the note on contributing to *The Handbook* and to the website, p. 312.)

Keep an energy awareness journal.

This can be a great experiment for novice and experienced facilitators alike. Make a record of the energy shifts and events of your day, noticing among other things:

☆ **when you felt connected or disconnected** from other people and if you feel warm or cold toward them now.

☆ **if you felt uplifted, overwhelmed, stressed, comforted, etc. by people or situations you encountered** (if you're already familiar with bonding patterns, write down an energy account of what happens when you become involved in one).

☆ **when the words you heard matched the energy you felt coming toward you** from another person (and when they didn't), and how that felt to you. (Of course, it's harder to notice when the energy *you* sent out didn't match the words that you were saying, but it's really enlightening when you can!)

☆ **which people had a strong energetic effect on you,** on someone around you, or on a whole group.

☆ **ways that you influenced other people's energy** – did you calm someone down? get playful energy going? inspire confidence? pick up someone's spirits? increase or decrease tension and anxiety around you?

☆ **how "grounded" or "ungrounded" you and others seemed** – especially notice if decisions were being made from an energetically balanced place or from a frenetic place.

☆ **how your own energy tends to change** at work, at home, at a party, on vacation, in a crisis, with children, with the elderly – and what changes you notice in others' energy in these different situations.

☆ **what physical changes go along with energy shifts** in yourself and others – do you notice tension in certain parts of your body, a change in stance, a shift in tone of voice?

☆ **when do you find yourself in an internal energetic struggle between different selves** – doing something when your "heart isn't in it," or pushing yourself forward when a part of you is really scared.

These are only a few of many possible ways to recognize energy, and if you keep an energy journal you will probably discover many more. You may be quite surprised at how deeply an "energy journal" invites you to look at yourself and the people in your life. Energetics, after all, reveal the hidden agendas, the unspoken motives.

"Reading the energy of a situation reveals the disowned selves that we try to keep hidden as well as the primary selves we want to express."

Or we could say that *reading the energy of a situation reveals the disowned selves that we try to keep hidden as well as the primary selves we want to express.* Keeping an energy journal, even for a short time, will make facilitating more natural and easy, plus you may find it's a lot of fun. If you have a video camera, it might even be very educational to film yourself and your family and then look at your "documentary" from the point of view of energy. (If your family doesn't want to play, those old home videos might do just as well or better!)

Learn to "tune in" to the person you are facilitating

Beyond paying attention to observable changes in yourself and in the person you are facilitating, it is possible to obtain energetic information directly *by simply being open to it and inviting it to come into your consciousness.* Tuning in is like listening to your intuition, to the proverbial "still small voice within." Only in this case you are listening for a message about a person other than yourself. The vehicle for that message to come through is once again that intangible, never-quite-definable stuff called energy.

Even though most everyone has an understanding of what intuition is and how to use it, probably no two people do it in quite the same way. The same thing goes for tuning in and receiving non-verbal, non-physical information. Here's one person's description of his way of tuning in:

> When I tune in to a person (or situation), I infuse myself with their presence – it's like inhaling a gas that fills my mind and body with its essence. I invite in the image of what I am trying to tune into and shift energy in my brain and body to a place of receptivity. It displaces personality because I am filled with the other, my whole self is focused on being one with whatever it is I'm tuning in to. Then I quietly ask questions or look for images. If I don't "take off the clothing" of my own personality in the process of tuning in, then there is a struggle to determine how much of the information I get is my own projections and concerns rather than living imagery coming from the person or situation I am holding in resonance. (Richard Berger)

Everyone's experience of tuning in is different, but some aspects such as making oneself quiet and receptive and feeling a sense of resonance with another person are quite common. Many people also start out doubtful about the accuracy of the information they receive. "How do I know I'm not just making it up?" is a question beginning facilitators often ask. *Over the years I've learned that tuning in is a creative process and that the feeling of "making it up" is part of how my intuition works.* Just as artists feel inspiration coming from both inside and beyond themselves, tuning in combines my own intuition and imagination with what I'm able to receive from another person. I've learned to trust that what comes to me is worth offering to the person I'm facilitating. Like playing the child's game of "you're getting warmer… no, now you're cold… now you're really hot!" you'll find that you start to get a sense over time of when your intuition is accurate. The people you work with will give you feedback, and as your batting average goes up, you'll naturally become more at home with the process. Sometimes you'll be very clear and other times your own selves will cloud your ability to tune in and you'll have to refocus and go in another direction.

It is essential, however, to offer your perceptions without any expectations or investments in how they will be received. The facilitator can simply offer what he senses in a very neutral way so that the subject has total freedom to receive or dismiss it: "I don't know if this rings true for you, but I sense that…" "I just had a thought that may or may not seem relevant, but let me offer it in case it's useful." The subject may find your perception very helpful, or it may not "ring" for them at all, and you have to be okay with that. Psychologist, Betty Bosdell, Ph.D., who has worked for years with Voice Dialogue, tells the people she facilitates that when something pops into her mind several times, it's her rule to mention it even if she isn't at all sure what it means or why it might be important. Mentioning it, however, does not imply that the person she is facilitating needs to pick up on it. In this way she honors the intuitive process and the information her intuition brings without at all obligating the people she facilitates to accept it or follow any particular direction.

Here's a list of guidelines to help you create your own personal recipe for tuning in:

♦ **Quiet your mind and body** and find a place of neutrality in yourself.

♦ **Open to the person** you are tuning in to.

♦ **Enter a state of receptivity** and listen to whatever comes into the space you are creating in your awareness.

♦ **Free your imagination,** make something up and trust that it's part of the process.

♦ **Honor the information you receive** – thoughts, images, feelings, etc. – don't discard it.

♦ **Be present, patient and unhurried,** and become comfortable with silence.

♦ **Experiment** – risk expressing questions and suggestions based on what "came to you."

♦ **Remember that the information you receive is just one possibility** – remain flexible, making it easy to change direction.

♦ **Verify your experience, get feedback** – see where your tuning in worked, and where it didn't. Be unattached. (This will deepen your ability to tune in and further trust the information you receive.)

Tuning in can make the difference between a Voice Dialogue session that is quite good and one that is a profound gift to the person being facilitated. Before starting your session ask yourself the question, "What can *I* contribute to this person today?" and listen inwardly as the session progresses. *Though other facilitators might recognize the same primary and disowned selves in this person, the information you receive from tuning in is unique to you in this facilitation and unique to this one moment in time.* Your internal guidance might be something quite ordinary like "Just stick with the inner critic today, really give it some time, don't hurry." Or, something quite out of the ordinary might occur to you such as, "Try going deeper and see if you can have the subject access the voice of that very straight spine, let the backbone talk." Either way, when you tune in and listen and follow the information that comes to you, you offer the best of yourself on all levels to the facilitation, and imaginative, creative, powerful work is often the result.

Take the time to do some "energy exercises."

Most, if not all, trainings in Voice Dialogue that are available around the world include in their program exercises in energetics – opportunities to experience and identify clear shifts in energy and learn to consciously manage one's own energy field and energetic communication. It is definitely easiest to learn about and work with energy in a group situation where people can work energetically with each other, but the exercises included here will help you get started and may also offer you some new ideas for talking about energy with the people you facilitate.

Exercises in energetics

Energy follows thought or intention...

(Try this exercise the first time alone in a familiar safe place. Then the next time you may want to try it with another person or even see how it affects other people around you in a more public environment. If you do this with a partner, take turns, so that only one of you at a time is going through these changes and the other is feeling the energy shifts and giving feedback.)

To demonstrate to yourself how it is that energy follows your thought or intention, take a few minutes to experiment with thinking about different aspects of your life and then seeing what energy follows your thoughts. Working with this exercise over time will help you become more energetically flexible, able to easily shift your energy to match the selves of the people you facilitate.

> *The following exercise will work best if you allow time to follow the directions one sentence at a time and answer each question as it comes up before moving on.*

Start with simply noticing how you feel right now. Is your energy down or up? Do you feel open, closed, neither? Are you agitated, peaceful, tired, wired? *It's important to take note of your starting point so you'll be able to compare and notice the changes.*

Next, think about someone you love dearly and imagine being with them, wanting to reach out to them, feeling loving toward them. Notice how your body feels when you do this. We talk about feeling "warmth" toward the people we love. Can you actually feel any part of you get warmer? How does your heart and the area around it feel? Do you feel more expanded or contracted? If you're doing this with another person(s) in the room, do they seem to warm up to you? How does the space between you feel different?

Shift now into thinking about a situation that really frustrated or irritated you. Let yourself go back into that energy of annoyance or anger. Where do you feel tension in your body? What happens to your energy field when you change your focus in this way? Can you actually feel something change out around your body? If someone walked in right now, could they walk up and hug you, or do you have a sort of invisible sign out around you that says STOP HERE! If you are doing this with a partner, ask them to tell you about what they felt as you shifted from loving to irritated energy. Let yourself go back to "neutral" before you shift into the next energy.

Experiment with recalling a time that you felt anxious or afraid. What happens in your body the moment you bring that memory back? Anger and fear are very different from each other, connected to different organs, different acupuncture meridians, different body postures and gestures, so it's quite likely you'll feel a real shift as you bring yourself out of the energy of anger/irritation and into the energy of fear/anxiety. How protective does your energy field feel to you now – can you still keep people out, or do you feel like a soft-shelled crab without your usual protection? If you're doing this with a partner, did it feel to you that your *partner* changed in some way? Did their energy suddenly seem more invasive when *you* changed? Talk about your experience with each other.

Try bringing in a very peaceful, grounded energy perhaps by recalling a favorite place in nature where you like to relax and enjoy your solitude. Let yourself imagine birdsong or forest smells or waves or peaceful fields or a running stream or waterfall. What happens in your body as these images and memories come into focus? What happens to your center of gravity? How would you describe your energetic relationship to the world around you? If you're doing this exercise with another person, did you forget for a moment that they were here? *(Remember to take turns with your partner so that both of you can experience the whole process. Also take time to talk together and compare your experiences.)*

You can continue this exercise on your own by imagining any number of different experiences and then observing the ways in which your energy changes as a result of your thoughts. Try a spiritual focus or a playful one. Try some sensual/sexual energies or a businesslike energy or one that is very competitive. Doing this is very much like bringing the selves into the Aware Ego (See "Learning to access the selves through the Aware Ego" in Section Four, p. 265.) and will help you to become more skilled at recognizing and inducting different energies when you are facilitating.

Once you become adept at doing this, begin to pay more attention to the ways in which you affect other people's energy when you change your own. Notice also how *you* change when someone else does. What happens to your energy field when your partner gets angry or someone you love is frightened or a store clerk is very brusque and impersonal? And, notice what happens to the other person's energy if you *don't* respond, if you remain unaffected by their energetic changes. Experimenting in this way helps us to become more aware of our energy and more able to choose how we want to express it.

Working with your energy field…

(If you can, find someone to work with you. It's easiest to try these exercises first with a partner. If not, it's also possible to experiment with your energy field on your own or even with other people who do not have to be aware of what you are doing.)

The following exercises help you to feel your own energy field and the field of the person sitting across from you. You will practice paying attention to the energetic connection between yourself and a partner (a friend or colleague), and learn to recognize when you have made "energetic contact" with another person. Most likely you already feel this energetic connection even if you are not intellectually conscious of it. Most of us can sense when the space between us and another person feels "empty" and kind of flat, and we also know when it feels "full," maybe even electrically charged. (A lot of poems and songs have been written about the invisible energetic feeling between two people when they are excited about being together.) Doing these exercises will help to make you aware of the subtle changes in energy between yourself and another person, including when the other person "shuts off" and their energy is no longer available to you.

1) Sending and receiving energy:

You can exercise your energy field just the way you exercise your body, only instead of building muscle you'll be developing control of the subtle unseen ways that you interact with your environment. The only equipment you need in order to do the following exercises is your imagination and your awareness. Sit down facing a partner (close, but not touching). If you have no one to do this with, you can try it alone or with an animal or a tree. I've even experimented with expanding and contracting my energy on a crowded bus or waiting in line to buy movie tickets. Follow the directions one step at a time and take time to notice what happens before moving on to the next step.

Working with a partner, decide who is going to send energy first. The easiest way to do the exercise is for one of you to do the entire process while the other person remains silent (except when reading the directions out loud) and feels what it's like to be on the receiving end of these energy changes. Both of you may want to leave your body posture open, no crossed arms or legs, so as to help open your sense of energetic flow. And, though it's not necessary to have eye-contact to feel energy, *begin* with eye-contact so you can take advantage of all the cues you can get while you're still in the process of learning something new.

Begin with both of you letting your energy field be neutral, very much the way you would take a vehicle out of gear. It's easy to do this. Just take your attention off of other people and things and think of being in a sort of in-between place where whatever has happened is complete and the next thing hasn't started yet, sort of an "energetic holding pattern."

Directions for the person who is sending energy:

Now expand your energy field out around your body. Simply *imagine* that you have an energy field and that you can make it bigger. It may make it even easier if you picture an image that appeals to you personally. You might think of it as light around your body or a big balloon or bright color or you might not need an image at all – whatever works for you. Notice if anything in your environment feels different to you when you begin to expand your energy field. Notice if anything changes in your body, in the way you feel physically or emotionally.

Extend your energy field forward, straight toward your partner. Have your partner indicate nonverbally to you if/when they feel it (later they can talk about how that felt to them). Notice when you feel your energy come in contact with their energy field. (If you try this with different people, animals, even trees or plants, you may notice that your energy seems to be able to get much closer to some people than to others – the more you play with this, the more aware you'll be of the energetic diversity in the world around you.)

Shift your energy now and pull your energy field in, really close to your body. Again have your partner indicate when they feel the change (or if you're on your own, notice when something changes in your relationship to your environment). How does it feel to you when you pull your energy in, both physically and emotionally? What about the space between you and your partner. Does it feel empty now that you've taken your energy out of it? Do you enjoy this more or less than having your energy extended?

Try some variations in extending your field – imagine you can send energy out from your different energy centers (or chakras). Drop your attention down into your belly below your navel and imagine you can beam energy out from this spot. In many martial arts this part of your body is considered to be the energetic center of your being. How does it feel to extend energy out from this place? Does your relationship to your partner or to your environment change in any way?

Pull your energy back in, and then move your attention up to your head, to the middle of your forehead. Send your energy out from here and see what that feels like in your body. Does the world around you look and feel any differently to you when you send your energy out from here? Do you feel anything new? You can also try pulling your energy back and then move your attention into the area of your heart or heart chakra, the energy center in the middle of your chest. Does simply bringing your attention here make you feel anything different? Try beaming your energy field out from this place. Ask your partner to indicate when they feel this new energy. How does the space between you feel now? What else do you notice?

Take some time to share with each other what this felt like and then switch roles. Feel free to improvise with this exercise, try out other ways of focusing and sending energy. Play with moving to extremes – flooding your partner (or the whole room) with your field and then drawing your energy almost completely back inside yourself.

Note: *Being the observer is as useful as going through the energy changes, perhaps even more so, because as a facilitator you want to become skilled at recognizing energy shifts in other people and develop the ability to shift along with them.*

2) Opening and closing the field:

One of the first steps toward energy awareness is becoming conscious of when your energy field is open and when it's closed. Once you have this awareness, then you'll be able to adjust your energetic openness as you go through the day, opening up to energy that nurtures you and closing down when the energy coming toward you is overwhelming. With some practice you will be able to open and close your energy on your own in any situation, but at the beginning it helps to practice with a partner. As a facilitator you will be teaching the people you facilitate to regulate the amount of energetic connection they have with you, so it's important that you develop familiarity with and confidence in regulating your own energy.

Together with a partner, read through the exercise a couple of times so you have a clear idea what it is you are going to be doing. One of you is going to send a steady stream of energy to the other. The other partner is going to alternate opening up to receive the energy and then closing down their own field or turning down their end of the connection. *It will help if both partners nod or signal to each other to indicate when they feel the energetic changes.*

Both partners begin with their energy in neutral, sitting across from each other, close but not touching, simple eye contact, and just allowing your energy fields to be "normal."

The partner whose job it is to send energy begins extending their energy field out toward the other just as we did in the previous "sending and receiving energy" exercise.

Directions for the partner who is going to open and close their energy field:

Begin by opening up to the energy that is coming toward you. Literally imagine your energy field opening up to your partner's energy, enjoying it like sunshine on a summer's day. Let yourself bask in the warmth of their attention, let your energy field blend with theirs. This is what it's like when two very personal selves connect – lots of warmth and no boundaries.

After a while imagine that you've had enough connection, it's getting too close and too hot, and you'd like some "energetic shade." You need some space, a clearer sense of boundaries, so you pull your own energy back in and have a definite sense of shutting theirs out. Stay there for a little while with both of you noticing how it feels.

Now let's do it again, differently. Open up again to your partner who is still sending a constant stream of energy your way. Once again let your energy blend with theirs and relax into the warm feeling of being connected.

This time when you decide you are ready to disconnect, you don't want to be "energetically rude" to this sweet person who is beaming so much lovely warm energy toward you. Instead of pulling your energy away abruptly, you imagine that you have a valve or dial or lever that you can use to just turn down your energetic connection with them. As you gently and slowly turn your end of the energy down, notice what seems to happen to the energy field between you. Are they able to maintain as strong a connection, or do they naturally tone their energy down too? Take some time to talk with each other about what you experienced, and then switch roles and repeat the exercise.

Learn more about energy fields and energy centers (chakras).

For a long time now our culture has been used to the idea that "energy" (all kinds of energy from the energy of love to the energy from power plants) is both literally and figuratively what makes the world go round. We accept scientific concepts of energy (whether we understand them or not) that account for everything from our planet traveling through the universe, to driving a car on the highway, to turning on a light bulb or a computer. Modern science, in fact, has explained to us that on the most basic level all matter is actually a form of energy – that all there really is in the universe is energy. So it's not a huge leap to understand that there is a human energy system too, that we ourselves are, at our most essential level, energetic beings.

The study of human energy systems is really just beginning to be "discovered" in European culture – western science has only recently begun to confirm the existence of human energy fields and energy centers. By contrast, there are many eastern and indigenous cultures around the world where working with the human "energy field" has been widely understood for hundreds, and often thousands of years. As you become more familiar with your own energy and develop your knowledge of facilitation, you may want to study some of the fascinating ancient systems of energetics that come to us from other parts of the world. You can enhance your awareness of energy by reading more about energetics or inquiring into one of the many systems of working with energy. Yoga, T'ai Chi Ch'uan, Aikido, Huna, Reiki, Chi Kung, Polarity Therapy, Bio-energetics, and almost every form of meditation are just a *few* practices and healing modalities that focus on ways of working with your own energetic expression and balance, and that teach about the energy field and energy centers (or chakras as they are called in Sanskrit).

There are so many traditions of working with energy that it's quite easy to find one that appeals to you. Learning about energetics and about our "energy anatomy" is deeply absorbing in and of itself, and it has the added value of enabling the facilitator to better understand and work with energy in her Voice Dialogue sessions. Because you will be teaching the people you facilitate about energy, it's always useful to know as much as you can so that this information is familiar and comfortable for you. The more at home you feel with the subject of energy, the more easily you will develop effective ways of communicating about energy to others. Remember, as you start to explore, to take it easy and keep it simple. You'll learn as much about energy by

We have an energy anatomy just as we have a physical anatomy…

If you look into some of the books on human energy, you'll find that it is generally accepted that we humans have an energy field that extends beyond our physical bodies anywhere from a few inches to several feet. This field exists around other living things as well and has even been photographed with specialized cameras. It is also widely agreed that we have at least seven energy centers (see illustration) going up the center of our being, beginning at the base of the spine and going up above the top of the head. Around the body is an energy field that has layers which correspond to these centers (or *chakras* as they are called in Sanskrit). The *chakras* are in most systems associated with different levels of awareness and of emotional and spiritual development.

The energy field and energy centers together constitute an "energy body." Our energy bodies can be healthy or ill, strong or weak, active or inactive. And yes, it's possible to do "energy aerobics" and get yourself energetically "in shape." To work with energy as a facilitator you don't have to become an energy expert, but it really helps to explore and learn at least enough so that:

♦ **you can feel an energy field around your body** and expand or contract it at will.

♦ **you know where your basic seven *chakras* or energy centers are located,** can sense how they feel, and know what it's like when they are open or closed.

♦ **you can easily shield yourself from unwanted energy** and can "ground yourself" (anchor yourself to the earth's energy).

♦ **you can teach these same skills** to the people you facilitate.

It is beyond the scope of this *Handbook* to go into an in-depth discussion of all the different ways to work with energetics. Some ways of working with our human energy fields and *chakras* have been developed over thousands of years and are very complex and sophisticated. *What is most important is to begin learning about your own energy and to get good at sensing energy in the people you facilitate.* Beyond that, let your natural curiosity draw you toward studying other systems and ways of working with energetics.

noticing the energetic shifts in your own life and by working with facilitation as you will by reading or studying, so don't let one of your overly ambitious selves drive you into learning more than you need to know.

It's as natural to understand how our energy works as it is to know about how our bodies function. Even though much of our knowledge has come from foreign spiritual traditions and may be classified with esoteric information in your local bookstore, this does *not* mean that energetics itself is a big secret or difficult for ordinary people to understand. Dr. Sidra Stone in her book, *The Shadow King*, talks about becoming conscious of our energy fields and learning to manage them. Her explanation of a human energy field is simple and direct.

> *When I talk about our energy fields, I am talking about the energies that extend beyond our physical bodies and are usually invisible to the naked eye. We can see our physical bodies because the energy of our physical body vibrates at a rate that can be detected by our eyes. We can see the colors red or blue in the visible spectrum in much the same way; the vibrational frequency of red or blue can be detected by the mechanisms that operate in our eyes. The part of our energy fields that extends beyond the body is different, however. It is like the infrared or ultraviolet light, or like x-rays. Most of us cannot see them with the naked eye, but they are vibrating energies, nonetheless, and you can experience the effects that they have on your body… We all experience these energy fields even if we do not know about them. We feel the warmth of someone whose energy field is touching ours or the coolness of someone whose energies are withdrawn from us. We may not have words for this, but the sensations are well known to us.**

In our external world nothing runs without energy and it's just the same on the inside. The "management" of physical energy and energy resources is seen by corporations and nations alike, to be of the highest priority. We might be quite wise to make our personal energy expenditure and conservation an equally high priority.

"We can quite literally become energy masters instead of energy victims, working creatively with energy rather than being at the consequence of it."

With the popularization of energetic practices such as martial arts, yoga, meditation, energetic healing, and using visualization techniques for competing in business or winning in sports, we are beginning to develop at least an unofficial acceptance of the reality of energy even if our science doesn't always acknowledge it or approve. One could say that on the most basic level, it really doesn't matter what the official word is on energy because our experience of it remains personal, regardless of how it is explained or analyzed. What is important to understand as a facilitator is that the more conscious we become of energy and energy fields, the more options we have. *We can quite literally become energy masters instead of energy victims, working creatively with energy rather than being at the consequence of it, creating new choices and opportunities.* And, as facilitators, we can help those we facilitate to become aware of their energy and work with it intentionally and effectively through the Aware Ego.

*Dr. Sidra Stone, *The Shadow King*, p. 178.

Summary

To guide others in becoming not only conscious of their energy but graceful in the way they express it, the facilitator needs to become conscious of his own energy as well as sensitive to theirs. As facilitators, our job is first to do our own work, to separate from our selves and birth our own Aware Ego. We want to become as conscious as we can, over time, of our own energetic presence and expression. One of the most dynamic and satisfying aspects of being a Voice Dialogue facilitator is that since it's required that the facilitator do the work too, he gains as much or more from the Voice Dialogue process as do the people he facilitates. *It's not required, however, that you "first become perfect before you can teach others."* It's much more experimental and more fun than that. Many facilitators find that as soon as they separate from a particular self, someone turns up in their facilitation practice wanting to do the same piece of work that they just did. It's quite possible that it's the "energy" of their shifting and growing that attracts other people who need to shift and grow in the same way. We are on a journey together in the evolution of human energy and consciousness, and not only we but the work itself are still growing and changing. Instead of having to "have it all down" and know all the answers, *what is most important is simply the facilitator's non-judgmental dedication to the consciousness process and his supporting the unfoldment of the Aware Ego both in himself and in others, because that is the central goal of the work.*

Thinking about energetics may be new, but the basics of working with energy are already familiar. We simply need to bring our natural experience of energy to awareness, develop a language of energy, and begin to use our knowledge consciously. Anything that increases awareness of energy – of energy centers in the body, of energetic boundaries around the body, of the way energy shifts in a room when certain people walk in and out of it, of how energy moves between people – will aid in the process of our *learning to be energetically sensitive Voice Dialogue facilitators.* From there it's possible to enhance energetic awareness through many teachings about energy, both modern and ancient, but the fundamental information we need to work with energy is really completely available in each Voice Dialogue session.

If developing an Aware Ego is essentially an energetic process, then it works well to begin paying attention to the phenomenon of energy in ourselves, in our relationships, in our Voice Dialogue sessions, in the movies, in politics, in animals, in all of life. We are already familiar with energy changes, we just have to recognize and pay attention to them. *As you develop your skill at working with energy, you'll achieve empowering results in your own life and facilitate that empowerment for others.* Being conscious of energy and being able to use it intentionally opens new worlds of possibility. It is almost like learning to breathe underwater or having wings to fly because in a very real sense a whole new dimension of life becomes available to us. You'll find as your mastery of the language of energy grows that you become:

☆ **more able to have your energy and your words be congruent.**

☆ **more adept at determining the degree of your energetic involvement** with the people in your life.

☆ **less vulnerable to sudden energetic "take-overs"** by different parts of yourself.

☆ **able to experience a new kind of empowered intimacy** that allows you to have boundaries *and* stay energetically connected to others.

Developing an awareness of energy, and skill in working with it, basically involves comprehending *simple principles,* even though the results may be dramatic. We can start by discovering what we already know and by recognizing the abilities that are intrinsic to our nature, building on the reality that we humans are essentially energetic beings, expressing our energy through intellect, feeling, sensuality, and spirit.

Introduction to Section Three

Now that we know the ground rules and have explored energetics (the hidden ingredient that makes facilitation powerful and effective), we're ready to look at a Voice Dialogue session in detail and begin to use what we know.

Every Voice Dialogue session is different. Some sessions may include working with several selves, other times the facilitator will stay with one self for the whole facilitation. In some sessions the major focus will be on energy work (for example channeling the energies of the selves through the Aware Ego), and in another session the focus might be almost entirely on dreams. The work is always changing and is rich in possibility – it is open for imagination and creativity on the part of both facilitator and subject.

However, just as there are ground rules for all Voice Dialogue work, there are also basic elements that are foundational for each Voice Dialogue session. When the facilitator is familiar and comfortable with these basics, she can improvise freely. To make sure that we know what these basics are, Section Three takes us through all the *foundational components* of a Voice Dialogue session so that we can see and understand the structure of the facilitation process. Whether you have just begun facilitating or have been doing this work for a long time, you may find looking at a Voice Dialogue session in this way to be a real eye-opener. I know that I gained a great deal more awareness of myself as a facilitator by breaking the work down into all its fundamental parts and observing the internal logic of what I have been doing for so many years. Even if you're an "old hand" at facilitating, I invite you to do the same.

We will be moving through a Voice Dialogue session from beginning to end, but please don't hesitate to read and use the material here in the order that best suits *you*. For instance, you may want to jump ahead to a particular part of facilitating where you have the most unanswered questions. If you are entirely new to this work, I encourage you to take it easy, focus on one step of the process at a time, and allow yourself to relax and enjoy what you are learning. Of course, in an actual facilitation, it's unlikely that you'll think about all these separate steps as you work with your subject. Remember learning how to drive? You had to pay attention to your hands and feet, your peripheral vision, the gears, the other cars on the road, etc. until dealing with the demands of driving became second nature and you could relax and enjoy the journey instead of always thinking of how to operate your vehicle. You can expect facilitation to be much the same. The more you facilitate, the more the process will seem as natural as a conversation that just comfortably flows along, and the less *conscious* attention you'll need to give to the structure and dynamics of the work.

The chapters in this section are full of opportunities for you to participate in the facilitation process. In particular, with each of the facilitation examples there are questions followed by "discussion" rather than by "answers." The questions invite you to think about what you have read and to create your own approach to the various facilitation situations. You may want to take the time to think through your own answers before going on to the discussion which follows. The discussions in each chapter address some (but not all) of the questions. Rather than giving definitive answers, the discussions are intended to initiate an exploration of ideas and facilitation approaches that you can continue on your own or with your colleagues.

One final note before we begin: If you have not already read "A word about grammar" at the beginning of *The Handbook*, this would be an excellent time to do so. In order to help sort out the subject from the facilitator and the subject from the selves, I have taken certain liberties with conventional grammar, such as using the plural pronouns "they" and "their" to refer to a singular subject which helps to distinguish the people being facilitated from the facilitators who are referred to as "he's" and "she's." I have done this so that you can more easily follow who is who and won't end up floundering in a sea of pronouns. Also for simplicity's sake, selves are universally referred to as "it," even though in a live facilitation the facilitator would probably point to the place where a particular self was sitting and say *"she* felt angry about…" or *"he* doesn't like…" etc. On paper, without the benefit of gesture, it's much harder to keep track of who or what is being referred to, harder to know if a "he" or "she" refers to the subject, to one of their selves or to the facilitator. It's a good reminder, too, for the facilitator not to jump to identifying selves by the gender of the person she is working with – both men and women have opposite gender and non-gender selves.

Beginning at the beginning

Where does a Voice Dialogue session begin? Does it start when the person being facilitated moves over and the facilitator begins to speak with one of their* selves? Or does it start earlier, when the person first walks in the door? Is the conversation between the facilitator and the subject also part of Voice Dialogue work? What about before the subject arrives – does the work begin with the facilitator?

We already know that the ground rules say facilitation actually begins with the facilitator *being facilitated.* Unless the facilitator has initiated her own Aware Ego process the work will consist of one group of primary selves (the facilitator's operating ego) trying to facilitate more of the same. If you have not yet begun the process of separating from your own primary selves, another difficulty is that your inner critic, pusher, and perfectionist may make facilitating quite a trial and tribulation for you! After all, how much attention can you give to the subtle changes in someone else's conversation if you have voices in your own head judging your every move as a facilitator? *There really is no better way to prepare for facilitating someone else than by being facilitated yourself.*

Familiarity with the work builds confidence. There are other advantages to being facilitated on a regular basis. One is that it makes you accustomed to noticing changes in yourself and in other people. This in turn makes it much easier to identify the different selves that emerge in the course of a conversation with the person you facilitate. You'll actually be able to notice "who *you* are" before they walk in, and then quickly and easily pick up on "who is talking to you" once you greet them and sit down together.

Take time to become aware of yourself before you start the session. Being aware of how you're feeling, where your energy is, will help you avoid unpleasant surprises in the middle of the session such as "spacing out," or going off into one of your own selves, "going into voice." Take care of your own needs first! If you've been in the habit of functioning in high gear on a mental level, take the time to slow down and get centered in your body. Remember it's the mind that is capable of taking off at top speed, leaving the body and the energy field behind – sort of like someone who gets in the car and drives off without checking to see if all his passengers are

---

*See the previous page for an explanation of why plural pronouns are used here to refer to singular subjects.

actually with him. Notice your breath and how deep it is. Pay attention to the sensations in your body, how you are feeling and what you are feeling.

It's also possible to call in a "facilitator self" before you begin the session. Facilitators are all so different from each other – some of us find facilitating completely natural as if we had always been doing it and others need to overcome anxiety about doing something that feels a bit strange and unfamiliar at first. One approach that many people have used with success is to get in touch with a facilitator self in their own Voice Dialogue work. They then bring in the energy of this facilitator self *through their Aware Ego* before beginning a session. One might think of this approach as a stabilizing technique that becomes less necessary as we become more practiced and at ease with facilitation over time.

 *A Voice Dialogue session begins with the facilitator's own work and internal preparation, being aware of his own selves and ready to observe and connect energetically with someone else's.*

"Warm-ups" for the facilitator

The following are a few suggestions for ways in which the facilitator can prepare herself for a session. (These are, of course, only suggestions and not necessary prerequisites or even a recipe to be followed.) You may want to try your own version of one of these ideas or simply use them as a reminder to focus yourself energetically before beginning facilitation.

☆ **Facilitate yourself** before your subject arrives for their session. If you are on a tight schedule, this could be a simple and very quick exercise, or it could be something longer and more elaborate depending on what you have time for and want to do. If, for example, you can feel a part of you that is anxious about being a good facilitator, you can actually move over to another place in the room and have that self talk. After you come back to the Aware Ego, you may want to either move over into an impersonal self or pull some impersonal energy into your Aware Ego to help give you balance. There is great value in doing this as it gets you very actively in touch with your own Aware Ego and re-separated from some of the primary selves that can crowd in on your facilitation. With this simple preparation, these selves are much less likely to come in and surprise you while you are in the middle of a session.

☆ **Practice bringing different energies in and out of the Aware Ego.** Once again, this puts you solidly in touch with your own Aware Ego process before you begin facilitating. It also gets your own "machinery" running so that you're ready to bring in the appropriate kind of energy to induct, support, and communicate with each of the selves you facilitate during the session. (If you are not yet familiar with bringing the energies of the selves into the Aware Ego, refer to chapter on "Learning to access the selves through the Aware Ego" on p. 265 in Section Four.)

☆ **Play and experiment with your own energy field,** expanding and contracting your energy from the different energy centers in your body. Use abbreviated versions of some of the exercises in the chapter on energy.* These exercises will sensitize you to energy in general so that you'll be warmed up and aware of both your and your subject's energy during the session. Also, if you are tuned in on the energetic level, you'll be more conscious of linking your energy with the person you are facilitating and more able to teach them to do the same with you.

☆ **Map out your own primary and disowned selves on paper**. If you've never taken the time to do this before, you'll find it very enlightening. Not only will you have a clearer idea of who your selves are, but the process of identifying what is going on inside yourself will make you all the more observant of how the selves constellate in others.** Keep your map handy so that you can refer to it on a regular basis. Your selves will become more familiar to you this way, and you'll notice them more quickly when they make a surprise appearance in the middle of your facilitating a session.

*See "Exercises in energetics," on p. 68.
**See the maps of Glen's selves on pp. 100-101, for some quick and simple mapping ideas.

Beginning to build an energetic connection...

Connecting energetically
with the person you facilitate

The facilitator and the person he is about to facilitate need to connect energetically with each other. This may seem like stating the obvious, but many of us are not yet used to paying attention to our energy and our energetic linkage with others. Instead, what many people are used to in everyday life is a lot of unconscious energetic collisions as if we were driving bumper cars at the fair. If you remember our conversation about the feeling/linkage selves and the mental/non-linkage selves in the chapter on energy,* you'll understand that many people just aren't "tuned in" to the way they relate energetically with those around them. It may even take a few sessions before these people understand anything you tell them about linkage, while some may pick up on it right away.

The Voice Dialogue facilitator's goal is to teach people how to use their energy consciously and gracefully. The facilitator makes it easy for the subject to become more aware of energy by modeling conscious energetic linkage right from the beginning of the first session. The subject may not be aware of their own energy and they may have no attention at all on the facilitator's energy, but laying the energetic groundwork for linkage at the beginning *will* have an effect later on. Once we've worked with some selves and returned to the Aware Ego, we'll be ready to talk directly with the subject about energy and begin teaching them** about linkage.

At the start of the session, the facilitator pays attention to both his own and the subject's energy. As the facilitator, you are familiar with ways of communicating energy that the subject has not yet experienced, so it is *your* responsibility to pay attention to energy in the session at first. Then you can help the subject become conscious of energy as soon as they are ready to learn. As the facilitator you can:

♦ **pay attention to energy** from the moment the subject walks in the room and you say hello and sit down to talk.

♦ **use your imagination** to get a sense of the space between your bodies, how empty or full it feels, whether you feel the other person pushing toward you or pulling away, whether you feel "met" on an energy level or, in contrast, if it feels as if there's no one out there.

---

*See "Linkage – energetic connection and communication" on p. 61.
**See "A word about grammar" on p. xix for an explanation of why plural pronouns are used here to refer to singular subjects.

♦ **create a container of energetic safety** for the session. You know this container is working when the subject feels relaxed and trusting in your presence even though they may not yet have an understanding of what energy is all about.

♦ **balance** an overwrought or excited person by "grounding" your energy, imagining a connection to the floor or the earth.

♦ **notice if something feels energetically "off."** If you sense there is discomfort between you and the person you are about to facilitate, take the initiative to clear this up before the facilitation starts.

♦ **extend your own energy in welcome.**

Working with energy in some of these ways may feel like you're "making it up" at first, but the more you focus on something, even something "invisible" like energy, the more easily you'll notice openings, shifts, changes. You'll find that you become adept at offering energetic support (sending energy to link with the subject and holding an appropriate energetic tone) even before they are ready to pay attention to their own energy or how it is interfacing with yours. By staying conscious of the energetic exchange (or the lack of one) between you and your subject, you'll become very sensitive to how they are learning and changing. You may find, for example, that after facilitating a very strong rational primary self which does not link at all with other people, when the subject comes back to the Aware Ego there may be a sudden feeling of warmth and aliveness between the two of you. You can simply ask if they feel it too, and if they do, you have a natural opening to begin explaining energetic linkage.

Linking energetically usually only takes a few moments' time. It's often as quick as taking a breath, relaxing into your chair, making eye contact, and opening your energy to the other person. Because "energy follows thought," you can link with another person *by simply thinking and intending to do so.* Once you become used to experiencing linkage, it's hardly noticeable that you are doing anything at all or that it took any time to do it. However, at that point, it will be very noticeable if you *don't* connect energetically. You'll miss it! The facilitator who can detect this difference easily and feel what kind of energy is coming back at her is way ahead of the game. Before a conversation even starts, she'll sense what selves are "out and about" and know where the subject is coming from. As the work unfolds, she'll be able to help the people she facilitates to reach this level of sensitivity as well.

> *"It may feel like you're 'making it up' at first, but the more you focus on something, even something 'invisible' like energy, the more easily you'll notice openings, shifts, changes."*

Don't expect a first-time subject to understand what you mean by energetic connection, and certainly don't bother giving any long explanations about energy to the operating ego before a separation from the primary selves has occurred. In the chapters on "Returning to the Aware Ego" (p. 169) and "Teaching the Aware Ego to work with energy" (p. 185) we'll explore how to communicate the concept of energetic linkage once there is an Aware Ego present and able to understand what you're talking about. *For now, though, you need to be fully energetically available to your subject whether or not they are ready to reciprocate.* The facilitator needs to model the ability to link, to connect, to be fully present, so that right when the subject walks in the door, they feel welcomed and can relax. It may take a few sessions, but sooner or later the person you facilitate will be able to start consciously connecting with you too.

An essential part of the ongoing work is learning to be conscious of our energy and how we use it in our relationships, and the Voice Dialogue session is the easiest and most obvious place to practice. Eventually, after some solid groundwork, it will be more likely that the subject will come in ready to link energetically with the facilitator right at the beginning of the session. On the other hand, the subject may be focused on a crisis or situation that has brought them to the session. They may be entirely "in voice" and have no capacity for linkage with the facilitator when they walk in the door. It is definitely worth attempting to link energetically at the beginning of every session, as long as you are not invested in the subject being able to link with you as well. It is important to remain aware that the subject *may* not be able to focus their energy (or even notice you're there!) until you've worked with the self that's "out."* Because so many of us are so deeply absorbed in our own selves and their concerns, the facilitator's energetic outreach may be a singular experience in the subject's life. Let your own energetic awareness and presence stand as an unspoken invitation to the people you facilitate, and you may be surprised how quickly they learn to respond.

> *"The facilitator needs to model the ability to link, to connect, to be fully present, so that right when the subject walks in the door, they feel welcomed and can relax."*

Linkage – energetic connection between the facilitator and the person being facilitated – is the second essential step in a Voice Dialogue session. It doesn't take much time, but it lays a foundation for the facilitation and initiates the subject's training in learning to use their energy consciously.

Four opening scenarios

The following are only four out of innumerable ways a Voice Dialogue session might begin, but these four do illustrate different degrees of linkage between facilitator and subject. In terms of linkage, these four examples of beginnings can be categorized as:

❶ **practiced and adept**

❷ **starting to get a feel for energetic linkage**

❸ **taking care of other more pressing energetic needs**

❹ **going off into a mental reality rather than an energetic connection.**

Describing how energy feels is next to impossible because the experience is so individual. However, I have included interpretations of what the energy *might* feel like to these facilitators and their subjects with the idea that, like poetry, a sensual description may help you get more of a feel for what energetic linkage is. Please *place yourself in the facilitator role* as you read further and see how you might like to proceed with Matt, Kirby, Amber, and Mallory.

*A self is said to be "out" when the subject is relating to the world through that particular energy.

❶ Facilitator and subject link energies easily. The facilitator greets Matt with a warm smile when he walks in the door. They've been doing Voice Dialogue work for some time.

> **Matt:** (*sits down and smiles back looking tired but present*) It's been a long day, but I'm here!

> **Facilitator:** (*without even thinking about it, extends her energy out to Matt – if she were to try and describe how that feels it might be a soft attentiveness through the eyes and a wave of warmth flowing out from the center of her chest – they both relax for a moment, making eye contact, without saying anything*) It's good to see you again. How have you been?

> **Matt:** (*his voice even-toned, and his attention fully on the facilitator*) I've been okay, but it's nice to be asked. I've been looking forward to our session.

Note: On this end of the spectrum where there is a lot of energetic connection, there are very few words that need to be said. On the other end of the spectrum where the rational mind resides, there may be no energetic linkage and a tendency to fill the space with talking.

❷ The facilitator helps the subject build on the work they've done before and reconnect energetically. Kirby arrives for his session – he's been to an introductory Voice Dialogue workshop and has been coming for private facilitations for about a month now.

> **Kirby:** (*a little breathless and distracted*) Sorry I'm a little late, I had a hard time finding a place to park.

> **Facilitator:** (*centering himself by breathing more deeply and sinking his weight into the chair*) Actually, by my clock you're right on time. Catch your breath and take a moment to get here.

> **Kirby:** (*smiling and taking a deep breath too*) Thanks, I could use a reminder.

> **Facilitator:** Sure...* let's take a moment to just be present with each other, to link energetically the way we did at the end of the last session. That way we'll be sure we're both really here.

> (*The facilitator and Kirby take a moment in silence, looking at each other and opening to each other's energy. If Kirby were to try to describe it, he might say that he could feel his own shoulders drop down a notch after the tension of driving and that the room and the facilitator seemed to come more clearly into focus. The facilitator might say it felt as if he had extended an invisible hand to steady Kirby and help him fully "land" in the room. Plus, the facilitator would sense more relaxation in his own body. Both of them, if they stopped to notice it, might be aware of a feeling something like satisfaction or ease.*)

> **Facilitator:** I can really feel you here now and connecting with me. How do you feel?

> **Kirby:** It feels peaceful and so simple. I know if I remembered to take a moment like

---

*The use of ellipses in our facilitation examples indicates a silent pause and not that anything is being left out of the conversation.

this at home, I'd be happier and more relaxed. I get so caught up in stuff.

Facilitator: Well, give yourself time to learn. Enjoy it when you remember to use it and go easy on yourself when you forget. It takes time.

❸ **The subject arrives at the session completely "in voice" and the facilitator decides to "go where the energy is."** This is Amber's third Voice Dialogue session. She arrives a little late, fairly agitated, walks into the session room and heaves herself onto a chair with a huge sigh.

> **Facilitator:** *(already feeling Amber's agitation in his own solar plexus or 3rd chakra area)* Amber, good to see you. You look like you had a struggle getting here.

> **Amber:** *(not really looking at the facilitator)* I've had a struggle all day – getting here was the least of it.

> **Facilitator:** *(taking a deep breath and centering himself)* Well, catch your breath and tell me what's going on.

> **Amber:** *(not really talking to the facilitator, more just generally downloading energy)* Those jerks at work give me so much trouble and I've tried so hard with them. I can't believe how dumb this whole program is that they're doing.

> **Facilitator:** *(sensing that there is a self which is clearly out and isn't going to go anywhere soon, the facilitator concludes that there won't be any chance of connecting with Amber until he talks with this self – he switches gears)* You know, it might make things easier to just go straight to the self that is so upset about work and hear from that part directly. How about moving over so we can talk with the part that's angry about work.

> **Amber:** It feels like all of me, but I'll move over.

❹ **The subject inducts the facilitator into a mental energetic and there is no linkage between facilitator and subject.** Mallory has had one session before today. She's a lawyer and very much identified with her intellectual selves. The facilitator actually finds Mallory's assertiveness a little intimidating though she hasn't stopped to notice this or figure out why she feels vaguely uncomfortable. Their first session seemed successful, so the facilitator isn't sure why she's feeling a bit anxious about seeing Mallory again.

> **Facilitator:** *(feeling tense in the back of her neck and shoulders but not really paying attention to it)* Good to see you again, Mallory. How have you been since our session?

> **Mallory:** *(very much her courtroom self, notebook in hand with a list of questions written out – if we could take an energy picture of the room, Mallory's energy would be taking up most of the space, but not at all connecting with the facilitator)* I've been okay. I'm not sure I understand everything we did last time. I have a few questions I've written down. First...

Put yourself in the place of the facilitator in each of the above scenarios and ask yourself these questions with each one:

What seems effective/ineffective about this facilitator's approach?

What energetic cues did this facilitator pick up on or miss altogether?

Have I experienced a similar situation facilitating?

What would I do differently and why?

How do I develop my ability to work with energy?

The following are a few ideas to help you develop your own energetic skills and make it easier for you to link with the people you facilitate:

➡ **Make sure you are energetically clear before the session starts.** Make your work easy by giving it your undivided energetic attention as well as mental focus. It's enough of a challenge to pay attention to the subject's selves without having various parts of yourself clamoring for attention. (See "A Voice Dialogue work list for the facilitator," p. 301, for guidance in getting your own energy free and clear. You'll find, too, that rereading chapter three of the Stones' basic Voice Dialogue manual, *Embracing Our Selves,* is very helpful, as is listening to the audio tapes in the "Mendocino Series.")

➡ **Attention and intention are key.** Remember that "energy follows thought." This is what makes working with energy easy. If you are paying attention to energy and you intend to link energetically with your subject, most of the time this will happen quite effortlessly or you will at least be very clearly aware when it is not happening. You can then point out what occurred energetically, what changed and shifted, to the person you are facilitating.

➡ **Practice observing energetic linkage in daily life.** This could be after the fact, noticing that the half hour you spent sitting with your partner after dinner or the time you spent with your child on the weekend really was very unhurried, deeply connected, quality time together. See if you can figure out what you did differently from the times when you don't seem to connect in this way. Also observe times when you feel really disconnected from others. *You want to get to the point where you notice energetic linkage or the lack of it as easily as you notice whether someone said "hello" or not when they walked in the door.*

➡ **Experiment with your energy.** Sometimes when you are feeling hurried and disconnected from the person you're with, stop for a moment and try experimenting with your energy. Take several big breaths and settle more deeply into your body. Does it feel as if everything is going on in your head? Bring your energy down into your heart center. How do you do this? Remember that energy follows thought and intention, so energy will flow to the place you put your attention. (Notice if when you do this you shift from one self to another!) Imagine you can reach out to the other person with your energy field as if you had an invisible "energy hand" that could actually touch them.

By now, even if you haven't said anything to the other person about what you are doing, they will probably notice it and respond. However, they may not be aware of anything different coming from *you*. Instead they might sigh and feel more relaxed because you've released some of the tension and pressure that were in the space between you and replaced those energies with warmth. If the person you're with is open to trying this with you, take the time to do some energy exercises together.*

Let yourself have fun with this! Pay attention to your energetic interactions with people at work, at the grocery store, even on the bus. Practice pulling in your energy field in situations where you want more space and more privacy. See if you feel differently doing this and/or if you get usual or unusual reactions from others. Actually, everyone extends and withdraws energy of one kind or another most of the time, but when you do it consciously you can watch the results and learn a lot as well. *The goal is to be as naturally aware of what you're doing with your energy as you are of where you place your feet – not obsessively watching every step, but not tripping all over yourself either.* To reach this natural state of being in a culture that doesn't directly teach us about energy takes a certain amount of attention and practice in the beginning stages. Take your time. As you personally begin to enjoy more and more of the benefits of being able to extend or withdraw energy, you will more naturally and easily be able to teach this to others.

> *"The goal is to be as naturally aware of what you're doing with your energy as you are of where you place your feet – not obsessively watching every step, but not tripping all over yourself either."*

See "Exercises in energetics," p. 68.

Voice Dialogue is always a natural organic process...

Talking with the operating ego

When the person you are going to facilitate walks in and sits down with you, they will most likely be in the operating ego, that group of primary selves that functions as a single personality and runs our lives for us. The operating ego is there *before* we begin to develop an Aware Ego and also whenever we are *unable* to access the Aware Ego.* The place where the subject first sits down in front of the facilitator is called the "ego place (or space)." This spot is reserved for the subject and none of the selves are allowed to sit here. Both facilitator and subject refer back to this place by the subject's name (e.g. "That's where Mary is sitting...") – it is essentially "home base" for the work. At the beginning of a session it is usually the operating ego that sits here, and then later, after a self has been facilitated, the subject will return to this same place as an Aware Ego. The Aware Ego then occupies the original spot that the operating ego was sitting in. *The operating ego and the Aware Ego share this same physical space just as they share the role of directing our lives.*

Taking time to talk with the subject in the operating ego gives the facilitator clues about what opposites are functioning in the subject's life and which selves to work with in the session. Listening to the subject talk about what is going on in their life, the facilitator begins to observe which selves/energies are primary (what the subject is identified with), and which are disowned (what the subject under- or over-values). Their conversation is very much like a friendly interview where the subject is doing most of the talking. The facilitator listens very attentively, on the lookout for energy shifts (indications of "who" is talking and how big or small a part each particular self seems to play in this person's life).

The facilitator listens to the subject and observes which selves make their appearance. Right from the beginning when you reach out to link with your subject, pay attention to what kind of energy comes back at you:

- ◆ Who is it you are connecting with?
- ◆ What does it feel like being with this person today?
- ◆ Which subpersonalities do you feel are talking with you, are present energetically?
- ◆ What inner opposites are you starting to notice in this person?
- ◆ Do you hear this person saying one thing in words and notice that their gestures, body language, and voice tone are saying something else?
- ◆ How much space do they seem to take up in the room – can you sense their energy shrinking or expanding in the course of your conversation?
- ◆ If you've seen this person before, do they feel different to you today?

*You may want to review the explanations of the Aware Ego and the operating ego on pp. 5-8.

If it is the subject's first Voice Dialogue session, the Aware Ego won't be around yet even as a concept, let alone a reality. In fact it's rare, even with a subject who has done Voice Dialogue work for a while, to have them walk in and sit down in an Aware Ego at the *beginning* of the session. After all, on their way over to see you they've been thinking about issues in their life that they want to explore, and that process tends to bring the selves involved in those issues (and their feelings) to the fore.

The facilitator asks the subject questions, all the while listening to see "who" answers. Often the subject will start automatically talking about their concerns, but if they don't, it's easy to ask questions that will get the conversation going and then listen and detect which selves are responding. Use simple questions to open a discussion:

> *"Tell me about yourself."*
> *"What got you interested in Voice Dialogue?"*
> *"What would you like to explore today?"*
> *"What would you like to work with? What's up for you right now?"*
> *"How do you see yourself in the world? in your life?"*

Remember that the words you use aren't nearly as important as a tone of openness and holding an energy that invites easy communication. Words are also only one part of the subject's response – body language, gestures, posture, facial expressions, and so on, all contribute important information as well.

The facilitator will begin in her own mind to map out the territory of the subject's personality (what the Stones call creating a "psychic map") as she continues talking with them, paying close attention to which selves are primary and which are disowned as well as to the energetic patterns of their appearance and interaction. As facilitator, you understand that the Aware Ego develops in relation to specific pairs of opposite selves within us, and you want to be able to guide the work in a direction that will be meaningful *and* nonthreatening for your subject. You really need to notice not only which selves are talking but also how often each self comes back into the conversation, how much power it seems to hold in the living of this person's life. In this way you will be able to safely begin facilitating the primary selves while holding an awareness of their opposites. In *Embracing Our Selves* Hal and Sidra Stone comment:

> *As in the exploration of any new territory, it is helpful to have the orientation [that] a psychic map provides [in order] to gain a sense of what we as facilitators are moving into. This is an important safeguard in the work because it means that as facilitators we are not going to jump into working with any one particular area before we have at least some idea of how it relates to the whole person.**

As you become more experienced in facilitating, you will probably map out the selves in your mind quite easily, very much the way you might observe the dynamics in a new social situation before jumping in to participate. If this seems too subtle and complex to you, if you have a primary self that "never was good at psyching out social situations," you might want to practice drawing some actual maps on paper. There are two sample maps at the end of this chapter. Try using them as a model to create maps for people you are facilitating or for yourself.

*Stone & Stone, *Embracing Our Selves*, p. 51.

94

You can also map out the selves of some of the sample subjects in your *Handbook*. Even if you have already done quite a lot of facilitating, committing your observations to paper once in a while can give you new insights and help fill out your picture of the selves in helpful and sometimes unexpected ways.

Once you have a sense of "who" is talking, you can report some of your observations. Your feedback, first of all, helps to build the subject's awareness of their selves right from the beginning of the session. When you communicate your perceptions in a non-judgmental way and with a real appreciation, most people are pleased that you have given them your full attention because they really feel "seen."

> *"I'm already hearing a part of you that cares deeply about your work. And then there was also a hint of overwhelm and wanting to get away, though that part doesn't seem to get out much."*

> *"You seem to have a lot of responsibility, and I'm noticing a part of you that seems to be very critical of you and dedicated to perfection."*

> *"What I'm observing as you talk really confirms what you were saying about being in a quandary about relationships. When you first started talking about why you don't want to get involved in another relationship, there was this real "no nonsense" tone in your voice, and then your tone and expression changed completely, became really soft, when you talked about being lonely and missing someone to snuggle with on Sunday mornings. I think I may even have heard another part in there that seems to think you ought to have a relationship and if you don't, you've failed."*

People can also be quite amazed and delighted when a facilitator detects the different selves' presence from just 5 or 10 minutes of conversation – it literally opens a doorway to a new way of seeing themselves. In addition, your perceptions will help both of you decide where to go with the session, what selves need to speak, what issues are most energetically available to be explored. As you gain experience facilitating, you will probably notice far more about the person you are working with than would be appropriate to tell them all at once right at the beginning of the session. You'll need to sort out what is helpful feedback to the subject in this part of the session from what is information for *you* to keep in mind as you meet and talk with the different selves.

> *"As you gain experience facilitating, you will probably notice far more about the person you are working with than would be appropriate to tell them right at the beginning of the session."*

Part of the fun in Voice Dialogue is being relaxed and imaginative in exploring options for the work. As facilitator, you can suggest any number of possible directions for facilitation *and* also be easygoing about whatever response you receive. If you propose a place to start, the subject will either feel fine about going in the suggested direction or a self that wants to do something different will speak up – perhaps a part that feels more secure taking control of the process rather than following directions. Having a self show up that wants to be in control is a gift for the facilitator because control is a perfect primary self to begin working with. In fact, *just by being relaxed and attentive, you'll find that it's almost impossible to go wrong. Whatever you suggest, a primary self will show up to either agree or disagree with it. Then it's easy to follow the lead and take it from there!*

It will also be obvious in talking with the operating ego if Voice Dialogue is not right for a particular subject or session. The first time you meet with a subject, you will want to get a solid sense of their personal history before beginning to facilitate any of the selves. Re-

"Whatever you suggest, a primary self will show up to either agree or disagree with it. Then it's easy to follow the lead and take it from there!"

member that the Voice Dialogue method does put people into an altered state of consciousness, so you want to be quite certain that it's a suitable method to use with this person at this time. Nothing says that you have to continue with facilitating selves if it seems inappropriate. The facilitator should never push or force the process because that would violate the ground rule of honoring the primary selves and protecting the person's vulnerability. (You may want to reread the chapter on "Ground rules," p. 35, and especially guidelines on "When not to do Voice Dialogue" on p. 47.)

The direction of the work will flow organically out of the initial conversation. Having a conversation is all that's needed to prepare for facilitating a self. There's no need for elaborate explanations or instructions, or guided meditations – *just a conversation with the ego, observing "who's talking" and suggesting which primary self to facilitate.* Even as you begin to branch out into working with dreams, images, movement, and other creative improvisations on Voice Dialogue work, you will still need this basic step of having a conversation with the person you are about to facilitate. Once you have talked together, you're ready to choose a primary self and have the person move into it (unless they are entirely new to Voice Dialogue and need a bit of explanation about the process before you can begin).

SUMMARY *The facilitator links with the subject and engages them in conversation. He notices which selves are present, and talks with the subject about what he perceives. The facilitator begins to identify which are primary and which are disowned selves, and he starts to create a mental map of the personality. This initial conversation deepens the energetic linkage between facilitator and subject and opens the door for awareness of the selves.*

Some initial conversations between facilitator and subject

Let's listen in on a few different facilitators talking with their subjects at the beginning of a Voice Dialogue session. With these examples (as with all the examples in your *Handbook*), it is valuable to take the time to put yourself in the role of the facilitator and imagine what direction you would decide to take.

Kelly

Kelly is just starting Voice Dialogue work. She went to a weekend workshop and this is her first private session with an experienced facilitator. After catching her breath and talking about how rushed she was getting here, Kelly explains that she's feeling pretty anxious about her two children leaving for summer camp for the first time.

Facilitator: *(notices that Kelly looks more tired than she sounds and that she never seems to catch a full breath – the facilitator checks inside herself and feels tension in her own shoulders and a tightness in her stomach, feelings that weren't there before the session started)* This is a big change for you, having both your kids go away for the first time.

Kelly: Well it's not like I don't know anything about the camp. My closest friend's daughter is a year older than my oldest and she's already been to this camp, plus my kids will have other friends there too. I'm trying not to be a mother bear, but I just can't help feeling anxious. I'm not even sure I'll know what to do with myself when they're gone! *(laughs suddenly and her voice becomes a bit girlish)* It's been so long since I've had any time to myself. *(Kelly's voice changes again to a responsible adult tone and she straightens her posture)* Of course, I'll drive down for Parents' Day and there's still a lot to look after even without the kids.

Facilitator: I can hear a lot of different selves talking already. You definitely do have a "mother bear" who is really concerned about the children and about taking care of everything at home. Then there is another part who tries to keep you from being "overbearing." *(they both laugh at the pun)* And I can also feel at least a hint of someone who is really excited about having time to herself, but I don't think that one is around much.

Kelly: No, that one hasn't had any chance to be around – I've been a full-time mother and wife for quite a while. I certainly didn't realize there were so many different parts. Most of the time it all just feels like confusion and pressure to me. I wouldn't even know where to start.

Questions

Why would the facilitator call Kelly's self a "mother bear" instead of a caretaker?

What other selves do you detect in Kelly besides the ones the facilitator mentioned? Can you match them up in pairs of opposites? Are some of the primary selves opposite to each other?

Which self would you <u>not</u> want to facilitate first? Why?

Discussion

The facilitator could call the anxious protective part of Kelly by any number of names, and it always strengthens the work to pick up on non-judgmental phrases, names or images that the subject may use in reference to their own selves. This makes it more personal and the subject feels that they are being heard and that you are honoring them by paying attention to what they say and quoting their terminology.

The mother bear is a primary self and so is the part that wants Kelly not to be overbearing. Keep in mind that lots of times we have pairs of opposite primaries* as well as opposite primary and disowned selves. Unlike disowned selves, opposite primary selves

---

*See "How to work with opposites without upsetting the primary selves" on p. 153.

each have their own territory, their own place on the psychic map where they are permitted to function. Probably most of the time Kelly tries to be a model mother who isn't overbearing, and then the mother bear comes out when there is a big change or a perceived threat of danger.

Joan

Joan has worked with her therapist for a couple of months and just recently he has started to do some Voice Dialogue facilitation with her. Last session they spent some time talking with Joan's inner critic. Today Joan was sitting very quietly in the waiting room, sort of daydreaming, but when the facilitator opened the door and invited her in, she clicked into gear, becoming very animated, almost bubbly, talking about work, friends, trips.

Facilitator: *(notices a sad feeling in himself that doesn't seem to match Joan's outward energy)* I'm glad to hear that your trip went so well. What were you thinking about focusing on today?

Joan: *(her voice suddenly flattens a bit, as if the fizz had gone out of it, and her body sinks down as if gravity were pulling harder on it than usual – it feels to the facilitator as if the bottom is literally dropping out of the energy in the room)* Work is going okay, but then I feel *so* tired at the end of the day. I just go home alone and sit there eating ice-cream and I don't even want to go out. I guess I just feel sorry for myself when I'm not all caught up in work.

Facilitator: *(simply holds the energy that he is feeling by allowing that heavy flatness to be present in his own energy field and doesn't say anything)*

Joan: *(with another burst of the bubbly energy)* I did start playing tennis again which is great because it gets me out, and at least I see some people who aren't connected to work. The truth is I hardly have time to see people, which is probably why I don't meet very many. *(going flat again)* I guess I don't really know what to do about myself and I feel embarrassed about it. Nobody who knows my take-charge working self would recognize what a blah couch potato I am at home.

Facilitator: I certainly notice that there is some part of you that tries to keep your energy up and moving all the time and is very focused on doing, on activity... And then it seems the rest of the time you run out of steam. It does seem that your work persona and who you are at home are very clearly opposites of each other.

Joan: Boy, is that true. I don't even feel like the same person from one place to the other. I keep going and going and then I drop like a ton of bricks when I'm out of active mode.

Questions

Why did the facilitator stay silent at times? Have you ever tried holding the energy without saying anything out loud? What does it accomplish here?

How does the facilitator show respect for the primary self?

What, if anything, would you do differently in talking with Joan?

Discussion

If the facilitator had started to respond to Joan's flat energy at this point, he would not have had an opportunity to observe her energy pattern, the way she typically pulls herself out of her depressed energy and then falls back into it again. There's a lot to be learned by simply observing and time enough to ask questions later.

Glen

Glen was referred by a friend to a Voice Dialogue facilitator and has no background experience with Voice Dialogue at all. The facilitator doesn't try to say anything to Glen about energy or linkage, but she does center herself and think to reach out with her own energy toward Glen. He sighs and settles in more.

Facilitator: I know we talked some on the phone, but now that you're here, tell me a bit more about yourself and what you're hoping to gain from Voice Dialogue work.

Glen: Well, I mentioned my friend, Alice, told me about you. I'm not sure I really understand yet what Voice Dialogue is and I'm a little nervous about it… but I know Alice got a lot out of it, and I could use some help sorting my life out right now.

Facilitator: *(the facilitator thinks that she wants to be more supportive of Glen, and since energy follows intention, her energy becomes both softer and more solid – it's not consciously perceived, but as a result some part of Glen instinctively feels more safe)* What kinds of things are you trying to sort out?

Glen: *(another sigh and his shoulders sink)* It seems like everything all at once, really. I made a job change that I thought would be great, but it's not working out that way. I thought working for myself would give me a lot more freedom, but not as many contracts came through as I thought and now I'm worried about money. I used to be a lot more confident, but now I guess I'm worried too that I don't really have what it takes to be successful… I'm pretty overwhelmed, and my girlfriend and I are having a hard time too – we're *so* different. The more she wants to talk, the more I clam up…. *(the facilitator notices that Glen's breathing has tightened and can feel herself tensing with him)* To tell the truth I'm embarrassed to be telling anyone about any of this. I don't usually talk about my problems, not even with my closest friends.

Questions

Which different selves do you notice in this short conversation? See how many you can jot down before reading on.

If Glen were your subject, where would you go from here? Would you begin by explaining Voice Dialogue to him? Would you start facilitating a self?

Discussion

It's so typical that when we run up against big challenges in our relationships, careers, health, etc. that primary selves (such as the inner critic, the protector/controller, the financial conservative, and others) stage a backlash against the selves who dared to put us at risk in the first place. Ouch! The primary selves do this in an effort to protect our exposed vulnerability. A lot of Glen's protective, controlling selves are upset right now about events in his life, and these parts of him will have to be willing for him to participate in the facilitation process. Probably some explanation about Voice Dialogue and then starting with the self that feels nervous about being here will do a lot to break the ice. In the next chapter we'll discuss how to explain Voice Dialogue to the first-time subject.

One simple, basic way to map Glen's selves:

Glen's main group of primary selves

Protector/Controller
Hesitant self
Pusher
Loner   Inner Critic
Rational mind

Less dominant, but still primary

Calculated risk taker
Businessperson
Self improvement
Confident self
Overwhelm/withdrawn

Disowned & vulnerable selves

Feelings/personal
Adventurer
Communicator
vulnerable child

A map of opposites – the facilitator's notes to herself:

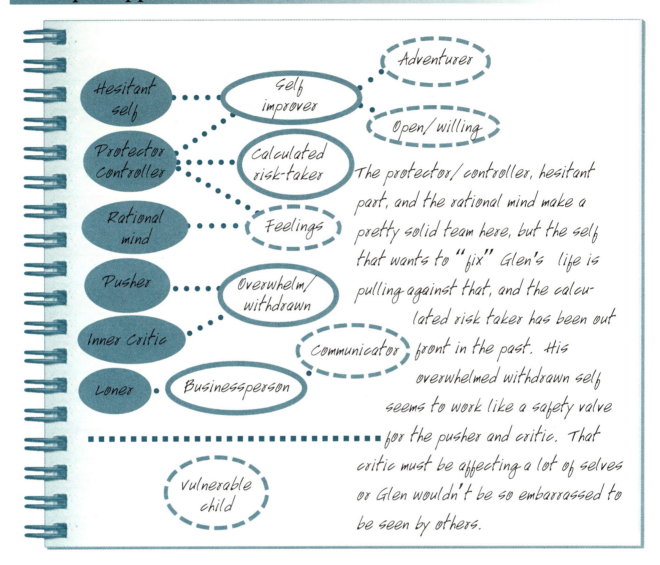

Hesitant self

Protector Controller

Rational mind

Pusher

Inner critic

Loner

Self improver

Calculated risk-taker

Feelings

Overwhelm/withdrawn

Businessperson

Adventurer

Open/willing

Communicator

vulnerable child

The protector/controller, hesitant part, and the rational mind make a pretty solid team here, but the self that wants to "fix" Glen's life is pulling against that, and the calculated risk taker has been out front in the past. His overwhelmed withdrawn self seems to work like a safety valve for the pusher and critic. That critic must be affecting a lot of selves or Glen wouldn't be so embarrassed to be seen by others.

On the previous page is one quick and easy way to map out the inner selves. The solid-colored circle has in it all the primary selves that seem to be most active in Glen's life. The selves inside the circle with the solid-color outline are also primary selves, but at least right now they play a smaller role. Inside the circle with the broken outline are grouped the disowned and vulnerable selves. This map gives the facilitator a simple way to categorize and remember Glen's selves, but it doesn't show very much about how they interact with each other.

In the second diagram above, the facilitator has taken the time to map out Glen's selves along a continuum of primary to disowned energies, primary on the left moving to disowned on the right. It's interesting to realize that the "hesitant self" is actually very powerful – it's always coming in to protect Glen (in fact it appears over and over in the session). One of the hesitant's self's opposites is a "self-improver" which has at least enough influence to get Glen to go to a Voice Dialogue session. The adventurer, on the other hand, is truly disowned. All the primary selves are involved in protecting the vulnerability, which appears down at the bottom of the page, showing that vulnerability underlies the whole internal patterning of the personality.

Explaining Voice Dialogue

The facilitator is also a teacher who introduces the Psychology of the Aware Ego to the people he facilitates. It is through your demonstration of the work, modeling of the Aware Ego, and explanation of how the system of selves develops, that the people you facilitate will come to understand what Voice Dialogue is all about and see how to apply this work in their own lives. As we have already discussed at length, the nature of Voice Dialogue facilitation is primarily energetic and the most important learning comes through the actual separation from the selves and the experience of being in an Aware Ego. A great deal of talk about theory without the actual practice of facilitation can result in increased awareness but not in the development of an actual Aware Ego.

At the same time, not having any explanation of the process can leave the subject confused about the purpose and meaning of the session. Simply talking with one or two selves and then having a fleeting encounter with the Aware Ego probably won't be enough to ground the experience. The subject may be very interested in Voice Dialogue work, but they will not be able to hold on to an understanding of the work if they have nowhere to "file" this new information in their consciousness. Each person needs to hear *something* about Voice Dialogue to help anchor the facilitation *in their known world.* If the subject has a very strong rational mind, they may require a longer, more intellectual discussion in order to trust the validity of the process. If the subject is more oriented toward the feeling side of the personality, they may want to start out with reassurances about the facilitator's role and a picture of what the session will feel like.

It is up to the facilitator to listen to each subject and then explain Voice Dialogue to them at a pace and in a way that suits their individual needs. You will have to decide how much conversation with a subject about selves and how selves develop is appropriate at the beginning of the first session and what to save for the end of the session (when there's a little bit of experience to refer to). Then you will also have to think about whether to explain very much about energy, linkage, the Aware Ego, etc. or to save that discussion for other times. Even though each person you facilitate will be unique and you may never introduce Voice Dialogue *exactly* the same way twice, here are some general guidelines for explaining Voice Dialogue work in the first and subsequent sessions. Please keep in mind that this chapter is full of suggestions for *possible* ways of introducing Voice Dialogue work. *It would not be a good idea, or even possible, to try to include all of these suggestions in any one session – there wouldn't be any time left for facilitation!* Instead use this chapter as a reference, trying out different approaches at different times, choosing what works best for you, and coming back to it from time to time for new ideas.

Explaining Voice Dialogue
at the beginning of the first session

A good approach is to start by finding out what the person you are going to facilitate already knows about Voice Dialogue and what they think it might offer them. At the very beginning of the session you can simply say *"Tell me a little bit about yourself and what made you decide to try doing some Voice Dialogue work."* As the subject talks, listen for what the primary selves need to know and let that be your guide for how much explanation to give. Some first-time subjects may come to you because of an enthusiastic recommendation from a friend and they really do not have a clear idea of the nature of the work. Other people come to a facilitator *after* reading the Stones' books or hearing their tapes, so it's quite possible that some of your first-time subjects will already have quite a sophisticated understanding of the Psychology of the Aware Ego and the Voice Dialogue method.

If the subject has no background in Voice Dialogue, you will need to offer them some explanation of what the facilitation process is and what a facilitator does before you can choose a direction together and then move out into one of the primary selves. After connecting (linking) with your subject and hearing their story, you may want to:

☆ **Talk briefly about the concept of inner selves, primary and disowned, and explain how these develop in our lives.** You will undoubtedly invent your own favorite way of talking about how the selves evolve, but remember that this kind of description can be most effective when you add in examples from the story the subject just told you about themselves. For example, *"You were talking about your need for independence and how it keeps you from forming close relationships. That independent part of you is what we would call a primary self, one that developed to protect you from being too vulnerable and dependent on others. The kind of person who can be emotionally very close to other people and who might even be needy, carries what in Voice Dialogue we would call one of your disowned selves."* (The illustrations from the first chapter on "What is Voice Dialogue" can give the people you facilitate a visual picture of an inner family of selves.)

☆ **Take the discussion of selves further by introducing the idea of a map of the psyche on which the selves live.** You can draw a simple diagram like those of Glen's selves in the last chapter, or you may want to invent your own way of charting primary selves and their opposites. The "Map of Persona" at the end of this chapter is also available as a full-color poster* that is designed to be used as a lighthearted visual aid for talking about how our selves develop, where they live inside of us, and how the selves function in our relationships. The color poster is also an ideal way for people to introduce the idea of selves to their partners and families – friends, couples, parents and children can all have a lot of fun locating different parts of themselves on the map. Lots of suggestions come with the map for ways to use it as a teaching tool with those you facilitate.

*"Picturing the Process," p. 11, and "The Island of Persona," p. 111, are designed as teaching tools for you to use in your facilitation practice or give as a handout for workshops and classes. See p. 312 for information on ordering a facilitator's kit that includes ready-to-photocopy text and illustrations of these two mini-chapters, plus a full-color poster of Persona.

☆ **Tell the subject that the Voice Dialogue method involves their physically moving over to allow various parts or selves to talk** and then moving back again to where they started out. You can explain that moving into a self will actually help them to know this part of themselves better and to get some distance from it. (If the operating ego seems relaxed with this much explanation, you may not want to go into additional, more complex information about the Aware Ego or energetics until after you've worked with a self and come back to the ego place.)

The person you are facilitating needs to know about you too and what it is exactly that a "facilitator" does. Once the subject has some idea of what Voice Dialogue is and what we mean by primary and disowned selves, you may want to explain a *bit* about what you do as a facilitator. This can be a sentence or two saying something like:

"While you were telling me about yourself, I was listening for which different parts of you were talking. My job is to notice what we call your inner selves and see if I can tell which ones seem to be around most of the time – those are ones that we would call primary selves. Once we've figured out some of the primary selves, we'll choose one of them to talk with directly."

This might be a good moment to point out a few of the selves you've noticed so far, and then you might want to go on with a little more explanation of the facilitator's role.

"One of the most important results of doing Voice Dialogue work will be for you to become aware of these different parts of yourself and have more choice about when they are present. My role as facilitator is to help you identify these different selves and become more conscious of them."

It can also work well to ask if the subject has any questions at this time about your role as facilitator or about Voice Dialogue. Again, if there are hesitations they will show up when you ask this, and *most hesitations will lead you straight to a primary self.* Of course, there is a lot more to the role of facilitator, and later, as the process of working together organically unfolds, you will want to explain other aspects of facilitating, such as teaching people about energy management and modeling the Aware Ego for them.

> *"If the subject has hesitations, they will show up at this time, and most hesitations will lead you straight to a primary self."*

You don't need to answer every question that is asked, however you do need to respond. It is helpful to answer questions *now* that will support the process and save for later answers that would only be confusing at the beginning of a session. It's fine to say, "Let me tell you a little bit about that now, and then after we actually have an experience of meeting one of the selves it will be easier to explain more." It will be far, far easier to point out energetic and feeling aspects of the work in retrospect than to try to explain them in advance.

Creating a comfort zone for Voice Dialogue work

The primary selves need to know what is going to *happen* in a session so they won't be nervous about getting into the unknown. When someone is completely new to being facilitated, you need to offer them some explanation of what it is you are planning to do – *otherwise the primary selves may be very concerned and worry about what they're getting into.* The primary selves are always protective of the subject's vulnerability, and in a new situation they want to hear what's going to happen next so they don't have to be on guard against surprises.

Simple, straightforward descriptions tend to be most effective. You will undoubtedly develop your own natural way of talking about the process, but here are a few examples to help you get started.

> *"This is a process where we get to talk with different parts of you, each of which probably sees your life and the world in its own particular way. And, each of these parts will have its own physical space in the room."*

> *"The place where you're sitting now is going to be your place – it's called the operating ego or Aware Ego place. Wherever you move during the session, you'll always get to come back here."*

> *"We'll talk more about the Aware Ego later because it will be much easier to explain once you've had a little bit of experience with it. What else would you like to know before we begin?"*

By taking your cues from your subject's questions, you can be sure you're telling them what they need to know, and not a lot of information they don't want or need now. It is important not to ramble on just to satisfy one of your primary selves, perhaps a perfectionist or a part that feels insecure about facilitating. Your own mind can also become excited about the theory of the Psychology of the Aware Ego and get a little carried away talking about it in detail.

The facilitator's linkage with the subject is perhaps the most important ingredient in creating comfort and safety for the work. The subject may not be able to respond at first to your energetic outreach, but by paying attention to energy, your own and the subject's, you will create an energetic container to hold the new experience of Voice Dialogue.* Linkage can help a person to feel comfortable, easy, and open with the facilitator – and ready to try something different. In contrast, giving a subject a lot of information, *without* any energetic connection, may simply lead to their being overwhelmed by new ideas and nervous about exploring something unfamiliar. Or, it might induct their mind without helping them to separate from the mental self and create an Aware Ego in relation to it.

> *"By paying attention to energy, your own and the subject's, you will create an energetic container to hold the new experience of Voice Dialogue."*

As facilitator, if you pay attention to linkage right from the beginning, you may find as a result that your subjects are more relaxed and need to ask fewer questions. Many people ask a lot of questions at the beginning of the work more to orient the primary selves and make them feel safe than to acquire needed information. You will be able to sense more easily "who" is asking a question if you are in linkage. If you are energetically tuned to your subject, you will be able to know what kind of answer or information their primary self needs in order to feel safe with the work. A rational mind, for example, needs a different kind of answer than a very feeling self that is shy about doing something new. You don't have to go into detail about the fine points of Voice Dialogue method or theory, you just have to speak to the self that is asking the question in a language it can understand. If there is a self that is hesitant about doing something new, you will probably want to begin with that part. Depending on the person you are facilitating and how they feel, you may also find that you need to:

➥ **give reassurance that Voice Dialogue is a very non-invasive, respectful process**
and that they don't have to engage in any behavior – or even say anything – that feels uncomfortable to them. Let them know that this work is for *them* and they are in charge of "how far we go with it."

*See "Linkage – energetic connection and communication," p. 61, in the chapter on energy.

106

➡ **establish that the process is easier than it sounds** and any attempt the subject makes will work just fine. Some people express disbelief about being able to move into different selves. "I'm willing to move over, but I don't know if anything will happen" or "I'm sure other people can do this, but I'm not sure I can" are common doubts about facilitation. You may need to give your subject reassurance that you are confident Voice Dialogue is something that *they* can do, and that it is *your* job to help them with the process – "After all that's what I'm here for."

➡ **clear up any misconceptions** such as the common fear that working with selves will be fragmenting for the personality, or the idea primary selves often have that this work is designed to get undesirable parts of the personality in line and make them behave, or (even worse) eliminate them entirely. Here too, you don't need to argue these points, but simply offer what you know to be true about the process and invite them to try it out before getting deep into discussion.

➡ **remember that the self that signed up for facilitation may not be the one who arrived for the session!** If the subject seems resistant to the process (I've seen this happen more often in workshops than in private sessions), you can suggest beginning with a part that feels uneasy about the Voice Dialogue process or a part that just doesn't want to be here doing this right now. I've never actually found anyone who was reluctant to take this option (in fact, that was the first self anyone ever facilitated in me). However, if the subject really doesn't feel okay about moving over and letting a self speak, even a very resistant and protective self, then this might not be the right process for them or the right time to approach it. Stay in the ego place and be ready to either work differently with this particular person or perhaps not at all.

If you are a therapist and are integrating Voice Dialogue work into your practice, the same principles apply. You never want to spring something new on the primary selves of any of your clients, so a brief description of what Voice Dialogue work is and why you think it would be useful for this individual at this time is appropriate. *To honor the primary selves, Voice Dialogue needs to be offered as an option which the subject is free to reject, even if you are enthusiastic in recommending it.* If the client is interested but hesitant at the same time, an ideal place to start facilitation is with the hesitant primary self. Honoring the conservative hesitant part, listening to it, and creating even the beginning of an Aware Ego in relation to it, can be a surprisingly powerful piece of work.

> *"To honor the primary selves, Voice Dialogue needs to be offered as an option which the subject is free to reject, even if you are enthusiastic in recommending it."*

What about the rational mind – doesn't it need to hear more explanation in order to feel at ease about participating in the session? This is a very important question. On the one hand, many intellectually oriented people are attracted to Voice Dialogue work, and it's important to honor their primary selves' need for solid rational information about the work. If the facilitator disregards the rational mind, the mind will be just as upset as any other primary self that a facilitator might ignore or neglect. The subject's operating ego might decide in this case that the facilitator is too "intuitive," too "flaky," or too "New Age" and will not pursue working with him or with Voice Dialogue any further.

On the other hand, if the mind is a very powerful primary self (and especially if it has joined forces with the subject's controller), the tendency may be to ask as many questions of the facilitator as possible and keep the session on safe, familiar, intellectual ground. The facilitator has to be quite sensitive and give the best answers he can without getting all caught up in a long involved intellectual discussion about the Psychology of the Aware Ego or what energetics is. If a subject has a great many questions, one option is to ask if they would like to move over and let you speak directly with the part of them that is asking the questions. In this way the primary self will be heard and get its questions answered while the subject begins the process of separating from the self that needs to hear the explanation.

Talking about Voice Dialogue at the end of the first session

You may notice that up until now we haven't mentioned explaining anything about the Aware Ego. It's much easier to talk about the Aware Ego toward the end of the first session, once the subject has actually separated from at least one primary self and *can feel the difference in their energy when they come back to the place they started.* No amount of theory and descriptive language will substitute for actually experiencing the disengagement from a primary self and the sense of spaciousness that comes with the initiation of the Aware Ego process. It would be like trying to explain snow to someone from the tropics – of course they'll understand the *concept*, but it's not the same as being in a snowfall and feeling snowflakes on their face.

"Remember that the Aware Ego doesn't spring up fully formed overnight, and learning about the Psychology of the Aware Ego doesn't have to be rushed either."

At the end of the very first session it may be enough to simply point out any changes that have occurred and answer any questions about the selves or the Aware Ego. It often feels more organic to let the work settle in, and then the subject can come back with more questions at the beginning of their next session. *Remember that the development of the Aware Ego is a gradual and ongoing process. It doesn't spring up fully formed overnight, and learning about the Psychology of the Aware Ego doesn't have to be rushed either.* Here are a few thoughts about "do's" and "don'ts" for first sessions in general:

☆ **Seed the idea that Voice Dialogue work is about consciousness and communication.** It is about embracing *all* of our selves rather than trying to get rid of what we (i.e. our operating egos) don't like. You can plant this concept at the outset without worrying about whether it's fully understood. Sometime later the subject will very likely remember what you said and comprehend it much more fully within the context of their ongoing work.

☆ **Save the Voice Dialogue terminology until it makes sense in the context of the work.** By the end of the session the subject will have a direct experience to refer to, and it will be natural and organic to begin using words like "energy" or "awareness." Before they have the experience of moving to a self and coming back to Aware Ego, hearing new terminology may just seem like alienating jargon. Terms like "energetics" or "linkage" can be off-putting to many people if you use this terminology before it means something real to them. It's the experience of being facilitated that will communicate the essential nature of what these terms mean.

☆ **Never underestimate the power of a small simple piece of work!** A friend of mine, after facilitating a first-time session, lamented about how ineffectual he felt trying to sort out all the energies and thought that he had failed to offer the woman he facilitated anything meaningful. He was bemused and astonished when he ran into her several months later and she exclaimed that the session with him had changed her life. It was the first time that she ever had a sense of her family of selves, and the work had opened for her a new appreciation of her own vulnerability. The initiation of the Aware Ego process can happen in relation to working with any single primary self even in a very "simple and ordinary" session.

☆ **Do a mini internal facilitation for yourself** if you find that you are pushing to do something big, impressive, brilliant, important. You might try calling in a wisdom self to help you regain your balance:

> **Facilitator:** Some part of me is feeling anxious that this person isn't going to get how significant this work is if we don't do something bigger and more dramatic.

> **Wisdom self:** While you're worrying about that, it's easy to lose connection with them. Take a deep breath and feel the energy between you.

> **Facilitator:** That feels better! I think I was too determined to accomplish something "important."

Teaching the Psychology of the Aware Ego is an ongoing part of Voice Dialogue

Every Voice Dialogue session is an educational opportunity for the Aware Ego. As a facilitator, you want to be asking yourself all through each session, "How is what we're doing and/or talking about right now supporting the Aware Ego process for this person?" Even though you may not verbally explain a great deal about the Aware Ego at first, if you keep this question in mind, it will help to guide you in choosing a direction for the work. This simple question by itself will support you in intuiting ways to communicate to each subject the nature and meaning of the Voice Dialogue work and the Aware Ego process.

Every subject has their own reasons for pursuing Voice Dialogue. The motivation for seeking out your services as a Voice Dialogue facilitator may range from stress-relief to a very active focus on the development of consciousness. And, someone who starts out just wanting to ease the stress in their life, may develop a deep interest in consciousness. The context for Voice Dialogue work also varies widely; it includes business consulting, personal growth, relationship counseling, acting classes, body work, traditional therapy, art and movement, to mention only

"As a facilitator, you want to be asking yourself all through each session, 'How is what we're doing and/or talking about right now supporting the Aware Ego process for this person?'"

a few possibilities. Obviously, not every subject will have the same degree of interest in learning about the Psychology of the Aware Ego, so it will be up to you as their facilitator to introduce information as you sense it is appropriate for each individual.

Although it is certainly not necessary for the work to be effective, having the subject read books and listen to tapes can be very supportive of the Voice Dialogue process. For those who want to learn more, the Stones' tapes and books are an invaluable tool. Suggest that they start with the basic tapes on "Meeting Your Selves," and "The Dance of the Selves in Relationship." The books, *Embracing Our Selves, Embracing Each Other,* and *Embracing Your Inner Critic* are each in their own way an excellent introduction to the Psychology of the Aware Ego – use your intuition in deciding which one to recommend to a particular subject. As specific issues come up in the work, you may want to suggest listening to additional tapes such as "The Voice of Responsibility," "Meet the Pusher," or "Children & Marriage," or perhaps reading Sidra Stone's book, *The Shadow King*, on the Inner Patriarch. "The Map of Personia" at the end of this chapter can also be used as an intriguing and fun way to track the exploration of one's inner selves over time. The illustrations and accompanying text in the "Picturing the Process" section from the first chapter on "What is Voice Dialogue" are a helpful visual aid in teaching people about how selves function and how the Aware Ego begins to develop.

Remember that most of the teaching comes in *doing* the work. Your first priority in each session is to link energetically with your subject, remain non-judgmental, and create opportunities for the Aware Ego to evolve and grow. Occasionally, with someone new, a session may feel a bit chaotic to you. The subject may not be going fully into the self or you may be dealing with a cluster of selves that you haven't quite sorted out. At this point your confidence level may not be at an all-time high. It is important in any situation to remember that as long as you follow the ground rules, a certain amount of separation will occur in the work regardless of how challenging it appears to you. Remember that even the smallest opening of the Aware Ego process can be a monumental step in a person's life.

The Island of Personia

Mapping Your Inner Selves

(This section is available in ready-to-copy format for use as a teaching tool for your clients and students. See p. 312 for ordering information.)

Welcome to Personia

The mythical Isle of Personia was invented in order to help you identify and locate your subpersonalities. You are invited to take a journey of the imagination and explore this land- and sea- and sky-scape as if it were an inner country where your primary and disowned selves live. On your first visit, you may only meet a few of the local residents – probably the parts of you that have the strongest positive or negative reactions to different areas of the map. As you get to be a regular visitor, and as you continue with your Voice Dialogue process, you'll probably find more and more of your selves reflected in Personia. Take your time and enjoy your adventure!

The perspective of Personia is designed so that you, the viewer, witness the landscape from above and outside – from a place of awareness. And, although everyone inhabits their own island of the personality differently, you'll find with a little help from your imagination, that Personia has room for many if not all of the different parts of yourself. Each of us has certain areas of Personia (i.e. of our personalities) where we take up residence, other areas we visit only occasionally or on vacation, some places that scare us because they seem dangerous, and others we "wouldn't be caught dead in" because we'd get in trouble or be ashamed to be seen there. There are also parts of the landscape of our personalities that we just don't know yet, and we've been too focused elsewhere to even think about exploring them. Some of our map is on conscious "ground" where we know what we like and don't like, other parts are in the Ocean of the Unconscious that surrounds our island, or in the Sky of our Imagination.

> **A travel advisory:** Notice the responses your selves have to different parts of the island, but don't get carried away. Keep an eye on your Responsible self so it doesn't turn your visit into "homework!" Look out for that Pusher who could take you on such a fast ride around the island that you wouldn't get to enjoy being there. Personia is a place for discovering and balancing opposites in yourself. If you find that you are caught up in any particular self while exploring, it may be time to take a break or at least refocus on a different energy somewhere else on the map.

Let's take a look at how different energies or selves are connected to the landscape. Some associations are so obvious they have become clichés in our culture. The person whose primary selves grew up on the farm may be quite uncomfortable traveling into the city, dealing with traffic, fast paced living, intensity and noise. If they do venture into town they may feel awkward and out of place. The same "country bumpkin," however, who may feel scared and inadequate in the city, might make fun of the "city slicker" who comes out to the country, gets lost, doesn't know a pig from a pumpkin, and can't survive a day on their own without a restaurant to feed them and a taxi to take them where they need to go. The farmer most likely will have a disowned city person and vice versa.

Each of us has a whole group of primary selves and a corresponding group of disowned selves that inhabit the island of our personality. Let's say the farmer we mentioned above is named Bill. "Country person" and "farmer" aren't Bill's only primary identifications, and the "city slicker" isn't his only disowned self. You may find another one of Bill's primary selves in the fundamentalist church his family belongs to and an opposite and disowned self might be one of those "godless intellectuals" who teaches at Personia University (PU). Farmer Bill is also very much a do-it-yourself kind of person, independent, self-sufficient, and hard-working. That part of him can't stand big government telling him what to do, and he also has no patience with anyone who doesn't work hard for a living with their hands (in this case both the lawyers in the Federal Building and the bums in the park could be Bill's disowned selves). Bill's wife, Betty, is a homemaker, a mother, and very proper. Her disowned selves might include both the career women in the big office buildings and the "live girls" who dance over by the race track at the X-rated theater. Betty has a beautiful singing voice, and when she was young she always wanted to go to music school, but her good girl self never even let her think about going away from home. In her day responsible daughters just didn't do that sort of thing. A positive disowned self for Betty might be the opera singer who performs at the concert hall.

Children develop their own set of primary selves, either taking after their parents or becoming quite their opposite. Bill and Betty's daughter, Amy, takes after her parents in some ways and not in others. She has her dad's spunk and independence, but not his conservatism, and she certainly doesn't agree with his politics. Amy is the first person in the family to go to college (on scholarship and against her father's wishes), and this is where she met Gene Jr., a banker's son. Amy is bored with life in the country and she is definitely not going to be a good girl like her mother! She is full of curiosity about the big world of the city that her parents distrust and she rebels against the constrictions of the church. As you can see, Amy has her own set of primary and disowned selves, located on various parts of the map. When Amy and Gene Jr. have kids of their own, the story increases in complexity as more and more primary and disowned selves play off against each other and more members of this growing (inner and outer) family experience the mystery and challenge of what it is to be human.

How to find your own selves on the map

The map of Personia is specifically designed for you to use in working with your inner selves and your Aware Ego process. The following are suggestions for ways to use this map as a companion to your Voice Dialogue work. You may find that the large color copy of the map gives you much more room to picture the interrelationships of your selves and is more fun to work with.

① **Notice your first response.** What part of the "landscape" appeals to you – city, country, ocean, sky? When you first look at the map, where do you feel drawn? Are there places or buildings that are attractive to you? Are there any places that look like home? Where do you *wish* you could live? What looks like a place where you *do* live? One friend took a quick look at the map while we were still constructing it, pointed to the mountain climbers and said, "That's me!" with a tone of glee in his voice. Where do *you* look and feel "That's me!"? The places you identify with most strongly are probably either where your primary selves live *or* are home to your positive disownments.

② **Notice your second response.** As you look at the map, is there any part that makes you feel uncomfortable or nervous? What part do you avoid looking at? What seems unappealing or even distasteful to you? If you lived on this island, where would you be *least* likely to go? Think of somebody you really don't like, someone who "pushes your buttons" – where would they most likely live on this map? These areas hold your negatively disowned selves.

③ **Notice your third response.** What haven't you noticed at all until now? True, it may be something really tiny like the fishermen on the lake or the junk yard or the protesters in front of the government building, but it also might be something really large like a whole mountain, or the golf course, or Solitude Island that somehow just didn't register in your consciousness. These things may represent either deeply disowned selves that you tend not to see at all, or they may simply be so outside the issues you deal with in your life, that you tend to tune them out entirely.

④ **Make a list of the inner selves you have been working with in your Voice Dialogue sessions.** Don't worry if you can't think of *all* of them now, just write down as many as you *can* think of, and then begin to look on the map for where they might live. The rational mind might gravitate toward the university, the museum, or one of the tall office buildings. A free spirit, adventurer, or a part that simply loves the outdoors might be off in the mountains, at the campground, traveling in the caravan, fishing on the lake, riding horses, or living in the commune. A very responsible self might be hard at work downtown or out on the farm or in the industrial section. A responsible mother self might be at home, or driving the kids to school or to the museum. Another kind of nurturing energy might fit right in at the hospital. A part that is very conscious of health and fitness might belong to the gym and go to the natural health clinic or the health food store. Your spiritual selves might find a home in the churches, at the ashram or the sacred circle, out on Solitude Island, or perhaps doing service work among homeless and poor people on the "seedy" side of town.

If you are new to Voice Dialogue work, it's likely that most of the selves you have explored in your sessions so far will be primary selves. Primary selves are the parts of you that you identify with – the ones you recognize as being "who you are." They are the ones that protect you, keep things under control, organize your activities, push you toward success, try to please others, take care of responsibilities, criticize your progress. When you look at the map, your primary responsible self, for example, will in all probability settle right down to business in some very work-oriented part of Personia and not want you to even look at the spa or the resort or, God forbid, the race track or the pool hall! Primary selves can make it difficult for us to look *directly* at what's on the other side, what we've disowned. So instead, we often get to see the reflection of our disowned side by looking *indirectly* through the mirror of other people's lives.

⑤ **Think of the sort of people you really don't like and list some of the qualities or behaviors in them that you tend to find disturbing.** Are you put off by aggressive or insensitive people? Do sweet, gushy people annoy you? Do you "have a thing" about wealthy people or politicians or panhandlers on street corners? Think of someone who "pushes your buttons," who evokes a strong emotional reaction from you every time you encounter them. It might be a person you work with, a family member, an old friend, a new acquaintance, even a public figure you have never met. *People you strongly dislike hold the energy of your negative disowned selves.*

114

It may help you to see and understand these negatively disowned energies in yourself if you look for where on the map you might find the people who upset you. Perhaps your sister, who you always thought was self-indulgent, extravagant, and lacking in meaningful values, lives in the ritzy condos on the waterfront and spends all her time shopping or at the spa. You never liked her husband either. He's a shipping magnate, has three cars, a place on the beach and goes hunting in the mountains. If *you* were going to go into the mountains, it certainly *wouldn't* be for hunting! And on it goes… *One person's primary self is another person's disowned self,* and it's remarkable how the same person can hold *negative* disowned energy for you and those same qualities might be a *positive* disownment for someone else. If your brother-in-law were to do something as out-of-character as mapping his selves, where would he place *you* on Personia? You can have a lot of fun (and learn a lot too) by imagining how other people might see you and where they would place you on the map.

⑥ **Continue to explore your disowned territory by listing any people you admire so much that you overvalue them – these people carry your positive disowned selves.** Think of someone you set up on a pedestal, someone you think of as being "amazing," "intelligent," "spiritual," "sensitive," "gutsy," etc. in a way you could never hope to be. This person carries a *positive disowned energy* for you. Some public figures hold a positive disowned energy for the whole culture. Mother Theresa, for example, represented a kind of pure selflessness that very few people could ever hope to emulate. If she is one of your positive disowned selves, where would you find her on the map? As you think about who might hold a positive disowned self for you, remember that what seems positive for you could be negative for another person. Look at our demonstrators, for example, the ones marching in front of the government building by the park. A friend of yours might find "those radicals" a threat to the community while you might really admire their willingness to stand up for their beliefs and wish that you had that kind of courage.

Until we begin to develop an Aware Ego that can both draw from and balance between our primary and disowned selves (i.e. make choices separate from what the selves might want to do), our primary selves operate as if they were the whole story of who we are. This is what goes on unconsciously and internally in all of us, but we can also observe many external examples of the same phenomenon. Take, for instance, the American political parties, the Democrats and Republicans. Each thinks their way is the best way and that the other side is either anti-American or just plain wrong. A larger truth, however, is that these two parties are both essential, and eliminating either one would damage the fabric of the whole country. Once you begin to notice the reality of different energies or subpersonalities in yourself and others, you may also start to see various opposites playing off of each other in your work place, your community, your local and national government, and between different cultures around the world.

⑦ **As you start to find both primary and disowned selves on the map, look for pairs or groups of opposites.** The Aware Ego develops as we separate energetically from each primary self and become aware of its opposite(s). In fact, we can only say we "have" an Aware Ego *in relation to particular selves* from which we have begun this separation process. *It is the Aware Ego that is able to stand between opposite selves and is in charge of managing the energies from both sides. The Aware Ego is capable of feeling these energies yet remaining unattached to the emotions and agendas that the individual selves hold.*

As you work with your map, see if you can find hints in the landscape about where your pairs of opposite energies reside. For example, if you see yourself basically as an "outdoors person," and spend most of your time in the garden, on the road, out in the woods, etc., then it's a sure bet that you will find opposites to these selves in the city. You might find, though, that it's not only a love of outdoors that keeps you focused in the garden. You might have a strong, peace-loving, spiritual self that is attached to the garden and is quite the opposite of a very different sort of "outdoors person" who is stationed out at the military base or camping with a survivalist group in the mountains. Once you locate a few of these pairs of opposites, expand your horizons and look for larger patterns of relationship as well. See if you notice a whole cluster or family of inner selves grouped together in one area of the map. The more you look at where your selves are on the map and consider how they relate to the surrounding landscape, the more easily you will discover the natural oppositions and energetic relationships that are alive in your own personality.

⑧ **Use the map to track your own process over time.** In playing with the map you are plotting the changing landscape of your own consciousness. You may want to log your journey through Personia in a journal, and as you continue to explore your inner selves through Voice Dialogue and other methods, the map can be used as a companion tool for your process. You may feel very differently about parts of Personia over time. A place that was very threatening a couple of Voice Dialogue sessions back may now feel neutral, or you may find you are no longer as entranced by another area as you used to be. The map may serve as an ongoing reminder of what territory you have covered in your facilitation, what areas the primary selves don't want you to go into, what places you've never had the opportunity to visit. Putting such clear attention on your process can deepen and even accelerate your Voice Dialogue work.

Try sharing the map with people who are close to you – let it provide a humorous and intriguing way to talk about your differences and similarities. Couples can learn a lot about each other simply by noticing what parts of Personia do or don't attract them.

⑨ **Add to the map.** Try writing the names of your different selves on Post-it® flags and plot them on the map. Like those generals in the old war movies, plotting the position of their troops on a map with little flags, *you can begin to locate the distribution of your energies*, both primary and disowned, on your personal map of the psyche, your own Island of Personia. You may want to use different colored markers to indicate primary and disowned selves. (Try using a third color flag or marker to indicate new selves that come into your life, new territories that you are just beginning to explore.)

You can also personalize your map by drawing in aspects that you feel are missing and that are important in your life. Use arrows to indicate selves that live in hidden parts of Personia – perhaps in a valley that is out of sight on the other side of the mountains or in an office in the middle of one of the skyscrapers. Use a non-permanent glue to paste on pictures so that your map becomes an ever-changing collage of your life, including dream images out in the Ocean of the Unconscious. A story will begin to unfold that will give you extraordinary information about your inner journey as it stirs the unconscious and stimulates a new awareness of your process and your progress.

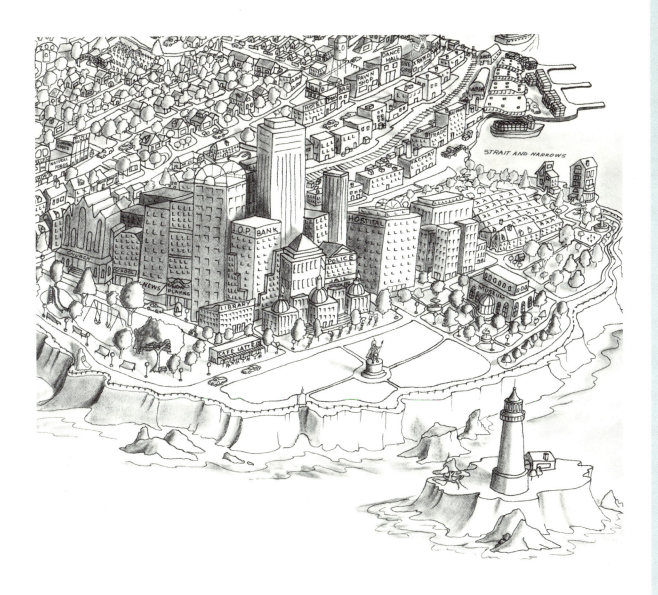

Southeast Personia is the busiest part of the island. Can you identify with the people working in the office buildings? There may be certain primary selves in you that occupy the lower part of the skyscraper. These may be parts of you that try to please others, that are conservative and want structure, that avoid risk, etc., while an entirely different sort may occupy the big offices at the top, perhaps the inner power broker, risk taker, pusher, entrepreneur, etc.

How many of your selves (both primary and disowned) can you find in this one part of the map? Do you identify with the people in the government buildings or with people protesting in front of them? Would you feel more at home in the high rise apartments overlooking the water or in a factory? in the museum or the shipyard? in the police station, the lighthouse, or the playground?

Southwest Personia is where you can go for an education or recreation, retirement or health care, to mention only a few possibilities. How many of your different selves (primary or disowned) can you imagine placing in the university, the spa, the golf course, the natural health clinic, or the sports stadium?

Are you someone who heads for the beach at the first opportunity, or do you only wish you could? Perhaps you have a vacation self that is primary when you're on vacation for one or two weeks, but does it then take a back seat to the opposite and more dominant primary energies of responsibility and work that rule the other 50 weeks of the year?

Would you be likely to use the holistic health center or the natural food market, or does just the idea of this sort of place make you want to run to the nearest ice cream parlor? Does the university appeal to your rational mind? Or, would you be cheering for the football team in the stadium? How do you feel about the Live Oak Retirement home? Would your nurturer or responsible self be active there? Do you have a disowned elderly person you're afraid might end up there or another self who wants to go there now just to be taken care of?

Dream Cove is a place where the deep Ocean of the Unconscious touches the shore of our waking reality. Here where it's shallow and safe to go in the water, dreams surface and we can bring back their messages from the Unconscious to energize and inform our lives. What do you think may be living in your own Dream Cove? Would you sit quietly on the shore, take a walk, or go for a swim?

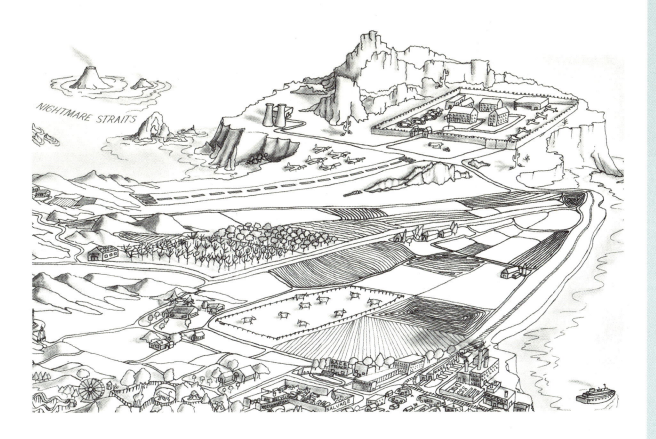

Northeast Personia is a place of contrasts, encompassing everything from the race track and the salvage yard to the zoo and amusement park. There is a military base and a nuclear power plant. It even has its own active volcano offshore. There are factories, farmland, a railroad and ships. Are there parts of you that feel at home in certain of these areas and not in others? Do you find more of your *disowned* selves living on this part of the island? If so, name a few of them and place them where you think they live.

If it doesn't appear that any of your selves live on this part of the island, do military people, gamblers, farmers, or volcanoes show up in your dreams? Maybe these dream characters are appearing to balance other parts of your life. Many people, for example, who are attracted to consciousness work find themselves in opposition to the kind of choices that could lead to a career in agribusiness or the military or factory work, but that doesn't mean that they don't need some of the energy that these occupations embody. Could you use a *little* more authority, discipline, connection to nature, assertiveness, working with your hands, etc.? What other energies from this part of the map could offer more balance in your life? (In small doses of course!)

This part of Personia may be where many of your inner children can enjoy themselves. Do you have a part of you that longs for some fun, a day at the park, a trip to the zoo? Do you remember climbing apple trees or playing with animals on a farm? Is there an inner boy who is fascinated with trains or airplanes, or wishes he could go to sea? a girl who dreams of horses in the country?

Northwest Personia is full of alternatives to the busy city which is its opposite. If you have a loner self that really wants to get away from it all, there is Solitude Island off the coast of Personia or the hermit's hut way up in the mountains. What part of you could live a simple life in a fishing village? Who would go hiking or hunting in the forest or sailing on the lake? Can you even imagine that you have such a part?

Do you think of yourself as creative? Would the artist in you love to live in an artist's colony or out in the country? If you can't imagine yourself doing that, do you have a friend or family member or associate who lives out that energy? Do you judge or admire them for it?

Is there a part of yourself you see as spiritual? Is your religion the foundation of your moral and spiritual life? Would you belong to the big church in the city or to the little country church, or are you attracted to meditating in the ashram at the foot of the mountains? Perhaps religion and spirituality are disowned selves for you and you want nothing to do with "unscientific beliefs." On the other hand, maybe there is a part of you that really feels most connected to spirit in nature. Is that a medicine wheel or ancient stone circle up on the cliff, and is there a part of you that would perform a celebration there? Or does some other self consider that sort of thing to be a lot of "New Age craziness?" However you feel about these questions, answering them will help you find more of your inner selves, both primary and disowned, on the map.

Our intention is to find the easiest and most organic place to start...

Choosing which primary self to facilitate

A Voice Dialogue session is by its nature a relaxed, organic and creative process for both facilitator and subject. You meet and connect, listen to what is going on in the subject's life, talk a little bit about what Voice Dialogue is (if the subject is new to the process), and then move on to choosing a primary self to facilitate.* Usually after ten, fifteen, twenty minutes of conversation at least one or two if not several primary parts will have shown themselves to the observant facilitator, and the task will be to determine which is most energetically available and most connected to the issues this person would like to explore today.

Picking up on the energy changes is the key to making this part of the session easy. The more you notice energetic changes during your initial conversation, the easier it will be for you to choose a primary self to facilitate. By paying attention to energy, you'll see which voices are most "up and out." You can identify which parts are primary not only by what they have to say, but also by their energetic predominance. Use your perception of body language, voice tone, and how the energy feels to you to confirm your sense of which primary self seems to be most present and most important for the subject to explore in this session. And remember, *you don't have to figure this out alone.* You can talk with the person you are facilitating to see what part feels most familiar and primary to them. If you see a couple of good options, tell your subject what you perceive and right away you'll get a response that lets you know more about where this person wants and needs to begin.

Almost invariably, the very first primary selves you'll choose to facilitate are the "gate keepers," the ones that control access to the rest of the personality and that will reveal the rules this person lives by. These selves also carry the conditioning of the family and the culture. *They are the selves that are so central in the personality that the subject often doesn't even know they exist* – "It's just the way I *am.*" On the other hand, these parts of the personality are easy for you, the facilitator, to detect because they announce themselves as soon as you meet your subject. Keep in mind that it's often quite a startling concept to the person being facilitated that something so basic to their personality could actually not be *all* of who they are. It may be a revelation to discover that it's possible to separate out from these most fundamental primary selves and at the same time feel them more clearly and fully than ever before.

---

*Note: In *The Handbook, Part I*, we will be working *only with primary selves.* Facilitating disowned selves will be introduced in *Part II.* Although in long-term work with most subjects there comes a time when it is organic to work with the disowned selves, it is important to remember that the primary selves *don't like it* when you go to the disowned selves, and you and the subject can create a "primary self backlash" by going to the disowned side too soon. It is important also for the facilitator to be experienced with the facilitation process and comfortable working with primary selves before attempting to work with the disowned energies directly. Please remember that the goal is to enhance the Aware Ego process and not simply to explore as many selves as possible. A huge amount can be accomplished by separating from primary selves (especially pairs of opposite primary selves, see p. 153).

It works best to keep the process of choosing a direction really simple, especially if both the facilitator and subject are new to Voice Dialogue work. Most often, as we have seen in the beginnings of our sample sessions,* your initial conversation will give you an obvious place to start, but if it doesn't, the following are tried and true places to begin:

♦ **The rulemaker** – you can simply ask to speak with the "rulemaker," the self that has rules about what is and isn't okay for this person to do in any given situation. The Stones say,

> *This may be the single best self to start with in facilitation because this self is what manages the person's value system, and it doesn't upset any of the [other] selves in the system to talk with this part. You start to ask it questions about what it wants and doesn't want, what it will and won't allow, and you've entered a "gold mine." Basically it will give you a list of all the primary selves as it outlines its requirements.*

♦ **The protector/controller** – any self that is in charge of protection, safety, or control will be a safe and productive place to begin the work. Important information to learn from this self is what its concerns and fears are and how it goes about protecting the subject from the dangers it perceives.

♦ **The responsible and/or caretaking part** – no one is offended if you ask to speak with the self in them that is responsible and/or takes care of people. And, in talking with this self you will inevitably discover sources of anxiety, pressure, and stress.

♦ **The part who arranged to do Voice Dialogue work** – you can ask to speak with the part who is most interested in doing Voice Dialogue, the one who called up and made the appointment. You'll be able to ask this self what other things it organizes in this person's life and to what purpose.

♦ **The hesitant/resistant self** – if the person being facilitated has some hesitancy about or resistance to doing Voice Dialogue work, start with the hesitant or resistant self. In this way you will honor this self's caution and find out what its other hesitations are.

Facilitator and subject together choose where to begin. The process of deciding where to start the facilitation needs to be a graceful energy dance between you and the person you are facilitating. It's very important, especially if the subject is new to Voice Dialogue, for the facilitator to talk about her initial observations and make clear suggestions. If you simply ask the subject what self they want to go to first, you may get confusion or inappropriate choices as a response, *so your leadership and guidance here are essential.* However, if the facilitator can see two equally good directions to take, it's smart to ask the subject which one appeals most to them. Someone who has already been facilitated a few times may have a very clear sense of where they want to go, while someone new to the process will know if they feel uncomfortable with the facilitator's choice, but may not be able to come up with their own choice. I often listen to the person I'm facilitating talk for a while and then quite spontaneously say something like, "Ah, the part of you that just made that remark

"It's very important, especially if the subject is new to Voice Dialogue, to talk about your initial observations and make clear suggestions – your leadership and guidance here are essential."

*See "Some initial conversations between facilitator and subject," pp. 96-100.

about comparing you to other people – I'd really like to meet that self and talk with it more. Would that be okay with you?" *It is important that the people you work with know that they can count on you to be ready to shift gears and go in another direction if they are the least bit uncomfortable with any suggestions you make.* In this context of safety and respect, you will be able to use your intuitive abilities fully and will very likely find that your subjects are willing to follow your suggestions more often than not.

> *"It is important that the people you work with know that they can count on you to be ready to shift gears and go in another direction if they are the least bit uncomfortable with any suggestions you make."*

What if you make a suggestion the primary selves don't like? Every facilitator makes some proposals that get rejected, and this can be a very positive part of the process *because the rejection leads you straight to a primary self that is uncomfortable with what you suggested.* You really can't go wrong! When this happens to you (and it's certainly happened to me *lots* of times), you'll find *if you keep your energetic linkage with your subject strong* (even if they aren't consciously aware of linkage yet), you'll move through the bumpiest part of the road with resourcefulness and humor. When the uncomfortable primary self comes to the surface, verbally and/or energetically expressing hesitation, discomfort, confusion, etc., it's necessary to shift directions easily, *to gracefully follow your subject's lead.* By "gracefully," I mean that the facilitator is gracious and respectful. She is not invested in either the direction or outcome of the work, and makes it clear that there's no need to start anywhere that causes discomfort and that the subject did nothing wrong. The facilitator can simply say something like, "Well, we certainly don't have to go in a direction that makes some part of you uncomfortable. In fact, would it be okay to begin by talking with the part that feels uncomfortable and find out what concerns it?"

A few things to keep in mind...

Even when a person has been facilitated many times by an experienced facilitator, it's still preferable to begin *each* session with a primary self. Whatever issue the subject wants to focus on, it's best to start facilitating the most dominant primary self. If you don't, it's quite likely that the most dominant primary self will barge in anyway, taking over the space of another self or coming in quite forcefully when you return to the Aware Ego. Think of the primary selves as literally having seniority because they have been around so long in the subject's life, and it would be rude to walk past an "elder" and ignore them without at least stopping briefly to check in with them first.

> *"At the beginning of a facilitation relationship, you are building trust between you as facilitator and your subject's primary self system. It's more important to develop that trust than to go after emotional release."*

If there is a choice between two primary selves, go with the one that is least likely to trigger vulnerability, especially for the very first session. For example, with some people, a rulemaker or organizer might be a better choice to start with than a very powerful critic. All of these selves are primary, but in working with the critic there is often a vulnerable self "waiting in the wings" that can feel devastated by all the critic's internal judgments. *Especially at the beginning of a facilitation relationship, you are building trust between you as facilitator and your subject's* *primary self system. It's more important to develop that trust than to go after emotional release.* Many people have allowed their protection to be violated by therapists or teachers who believe it's good to get rid of defenses or to go through a cathartic release of emotions. You can count on it that the protective/controlling selves will be waiting to see if *you* are going to push to uncover vulnerability the way other professionals may have in the past. The primary selves want to know if you mean what you say about honoring their limits.

What if the subject seems eager to explore their vulnerability, pain, shame, shadow, etc.? What if they've read all about their disowned selves and are ready to embrace them? Think for a moment what you would be inclined to do... My first choice would be to speak with the self that is eager to explore these areas. I would ask it what it hopes to gain by working with disowned selves and what additional goals it has for this person. What does this self fear if the person *doesn't* succeed in dealing with all their pain and shame? Usually when I do this, I uncover a perfectionist/pusher who has read a great many books or gone to lots of workshops and is determined to find a way to make this person okay in the context of the "self-help subculture." The Stones have nicknamed this self the "New Age Pusher," and you'll find that its bottom line concerns are the same as any other primary self – protection, safety, control, acceptance.

> *"It is the responsibility of the ego (Aware Ego and/or operating ego), and not the individual selves, to deal with difficult events and strong emotions."*

Remember too, that people most often arrive for their sessions "in voice," and the particular energy they arrive in may be very vulnerable. If a subject walks in the door on the edge of tears because of something that just happened that day, *have them stay in the ego place* while they are talking about what happened and expressing their feelings. If you were to have the person move out into a vulnerable self, that would violate the primary selves' need to protect the vulnerability. By keeping the subject in the ego place, you *reinforce that it is the responsibility of the ego (Aware Ego and/or operating ego), and not the individual selves, to deal with difficult events and strong emotions.*

If it doesn't seem obvious where to go with the work, if it feels like a struggle or an effort, *you are probably trying to make something happen rather than simply following the energy of the person you are facilitating.* You may want to reread the chapter on energetics (p. 51) to internalize a deeper understanding of how facilitation works, or work through some of the questions that follow the sample facilitations to help you find your own natural ease in facilitating.

Facilitator and subject together decide which primary self they would like to talk with first. The facilitator may suggest a direction based on her observations of the selves, and she follows the subject's lead as to what feels comfortable to work with. Even when the subject has done a lot of Voice Dialogue work, it is still advisable to begin by facilitating a primary self.

124

Kelly, Joan, and Glen continued...

Kelly

When we were talking with Kelly earlier (we last worked with Kelly on p. 96), did you decide what self you would facilitate first? Following our ground rules, we know we wouldn't want to start with the part that is excited about having time for herself because that part is disowned. The facilitator could ask to speak with a generally responsible self or even with the part of Kelly who organizes all her responsibilities and obviously packs her schedule pretty tightly. It may seem irresistible to go with the "mother bear" because this self is central to the issue Kelly is dealing with, though if you read "More possibilities for working with Kelly" on the next page, you'll see that there are a lot of good choices for how you might proceed with this facilitation. Here's how Kelly's facilitator continues:

> **Facilitator:** I know what you mean. It really does help to separate from these selves, though, and get some distance from them so they don't crowd in on us so much. I think we might want to start by talking with the self that feels anxious, the mother bear, because she's the one that seems to be most strongly present today and probably a lot of the time lately. How does that feel to you?

> **Kelly:** Well, that part of me has certainly felt very present. I'm not so sure I know how to be a bear, but I'm willing to try.

Joan

It's actually common for people to have a different primary self (or set of primary selves) at home than they have at work. (We last talked with Joan on p. 98) Joan's colleagues at work probably wouldn't even recognize the "couch potato." Since both of these selves are primary in different parts of Joan's life, how do you decide which one to facilitate first? Think about it for a moment before reading on...

The facilitator in our example suggests beginning with the part of Joan who pushes her energy up, the one that makes her go play tennis, who clicks her into gear and keeps her schedule full. He suggests working with this self because it seems to him to have the strongest energetic presence – every time Joan would flatten out while she was talking, this self managed to pick her up and get her going again. However, it's just as easy to look at it the other way, that every time the bubbly energy would get going, eventually the more lethargic part would come back and flatten it out. Since both energies are primary for Joan, the facilitator can safely suggest either one as a starting point.

> **Facilitator:** I think it would be very interesting to meet the self that keeps you up and moving because it's such a prominent part of your personality.

> **Joan:** I've never actually thought about it, so it would be interesting to see who that is.

> **Facilitator:** Well, if that feels okay to you, let's start with the "up and moving" self.

> **Joan:** Sure. Do you want me to move over?

More possibilities for working with Kelly…

Even though in every session there are several valid and useful directions to take with the work, it's really easy to read the sample facilitations throughout *The Handbook* and *assume* that each is somehow the one best way to go. To help us get out of that mindset, let's start right at the beginning with our first subject, Kelly, and try out some additional choices for her session. Here are three other possible lead-ins for facilitating Kelly. *An excellent exercise for developing your facilitation skills is to imagine following through with any one or all of these lead-ins, move Kelly into the self, and complete the facilitation.* You may also want to review Joan's and Glen's sessions too and see if you can come up with a couple of additional directions for working with them.

Another possible lead-in:

Facilitator: You know one self I'm kind of hearing behind the scenes is your inner critic. *(Kelly rolls her eyes and nods her head, and the facilitator has that sense of a recognition "clicking in")* You haven't mentioned it, but I get the sense that there's a part of you that is really critical of you as a mother and probably in other areas as well.

Kelly: Boy, that's for sure. Sometimes I feel I can't make a move without passing some sort of inner inspection!

Facilitator: Maybe that would be a good place for us to start. *(Kelly nods assent)* How about moving over to where you think that critical self might be.

Another possible lead-in:

Facilitator: What do you think about starting with that anxious, mother bear part of you? *(Kelly's energy withdraws a bit, the facilitator can feel something tightening up in herself)* Does that feel okay, or is that too much to start with?

Kelly: *(looking a bit nervous)* Well, I'm not sure. When you said that I kind of felt it was too personal – I joke about being a mother bear, but I think I'd feel kind of dumb trying to actually be one. Maybe if we didn't have to call it a bear.

Facilitator: *(paying attention to her energetic connection with Kelly so wherever they decide to go, Kelly will feel the facilitator supporting her)* Absolutely! We want to start wherever it feels most comfortable to you *(Kelly breathes more deeply and lets her shoulders down a little bit)* – maybe it would be good to simply begin with the responsible part of you.

Kelly: *(nodding her head, taking another deep breath)* That sounds good. I feel okay with that.

Another possible lead-in:

Facilitator: You know, as I listen to you, Kelly, I can really feel you're under a lot of pressure! I feel it myself just talking with you. You've taken on quite a load to be doing and organizing so many things in addition to taking care of your family.

Kelly: *(a real mixture of feelings on her face, everything from pride to a hint of tears)* I know… I love all of it, but sometimes it feels like there's just no breathing space. I had this friend who used to say, "It looks good on paper…"

Facilitator: *(the facilitator feels Kelly's tension and also has a sense of a door opening up here)* Well, we know there's a part of you that's starting to really feel the effect of all the pressure in your life. You probably remember from the workshop you went to that we always start with the primary selves first, the ones that have been "running the show" in your life. Some part of you obviously takes on a great deal and puts you under a lot of pressure.

Kelly: *(taking a big breath and nodding agreement)* Boy does it ever! I don't know how I could ever get away from that part of me – it will probably run me into the ground first.

Facilitator: Well, fortunately it's not necessary to try to escape that part of yourself. Instead you can move over and *be* the part of you that puts all the pressure on. That way you'll become more aware of that self and be able to experience some separation from it. Want to give it a try?

Kelly: Sure, that sounds like something I could really use.

Another possible lead-in (an exercise for your imagination):

Facilitator: …

Kelly: …

Etc.: …

Glen

Isn't it amazing that we were able to see so much of Glen's "psychic map" from such a short and casual conversation. (The maps of Glen's selves are on pp. 100-101, and our conversation with Glen is on p. 99) On the primary side, we have a self that has decided Glen needs to get his life "sorted out" and a self that is protective, concerned about embarrassment and vulnerability and wants to stay in control of whatever the Voice Dialogue process is. Some part of Glen got him into a relationship, but communicating, especially about his feelings, is definitely disowned. Certainly Glen's rational mind is primary and he must be able to communicate enough to be in business for himself, though he has a definite loner that is also primary and wants to work on his own to get away from people.* There is also a self that is concerned about Glen's financial stability, a critic that finds him lacking in several areas, and some self (or selves) that feels very overwhelmed. The parts of Glen who were confident, adventurous, risk-taking, etc. may have been around a while back, but at present he is having a hard time accessing those energies. Underneath all of this is Glen's vulnerability, which is very disowned, though its energy drives the whole system.

Like many of us, Glen ventured into new territory, some of it risky and somewhat disowned (like getting into a relationship or going into business for himself), only to find his primary selves coming back in full force as soon as they felt threatened by financial difficulty or stress with his girlfriend. *This bouncing back and forth between opposites is very different from Glen developing an Aware Ego process and learning to access, use, and balance these opposite energies.* When we are able to embrace our opposites from center, life goes along more smoothly and we are much less vulnerable to being suddenly taken over by anxious and upset primary selves when things "go wrong."

> *How would you proceed with Glen's session and how much explanation would you give Glen about Voice Dialogue?*
>
> *Where would you start? Think about your own approach before following our facilitator below.*

Facilitator: Did your friend, Alice, explain anything to you about how a Voice Dialogue session works?

Glen: She said I'd get to meet different parts of myself, which sounded a little strange to me. I hope it's not role playing because I don't think I'd be any good at that sort of thing.

Facilitator: Well, I've only done a little role playing so I'm not an expert on it, but I do know it's not the same as Voice Dialogue. I can assure you that this process is very natural and easy and doesn't require you to do anything that doesn't feel okay to you. Actually you don't have to do anything really different from the way you've already been talking to me except that each part of you will get to talk *separately* and from its own place in the room. For example, we could start by meeting the part of you that is interested in getting your life "sorted out."

*See p. 153 for an explanation of opposite primary selves.

Glen: *(tenses slightly at this suggestion)* What would I have to do?

Facilitator: Well, it's pretty simple. All you have to do is move your chair over and continue talking as the part of you who wants to sort your life out. We've already heard some of what that self has to say and this way we'd get to listen to more of it. *(Glen still seems uncomfortable and the facilitator begins to feel a corresponding tension in her own body – something doesn't feel right)* You know what? I think it would be even easier to just go ahead and meet the part of you that feels hesitant about Voice Dialogue and being able to do it right. That seems to be your first concern and we can look at other parts later.

Glen: *(seems relieved)* That sounds okay. I appreciate your being patient with me – this sort of thing is very new to me.

Facilitator: *(relaxing too)* Sure, please let me know if anything doesn't feel comfortable to you because I want to be respectful of your concerns... It's an essential part of doing Voice Dialogue work together.

Glen: *(the first hint of a smile since he walked in)* I'm relieved to hear that. I've never tried any "personal growth" stuff before because I was afraid it would push me to be something I'm not.

Facilitator: *(feeling the clearest energetic connection to Glen since he walked in)* I hope you'll let me know if that happens here. I think that I'm already hearing a lot of what the hesitant part of you has to say, and if it's okay with you, we could go ahead and move into that self now.

Glen: Okay, I'm game.

It is essential to move physically into the selves ...

Moving into a primary self

Once you choose where to go, the person being facilitated has to physically move!
Getting up and moving to a different part of the room, even if it's only a few inches away, is a basic and essential part of Voice Dialogue work. *Moving* to another self makes the separation real on a physical and energetic level in a way that talking about it just can't do. After facilitator and subject have discussed the selves and agreed where to begin, the facilitator needs to explain clearly to the subject that *they* will be moving into a self.* For example, "In the next part of the session you'll have an opportunity to move to another place in the room and *be* the part of you we were talking about that is very organized and efficient. This will give the organized self it's own space, and we'll have a chance to meet this part of you and hear what it has to say, separate from the rest of you. Does this feel like something you are ready to do?"

If there has been a clear process of talking and identifying a primary self with which to start working, most subjects will be ready to go right into the self. Some will naturally pick up their chair and move it or find a different one they like without any more prompting from the facilitator. Some people look to the facilitator for either direction or reassurance that it's okay for them to go ahead and go wherever they feel like going, and there are others who say "Okay," and then just sit there without budging because they didn't really understand that you are actually asking them to get up and move their bodies to another place. *Whatever response you get, make sure if you need to give repeated or additional instructions that you do it without making the person feel foolish or wrong.* Remember this is a very new process for many people and it may take a while for it to sink in and make sense to the different selves.

There are no rules about where a self can be located except that they can't stay in the ego place and can't take over the facilitator's space. Part of the fun and surprise of facilitating is seeing the energy of the self emerge right from the beginning as it chooses a place to sit (or stand or even pace). If you are working in a room with a lot of different seating choices (hard chairs, soft sofa, pillows on the floor, etc.), the different selves will each choose what they like best and you'll learn something about them before they even begin to speak just by watching where they decide to go. If there are only two chairs, yours and the subject's, the self can still pick up the subject's chair and move it closer or farther away. (It's important to have a chair that moves easily if you only have one!) They may flip it around and straddle it, stand on it if they want to get up above the other selves, or leave it altogether and sit or even lie down on the floor.

> *"Part of the fun and surprise of facilitating is seeing the energy of the self emerge right from the beginning as it chooses a place to sit (or stand or even pace)."*

I've worked with vulnerable selves that could only be present with their back to me, huddled in a corner. I've seen sensual selves that writhed and wriggled around on a soft carpeted floor,

---

*See "A word about grammar," p. xix, for an explanation of why plural pronouns are used for singular subjects.

physically active selves that moved around the entire room, and very prim and proper selves that sat bolt upright only a few inches from the ego place.

It's best if a self picks its own place, but the facilitator can help if needed. Certainly there's no need to make a big deal about choosing a spot for the self to sit. The facilitator can make a suggestion such as, "You know, you were kind of looking over your right shoulder when we decided to talk with the part that makes the rules, so maybe moving a little back and to the right would work fine. It's really not too important which place you choose as long as you do move." If the subject does feel it's a big deal to move to the

"If the subject does feel it's a big deal to move to the 'correct' place, you may want to suggest first talking with the part that is anxious about making the right choice."

"correct" place even after you reassure them that any choice will be fine, you may want to suggest first talking with the part that is anxious about making the right choice. This will be an excellent primary self to begin the work, so please remember as facilitator that when you follow your subject's energetic lead, *you* can't go wrong! Your work will be clear and organic, and you'll both be more relaxed with the process.

Sometimes a primary self will not want to move at all. After all, they think that they *are* the whole person, and why should they move? With this kind of self it's essential to create a real physical separation so that space opens up for the Aware Ego to develop. First acknowledge that the self is indeed of central importance and then ask the self to move over just for the purpose of doing Voice Dialogue work. For example:

♦ "I know most of the time you *are* Sue, but how about moving over a couple of inches right now so you can have your *own* place in the Voice Dialogue work."

♦ "You're a part of John who is definitely right in the middle of everything he does, so I understand why you wouldn't want to move away from him. It will help John, though, to have more awareness and appreciation of what you do in his life if you move over just for now so we can talk with you separately."

♦ "I know that you really are the biggest part of Melinda, but there must be some other parts of her too, or Melinda wouldn't be experiencing the problems I've been hearing about. After all, you're the part of her who keeps everything under control so I can't imagine that *you* would be the one who is forgetting appointments."

"No, that's true. I certainly wouldn't do that, and it upsets me."

"Well, I'd like to help Melinda have more awareness of how you function, and to do that it works best if you move over just for a little while so I can talk with you separately from her."

"I guess I can do that as long as I get to go back again."

"Of course you do – nothing is going to take away your central place in her life."

If a person moves so little that they can't find the energy of the self, you may want to suggest that they move just a little bit more. Usually the self will "click into place." There's no rule about how much a self should move, and a few inches will usually be enough at first –

just to initiate the separation. You want to make sure there is enough distance for the Aware Ego to perceive a clear separation. As the work progresses you will probably find with some people that the selves naturally move farther out to their own favorite places and with others that they are able to accomplish the same separation with relatively little movement.

The facilitator shifts *energetically* as the subject moves *physically*. As facilitator, you don't get up and go anywhere when the subject moves into a self. However, *the way you move your energy* makes all the difference as to how fully the self will be able to come out. It's the facilitator's job to "match the energy" of the self, and the time to begin doing this is as soon as you know which self you are going to be facilitating. In a sense, by shifting your own energy to resonate with the particular self you want to induct, you create an energetic welcome that helps the self to become more fully present. Because you have modeled the shift, the self will feel invited in energetically and the subject will feel more comfortable moving into each part you facilitate.

What do we mean by "matching the energy" of the self? Let's demystify this basic skill before it starts to sound too esoteric or complex. Matching energy can really be very simple and very similar to the way you *normally unconsciously shift your energy* as you encounter different people throughout the day. Think of walking into a family gathering, giving your grandmother a genteel, respectful hug and a peck on the cheek, then slapping your brother on the back with a hearty hello, and finally squatting down to greet your two-year-old niece, changing your tone of voice to one that's appropriate for being introduced to her favorite dolly. Making similar kinds of changes in your energy, tone and body language when you

" By shifting your own energy to resonate with the particular self you want to induct, you create an energetic welcome that helps the self to become more fully present."

facilitate selves (though, of course without the physical contact) makes each self feel at home in the same way that your change in tone and energy makes each member of your family feel comfortable with you.

As you practice some of the energy exercises in your *Handbook** or ones that you have learned at workshops and trainings, *you will become adept at simply shifting your energy field without having to make any overt change in tone or gesture to go with it.* Remember the principle that "energy follows thought and intention." With practice you'll find that you can make big shifts that can

*See "Exercises in energetics" on p. 68.

be felt by the people you facilitate just by moving your focus high or low in your body or imagining that you are sending out a particular kind of energy, or even by simply changing your breath. As you experiment with energy, you may soon find that shifting energies in a Voice Dialogue session becomes second nature like changing your approach with different people at family gatherings and other social situations.

Does the self appear just because the facilitator asks it to? The concept that energy follows thought and intention is a principle that works for the subject just the same as it does for the facilitator. You'll find that even though your subject simply moves to another spot in the room, maybe only a few inches away, *it really feels as if a different person has appeared on the scene.* Does this shift happen automatically when the facilitator directs the subject to move into a self? The process *can* be that simple, *but it is not automatic.* Often more of an orientation by the facilitator is needed to help bring out the self. Remember tha*t just because you invite a self to appear, it doesn't mean that particular self will be the one that shows up. The facilitator has to stay on her "energetic toes" and be alert to what energy is actually arriving on the scene.* When a facilitator asks to speak with a certain self, and that part *doesn't* show up, there may instead be a part that was triggered by the idea of the other one coming out. Or, it may simply be that this one was ready to come out and nobody noticed it. The facilitator who goes on automatic can find himself in the embarrassing position of talking to a self that isn't present, who isn't the part he was expecting. If you've ever thought you were talking with one person at a party and then discovered they were someone else, you know how awkward it can feel!

> *"Just because you invite a self to appear, it doesn't mean that particular self will be the one that shows up. The facilitator has to stay on her 'energetic toes' and be alert to what energy is actually arriving on the scene."*

Let's look at an example. Julie's facilitator asked to speak with the part of her that likes to have everything organized and can't stand her sloppy sister. Julie moved over and the facilitator began by asking the self questions about how it organizes Julie's life. The facilitator was so focused on the content of the conversation that he just didn't notice at first that the answers coming back seemed vague, not the sort of reply one would expect from a highly organized individual. Fortunately, as long as the facilitator stays energetically open to the self that *is* there, it's not hard to extricate himself. He might just stop and say, "You know, I can feel I'm asking you the wrong questions. You seem different from the organized self I thought I was going to be talking to. Why don't you tell me about yourself?" This works because there is linkage between the facilitator and the self and because the facilitator doesn't make the self wrong for not turning out to be the part he was expecting. Certainly, whatever the reason for the change, the facilitator can't just pretend he's talking to someone who isn't there – he has to notice the change and "tune in" energetically to the self that has actually appeared.

 *After choosing a self to facilitate, the facilitator asks the subject to physically move over and be that self. While the subject moves physically, the facilitator shifts energetically to match and support the self that emerges.*

Helping Kelly, Joan, and Glen move into a primary self:

Turn back to where we left Kelly, Joan, and Glen, at the end of our chapter on "Choosing which primary self to facilitate," (We last saw Kelly and Joan on p. 125, and Glen on p. 128) and take the time to write out just what you would say to each of our three subjects to direct them to move over to a primary self. When you have completed this exercise, you may want to answer the questions and read the discussion on the following page.

Kelly _____

_____

_____

_____

_____

_____

Joan _____

_____

_____

_____

_____

Glen _____

_____

_____

_____

_____

_____

Did you change your approach with each subject?

If you did change what you said to each subject, how do you imagine your energy would have been different with each one?

Do you think any of these three subjects would have had any difficulty understanding how to move into a self?

What are some of the different responses you have encountered in first-time facilitations when you asked a subject to move into a self? How did you handle these situations?

Discussion

Asking a subject to move over to a self and then to move back to the Aware Ego (or to move out to awareness and back*) are really the only times that a facilitator has to give directions in the course of a Voice Dialogue session. I always find that it doesn't matter if I get my tongue twisted or don't give the world's best directions as long as my energy is clear. If I am energetically linked with my subject, even a bumbling transition will be easy and lighthearted. And, in the same vein, the most elegant directions will be hard for the subject to follow if we're not energetically in tune with one another.

*For a discussion of moving to awareness, refer to the chapter on "The awareness level," p. 195.

Meeting a self is just like meeting a new person...

Talking with a primary self

Facilitating a self involves asking it questions, supporting its energetic expression and listening to it deeply on all levels. In other words, facilitation requires "presence," a full attention that comes from your physical body and your energy body as well as from your mind. Watching an accomplished facilitator at work makes this process appear deceptively simple. It looks and sounds like two people who have just met and are engaged in ordinary conversation – one person asks a few interested questions and the other communicates easily about what concerns them. *Maintaining the energetic connection is what makes this conversation seem so effortless.* However, for many of us, until we get used to it, trying to talk and pay attention to energy at the same time can seem like trying to pat your head and rub your stomach simultaneously – awkward at first, and easy to forget to do one or the other. And, of course, it's possible to get so tangled up in trying to pay attention to energy and to carrying on a conversation that you totally forget to *listen.* It's very important to be patient with yourself and bring along a good sense of humor.

Asking questions is probably the easiest part of facilitation because it's the most familiar. You've talked with all kinds of people all your life, and now you can build on your natural communication skills in learning Voice Dialogue facilitation. Start by asking questions that, first of all, feel comfortable to the self you are interviewing. These questions will be appropriate for this particular self's energy (i.e. the kind of question and tone of voice for an inner hippie might be different than what you would use for an inner patriarch!), and they will convey your genuine interest without pushing or prying. You'll want to focus your questions on whatever you feel will retrieve useful information for the Aware Ego. Often what is most helpful for the Aware Ego is discovering what motivates a self, how the self functions in the subject's life, what its history is, and what its presence feels like.

"Talking with a self is even easier when you realize that you don't have to do therapy for the self, don't have to solve it's problems or get it to change in any way. Instead, your job is simply to get to know this new 'person.'"

This helps the Aware Ego to separate from, recognize, and utilize the energy of a particular self. Talking with a self is even easier when you realize that you don't have to do therapy for the self, don't have to solve its problems or get it to change in any way. Instead, your job is simply to strike up a conversation and *get to know* this new "person." You'll find, once you get started, that the energy and comments of the self you're working with will naturally guide you toward the next inquiry. Good facilitation is a matter of following the lead of the subpersonality so you create an opening, an unfolding of the energy and information that is held by the self. *The key to relaxed organic work is to stay present, recognize the leads you're being given and follow them.*

The facilitator also has the advantage of being able to listen beyond words. Talking with a self is very important, but in Voice Dialogue we have come to recognize that words are only as powerful as the energy behind them. The observation, "It's not *what* one says, but *who* says it" has long been a favorite saying among people who do Voice Dialogue work, and sometimes knowing who is really there means reaching beyond what the self is saying and going with other cues. One of the most common problems encountered by people just learning to facilitate is being so concerned about what to do (what questions to ask, what direction to go, when to move, etc.) that they forget that perhaps the most important part of facilitating is *being receptive – listening and following.* For the facilitator to "listen" to non-verbal communication, she has to pay attention to her own feelings and to the changes in her own body experience, as well

How to get the conversation going...

"Facilitate" comes from Latin and means to make EASY! As a facilitator, you want your conversations with the selves to be relaxed, both for them and for you.

Stay with the energy –

As we have emphasized over and over again, the number one way to make Voice Dialogue facilitation flow is to link energetically with the person you facilitate. Once you have that connection, the key is to keep it going – keep your attention on the energetic communication between you regardless of the verbal topic of conversation. Take your cues and leads from the self, and then if you make a conversational blunder, the linkage will still be strong and it will be easy enough to backtrack and head down a more promising communication trail.

Remember the basics –

Even though we know that the first, middle, and last thing to remember is *energy,* it is useful to have a few helpful hints about how to get the actual conversation going (especially if you are new to facilitating selves). Here are some basic guidelines to keep in mind:

➡ **Words mean different things to different people,** so it's best to ask a self to explain what it means rather than assume that you already know. If you take this approach, then you will always look for clarification from the self rather than making up a possibly erroneous conclusion in your own mind. "What do *you* mean when you say 'you don't like risks?' What would be a risk for *you*?" "Now *you're* the part that 'wants to be romantic' – tell me what *you* find romantic." As often as not a self's idea of risks or romance or responsibility or what's required for a relationship, etc. may have nothing to do with what the facilitator thinks or feels about those things. Asking these kinds of questions avoids the possibility of "leaping to conclusions" and helps you to keep your projections on (or about) the subject to a minimum.

➡ **Ask the most obvious questions.** "How does that feel to you?" "What don't you like about that?" "How do you do that?" "How long have you been in this person's life?" "What do you worry about?" "Do you get to come out a lot?" "What do you see as your job?" etc. Simple, straightforward questions such as these will yield a wealth of information about the self and how it functions in the personality.

as observing how the self she is facilitating shifts and moves. You'll find that the chapter on "Locating the self in the body" in Section Four (p. 231) will be particularly helpful in learning to listen and see more multidimensionally.

The facilitator continues to match the energy of the subpersonalities throughout the whole session. In the last chapter we talked about the facilitator extending an energetic welcome to the self and matching the self's energy when it first comes out. *This isn't something*

➡ **Avoid putting a self on the spot.** This is simply good manners. Asking a self what it does or how it feels is very different from asking it *why* it does those things or *why* it feels that way. Getting to know a self allows for honestly curious questions but *not* for pressure or interrogation or analyzing its motives. You also want to always allow an easy way out for each self. If you ask "When was the first time you came out in this person's life?" pay attention to whether the answer pops right out or if the self seems to be having a hard time responding. You can simply say, "It's not important to know the exact first time – I'd be interested to hear *anything* you remember." Emphasize your interest and reassure the self that there is definitely no wrong way to respond.

➡ **Make sure you ask questions that are appropriate for the particular self you are facilitating.** If you are talking to a very mental and responsible part and ask them about feelings, you may lose them or induct a different energy or perhaps draw a blank. If your breath is high up in your body, if you talk fast and use long words, if you ask analytical questions or ask the self what it thinks, you may very well find that you confuse or lose a being self or a child or a part that is very personal and focused on feelings. Of course, if the selves came in full costume and really looked like their energy (if we could see an actual child or patriarch in front of us, for example), then we facilitators would be much less likely to make these sorts of errors. As it is, it's probably inevitable that some of your questions will be met with resistance. When that happens, just back off gently and ask the self what *it* would like to talk about. *It's fine for you as the facilitator to make a mistake or be embarrassed, and <u>not</u> okay for the self to ever have to feel that way. It is essential that you always accept the self for exactly what it is.*

➡ **It really helps to remind the self who it is and what it does.** Remember as facilitator that you need to energetically anchor the self, i.e. help the subject move into a self, be there, and stay there for the duration of the conversation. It's not unusual for a subject who is new to the work or who is dealing with a complicated issue to look at the facilitator point blank and say, "Now *who* am I supposed to be?" or "I'm forgetting what part I am now." If the energy seems to be fading out or the self starts to get confused about who it is, you may want to just flat out say, "You're the part of Chris who isn't happy about moving to a new home." Or you may also want to quote what the self said earlier in the conversation to remind it of what it was talking about: "You're the part of Chris who said you really like it here and you hate moving, and you folded your arms across your chest kind of like this (and repeat the gesture that the self made)."

the facilitator just does when the self first comes out – it is necessary for him to continue to sense the energetic reality of the self so he can notice when that energy fades out or disappears, or when some other self comes in. The more you imagine and appreciate each self as a real and distinct person, the more natural this will seem. Picture yourself at a social gathering. Certainly if you were talking with someone off in one corner, you would notice when their interest began to fade or if they actually got up and left. You would be very aware, too, if someone else came over and butted into your conversation. This is exactly what it's like in facilitating when you feel the energy shift and there are changes in tone and expression when a self leaves or a different one enters in. The key is to use your imagination and intuition because these shifts are all happening in one physical body and in one chair.

I'm not adept yet at all the subtleties of energy work. How do I know for sure that the self I'm facilitating is really here and ready to talk with me? Relax! You may *not* know for sure that the self you invited is here, but *some self* will be. As long as you remain observant, respectful, and connected you really won't go wrong. The facilitator has to be ready and able to:

- ♦ **pay attention** both to the subject and to her own feelings.

- ♦ **ask questions** and avoid making assumptions.

- ♦ **be ready to talk** or be with the self that *is* there.

- ♦ **reassure the subject** that they did nothing wrong if and when a change needs to be made.

- ♦ **make every effort to understand** and honor the self's concerns.

Paying attention means that the facilitator both listens to the words she hears and checks her intuitive sense of the self she is interviewing. For example, she watches to make sure that the tone and body language of the self match up with what the self is saying. *If you don't sense that a particular energy is there and you have been paying attention to the energy, then that self probably isn't there.*

Remember the goal: The most important aspect of talking with the primary self is helping to create an Aware Ego process. The more the self is out on its own, speaking as only one part and not as the whole person, the easier it is for the subject to experience a real separation from this particular self. The kinds of questions the facilitator asks the self will help this separation even more. For example, if the facilitator asks a very protective self, "When do you run into problems in trying to be protective?" the self may respond, "I have the hardest time when there's a lot of emotion, when she gets upset and cries." *In this question and answer is a built-in acknowledgment that there is more than one part functioning in the person* – there's the non-emotional, protective part and some part that is vulnerable and disrupts the protective part's "cool."

As the conversation moves along, the facilitator continues to interview the self out of genuine interest and a positive energetic connection. The intent in talking with the self is to get to know and appreciate it, understand its concerns and how it functions in the subject's life, and help the subject create an Aware Ego process in relation to each self that is facilitated. *During a facilitation, if you touch upon territory that makes a primary self uncomfortable, it's important to make it clear to the primary self that it is in charge and can stop the process.* As facilitators, we want to support the primary selves and empower them rather than go against their efforts. It is essential, as we have noted in the ground rules, to very genuinely look into the primary selves' worries and concerns. After all, when the subject goes home from the session, it's the primary selves who will be in charge of their life, not the facilitator. The Stones often remind primary selves, "You are responsible for this person's safety, not me." They also point out that the primary selves have to be comfortable with the facilitator in order for the work to progress.

The facilitator talks with the self, matching its energy, asking questions to bring out information that will be useful to the subject's Aware Ego. Talking with the self helps create the separation needed to initiate an Aware Ego process.

Working with the unexpected

Facilitation is often the art of moving gracefully with the unexpected. The self that appears may not be the one you were expecting. Or, the one you invited to come out may arrive and then not be able to stay. You may realize that you're actually dealing with several selves all rolled into one and have to decide whether to try to separate them from each other or not. Sometimes primary selves lose their control and an emotional energy comes bursting through. Often other energies will come in with giggles, contradictory comments, or other expressions of embarrassment, and interrupt the self that is talking. You may find, with some people, that no matter where you go, the same self will force its way in and take over every time. These are only a few possible causes for sudden energy shifts in the middle of a facilitation. *What's most important is noticing that something has changed.* Then, in the moment, the facilitator has a variety of options including to:

- ♦ **accept that the self which appeared isn't the one you were expecting** and work with this self instead.*

- ♦ **help the original self to return.****

- ♦ **return to the Aware Ego and then move to the new self.**

- ♦ **have the subject move directly to a different energy.**

- ♦ **go back to the ego place and let the new energy express itself in the safety of "home base."** (This is especially helpful if the self that appeared is very emotional or vulnerable and the primary selves are not ready to have this kind of energy facilitated.)

The facilitator models the Aware Ego's ability to stay in the center and relate to any and all energies or selves that come into the field. When the facilitator is able to be relaxed with whatever self appears, this helps to stabilize the subject's Aware Ego as well, and soon the subject will begin to have more ease with and separation from the inner selves. The shift to a

*For an example of this in a session, see Joan's facilitation on p. 159.
**See how the facilitator works with Kelly's "mother bear" self when another energy comes in, p. 152.

different self may be as simple as a rational mind coming in to explain "what the self really means." In this case, it's possible to hold the energy of the original self, point out that another energy came in for a moment, and then simply ask the subject to move back into the original self. It's important to keep paying attention to make sure that the self is fully present and stable so that you know what part you are facilitating and don't push for an energy that isn't there.

The situation you encounter may also be more subtle and complex. For example, when you talk with the subject in the ego place, you might clearly hear an inner critic already in high gear, but then when you ask the subject to move over, a cautious, guarded self shows up

How to keep the conversation going…

Once you begin interviewing a subpersonality, your goal is to discover what it likes and doesn't like, how it lives, what motivates it, how large a part it plays in the subject's life.

Use questions that open up the conversation –

The key to asking the "right" questions is listening and following the lead of the self that is talking to you. Each person you facilitate will give you clues about what to ask – so much so that the more carefully you listen to them, the less you will need to make an effort to think about what to say. There are some selves that don't say much at first. Others can talk your ear off without ever telling you what you most want to know. In both these cases, the facilitator needs to guide the conversation. Here are some general topics that can help focus the facilitation and lead to information the Aware Ego would want to know. A few sample questions are included to get the ball rolling – use them as ideas to help you get started, but certainly don't let them limit your own inventiveness and imagination.

➡ **Find out what the self usually does.** "Tell me about yourself." "Are you around a lot in her life?" "Are you involved in her work? her relationships? her spiritual life? in physical activities?" "What do you usually do when she gets into a difficult situation?"

➡ **Find out what the self remembers.** "How long have you been active in his life?" "What's one of the first times you remember being present?" "Can you remember ever feeling this way before in his life?" "What is your role in his life today? Is it different from what it used to be?"

➡ **Who did the self learn from?** "Is there someone you take after in her family?" "Sounds like you've picked up a lot of information – are you the part that reads most of the books?" "Did you have a mentor, or did you kind of learn what you know on your own?"

➡ **Play off the negative responses from a self.** A self may say, "That doesn't impress me." You can respond, "Well, what *does* impress you? Or a self says, "I'm not interested in that."

instead. This would also be a primary self – one that in this moment is preempting the critic and taking over the Voice Dialogue process to make sure the subject is safe in this situation.

If the self that's there doesn't seem to be the one you were expecting, you will have to discern whether it's best to work with the energy that *is* there or whether it would be more useful to refocus and help the original self come (back) in. *Most of the time you can trust the primary selves to know in what order they need to appear.* If one primary self is taking center stage, crowding others out, it's probably for a good reason. Let's say in our example with the critic and the cautious self, it's quite likely that the cautious self (a form of protector/controller) needs to

"Well, what *are* you interested in?" "No, I don't ever do that." "What *do* you do?" In a session with Roberta, her facilitator is trying to get to know a part of her that is very concerned about Roberta's relationships. The facilitator asks, "Are you a part that helps Roberta connect to people?" The self answers, "No, I don't really do that – I just *talk* to her *about* people." *A negative response is just as useful as a positive one.* The idea is that you want to get information, as specific as possible, for the Aware Ego. You want to facilitate the process going deeper, closer to the essence of the energy, so that the Aware Ego will be able to understand the self and use its energy appropriately.

➡ **Follow up on comments that the self makes.** With a self that seems interested in relationship, "You seem to know a lot about what's important in a relationship. Can you tell me more about what you see as important for a good relationship?" Or with a spiritually focused self, "So apparently you have some ideas about enlightenment, can you tell me about that? What would that look like? How would that work in his life?"

➡ **Ask hypothetical questions** about what would change if this self were in charge of the subject's life or at least able to be more present. "If you had free rein to run her life, what would you change?" "How would things be different if you were around more?" "What works best for *you*?" "How would you change the way she is in relationship?"

➡ **Acknowledge the self's contribution.** Acknowledgments are very important, but are only effective if they are genuine. Do *not* praise a self because you think this is a requirement. Many subpersonalities will read this as energetically false and will come right out and say they don't believe this kind of "acknowledgment." And they're right! If, however, you listen to a self's story and understand how hard the self has worked to create its idea of safety and success in the subject's life, then it will be easy and natural to recognize and honor what the self has accomplished. Typical observations might be: "I can see that you've made a tremendous effort to protect her." "You've really been responsible his whole life – ever since he was 6 years old – what a huge job!" "Do you get much appreciation for your efforts?" When these comments come out of a genuine recognition of the self, then they are usually welcomed and often deeply appreciated.

ascertain that a Voice Dialogue session is a safe place to allow the critic to speak. After all, *inner critics may have very strong opinions, but they don't usually voice them out loud to other people. Facilitating any primary self will help the subject develop the Aware Ego process, so it's very important that you learn to shift directions easily and don't become attached to an idea of where you wanted to go in the session.* As facilitator you might simply say to the self that has appeared, "You seem to be more cautious than critical – I'd be very interested to hear your concerns." In the above example, the likelihood is that if the facilitator spends time with the guarded, cautious self first, it will be much easier to talk with the critic later in the session or at another time.

Follow leads and learn to be an excellent interviewer...

It's exciting once you begin facilitating to realize just how easy and organic it is to engage the different subpersonalities in conversation. Next, you want to guide the discussion in directions that will elicit the most interesting and useful information from the self.

Let your natural curiosity be your ally in facilitating –

Undoubtedly part of what makes a good Voice Dialogue facilitator is a true interest in people (both inner and outer). You can use your sincere delight in human nature to help you create linkage with the selves you facilitate and develop your interviewing skills.

☆ **Find out what the self actually *does* in the subject's life.** If a self talks about health concerns, you could ask it, "Are you the part of him that exercises and watches his diet, or is it more your job to *worry* about these things?" If a self has strong opinions about relationships, ask questions about its participation in relationships – "When she gets into a relationship are you there helping to pick out a partner for her?"

☆ **When a self says that it likes a certain activity**, find out if it actually gets to come out and do that activity. Don't assume because a self says it likes to go hiking that the person has actually been hiking in the last year, or even the past 10 years. "When did you last get to do that?" "How often does that happen?" And, if the person does go dancing or camping or swimming, find out if the self you are facilitating gets to participate. "When he goes swimming, do you get to go along?" (Often a child or a being self may love swimming, but it turns out only the pusher goes to the pool, does 80 laps before going to the office, and the playful child never gets to be in the water at all.)

☆ **"Tell me more about that..." is one of the most important questions you can ask.** "That's really interesting, tell me more about that. What is it that concerns you?" If a self says "I keep her from getting too involved in a relationship," ask, "How do you do that?" *Be a detective – follow your questioning through the many layers until you find out the specific details of what this particular self does and how it does it.* "Tell me more about what you do for Randy – what effect do you have on him?" "You were talking about Sarah's social life. Are you active in her social life, or do you work behind the scenes?"

As you acquire more experience facilitating, you'll become better at figuring out when a different self is insisting on coming in and when the subject is just going through a bit of energetic confusion before the self you invited out becomes fully present. *As always, it's the energy that will give you the best clues.* If you try asking a supposed critic some initial questions and the responses just don't *feel* like they're coming from a critic,

> *"When the facilitator is able to be relaxed with whatever self appears, this helps to stabilize the subject's Aware Ego as well."*

then it's probably not too likely that you're going to be able to get a critic to show up. You never know, though. You might say something like "You seem to me to be much more cautious and reserved than a critic. What part are you?" This *could* be just the right thing to kick the critic into gear! The critical self might bristle at the suggestion that it is being overly cautious – in fact, being overly cautious may be one of the things it criticizes in the subject. The critic may even start to criticize you for not giving clear directions! You have to be ready to roll with the energy and backtrack when you need to.

Acknowledgment is of key importance in relating to the self that does show up. When the facilitator recognizes and acknowledges that a different self has come in, the subject's Aware Ego will be able to make this distinction as well. *The beauty of this way of working is that however it turns out, you're still on track – you really can't go wrong.* Either way, the facilitator will get to a primary self and the work will go along just fine *as long as you don't mind not being in control of the process.* It truly doesn't matter if the transition into a self is a little confused or awkward, and it's important to remember that there isn't any way to avoid encountering some reactions (both negative and positive) from the selves. What *does* matter is learning to respond flexibly and gracefully to the reactions you do get. It's important that you pay attention, try to avoid making assumptions, be willing to go where the energy is strongest and make sure that you always make the selves feel accepted. *The subject and the selves should never feel that they did anything wrong.*

Checking in energetically with the self throughout the whole conversation helps the facilitator to roll along easily with any energy shifts and surprises. If paying attention to energy is a new concept for you, it's tempting to think when the self first appears that now you can ignore all that energy stuff and relax into a familiar mental mode of conversation. This may actually work part of the time, but it's not a good idea for several reasons. First of all, it's likely that the facilitator doing this will have gone "into voice," into one of his own mental selves, so he will be far more likely to miss the non-verbal part of the conversation

> *"It's important to make sure that the self is fully present and stable so that you know what part you are facilitating and don't push for an energy that isn't there."*

and less able to model the Aware Ego process. Plus, the energy may shift quite suddenly and if you're not paying attention, you may not even realize that this isn't the same person talking to you anymore! Selves can fade out or disappear altogether, especially when the facilitator loses energetic linkage with the self. Selves that are disowned or very new may have the greatest difficulty holding their ground because there will be primary selves that try to come in and take over, pushing them out of the way (another reason why it's so important to separate from the primary selves *first* before attempting to facilitate disowned selves). Primary selves can do this to each other too, as we see with Joan's competing sets of primary selves for home and work.

Sometimes you'll meet a primary self that is really two or more selves rolled into one. Very typical might be a self that is critical, pushing, *and* controlling – a combination I would call the "A Team." This kind of combined energy has a very powerful effect in a person's life. In the very first one or two sessions it probably isn't worth the confusion to try to separate these parts out from each other. Perhaps you can hear both an inner critic and a pusher coming out of one self, *but is their energy really very different?* Probably not. It may be best to talk to this combination self and point out later to awareness and to the Aware Ego that these selves are delivering a double whammy by teaming up together. Later on in the work it can be helpful (and easier) to begin to separate these selves out from each other. Combination selves will feel less oppressively powerful once they are unhooked from each other and then it will be easier for the Aware Ego to function in relation to them. The Aware Ego will learn, for example, that it's possible to move toward goals without a critic cracking a whip over one's head, and it will be possible to hear the inner critic without feeling compelled to take action in reaction to its judgments.

Getting to the bottom line...

Go deeper till you find out what is of most concern to each self –

Don't stop with a vague or superficial answer from a self or assume that you know what worries it the most. Actually, a useful rule would be, never assume – period! You can just ask outright what a self is most afraid will happen, but often the self won't be able to tell you, until through asking a series of questions you help it to get to the bottom line of its anxiety or concern. A good idea is to follow up any generalities or vague comments from the self with very specific questions so that you keep narrowing down the area of concern until you reach the key issue.

Facilitator: How do you feel about Ellen leaving her job?

Ellen's anxious self: I'm very upset with the idea.

Facilitator: What is it that *you* don't like about that?

Ellen's anxious self: Her new situation might not work out.

Facilitator: How are you afraid it might not work out?

Ellen's anxious self: Well, the contract might fall through, and it would be too late to go back to her old job.

Facilitator: What would be the worst thing that might happen then?

You'll be surprised as you gain experience in facilitating how many *different* answers there are to this last question. "She'll end up on the street totally broke." "People will lose respect for her

What if a disowned emotional energy comes bursting through? In such a situation an Aware Ego perspective is more important than any rule or guideline because the facilitator needs to hold the balance at center and be sensitive to a unique moment in the subject's process. In general, we know that it is best to work with the primary selves before going to disowned or vulnerable parts in order to honor the operating ego's need for safety and control, but the answer to what to do when the energy suddenly shifts into vulnerability in the middle of a facilitation is not always the same. The facilitator has to decide what to do based on her own experience level and on how far the subject has progressed in the work. Intuition also plays an important part when the facilitator *asks inwardly* what is the best course to take.

> *Has an emotional self come bursting through in a session that you facilitated?*
> *If so, how did you handle it?*
> *Do you feel the way you handled it was successful?*
> *Would you do anything differently next time?*

for making the wrong choice." "She'll be humiliated." "I don't know what will happen, and the worst thing is not knowing." When the self gives this kind of answer, it feels qualitatively different. It has a certain solidity and there is a sense of having come to the end of your line of questioning – in fact, if you keep asking more of the *same kind* of questions at this point, the answers will likely not go anywhere or circle around to this same place. If the facilitator is energetically tuned in to the self, she will sense a clear feeling state, a more basic kind of fear or sadness coming from the self than the more generalized anxiety in its earlier comments.

It's when you reach the self's bottom line concern or fear that you elicit a core piece of information about what truly makes this subpersonality tick. This is often the most important thing the Aware Ego can learn about a particular self because it reveals the true motivation that drives our selves (especially the protective, controlling, critical, and pushing ones) and what might be needed to allay their fears and concerns. It's quite common to find with primary selves that right underneath what may seem to be quite petty anxieties about family or health or work are much deeper fears about failure, abandonment, loss, old age, and death.

As facilitator/interviewer, once you discover a self's bottom line, you can question it further to find out what events are connected to its anxiety, what is the first time it remembers feeling this way, etc. Take your time and continue to ask questions as long as the self seems open to talking with you, the answers you're getting seem important, and you can feel the self's energy to be fully present. Remember that it's more important in a session to get to know one primary self really well than to move around and meet a lot of different selves. The goal is for the Aware Ego to come away with a clear sense of what this self's life is like, how it functions in the subject's life, what its essential nature is. Without being rude, ask the questions you're most curious about until you can feel an energetic shift that tells you it's time to bring the conversation to an end.

If this is one of the first times you are meeting with someone and they haven't yet separated from their primary selves, then it's almost always best to take them back to the ego and let the emotions be expressed in a safe, familiar place. Keep the flow of the work organic *but don't try to work beyond your subject's readiness or the level of your own training.* If, on the other hand,

> *"If the subject hasn't yet separated from their primary selves, it's almost always best to take them back to the ego and let the emotions be expressed in a safe, familiar place."*

you are an experienced therapist, trained in working with emotions, you *may* want to follow the vulnerable or disowned energy that has come through, *if* you can do this in a way that does not threaten or violate the primary selves.* Sometimes what may happen, if you have been working with the primary selves for a long time, is that the subject will go right through the layers of the primary self's defenses to the sadness of the vulnerability underneath. You'll be talking with a controller or a pusher or a caretaker or a responsible self and tears will start to come through, the subject's body will seem to soften or get smaller, and the voice will soften too. In this event it can work well to have the subject stay right where they are, in the protective place of the primary self, and both you and the self can be gently present with the vulnerability that is coming through. Later on there will be time, in awareness or in talking with the Aware Ego, to point out that there was a different part that came in with the primary self.**

CAUTION: If a strongly *disowned* energy, rather than another primary self, comes in unexpectedly, you don't want to guide the facilitation in a direction that would breach the primary selves' security system. It's not necessary to go back to the ego place at the slightest murmur coming from the disowned side of the personality, but if a disowned energy seems to be coming out in full force, the best thing you can do is to return to the ego place. Once the subject is back in the operating ego, if not the Aware Ego, you can talk together about the disowned energy within the safety and protection of "home base." Remember that the goal of the work is to teach the person you are facilitating to manage their energy from this central place – this means having choice about what self gets to come out and when it gets to come out – *and* being able to come back to center when a self tries to take over. Also check to see if you are unconsciously putting out an energetic invitation for the disowned side to come in because you think it's needed for a little balance. This may potentially create some complications. A subject's strong pleaser, for instance, might bring a more assertive part to the forefront in the session just to get the facilitator's approval, if it thinks that the facilitator wants to talk to an assertive part. This does not mean, however, that the subject will be able to be more assertive in everyday life.

---

*As we have stated before, in the Voice Dialogue process the selves are not seen as people who need therapy. The appearance of an emotional and/or disowned self should not be taken as an opportunity to jump in and do emotional release work or other similar types of therapy. If you are a psychotherapist combining Voice Dialogue facilitation with other therapeutic methods, it is best to be sure your subject is at least back in the ego place *before* you continue the session using any other therapeutic approach.

**We will be exploring how to work with vulnerability and disowned selves in much greater depth in *The Voice Dialogue Facilitator's Handbook, Part II*

With some people you'll find that wherever they move, sooner or later a particular primary self comes in and takes over. It might be an analytical part trying to figure everything out, or a spiritual self wanting to express certain values, or the voice of responsibility making sure the person doesn't stray too far. What would you do in this situation? I've usually found when this happens that it's a signal that I need to spend a whole lot more time with this one primary self until the person really can separate from it and develop enough of an Aware Ego in relation to this part to be free to move on to other energies.

Kelly, Joan, & Glen continue...

Now that we're ready to begin facilitating primary selves, let's return to our three subjects and see how they and their facilitators work together to access the energy of the selves and begin the separation process.

Kelly

Kelly has moved over to her "mother bear" self, sitting a little farther from the facilitator and off to the right where she can have her back to the wall instead of to the door. (We last worked with Kelly on p. 135.) The facilitator notices that Kelly really does somehow look bigger in the mother bear self, more massive and more solidly attached to the chair and the floor. If she could describe it, the facilitator might say that she feels her own energy field expanding and bulking up to make herself feel more of a match for a big mother bear. They both sit in silence for a minute – the mother bear seems to be settling in, becoming more present and the facilitator doesn't feel any urgency to talk.

> **Facilitator:** Hello… *(the mother bear nods in greeting)* You seem quite different from the protective energy that came out in the conversation a little while ago… much less anxious.
>
> **Mother bear:** *(voice is deeper than Kelly's and her breath is slower)* I don't really get to come out and just be by myself like this unless there's a major crisis. I'm usually behind the scenes on the alert for anything threatening and then other anxious parts of Kelly come in too.
>
> **Facilitator:** *(feeling that both she and the self are settling in to a deeper and more powerful place)* I see… So you're on the alert, but you're not really worried or anxious about anything.
>
> **Mother bear:** No, I can handle anything. Nothing gets by me if I'm around.
>
> **Facilitator:** Are there situations where you have trouble being around? What could prevent you from being present?
>
> **Mother bear:** I don't really like those worrying parts of Kelly, and I really don't like it when she gets emotionally upset. It makes it very hard for me to do what I do.

How to help a self separate from the subject...

Learning to facilitate can sometimes feel a little like learning to juggle. The facilitator has to keep track of the subject, the different selves, the Aware Ego, *and* at the same time manage to have a normal, relaxed conversation. This can seem even more complex when you are working with a powerful primary part that doesn't really want to separate from the subject – it sees itself as one and the same person as the subject and sees the subject's history, parents, relationships, body, home, job, etc., as its own. For example, a facilitator is talking with Harriett's nurturing mother, and this self refers to "my husband, my kids, my parents, my volunteer work at the hospital," etc. While it's true that this part of Harriett has a major involvement in all these areas, it's *not* Harriett and not the only part of her that is active in her life. Slowly, slowly the distinction between Harriett and this dominant primary part of herself will need to be made. Kyle, on the other hand, has a very strong proprietary self that takes control in as many areas of his life as possible. This self talks about "my wife" and "my children" even though it's quite clear that this is not a part of Kyle that really has a relationship with his wife or children – it doesn't "do relationship," it just takes charge. Working with these kinds of energies can be a challenge because on the one hand you know that your job is to facilitate a separation of the self from the subject, and at the same time, you don't want to annoy the self by incessantly attempting to create separation every time the self describes the subject's life as its own. Fortunately, clarifying the situation doesn't have to be a strain.

If you are just beginning to do Voice Dialogue work and find yourself becoming tangled up in trying to get people's selves to differentiate properly, relax! If the self you are facilitating keeps talking about the subject's family, friends, life events, etc. as if these were its own, don't rush to correct or intervene. Glen's facilitator (on p. 162), waited until there was something obvious in the conversation (that this self didn't like having a girlfriend) to clarify the separation between the self and the subject. Until the conversation reaches a place where a separation between self and subject will be obvious (or at least make sense), any corrections you make will probably feel annoying or confusing to the self you are working with. Once you find a *natural* opportunity to comment, you can try a remark like, "That must have been *Kathleen's* parents who took her out of school. Were you around when that happened?" or "I think it's actually *Stuart*, and not you, who works for the government, but is there a way that you participate in his work?" In this way you will both help the self to separate and come to a better understanding of how the self functions in the personality.

Sometimes the exact opposite occurs and a self will really be talking about its own reality, but will give the subject all the credit. In contrast to the selves that are so well established that they think they *are* the subject, you will find other selves that are just coming into their own and need to be acknowledged for the role they do play in the subject's life. For example, a facilitator is talking with what Paula calls her "creative self." The creative self says, "Paula really likes lots of bright colors." The facilitator responds, "I think that's *you* actually! Aren't you the part of Paula who loves color?" This kind of acknowledgment helps the self differentiate and helps to clarify who does what inside the personality.

150

You may also find that some selves are eager to cooperate with you as facilitator, and since they have gotten the idea that they are "supposed to" refer back to the subject in the third person, they refer *everything* back to the subject, whether it makes sense to or not. With these selves too, you'll find that you may need to gently remind them that there are some parts of the subject's life that really do belong to them. For example, Cliff's family-oriented self comments, "It's very important for Cliff to spend time with either his parents or his wife's parents every Sunday." The facilitator might respond, "Well, actually, I would think that *you're* the part of Cliff who thinks it's very important to spend time with the family. Aren't you the one who wants him to visit with his parents on Sundays?"

What about separating two or more selves that are grouped together? Especially with the "power brokers" of the personality (the inner critic, the pusher, the controller, etc.) it can seem that you're up against a consortium, or even a gang, of selves – every time you talk with one of them, you're talking with all of them joined together. If this is overwhelming for you as the facilitator, just imagine what it's like for the subject to live with this all the time. Hard to get a word in edgewise! The same advice that works for separating selves out from the subject works for separating them out from each other. *Wait till you find an organic opportunity for pointing out that there are actually several selves working together.* For example, Shane and his facilitator decided to talk with the part of Shane that pushes him to improve himself, to get ahead both in the world and in his own personal growth. Once Shane moved over and this part began to talk, it became clear to the facilitator that this self didn't just have an agenda for Shane to fulfill – it had a lot of criticisms of how Shane was handling just about everything in his life. In this instance the facilitator might simply comment on this teaming up of these two selves, so that it will be in Shane's awareness.

> **Facilitator:** I think maybe there's actually two of you working together here. You're the part of Shane who pushes him to accomplish a lot in his life, and I can also hear a part that is very critical of how Shane is doing.

> **Shane's pusher self:** *(shrugging)* I guess you're right... I think we always work together. I wouldn't know how to do things differently.

> **Facilitator:** That's fine. You don't have to do anything differently. It's just important for Shane to know that there are two parts of him working together. Then maybe at another time we'll get to talk with each of you separately.

After Shane moves back to the Aware Ego, the facilitator can talk with him about his inner pusher/critic team of selves. She can also point this out to him in the awareness position. It's not at all necessary to force these two selves to separate on the spot. Over time, working with Shane, there will be natural and easy opportunities to begin to sort out the inner power structure of these selves and create more and more Aware Ego in relation to each of them.

Facilitator: Tell me a little more about what you do.

Mother bear: *(drawing herself up a bit and looking around)* I look after her kids and the family and the house. I make sure everybody's safe and accounted for, and I protect them from *any* kind of harm.

Facilitator: How do you do that… How do you make sure they're protected?

Mother bear: Most of the time I'm an internal warning system.

Facilitator: So you let Kelly know on the inside and then other parts of her take action?

Mother bear: That's right, but if that isn't enough my energy comes right out directly. *(sounding quite proud)* A lot of people have said they can feel me, and if I have to, I frighten them.

Facilitator: You sound as if you enjoy feeling powerful. Do you look after Kelly too?

Mother bear: *(with a look that's a cross between indignant and surprised)* No! Of course not! She doesn't need it.

Facilitator: I was thinking about times you mentioned when Kelly gets upset or all worked up about something. It seems she could use help from someone like you then.

Mother bear: Maybe, but I can't help her then because I can't get through. It's actually easier for me when there is a really big crisis and all the other selves just shut up and let me handle it.

Facilitator: So, the children going away to camp isn't a really big crisis because if it were, all that anxious energy would get out of the way.

Mother bear: Exactly. When I get to come in and be in charge, I'm all business and nobody gives me a hard time. And I don't spend a lot of time worrying about what might happen – I pay attention to what's happening *right now*. But I don't like the fact that the kids are going away at all. I like to keep them in my range all the time. I'm a mother bear after all! *(at this the self suddenly giggles and looks sheepish)*

Facilitator: *(re-centers herself in her own "mother bear" energy by taking a deep breath and by focusing her intention on bringing the energy in more fully in order to help Kelly's mother bear stay present – the mother bear responds before anything is said, her expression and energy returning to the way they were before the self holding the giggle energy came in)* Some other part of Kelly came in there for a moment – somebody who felt embarrassed about being a mother bear. We can just let that go, and stay with you.

Mother bear: *(sighs and settles again in her chair)* Thanks. I used to be in charge, but now Kelly reads books that say it's not good to be "overprotective."

Facilitator: That must be very hard for you when protecting is basically what you do.

Mother bear: Well, it's annoying, but I don't care what anybody says about me as long as I'm able to keep track of her family.

152

How to work with opposites without upsetting the primary selves:

As facilitators, we know it's not enough to work with only one side of the personality because the Aware Ego develops in relation to a particular primary self and its opposite(s). The Aware Ego evolves and grows as we separate from our selves and become conscious of what opposites have been functioning in our psyche. We begin to see that we have either compartmentalized contradictory parts of our personalities, giving them separate domains in which to function, or we have repressed some selves altogether – banished them from the kingdom – and projected them onto other people or our environment. It is the Aware Ego's job to stand and hold the balance between opposites, to be aware of conflicting energies, and make choices in life that include and go beyond the limited view of the individual selves. We also know, however, from the experience that created our ground rules, that it doesn't work to upset the primary selves by pushing the work into the disowned territory, *so we need to start with opposites that are not disowned.*

A primary self can have several opposites, and these opposites can be either disowned selves *or other primary selves.* From our introduction to the Psychology of the Aware Ego in Section One,* we already have a clear idea of what primary and disowned selves are and how they develop in the personality. How is it, though, that we develop opposite *primary* selves? The answer is quite logical. We have already noted that the tendency among humans is to marry or partner with someone who carries our opposites, our disowned selves. The children who grow up in this family often model their primary selves on *both* parents, perhaps being just like one parent in one aspect of their life and the other in another. There is an internal tug of war, inherited from our parents, that goes on constantly within our personalities. These opposite primary selves provide a very effective place to begin facilitating both because they cause a lot of stress and because it's always safer and easier *at first* to stay within the primary self system.

Primary selves often function in matched pairs of opposites. Each primary self in the pair is active only in certain (mutually exclusive) situations in a person's life. A classic example of this is a man who takes charge at the office but becomes a little boy to his wife's mothering at home. Or, the reverse, a woman who is independent and impersonal in her professional role but can't seem to establish any emotional boundaries in her relationships with men. For the man, *both* his take-charge business self and his dependent son are primary selves. They are opposite to each other and each functions in its own place in his life. The woman's inner dependent daughter is primary in her personal life and her impersonal self is primary in her professional life. The primary self system does not allow the woman to be impersonal in her relationships or emotional at the office. Likewise, the man has inner rules that say he can't be a grown-up at home or a kid at work. *As long as each of these primary selves stays in its own territory the opposites are allowed to function in the person's life.*

*You may want to refer back to the first chapter, "What is Voice Dialogue," on p. 3.

A disowned self, on the other hand, is not allowed in the system at all.
Disowned selves are different from opposite primary selves in that *they have no space of their own in the person's life, no appropriate allowable place for expression.* In addition most, if not all, of the primary selves are heavily invested in keeping these disowned energies safely locked in the basement and/or projected onto undesirable people out there in the world. (Think of our illustration of the internal family of selves in "Picturing the Process," pp. 11-19.) To get a clearer idea of how this works, let's take the example of Bruce, who is identified with being very responsible and conservative in most of the social and professional arenas of his life, but has a laid-back, fun-loving character inside of him who comes out twice a year on fishing trips. Bruce's hard working responsible self doesn't mind the fisherman because he's planned for and safely contained within the limits of a structured vacation. The fisherman is an *opposite primary self* that has its own rightful (albeit small) place in Bruce's life, and *facilitating both the responsible and the laid-back primary selves will help Bruce in the Aware Ego to find an energetic balance between the two.* However, the parts of Bruce that are "really irresponsible," that would abandon his job, be inappropriately sexual, take dangerous risks, these are disowned selves and bringing them out prematurely through the facilitation process will only disturb the primary self system and perhaps lead to a distrust of the facilitator and of the work.

As a facilitator, how am I going to help the people I facilitate develop an Aware Ego in relation to their opposites, if I'm not supposed to facilitate disowned selves?
To begin with, it is valuable to understand that just separating energetically from any primary self automatically makes the disowned energy on the other side more available. Also, the confusion facilitators may feel about how to separate from the opposites without going to the disowned side stems from defining opposites only in terms of their outermost ex-

RESPONSIBLE SELF   FISHERMAN   PARTY SELF

tremes. If, instead, we think of primary and disowned selves existing on a *continuum* of energy, we'll find that there are different degrees of opposition and it will be easier to decide where we can safely and effectively focus our Voice Dialogue work.

To better understand this continuum of energies let's look at the illustration of Bruce's primary and disowned selves, running all the way from super responsible on one end to out-and-out derelict on the other. On the left side of the illustration we have the conservative, responsible primary self. A little further along the continuum is the laid-back fisherman. The fisherman may be an opposite to the responsible self, but it's not very far away on the continuum *because it still doesn't essentially break the rules of the primary self system.* If Bruce were to quit his job and spend all his time fishing that would be a very different story. Then his fisherman would be a disowned energy taking over (maybe a mid-life crisis), and it would seriously challenge his responsible self. An occasional fishing trip, however, doesn't really "rock the boat" or cause any big trouble.

So the fisherman is a primary self opposite to the responsible self. It's not so far along on the continuum and it's still included within the primary self system. A little farther down line, though, in a kind of gray area that isn't primary but also isn't totally disowned, is Bruce's occasional party-goer with a drink in his hand, a wink in his eye, and an off-color joke on his lips. This guy has only gotten out a few times in Bruce's adult life, and Bruce's inner critic always gives him a really hard time whenever this part of himself lets loose. Still farther along the continuum, and definitely in the disowned area, is a gambler, someone who would take big irresponsible chances with money, career, relationships. Bruce *never* behaves this way, but his brother (whom he can't stand) is exactly like this, and Bruce has ended up taking care of his brother's family and debts on more than one occasion. At the very extreme disowned end of the continuum is a derelict, someone who is really outside of Bruce's experience except in an occasional "bad dream." As a facilitator, if you talk with Bruce's responsible self and his inner critic and other similar primary selves, you'll

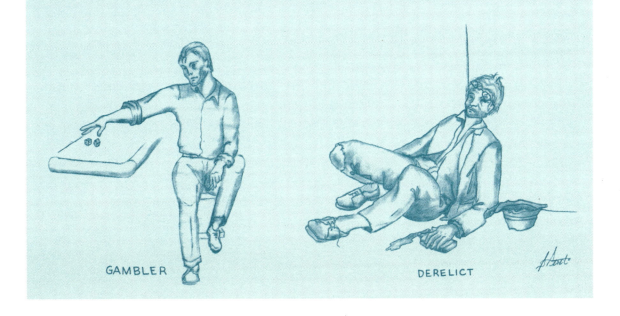

GAMBLER   DERELICT

find that this derelict is their worst fear and even the slightest let-up in control looks to these primary selves like a step toward total oblivion.

Begin your facilitation of opposites on the safe end of the continuum – begin working with opposite primary selves. This approach will help the subject to "unhook" energetically from the primary selves in a way that follows our basic ground rule of honoring and respecting the essential protective role these selves play in the subject's life. This ground rule was developed out of years of the Stones' and others' practical experiences with Voice Dialogue work. Over time it has become obvious that pushing past the protection of the primary selves to get at the more deeply disowned energies not only upsets the primary self system, *but is counterproductive to the goal of developing an Aware Ego.* Getting in touch with a disowned self without separating first from its opposite primary self may be very emotionally dramatic and seem to bring deep insight *within the context of the session,* but when the subject walks out the door, the effects of the work often disappear. Why is this? This question can be answered by another question: *Who is it who walks out the door?*

> *Remember that no matter how far the facilitation ventures into the disowned material, it is the primary selves (i.e. the operating ego), that are in charge when the person you are facilitating walks out the door at the end of the session.*

Developing an Aware Ego is an ongoing process, so it is fundamentally the operating ego that has to deal with the demands of home, work, family, projects, finances, etc. If we move too far and too fast in facilitating disowned selves, the primary selves will simply take over again at the end of the session and carry on as before. In the extreme, this kind of work may actually *entrench* these primary selves more deeply in their protective position, which is why people can sometimes do years of emotionally cathartic therapy and still not experience real change or real choice. In contrast, the more we listen to the primary selves (including primary self opposites) and separate from them, the more we channel and regulate their energy through the Aware Ego,* then, the more the primary self system will relax – and the easier it will be for the Aware Ego to create a new energetic balance in the subject's life.

When *is* it appropriate to facilitate the disowned selves, and not just the opposite primary selves? Disowned selves have an enormous effect on us, showing up in our lives where they create difficulties with our mates, children, siblings, co-workers, bosses, neighbors, etc. It is precisely because these selves have been repressed, out-projected, and disowned by the primary selves that they are initially experienced as so negative and can be so volatile in nature. Underneath all that perceived negativity lies the gift of what we are missing in ourselves, what we need in order to achieve balance and wholeness. Try telling that to a defensive and highly suspicious primary self that wants control and safety and doesn't want to hear about the supposed "gift" of letting go or taking it easy! Fortunately, it's not our job as Voice Dialogue facilitators to try to force the issue or confront the

---

*See "Learning to access the selves through the Aware Ego," on p. 265.

people we facilitate with our perceptions of what they need for balance. Instead we can work with the primary selves until there is a clear signal that indicates it's time to work with the disowned energies. As we will discuss in our chapter on dreams, the best and most experienced guide in this matter is the Unconscious.* Dreams will often show that the Unconscious wants the subject to begin looking more deeply at certain disowned selves. Also, pressure on the outside, "waking dreams" – perhaps in the form of a child acting out and getting into serious trouble, a dishonest partner, a loss, or an illness – may be clear signs that a disowned energy is surfacing in the subject's life and the time to work with it (once we've facilitated and separated from the primary selves) has come.**

A facilitator who finds himself *impatient* **to work with the "more exciting" disowned selves,** definitely needs to explore *which of his own inner selves* may be taking over the facilitation process. When the facilitator is able work from center, from an Aware Ego, there will be no attachment to having the process go any particular way and it will be much easier to focus on the basic groundwork of separating from the primary selves. As we have discussed all through your *Handbook*, stick with the ground rules as your foundation, and the likelihood is that you will organically move along a continuum of energy (between primary and disowned) in relation to any particular set of selves. You may very well find that helping a subject separate from a *primary* pair of opposites (like Bruce's responsible self and his fisherman self) will quite inexplicably (almost magically) affect and shift energy further along on the deep dark end of the continuum. For example, it may be that Bruce's learning to balance his controlled and easygoing energies through the Aware Ego will lead to more relaxation and less anxiety in the primary self system. After several sessions it may be quite acceptable and appropriate to facilitate the party-goer in a Voice Dialogue session, and then Bruce may come back in a week or two with a startling dream about his brother. It often goes this way where a very modest and gentle approach to the disowned territory "stirs the pot of the Unconscious" and then the way opens up organically for the work to go deeper.

Facilitator: What are you afraid might happen if you weren't there keeping track?

Mother bear: I don't know for sure and I *don't* want to find out. The world is a dangerous place. It's not like it was when Kelly was growing up. Now there are all kinds of awful things that happen to children. If I'm not around, then Kelly doesn't have my instinct to pick up on when things are going wrong.

Facilitator: Has anything ever gone really wrong? Is being alert based on an experience you've had or is it just your nature to be that way?

Mother bear: Well nothing's happened to her kids, I've made sure of that. But I don't really trust Kelly to take care of things without me. She's made mistakes in the past.

Facilitator: What kind of mistakes?

*See "Beginning to work with dreams in Voice Dialogue," p. 253.

**An in-depth discussion of facilitating disowned selves is reserved for *The Voice Dialogue Facilitator's Handbook, Part II*. Until *Part II* becomes available, there is a great deal you can learn about disowned selves in the Stones' books and tapes.

Mother bear: *(the energy changes here, as if something in the self tensed up, bristled — the facilitator can feel it sort of pricking up her spine)* She made a huge mistake when she was 9 years old. Her parents left her at home with her little brother who was only 6 and he climbed up the tree in their back yard and fell and broke his arm. If *I* had been there that would never have happened!

Facilitator: Did you come in after that?

Mother bear: Not really. I mean… maybe I got started after that, but I didn't really come out in her life until she had her first baby. Some part of Kelly has always felt anxious about being responsible for children and worried that she'd do something stupid again, and I'm here to make sure that doesn't happen.

Facilitator: So you actually make Kelly feel safe about being a mother, you sort of protect her from herself.

Mother bear: I guess that's true. I don't think about Kelly very much. I'm always focused on her family. But if she didn't have me she'd really be anxious.

Facilitator: That seems to me to be a very important realization. It sounds like you've taken the heat for being "hyper-protective," but you actually have a calming influence. It seems to me you've done a really good job.

Mother bear: *(suddenly the most relaxed she's been — the shoulders come down and there's a soft sigh)* Well, thanks for saying that… it's about time somebody did! And actually, I guess I wouldn't mind letting go a bit and just dealing with *real* danger if Kelly could just find some other way to calm down. It's really not my nature to be hyper at all. I just want her to be a good mother and to keep everyone safe.

Questions

Were you surprised by any of the facilitator's choices? Which leads didn't the facilitator follow? Would you have made different choices? If so, what is your reasoning or intuitive feeling?

What information has this self given the facilitator about other parts of Kelly?

What are some other primary selves you would want to explore? What disowned selves would you eventually want to work with as well?

Would you stop here or continue to talk with the mother bear longer? Why?

Discussion

Kelly is a made-up Voice Dialogue subject (as are Joan and Glen), but like a novelist writing a lively character, I found that she was just as alive and responsive as my clients. I was surprised by some of her answers myself! The facilitator could have asked the mother bear how she frightens people, how she warns Kelly, or how she learned to do what she does. It would be interesting to know if, over time, it has become easier or harder for the mother bear to do her job — do people in Kelly's life like it when this part comes out or do they give her a hard time when her mother bear energy is in evidence.

Certainly, this much conversation with the mother bear has already given the facilitator a lot of clues about other selves to explore. The part that is very anxious and worried, the part that was embarrassed, somebody who reads books about being overprotective (maybe a critic or similar part). The critic is probably one self that is afraid Kelly will blow her responsibilities, and somewhere there is undoubtedly a part that doesn't want any responsibility at all and hates being a mother. That self and the vulnerability that is connected to the trauma with her little brother are disowned, and it will take a lot of work separating from the primary selves before Kelly and her facilitator are ready to go there.

Joan

When the facilitator asked Joan to move over to her "up and moving" self, she pushed her chair back a bit and to the left. (We last worked with Joan on p. 135.) The facilitator had already started to gear up his own energy to match the self he had observed in Joan, the one that always seemed to jump start her into high activity. But when Joan moved over he didn't really feel much energetic change, so he's waiting to see what happens next.

Facilitator: *(pointing to the ego place)* We've left Joan over there, and are you the part of Joan who keeps her up and moving all the time? *(as he asks this, the facilitator begins to feel his own energy go down instead of up — he wonders if he doesn't have a different self here)*

Joan having moved over: *(looking suddenly like she's heavier, like there's a cloud around her)* You know, I'm not sure I'm really the one you want. I just don't feel very energetic. I don't feel like doing much of anything.

Facilitator: *(letting his energy sink down and level out to meet the energy he's perceiving)* Well, that's okay. I'm happy to be with you… *(sits for a little while simply connecting with this new part and the self seems to relax in the silence — he then speaks in a very quiet tone)* Tell me something about yourself.

Quiet self: *(speaking softly and slowly)* I feel like an anchor… a big weight… something holding Joan down or she'd take off like a rocket. *(shaking herself a little bit)* That other part moves so fast!

Facilitator: *(keeping his voice and energy quiet to match the self)* Are you the part Joan was talking about before, the one who likes to go home after work and sit around eating ice cream?

Quiet self: Sort of… Actually, if that up-and-moving part would leave her alone some of the time, we wouldn't need to eat ice cream. I just get her to eat sugar because it slows her down. It quiets her down too. I like it quiet.

Facilitator: Sounds like the only time it's quiet is when Joan goes home. You must have a hard time with her job.

Quiet self: I hate her job! I really don't like anything Joan does away from home – that's why I try to keep her home as much as possible. I wish she could work at home by herself.

Facilitator: Seems like you really don't like being around people very much.

Quiet self: Some people are okay. What I don't like is how wound up and hyper Joan gets. Plus, her job makes me nervous. She has too much responsibility – there are too many things that could go wrong.

Facilitator: Has Joan made mistakes at work?

Quiet self: Not yet... but I think the more active she is, the more she's asking for trouble.

Facilitator: What are you most worried might happen?

Quiet self: *(her tone and slow way of talking have stayed the same all through the conversation)* I'm not sure... I feel like everything could just cave in on her, that her whole life is just kind of an illusion, a big balloon that could burst... That's what happened to her father, and I guess I'm scared something like that could happen to her.

Facilitator: *(gently and quietly)* Can you tell me what happened to her father?

Quiet self: Her father got promoted and just a few months after that he had a nervous breakdown and got very depressed and had to take a leave from work... People didn't do that back then... it was very humiliating for the whole family... Her mother kept saying that people in our family just aren't cut out for big important jobs, that it was "tempting fate."

Facilitator: Were you around in Joan's life then?

Quiet self: I remember it happening, but I don't think I started being really present in her life till she was out on her own.

Facilitator: Sounds as if you really took her mother's words to heart... you've tried to protect Joan from experiencing anything like what happened to her father.

Quiet self: Well, I try... That other part is always trying to get her going so she'll get ahead and be different from her family, but I'm afraid she's just like all the rest of them and we'll find out the hard way. I don't like anything with responsibility or risk.

Questions

What was your first clue that the facilitator might get a different self than the one he asked for? Do you have any thoughts about why this self took precedence over Joan's other primary self?

What questions would you have for Joan's quiet self that the facilitator didn't ask? Try going through the facilitation step by step, asking your own questions and imagine what answers might come back at you.

What other names might you give this quiet self? What other selves do you imagine are related to it?

What other primary self(ves) do you feel would be really important to facilitate in Joan?

Discussion

The more you facilitate people's selves, the more subtle the cues you can pick up on – the words almost come as an afterthought. As soon as Joan pushed that chair a little to the left instead of picking it up and really moving somewhere, it already felt that this wasn't going to be a really active, outgoing part. It's interesting to see that even though this part wants everything quiet, it's not because this self is a "being energy" that enjoys peace and solitude. Joan's "quiet self" is much more involved in protection and control. I would want to ask this self more about how it feels in the body because I imagine it carries a lot of tension or heaviness, and, if Joan knows this, it will help her to be more aware of its presence.

It's important to note that a "small, quiet self" can energetically override a "large, loud, aggressive" part. It doesn't matter how big or small the self seems to you in the session – the real question is how much does it get to come out in the subject's life. The primary selves govern the personality, and, as in most any government, a lot of the power is behind the scenes. You may talk with a big energetic self that loves to travel, and then one of those quiet selves will come out and say, "that self thinks he's a real big shot, but he's not going anywhere. If I don't think it's safe to go, then we're not going!" How important and powerful a self is has a lot to do with how and why the self evolved, and how key its position is in providing the core protection for the vulnerability. In Joan, her quiet self is very much fueled by the fear and humiliation experienced by Joan's vulnerable selves, and probably the more effort she puts in at work, the more this self puts on the brakes. I'm guessing the quiet self didn't want to take any chances that the up-and-moving self would take over the Voice Dialogue process. These are opposite primary selves and they obviously struggle a lot to control Joan's life.

Underneath the opposite primary selves is the vulnerability that they are trying to protect. Right now, Joan's primary selves have two basic methods of dealing with her vulnerability: ignoring it at work while she forges ahead keeping super-busy, or anaesthetizing it at home with sugar and mindless exhaustion. As her Aware Ego develops, Joan will be able to become aware of and feel her vulnerability and begin to take care of it consciously. Also, once Joan separates from some of the primary selves, especially her inner critic, she may discover a part of her that really enjoys being quiet and being alone and is very different from the "quiet self" that is trying to anchor her and keep her from getting too big and moving too fast in the world.

Glen

After saying he was "game," Glen looked to the facilitator for direction and she suggested he just move over to the other chair that was right nearby. (We last worked with Glen on p. 135.) The facilitator's thought was to simply make the process as uncomplicated as possible. Again, Glen seemed relieved that the process was easy.

Facilitator: *(the facilitator focuses on keeping the energetic connection she has just established with this self)* So Glen is over there *(pointing at the other chair)* and you're the part of Glen who feels hesitant about doing Voice Dialogue.

Hesitant self: *(kind of pulling himself in and moving the chair back a little)* It's embarrassing. I don't really know how to do this and I don't want to make a fool of myself. God knows, everything else in my life is hard enough right now – I don't need to add to it!

Facilitator: *(keeping her energy soft and open, conscious of wanting to be supportive for this self and at the same time giving the hesitant self lots of space)* So it seems one of the things you do is protect Glen from embarrassment, from making a fool of himself. What other kinds of situations do you watch out for?

Hesitant self: I don't like anything where I don't know what I'm doing... at least not in public. If I'm alone I can try things out, but I don't want to be bumbling around with someone looking.

Facilitator: It must have been very hard for you when Glen decided to start his own business! There's a lot of trial and error in a new venture like that.

Hesitant self: Well, yes and no. At least if I'm on my own there's no one looking over my shoulder watching me mess up, but now that there isn't enough work I feel really mortified. Plus my girlfriend doesn't make it any easier. *(winces)*

Facilitator: *(the facilitator keeps sending a steady stream of supportive energy toward this self – she does this just by imagining she is sending a wave of gentle, grounded energy from her body to his)* How does Glen's girlfriend make things more difficult for you?

Hesitant self: She's always wanting me to talk about how I feel... She's very sympathetic, but I can also tell that she's disappointed in me and that makes me feel even worse about everything.

Facilitator: You may be the part of Glen she's disappointed in, but I don't think she's *your* girlfriend. I know you're used to thinking for Glen, but let's help you separate from him for a moment just while we do Voice Dialogue. I think she's really *Glen's* girlfriend and not yours because for one thing, you don't seem to me to be a part of Glen who particularly wants to be involved with a girlfriend.

Hesitant self: *(looking surprised but relieved)* That's true. I don't like relationships because it's another place I... Glen, can look like a fool. I don't like anyone to get to know him too well.

Facilitator: So you really are constantly vigilant in protecting Glen from experiencing embarrassment or humiliation. I can see you work very hard at it.

Hesitant self: *(his shoulders let down slightly and he takes a deeper breath than he has up to this point)* I do work very hard, but I'm not popular. Sally thinks I'm the part that keeps Glen from going forward with his life and his business, and it seems my way of managing things went out of style a long time ago… I can't help it, though… I just can't be like one of those people who blab about their problems on talk shows. It's totally undignified!

Facilitator: Well you could certainly never be like that! You're a part of Glen who is very conservative and very private. I imagine that's always been your nature… *(the hesitant self nods his head and lets out a small sigh)* How far back do you remember in Glen's life?

Hesitant self: *(stiffening slightly and looking a little guarded)* I think I've always been there, or at least since he went to school.

Facilitator: *(the facilitator relaxes her own energy by relaxing her breathing and her shoulders, and checking that she still feels the energetic link with Glen's hesitant self)* Do you remember protecting him from looking foolish in school? Did Glen have a hard time there?

Hesitant self: Schoolwork was easy except other kids made fun of me, of Glen, a lot. You know how kids are – if they get any information about you, they never let you live it down. I tried to keep quiet and make him invisible.

Facilitator: Seems your job hasn't changed very much over the years.

Hesitant self: *(sighs)* No, not really… I wish things could be easier. I would like not to have to be on guard all the time.

Facilitator: I can understand… You must be tired of paying such close attention all the time. You certainly were very vigilant at the beginning of *our* conversation. How has this worked out? Has it felt okay to be here talking with me?

Hesitant self: *(smiles a little, for the first time)* I'm surprised I feel so normal doing this. I thought it would be weird, but actually it's okay. I feel you respect me, you're not trying to get me to change.

Facilitator: *(smiles too)* You're fine with me the way you are – I wouldn't expect you to be any different… *(pausing to let the energy of what she said sink in)* Is there anything else you'd like to say before we go back to Glen?

Hesitant self: Not really. Just that I feel relieved this was so easy, and now I'd like a rest.

Questions

Where did you think following the part that was hesitant about doing Voice Dialogue would lead? Were you surprised?

Would you have tried earlier to get Glen's hesitant self to separate more clearly from him – when and why? What made it possible for the hesitant self to start talking about Glen in the third person?

What seems most important to you about this facilitator's style?

Why do you think the hesitant self tensed up when the facilitator asked about the past, and why did it relax again?

Would you want to talk with this self longer? What other questions would you pursue?

Discussion

Certainly this facilitator is relaxed and easy talking with Glen's hesitant self. She doesn't push too far in any direction, and as a result a surprising amount of information comes from a rather reluctant part. Also, she waits until they've reached a point in the conversation where the hesitant self can actually experience being different from Glen – i.e. not really enjoying or wanting to have a girlfriend – before she attempts to point out and encourage the separation. All in all, this primary self comes out of the facilitation with a very positive experience of being understood and respected, which is exactly what a primary self should feel coming from a facilitator.

Concluding the conversation with the primary self

It's the facilitator's job to bring the conversation with the primary self to a close. Our best social skills come in very handy at this point in Voice Dialogue facilitation, skills that enable the facilitator to gracefully end a discussion without rejecting or offending the other person (or in this case, a self). Occasionally, a self will actually say that it's done talking and wants to leave, but for the most part the facilitator needs to acknowledge his understanding of the self that has been present, ask it if it has anything else to share, and indicate that it's time to move back to the Aware Ego.

Questions to ask yourself before moving back to the Aware Ego:

♦ **Was this self completely present energetically**, or do I need to stay with it longer and induct it more fully?

♦ **Has this self been out long enough to create a clear separation from the Aware Ego?** (There's no rule on this – it could take five minutes or twenty.)

♦ **Has the subpersonality located itself in the body, given itself a name, identified itself with a place or time?** These are things that will help the Aware Ego to recognize this energy when it appears in every day life. (See "Locating the self in the body" on p. 231.)

♦ **Have we gone deep enough, gotten to the bottom line of what is important to this self?** Do we know what concerns and motivates it, when it comes out and why, how it functions in this person's life?

♦ **Have I, as facilitator, been fully present with this self?** Do I really understand and have a good rapport with it?

♦ **Have I worked with this energy long enough to have an organic sense of where we could go next?** This is a very important question. Often when you talk with a self a lot of information will spill out at first and then there may be an empty space, a silence. *If you can hang out with that silence instead of trying to quickly move on, the self may make a comment that really crystallizes what this energy is all about.* This may lead organically to a good place to go next in the work. (See "Silence – a key to getting good at energetics" on p. 243.)

Some of the very best information can often come at the end of your conversation with a self, when you ask questions such as, "Is there anything else you would like to say?" or "Is there something I haven't thought to ask you that would be important to know about you?"

Or sometimes, especially with selves that emerge from dreams or images, the facilitator might ask if they have a message for the subject, for the Aware Ego. This kind of question also allows you a natural segue if you are in need of one to move on.

"The question isn't, 'Has this self said all it wants to say?' but rather, 'Is the energetic picture complete, and has this self been here long enough to create a real separation from the Aware Ego?'"

"What if the self just keeps on talking? As the facilitator, I find it hard to know when to give direction and when to follow the self I'm facilitating." It's true that the facilitator needs to follow the *energy* of the self, but when that energy has run its course, then it's time to do some very gentle redirecting and move on. Certainly do not ask a self that rambles on forever if it has anything else to say! By the time you are at the rambling stage there's not a lot of new information or energy being revealed.

Deciding when to lead and when to follow can seem paradoxical to the person who is just beginning to facilitate, *especially if she is listening to words rather than feeling for energetic changes.* I often see people who are new to facilitation become trapped talking with a garrulous self – they look for all the world like someone who is stuck in a conversation at a cocktail party and can't figure out how to get out. It's obvious that the self has already said everything it needs to say but really loves to talk, and the facilitator is too unsure of herself to take charge and move on. In cases such as these, the question isn't, "Has this self said all it *wants* to say?" but rather, "Is the energetic picture complete, and has this self been here long enough to create a real separation from the Aware Ego?"

As you facilitate more, you will develop a natural sense of when the energy has run its course and it's time to move on. Don't be timid about telling the self it's time to go back to the Aware Ego. Any time we meet someone new (whether a person or a self) it's a normal tendency not to want to interrupt or appear rude, but *you are the guide here, and as long as you are respectful of the self it will follow your guidance.* Practice finding clear, clean, effective ways of bringing the interchange to a close without in any way insulting the self with whom you are speaking. For example, "I think I have a pretty clear understanding now of who you are in Janice's life and what you do. Thank you for talking with me and I'd like to go back now to Janice in the Aware Ego." You can point to the place where the Aware Ego sits – this makes it clear where the subject has to go and helps get the energy moving in that direction. As you get better and better at asking the questions that really count, the ones that give the Aware Ego the most complete experience of the self and the best understanding of how it functions in the subject's life, you will also become more sensitive to when to stay with a self and when to move on. Your decision will be based not only on the verbal information the self has to give, but on how full the energetic experience has been. And, as an extra benefit, the facilitator may find this skill carries over into her own social life.

 *The facilitator determines when the interview is complete, allowing for last-minute comments and revelations from the self. He then gracefully ends the conversation with the primary self and indicates that it's time to physically move back to the Aware Ego place.*

166

Directing Kelly, Joan, and Glen to move back to the Aware Ego

Turn back to the chapter on "Talking with the primary self," and read over the facilitation examples on pp. 149, 159, and 162. This is your opportunity to decide, as the facilitator, how you would like to conclude the conversation with each of these primary selves. How would you direct Kelly, Joan, and Glen back to the Aware Ego? You may want to jot down key words or write your entire conversation out in the space provided below:

Kelly _____

_____

_____

_____

_____

_____

_____

_____

Joan _____

_____

_____

_____

_____

_____

_____

_____

Glen _____

_____

_____

_____

_____

_____

_____

_____

Questions

How was your approach different/similar with each subject?

Did it seem natural and easy to guide these subjects back to the Aware Ego? Did any one of them seem more of a challenge than the others?

Have you run into any challenges in your Voice Dialogue sessions with ending a conversation with a self? How did you handle these situations? What would you do differently next time?

The facilitator is the midwife for the birth of the Aware Ego...

Returning to the Aware Ego

Facilitating the birth and growth of the Aware Ego is the heart of Voice Dialogue – it's what the work is all about. In essence, *our most important reason for meeting the selves and spending time with them is to develop an Aware Ego process in relation to them.* The magic of Voice Dialogue work is that a transformation takes place in the psyche *every time* a person separates from any one of their subpersonalities. Even though the subject starts out from an operating ego (a group of primary selves which operates as the individual), when they return to the place where they began the session *they are changed* – an Aware Ego is born out of the process of separating from the primary self(ves). To be sure, it's a small beginning of an Aware Ego at first, and they may not be able to hold on to it for very long. However, the process is initiated and the simple act of leaving the primary self over in its own place and returning to center without that self crowding in on one's consciousness is quite a significant shift in reality.

Having returned to the Aware ego place, it is now your job to communicate what the Aware Ego is to the person you are facilitating. This can be difficult because the Aware Ego is not a thing one can have and hold on to, but is rather an evolving state of consciousness and an ongoing energetic transformation. There are many strong primary selves that will be quite uncomfortable with this. The controller wants to know what an Aware Ego is and have it under control, the pusher will want to get it handled and done with, the critic will berate the person for not having an Aware Ego yet, the psychological and judgmental parent will berate the person's partner for not having being in an Aware Ego, and so on. As the Stones say, we have to

> *"The magic of Voice Dialogue work is that a transformation takes place in the psyche every time a person separates from any one of their subpersonalities."*

"embrace the Aware Ego as a journey, not a destination." The more comfortable you are with the open-ended nature of this journey into consciousness, the more you will put the people you facilitate at ease. You may want to think back to your own initial experiences of being facilitated. Did you feel surprised when you came back to the Aware Ego? Was there a sense of spaciousness, balance, or freedom? Did you feel a new and different connection with your facilitator and/or with your environment? These are only a few common experiences people have in the Aware Ego, and now you have the opportunity to facilitate others in this transformational process.

In this chapter we'll start with the basics of working with the Aware Ego:

(a) We'll learn to make sure the subject really *is* back to the Aware Ego and there isn't a self sitting in the ego place.

(b) We'll discuss how we can support the Aware Ego in separating from the primary self(ves).

Once we're clear about *how* to return to the Aware Ego, then in the next chapter following this one we will explore teaching the person you are facilitating to *relate to the world through their Aware Ego.* The goal is for the subject to become more and more familiar with their Aware Ego process so that they can access it on their own. Working with the information, facilitation examples, and questions in both these chapters will help you to facilitate the Aware Ego with ease, effectiveness, and enjoyment.

How do we know when we have successfully separated from our subpersonalities?

Separating from the selves is an on-going process, and "success" is in the doing of it rather than in some imaginary goal of "having it all done." In the beginning of this process, we find that we have *much more awareness than we have Aware Ego.* We gain awareness of our selves long before the Aware Ego has the ability or strength to act on this awareness. For example, you can be aware that your pusher has taken over again, but not have an Aware Ego to do anything about it. The pusher will still take over because the Aware Ego is not yet strong enough to maintain a separation or exercise choice.

The Stones suggest that "it takes two to three years to separate and create a [reliable] Aware Ego process." For many years I recognized my own Aware Ego more by the tracks it left on the ground of my life than by actually catching sight of it when it was fully present. I might notice in retrospect, for example, that I handled a situation with my friend, spouse, co-worker, etc. differently – I was more balanced, less reactive, or for the first time didn't become polarized. I only rarely noticed in the moment that "Hey! This is the Aware Ego right now taking action in my life!"

When a person first begins facilitation, the Aware Ego is mostly noticeable only in the context of their Voice Dialogue sessions. The Aware Ego seems to almost disappear when they go back into the commotion of relationships, work, responsibilities, and life in general. It takes a while before the Aware Ego process evolves enough to stabilize and be noticed as a new level of consciousness operating in our lives. Within the Voice Dialogue work, however, there is both the facilitator's supportive modeling of the Aware Ego as well as specific time and space allotted to it. In addition, moving out to a self and back to the Aware Ego creates a definite physical separation. At least for a short while in the context of the session, facilitator and subject can together enjoy a clear experience of being in the Aware Ego, balanced between opposites, and relating to each other from that place. This ability to access the Aware Ego gradually becomes more available in the rest of life (outside of a session), and over time it becomes easier and easier to access the reality of the Aware Ego without the support of a facilitator or the Voice Dialogue process.

Have in your consciousness that moving out to the selves and back to the Aware Ego is something that you and your subject do together. Remember that separating from the self and coming back to the Aware Ego place means leaving the reality of the self and *energetically,* as well as physically, moving back to center. This is easiest to do when a skilled facilitator:

   ① **gives clear instructions.**

   ② **energetically models the process** (brings his own energy back to center).

   ③ **makes sure the Aware Ego,** and not some other self, shows up in the ego place.

   ④ **supports the separation** between the Aware Ego and the self.

Your role as the facilitator is perhaps most significant at this very point in the session. Throughout the process of meeting, talking, and moving in and out of a self, you have been following the subject's lead (or energy), *but now it's up to you, the facilitator, to guide the subject into an entirely new experience.* Though it does happen sometimes that the Aware Ego emerges spontaneously on its own without any support, it will much more likely need verbal guidance and energetic anchoring from the facilitator to help make the experience of the Aware Ego real and lasting.

① *Giving clear instructions*

It's not a given that the person will leave the primary self and come back to the Aware Ego unless the facilitator instructs them to do so. Without this instruction the primary self may simply move back over to the ego place or another self may pop in instead. Often facilitators make the erroneous assumption that just saying to a self at the end of the conversation, "Let's go back to the Aware Ego," means that the subject will automatically arrive in the Aware Ego place. An inexperienced facilitator may start talking (often from the mind) to an assumed Aware Ego, only to find out sooner or later that there is no Aware Ego there at all. *You will notice in the sample facilitations that the facilitators always give very clear directions to leave the self behind, come back to the Aware Ego, and feel the separation.* Some people you facilitate will find this transition easy to accomplish. For others, or even for the same person on another day, it may be quite a challenge to leave the self and come back to the Aware Ego, and your guidance will make a big difference in their success.

> *"Without instruction the primary self may simply move back over to the ego place or another self may pop in instead."*

The most simple and obvious directions are often the most important. It really helps the process when the facilitator tells the subject first to come back to the Aware Ego and *then reminds them that they are now in the Aware Ego* once they arrive at the place where they were originally sitting. Remember that moving into a self puts one into an altered state of consciousness so it may take a moment for the subject to reorient themselves once they move. *Giving instructions on both ends of the move* can help the subject shift smoothly. The facilitator can then help the person he is facilitating notice the difference in how they feel *here* from how the self felt over there. Here are a few examples of typical comments from facilitators *after* the subject has moved back to the Aware Ego place:

- ♦ "Do you sense any differences between how you feel here and how you felt over there?…" *(pointing at the place where the self was sitting)* Can you describe how it feels?… Do you notice any change in our connection?"

- ♦ "Just let the pleaser stay over there now… and bring yourself back to the Aware Ego, right over here *(pointing)* where you started… Can you feel the pleaser self over there *(pointing)* separate from you?"

- ♦ "Now you're back in the Aware Ego – take a moment to bring yourself fully here… *(pausing, connecting energetically)* How are you doing?"

② *Energetic modeling*

Paying attention to energy, both yours and the subject's, will make your instructions simple to follow and the transition to the Aware Ego an easy one. Here's a brief exercise to help you in communicating energetically:

1) **Take a moment to quickly reread (from a mental place) the above comments** where the facilitator is addressing the subject in the Aware Ego.

2) **Now read these same comments again slowly** and allow yourself pauses and space for the energy to move.

3) **See if this feels any different** – how?

The facilitator needs to energetically guide the subject into the Aware Ego in much the same way that he inducts the subject into the selves – that means *the facilitator has to be in his own Aware Ego* and pay attention to whether or not the subject energetically shifts into their Aware Ego as well. If anything, it takes *more* care and attention to arrive in the Aware Ego, not less, because the Aware Ego is a new and unfamiliar place while the primary selves are the reality we are used to.

At this point in the session, having just "survived" the challenges of facilitating the selves, it can be tempting to relax your awareness of energy and start talking with the subject, without really noticing whether your instructions to return to the Aware Ego have actually been heard and followed. Add to this the habit many of us have of letting our minds rattle off

> *"If anything, it takes more care and attention to arrive in the Aware Ego, not less, because the Aware Ego is a new and unfamiliar place while the primary selves are the reality we are used to."*

instructions without necessarily noticing how these instructions *feel* or whether they have been received, and you have a recipe for getting lost on the way back to the Aware Ego. Of course, the subject won't have any trouble physically moving back to the Aware Ego *place*, but *arriving at the Aware Ego state of consciousness, separate from the selves*, most often requires guidance from the facilitator. This makes sense when you remember that the spot where the Aware Ego sits is the same chair the operating ego uses, so the only way you'll know the subject is really in the Aware Ego and not in a primary self is by paying close attention to their responses. A verbal response from the subject won't tell the whole story – tone of voice, body language, and their *energetic* response is what will confirm arrival in the Aware Ego. *There simply is no place in a Voice Dialogue session where the facilitator can stop paying attention to energy.* This makes it all the more important to take your time and make sure you are in *your* own Aware Ego – remember the old saying, "It takes one to know one!"

"Of course, the subject won't have any trouble physically moving back to the Aware Ego place, but arriving at the Aware Ego state of consciousness, separate from the selves, most often requires guidance from the facilitator."

It is very difficult to pin down what we are talking about here just by putting some words on this flat page. What we are describing is nothing less than *being present!* That presence allows you to be energetically tuned in and aware of yourself, your subject, and the space between you that is filled with invisible yet very real energy. Even though the subject physically moves over only a few inches or a few feet and then back, *energetically they may have traveled very far on the map of the psyche.* It's your job to first move your energy out with them to support the self in being present and then to bring your energy back to center to model the Aware Ego process.

> *Think about times when you have been the subject:*
>
> *Can you remember times when you moved back to the Aware Ego and could really feel a distinct shift, as if you definitely had left one place and arrived somewhere else?*
>
> *In contrast, has there ever been a time when your facilitator had you move your chair over and just began talking without paying any attention to the energetic shift?*
>
> *How would you describe the difference between these two ways of coming back to the Aware Ego? How did it affect the way the whole session felt to you?*

For the type of facilitator who is a natural with energy and shifts back to center without even thinking about it, bringing a person back to the Aware Ego is "as easy as falling off a log." Those of you who have this experience are probably wondering why I'm making such a big fuss about it! However, many beginning facilitators "lose it" when it comes to this part of the session. The tendency is to get the person back to the Aware Ego place, feel relieved that I "made it through all that energy stuff," and switch back into normal conversation mode (which for many people means switching back into the mind), forgetting that the Aware Ego place is where the energy education begins to really ground in. As we've noted before, *it's important to stay conscious of energy throughout the entire session* – otherwise, it's a little like taking your feet off the pedals and hands off the wheel while the vehicle is still moving!

"The Aware Ego place is where the energy education begins to really ground in, so it's important to stay conscious of energy throughout the entire session."

③ *Making sure you have a real Aware Ego*

The facilitator has to be able to recognize the beginning of an Aware Ego when it first appears. She senses when the subject actually arrives in the Aware Ego and points it out to them so that they can become familiar with it. This means the facilitator has to know what an Aware Ego looks like, feels like, sounds like. Conversely, she also has to know what responses definitely *don't* come from an Aware Ego and instead indicate that another self has surfaced. Let's look at some contrasting responses to a simple question such as "How are you doing?" or "How do you feel?" from subjects coming back to center after being facilitated in a self:

Aware Ego response *(holding center)*	Not the Aware Ego responding *("in voice")*
"Fine." *(calm voice tone)*	"Confused."
"More relaxed."	"Sad." *(or on the edge of tears)*
"I can breathe easier here."	"Uncomfortable." *(or nervous tone)*
"It feels more spacious."	"Exhausted."
"I feel okay." *(relaxed body & voice)*	"I can't stand that part of me!"
"I do feel separate from that part."	"I'm getting a headache."

The responses from the Aware Ego feel calm, relaxed, balanced, centered, and often there is a new sense of spaciousness and freedom that results from separating from a self. In contrast, the subject's responses when the Aware Ego is *not* present may come from any one of a number of selves, and there are many choices and possibilities for how the session may then proceed. The following are a few of the most common energies that show up instead of an Aware Ego, but they are by no means all of the ones you may encounter either facilitating or being facilitated.

☆ **A self that is opposite to the one that was just facilitated may jump into the ego place** – you can often tell this kind of self by its expressions of dislike or impatience for the subpersonality that was just facilitated. As the facilitator you may decide to have the person move over and do at least a short facilitation with this new self as well, and then when you bring the subject back to the Aware Ego, they will be able to separate from both energies and stand clearly between the opposites.

☆ **If the self that emerges when the subject tries to return to the Aware Ego is very vulnerable and/or emotional,** you most likely will want to keep the subject in the ego place out of respect for the primary selves and their concern for safety. You can direct the subject to feel the emotion of the vulnerable self *from center, from the Aware Ego.* It is much more important to teach the subject how to *be with this kind of energy from an Aware Ego place* than to have them move over into any new and intense self that shows up.

After all, the subject already has the experience in everyday life of being overtaken by strong selves. In the Voice Dialogue session they have the opportunity to learn that it's possible to maintain at least some small amount of awareness when emotion comes in – emotion and vulnerability don't have to completely take over. The reason the primary selves fight so hard to repress emotion and keep vulnerability hidden is that they are convinced (usually from past experience) that once these energies do come out they take over completely and are impossible to control. Once the subject has some experience of being able to feel both an emotional self *and* the part that is embarrassed by that and wants to hide it, then they are on the road to learning how to manage and balance these energies from an Aware Ego place. As their ability to do this evolves, the primary selves will become less controlling and the emotional side less likely to flood the whole system and take over.

☆ **A primary self may come back upset by an opposite energy that was facilitated.** If you started the session with a caretaker primary self, and then worked with a very fun-loving self, the caretaker may feel badly about the fun-loving self coming out. The caretaker may feel that it isn't liked or appreciated, or it may be afraid that its place in the subject's life will be usurped. When you try to guide the subject back to the Aware Ego, you may find that this caretaker primary self is upset and comes back in with a lot of feeling. A tried and true way to avoid this situation is (1) to spend lots of time creating a real rapport with the primary self so that it feels truly understood and appreciated by you, and (2) to make a habit of checking back with the primary self after facilitating its opposite, making sure the primary self knows that it is respected and valued.

☆ **If you have been facilitating a self that has a very powerful presence or if there has been a lot of emotion,** it may be difficult at first for the subject to separate from the self – the self may still be energetically present in the ego place. *In this situation it is particularly important for the facilitator to remember to shift his energy too.* After all, the facilitator has probably been extending an energy to match and support the self that was out. Now the facilitator has to also draw his own energy back in and ground himself in the Aware Ego. Often a clear modeling of energetic centering and separation from the self is all that is needed for the subject to be able to success-fully let go of the self and arrive in the Aware Ego place. We could say that the facilitator inducts the energy of the Aware Ego in much the same way that matching the energy of a self helps to induct that self. The facilitator can also suggest again to the subject to let go of the self that has been there. Because energy follows thought and intention, if the subject imagines letting the self go, they most probably will succeed. Moving their chair a little further away from where the self was sitting, taking a couple of deep breaths, or looking around the room can also be helpful in disengaging from a very strong energy.

☆ **Some parts that want and need to be in control may simply be overwhelmed by the Voice Dialogue process** (especially if you have facilitated two or more selves in the session). These selves may come in feeling confused or anxious (and some-times even tired, headachy, or nauseous) when you try to bring the subject back to the Aware Ego place. These are almost invariably primary selves and they often express worry about how to deal with all the new information the facilitation has brought forth. It's easy to point out that there is another self present who is worried about the process and have the subject move over into this new self so you can talk with it about its anxiety. The subject is often astonished to find when they finally do return to the Aware Ego that real physical symptoms such as tiredness, headache, or nausea that they may have felt just a few minutes ago are now actually gone! Like feelings, symptoms can sometimes come in with a self and then may disappear just as suddenly when the subject separates from that self.

When you can't get the Aware Ego to come in,
go with the self that's out...

If you've come back to center and it's clear you have a primary self sitting where the Aware Ego should be, most often the easiest thing to do is for the subject to move over and find out who the self is and what its concerns are. It certainly doesn't work to *pretend* you're talking to an Aware Ego! That would be counterproductive; and, as facilitator, you want to do everything you can to help the subject learn to distinguish between being in the Aware Ego and being in a self.

First of all, be sensitive when you break the news that it's a self and not the Aware Ego who has come back to center. It's so easy to make many selves feel as if they "did something wrong" by showing up when they "weren't supposed to." It's not unusual for the subject to look surprised and say, "Oh, this isn't the Aware Ego?" And the facilitator can assure them, "No, it's not the nature of the Aware Ego to be upset or worried, but *it's fine that we have another self here instead.* Let's just move over and see who *is* here." You may then only need to have a very short conversation with the part that came in and it can even turn out to be the most important part of the session.

Let's look at an example of a facilitator working with a subject named Barry. Barry has been doing Voice Dialogue work for some time, and in this session the facilitator has been talking with Barry's analytical mind. When they're done talking the facilitator suggests they go back to the Aware Ego.

Facilitator: How are you doing?

Barry sitting in the Aware Ego place: Well, I'm concerned that talking with that self really doesn't address the whole problem with my job that I talked about earlier. I suppose we can get to it in the next session.

Facilitator: You know, I think it would be good to talk for just a moment with the part who is concerned about that – how about if you move over to a different place for that self. *(Barry moves over and the facilitator is now talking to the new self)* We were trying to get back to the Aware Ego, but you're a part of Barry that had some urgent concerns and needed to come right out and talk about them. Tell me more about what worries you.

The more facilitating you do, the greater will be your energetic fluency in moving in and out of selves and back to the Aware Ego. Use your own experience being facilitated as a reference and a guide. Can you remember attempting to return to the "Aware Ego" and definitely being in a self instead? How did your facilitator work with that? What, if anything, would you want to do differently? And think about your own experience with facilitating so far – have you found yourself confronted with an unexpected energy when you asked someone to come back

Worried self: Well, he has a lot of problems at his job and I'm worried that he won't get it worked out – he has to make some decisions *soon*.

Facilitator: Sounds like you're the part of Barry who really feels the pressure.

Worried self: I do feel a lot of pressure and that analytical voice that was talking before can think and think forever and not ever *do* anything. I think a lot too, but I'm more practical. I'm concerned he won't make the right decisions, that he might lose his job.

Facilitator: I know it seems to you that talking with the analytical self won't directly help solve the problems that worry you, but I think that the more Barry can experience being in the Aware Ego place, the more likely it will be that he'll make good decisions. I don't know if that's any comfort to you right now.

Worried self: It is a comfort because I know I'm not so agitated when he's in the Aware Ego. I feel better now just from being here and talking about this. It's okay if we go back.

Facilitator: Thanks for being here, thanks for coming right out with your concerns. It's important to know what's going on with you because you're Barry's "early warning system." Let's go back to the Aware Ego now. *(Barry moves his chair back to center and the facilitator addresses the Aware Ego)* How do you feel now?

Barry in the Aware Ego: Better... more grounded. I really feel the difference being here now from how I felt when I sat down here before! I'm starting to get a much clearer sense of what it's like to be in Aware Ego and when I'm in a self.

Facilitator: You feel more grounded to me also, and I can feel more linkage with you now. Does the energy between us feel different to you too?

Barry in the Aware Ego: Yeah, I'm much more aware of you and of connecting with you now. When I sat down here in that worried self all I was connected to was all the things I was worried about... I didn't really have any energy left over to relate to another person.

to the Aware Ego? Were you able to move easily with the shift in energy or did it throw you off balance? Voice Dialogue work is always full of surprises, but as you can see from the contrast in our sample responses, most people will give lots of easy-to-read clues when the facilitator takes the time to ask how they're doing. *The key is for the facilitator to remember to check in rather than assuming the Aware Ego is there, and then to pay close attention to the response.*

④ *Supporting the separation from the self*

Once you have made sure the subject has separated from the self and come back to the Aware Ego, don't stop there! You can also enhance and continue the separation process by doing a few very simple things:

➡ **Direct the subject to continue the separation process:**

"As we're talking, the rational mind is starting to come back in because it likes to talk, so see if you can relax and just direct your rational mind to go back over there… (pointing to where the rational mind was sitting in the facilitation) that's right, just let it go while you stay here in the Aware Ego."

➡ **Keep asking the subject to notice differences** between the way they feel in the Aware Ego and the way they felt in the self:

"You certainly look and sound different here than you did as the self that organizes everything. What does the difference feel like to you?"

➡ **Point out differences *you* perceive** between the Aware Ego and the self:

"I can really feel you connecting to me from this Aware Ego place… It feels very different from the pusher energy we just talked to."

➡ **Build on their previous experience of the Aware Ego:**

"When you first sat down in the Aware Ego place, you said it felt like you had more room inside yourself. Why don't you take a moment to feel that more deeply, enjoy that spaciousness and see if you can even expand it?"

➡ **Use the body to help in the separation process:**

"Try taking a deep breath or looking around the room or even shake your shoulders a little bit, and see if that doesn't help you leave the responsible self behind and be more present in the Aware Ego place." (You can move your own body to demonstrate.)

These ways of helping the subject to work with the selves and the Aware Ego may seem almost too obvious to need any elaboration, but *we are engaged in an ongoing process, and we need to remember to do the simple and obvious things over and over again in order to reinforce the separation from the selves.* Any time we try to bring something out of the Unconscious in order to make it a conscious part of our lives, we find ourselves swimming upstream against the powerful force of our habitual (primary self) activity. As a result, it's the easiest thing in the world for the subject to slip right out of that Aware Ego place and even forget it ever happened. Every little thing the facilitator does to help make the process more conscious, more memorable to the subject makes a huge difference.* Remember the purpose of Voice Dialogue work is to support separation from the selves and cultivate the Aware Ego process. *It is essential to think of this time with the Aware Ego as the heart of the work and certainly not just "something you do after talking with the selves,"*

"It is essential to think of this time with the Aware Ego as the heart of the work and certainly not just 'something you do after talking with the selves.'"

---

* One of the most important ways to clarify and anchor the separation from the selves is to take the subject to the awareness level, a topic which merits an entire chapter of its own (see p. 195).

or as some sort of addendum to the facilitation. In the next chapter we'll pay special attention to the energetics of working with the Aware Ego and educating the subject to become more conscious of and able to use the Aware Ego on their own.

The facilitator helps the subject to return to what is now the Aware Ego position, making sure that the separation from the primary self has actually occurred. At this point, facilitator and subject may also decide to move to another self or to move to the awareness position.

Kelly, Joan & Glen: Returning to the Aware Ego

Shifting out of a self and into the Aware Ego is an *energy event,* so a lot can happen even though it might not take a very long time or require a lot of talking. Look for both similarities and differences as we return to our three subjects and follow their sessions into the Aware Ego place. Questions and discussion about all three facilitations are grouped together at the end of the chapter.

Kelly

How did you conclude with Kelly's mother bear self? Did you ask if it had anything else to say? Did she seem ready and willing to move back to the Aware Ego? (You worked with Kelly on p. 167 and our last facilitation was on p. 149.) Our facilitator simply acknowledges that she understands the mother bear's concerns, thanks the mother bear for talking with her, and says it's time to go back to Kelly, back to the Aware Ego. Kelly gets up and moves back to the place where she started.

Facilitator: *(the facilitator consciously leaves her own "mother bear-like" energy aside just by simply deciding to let that energy go and move back to her own Aware Ego at center)* Feel yourself come back to Kelly now… back to the Aware Ego… and feel yourself separating from the mother bear who is over there… *(pointing)* How does that feel?

Kelly in the Aware Ego: *(a relaxed smile on her face)* It's amazing – I really do feel smaller here… more human-sized! I feel fine, though… more relaxed.

Facilitator: It's true. That bear felt big to me, too. It sounds as if you do have a sense of being separate from that part… *(extending her energy field toward Kelly)* Let yourself feel the separation even more fully now. Half of getting to an Aware Ego is actually thinking to let go of the self that was here and consciously bringing yourself to this central Aware Ego place. *(the facilitator watches Kelly bring her energy more fully into center – even though this is an invisible process, it feels to the facilitator that she can actually "see" Kelly come back… the facilitator can feel the connection between them become stronger and more focused)* Can you feel a difference in our connection now too?

Kelly in the Aware Ego: *(her energy coming forward toward the facilitator, the way people are when we say they're "up-front" but not in any insistent or pushy way with their energy… available, but contained at the same time)* It's funny, but I feel I can see you more clearly somehow, as if the atmosphere between us changed. I feel I actually have space for a change to notice *you* and not just *my* problems. It would be nice to feel this way more often.

Facilitator: The primary selves have a lot to worry about, and it does feel more clear and spacious and easier to connect when we get some separation from them… Let's just stay here a moment and enjoy the connection.

Joan

Did you take the discussion with Joan's quiet self any further? Did it seem easy to move out of this self or did you get caught up in its inertia? Do you have a sense of where to go next with Joan's session? Take a moment to think about your experience working with the opposites of activity and inertia (your own or other people's) and imagine two or three possible ways Joan's session might continue from this point. (You worked with Joan on p. 167, and our last facilitation was on p. 159.)

To give you at least a small sense of how open-ended Voice Dialogue work can be, we're going to let Joan take us in two quite different (and equally likely) directions as she comes back to the Aware Ego. In completing his conversation with the quiet self, Joan's facilitator said he understood this self's concerns and wanted to know if there was anything else it had to say. The quiet self said it wanted Joan to make some quiet time in her work day, even just for 10 or 15 minutes, so that home wouldn't be the only place she ever slowed down. The facilitator said he didn't know if Joan would do that, but he would make sure to repeat the quiet self's request to Joan in the Aware Ego, and then he asked Joan to move back to the Aware Ego place. Here's one possible direction Joan could take in returning to the Aware Ego:

Joan returning to the Aware Ego #1

Joan: *(shaking herself as if she were trying to get rid of something)* God, am I glad to get out of there! I hate that part of myself!

Facilitator: *(shifting his energy back to its normal level quickly, very much like gathering oneself out of a quiet place and going to answer the phone)* Well, I can see you're certainly not in that quiet self anymore! It looks as if now we have the opposite energy coming in. How about moving your chair over to the other side so we can talk with the part that *doesn't* like to be quiet?

Joan: Gladly! *(picks up the chair and plunks it down a distance to the right)*

Facilitator: *(the facilitator can feel a different, faster energy coming in – he can feel his body waking up and speeding up after being with Joan's quiet slow self, and when he speaks, his voice* *is louder and faster than it was before)* You seem to have had about all you can take of Joan being in that quiet mode.

Active self: I'll say! I don't mind a *little* quiet, but that's like being totally stuck in the mud over there. If she didn't have a job to go to, we'd all just be swallowed up by that black hole – they'd find us as fossils in a million years! *(this self is louder, faster and feels as if it's coming at the facilitator – the quiet one felt as if it were sinking down and moving away)*

(After a conversation with the active self, the facilitator asks Joan to come back to the center again, to the Aware Ego.)

Joan coming into the Aware Ego: *(taking a deep breath and shaking her shoulders slightly, letting them drop down)* I think I'm back this time.

Facilitator: Good. *(he has a sense of pulling himself into center, into balance)* Get a sense of separating both from the active self over there... *(pointing)* and from the quiet self on the other side *(pointing again).* Notice what it's like to be in the middle between these two and separate from both of them.

Joan in the Aware Ego: *(takes an easy breath and looks very clearly at the facilitator)* I'm not sure when I last felt like this... not speeded up or slowed down, just kind of... here.

Joan returning to the Aware Ego #2

Here's a second possible direction for Joan's session – Joan is returning to the Aware Ego for the first time after being in the quiet self.

Facilitator: *(the facilitator turns his energy level back up to normal as Joan moves her chair back to the place where she was first sitting)* Feel like you're back to yourself? Back to the Aware Ego?

Joan coming into the Aware Ego: *(blinking and shaking herself)* I'm trying to get back, but that's a very strong energy for being so quiet. *(shakes herself again)*

Facilitator: *(extending his own energy field like a hand reaching out to someone who's trying to climb up out of the water)* Just think about letting that self go now, and... you know, you might try bringing your chair a little more to your right and towards me... you're not quite back in the actual place where you started.

Joan in the Aware Ego: *(moves her chair a tiny bit and this time she sits up straighter and looks more directly at the facilitator – she seems lighter, too, as if she really had climbed up out of water into fresh air)* That feels better... *(her tone is even and relaxed)* I feel I'm here now.

Facilitator: Good... *(pointing toward the quiet self)* Feel that quiet part over there, and start to strengthen your sense of being separate from it. Just thinking about separating from that part will help you be more present in the Aware Ego. *(the facilitator continues separating from the quiet heavy energy he called in to match Joan's quiet self – it's as if he's* *walking along an imaginary energy pathway with her, "holding her hand," and feeling her progress through his own energy field)* How do you feel now?

Joan in the Aware Ego: Better. I don't feel anymore as if I might slip back into that place. I think I would like that part of myself much more if it didn't feel like quicksand… if I felt I could get out.

Facilitator: You're already beginning to feel what that's like from where you are now, from the Aware Ego.

Joan in the Aware Ego: That's true, it does feel different right now.

Facilitator: That's really what separating from a self and having an Aware Ego is all about – being able to enjoy as much of a particular self as you like without being *compelled* to be there… *(there's a pause where the facilitator and Joan are in energetic communication, feeling each other's presence but not saying anything – it feels as if they are settling in, stabilizing)* I promised that self I would tell you that it wants to have 10-15 minutes of quiet time during the workday for balance. *(seeing a nervous look come over Joan's face)* I know we haven't talked with the active side yet, and that part might think it's way too much time!

Joan: Well, just hearing you talk about it, I can feel my work self coming in. I can tell she doesn't like the idea.

Facilitator: How about moving to a new place for that self so we can hear what that part has to say?

Glen

Glen's hesitant self made it really easy for his facilitator to direct Glen back to the Aware Ego. (You worked with Glen on p. 168, and our last facilitation was on p. 162.) *If a self says it's tired and would like a rest, that's a clear sign that "time's up" and we're ready to move on.* I have unfortunately seen many facilitators miss this very clear message and go right ahead and ask a self whether it has anything else to say, even though it has already said it wants to go. This leaves the self at best confused or at worst somewhat insulted that it hasn't been heard. This is where it's especially important to be listening to the self and following its cues rather than "going by the book" or by habit. Glen's facilitator simply directed Glen to move back to where he had been sitting at the beginning.

Facilitator: *(automatically re-centering herself)* Sit right back down where you were at the beginning of our session and take a moment to let go of the self we were talking to. Just imagine he's over there *(pointing to the place where the hesitant self was sitting)* and you are separate from him.

Glen in the Aware Ego: *(looking over to where the hesitant self was sitting and then at the facilitator, he takes a breath and stretches just a little through his upper back and shoulders)* Okay.

Facilitator: How are you doing?

Glen in the Aware Ego: Okay. I feel different… I'm not sure how I would describe it, but it feels all right.

Facilitator: Do you have a sense of being separate from the hesitant self?

Glen in the Aware Ego: *(nodding, relaxing a little more)* I do, actually. Normally I would think that was weird or silly, but I do have a sense of having felt one way over there and kind of lighter, clearer here. Is that what you mean by "separation?"

Facilitator: That's exactly it.

Questions

What did each facilitator do or ask in each of our examples to make sure the subject was actually back in the Aware Ego?

Thinking back over our three facilitations, how do you see each facilitator supporting his or her subject in the Aware Ego? What have you found to be helpful in bringing people out of a self and back to the Aware Ego?

What other possibilities can you imagine for each of these facilitations in returning the subject to the Aware Ego? What responses have you encountered in your facilitations when you brought a subject back to the Aware Ego place?

Discussion

Repeating directions can be really helpful. Telling the subject again that they are now in the Aware Ego place helps them to arrive and get grounded – it affirms the shift they have made. It may feel a bit odd to "repeat yourself," but remember that you're actually talking to a "new and different person." It's a testimony to how real and alive and distinct the selves are, that even though you may say good-bye to a self and give the instruction to return to the Aware Ego, when the subject sits down in the Aware Ego place, they may not recall what you said at all. Another reason for re-emphasizing the shift to the Aware Ego is to help the subject come back to ordinary present reality from the somewhat altered state of consciousness that occurs when they are "in a self."

There are lots of ways to make sure you have the Aware Ego and not another self coming in, but asking a simple question such as "how do you feel?" or "how are you doing?" in a matter-of-fact and easy tone can make the job of facilitating a whole lot easier. The Aware Ego feels "fine," "okay," "clear," "light," "more spacious," "relaxed," etc. – neutral states of being that are appropriate to the Aware Ego's position in the center, balanced between opposites. The Aware Ego doesn't judge the self(ves), it doesn't have big emotional responses, it's not overwhelmed or confused, and it doesn't develop sudden headaches, nausea, etc. The Aware Ego doesn't become wildly excited or enthusiastic either. If the person you are facilitating sits down in the Aware Ego place and is very reactive, emotional, judgmental, or experiences sudden symptoms, you've got another self and the subject is not in the Aware Ego.

Taking your time is so important when you work with the Aware Ego – allow for breathing and silence and not hurrying to say very much so that the subject's energy has lots and lots of time to re-configure and settle in. In the next chapter we'll focus on linkage and how to deepen our energetic experience of the Aware Ego process.

Teaching the Aware Ego to work with energy

Every time you bring someone back to the Aware Ego, you teach them through experience and their relationship with you, the facilitator, what an Aware Ego is and how to use it. The Aware Ego by definition both experiences the life of the selves and is also able to tap into the awareness or witness level. It has a natural ability to channel the energy of any self and use it with choice, but as with almost any talent, it takes consciousness and practice to turn natural ability into mastery, something you can count on to be there when you need it. Coming back to the Aware Ego in the Voice Dialogue session is just the beginning. The facilitator then begins to teach the subject how to recognize when they are being taken over by a self and how to find their own way back to center. *The facilitator helps the subject transform their experience of the Aware Ego from a momentary feeling of centeredness to a readily identifiable way of being that they can recognize and return to on their own.*

> " *The facilitator helps the subject transform their experience of the Aware Ego from a momentary feeling of centeredness to a readily identifiable way of being that they can return to on their own.*"

One person I facilitated said, "Aware Ego seems like a slippery place to me – kind of like a very narrow ridge with a drop on each side. I can feel the separation when I'm here with you, but I find it very hard to hold on to that when I leave." At this point in our session, having brought the subject back to the Aware Ego (whether for the first or hundredth time), we want to explore some ways in which the facilitator can help to continue broadening that "narrow ridge" into a plateau – a place where one can comfortably stand and not immediately slip into the primary selves and disowned selves on either side. Let's look at some of the key ways in which the facilitator can help the Aware Ego process to develop and stabilize. These include:

① *Modeling*

② *Repetition*

③ *Linkage through the Aware Ego*

④ *Learning to adjust the intensity of the linkage with the facilitator*

⑤ *Channeling the individual selves through the Aware Ego*

⑥ *Learning to adjust the volume of each self*

The first four of these – modeling, repetition, linkage, and regulating linkage – we'll look at in this chapter. The last two – channeling the self and adjusting its volume – we'll explore in the chapter on "Learning to access the selves through the Aware Ego," p. 265, in Section Four. As you read, keep in mind that many ways of working with the Aware Ego are still undiscovered and all the important questions on this subject haven't even been asked much less answered. All of us doing this work have the opportunity to contribute to the collective wisdom about the Aware Ego, and your own experience facilitating may be a source of inspiration in this evolving process. Please be aware, too, that your *Handbook* touches on only a small part of the knowledge we already have about the Aware Ego, and it really will enrich your work enormously to pursue all the available information on this topic – listening to the Stones' audio tape set, "The Aware Ego," is especially helpful.

"Keep in mind that many ways of working with the Aware Ego are still undiscovered and all the important questions on this subject haven't even been asked much less answered."

① *Modeling*

The facilitator models energetically what the Aware Ego is and how it functions. In a very real sense *the facilitator stands in for the subject's Aware Ego while the subject is developing one of their own.* The facilitator:

- **is energetically fully present** and extends his energy to the person he is facilitating without compromising his own boundaries.
- **is neutral,** non-judgmental, equally respectful of all the selves that are facilitated, and has no agenda about what the outcome of the work should be.
- **is willing to wait**, to hang out with the opposites and allow ambiguity without leaping in to resolve conflict.
- **has free access to the full range of his own personality** and, at least for the duration of the session, uses the energies of his various selves without becoming identified with or destabilized by any of them.
- **uses the gift of his own experience** to guide the work and is conscious of the opposite and disowned selves that have not yet emerged in the facilitation – the facilitator models the Aware Ego's ability to embrace the whole.

By the facilitator embodying the Aware Ego to the best of his ability within the context of the Voice Dialogue session, and as much as possible in his life as well, he powerfully supports the development of the Aware Ego in the people he works with. As a facilitator, you are the scout for a group of pioneers in consciousness – the people you facilitate. One could say that the subject's sense of their own Aware Ego will come in more easily from having been and continuing to be around yours. *After all, not only individuals but the entire culture is run by primary selves who feel most comfortable with a very clear black and white reality – each primary self thinks that it knows exactly what to do in regard to the problems life brings and doesn't want to hear about the other side.* In contrast, a Voice Dialogue facilitator is able to resist quick, easy answers and opt for living with the tension of opposites while honoring the concerns of all the selves. *As a facilitator, the more you are able to occupy this middle ground between opposites, then the*

"As a facilitator, the more you are able to occupy this middle ground between opposites, then the more you will be able to model the Aware Ego for the people you facilitate."

more you will be able to model the Aware Ego for the people you facilitate. If you can broaden your own "narrow ridge" into a place where you can easily stand, you will make this place more accessible and familiar to the subject.

② *Repetition*

Separating from the selves and arriving at an Aware Ego in relation to those selves is a process we repeat over and over. This is what strengthens the Aware Ego and helps it to evolve. The Aware Ego is not a permanent state we arrive at but an ongoing unfoldment in our psyches. The Stones point out that our experience of awareness, perhaps a big "aha" about something, is immediate and lasting. We may not be able to put our big "aha" into action, but it comes upon us quickly and stays in our consciousness. In contrast, the experience of the Aware Ego is at first fleeting, as it is a new and (r)evolutionary state of consciousness. It is one that we come to slowly and often find difficult to hold on to. We have to arrive at the Aware Ego again and again to build any functional permanence.

As a facilitator you want to give the people you work with every opportunity to become familiar with what it feels like to be "in an Aware Ego." This may mean designing your sessions so the subject can spend more time in the Aware Ego place. Certainly, talking in the Aware Ego, feeling the emotions of the selves through the Aware Ego, and especially linking energetically with the facilitator from the Aware Ego, all cultivate the subject's ability to access Aware Ego consciousness on their own.

> **Note:** As Voice Dialogue has developed over the years, the focus of the work has gradually moved from an emphasis on facilitating the selves to much more time and attention being devoted to working with the Aware Ego. When I first started facilitating, I would often have a subject move directly from one self to another and not come back to the Aware Ego until we were done with all the selves. Though there are still some times when I find moving from one self to another in this way is the most organic approach in a particular situation, I almost always now *come back to the Aware Ego after every self* and talk with the person I'm facilitating about the importance of separating from each self before we move on to the next one. After all, the essential purpose of facilitating the selves is to make it possible for an Aware Ego to experience those selves and be able to separate from them, and *each time we return to the Aware Ego it offers the subject the maximum opportunity to accomplish this.*

③ *Linkage through the Aware Ego*

Each person you facilitate will naturally start out more identified with either their linkage or non-linkage side, though it's rare at the beginning of the work that a subject will have any idea what linkage is or even the language to think about it.* "Linkage" is a term that simply connotes energetic connection between people. Some inner selves want and need this connection and others aren't even aware that such a connection is possible. The selves are usu-

*See p. 61 in "Energy, our hidden language" for a discussion of linkage.

ally quite *unconscious* about how they link or don't link with other people. Through Voice Dialogue work we have the opportunity to become aware of our energy and *learn to link consciously through the Aware Ego* rather than unconsciously through a self. Because the Aware Ego is by definition in touch with both sides, it has the capacity to bring in a non-linking self like the rational mind *and still stay linked to another person.* Likewise, the Aware Ego can bring in a very personal, linking energy *and maintain boundaries at the same time.* On their own, linkage and non-linkage selves would each stay locked into their separate ways of relating to the world. The Aware Ego, in contrast, is able to encompass these opposite energies and bring us much more freedom and consciousness in our connections with people.

As you develop your skills as a facilitator, start thinking about primary selves specifically in terms of their natural ability or inability to link energetically. From this perspective you will be able to help the people you facilitate become conscious of their energy and how they use it to connect with others. With each self you facilitate, notice the linkage or lack of it – this will not only tell you a lot about the self, but it will also give you important clues about its opposite. For example, if you are facilitating a primary self that is very much on the linkage side, by the nature of what is known about how energies balance each other (both in our psyches and in the world), you can assume there is an opposite (primary or disowned) non-linkage self. Even before you hear the whole story from the subject, you'll begin to have a clear idea of how they relate energetically and how you might help them find a new and more satisfying balance.

Both our linkage and non-linkage selves have their strengths and can make important contributions to our lives. What we want is to be able to decide freely when to use these different parts of ourselves. *By separating from linkage and non-linkage sides and developing an Aware Ego in relation to them, we are able to claim and use both our mental and feeling capacities with balance and choice.* The Aware Ego is always *able* to link energetically, and it can *choose* not to as well. It is not locked into either side. This means that the Aware Ego, which has access to both sides of the personality, can organically find a balanced middle ground of relating. This middle ground is not just a compromise or a "happy medium" somewhere half way along the path between the opposites. Rather it exists as a third point of perception, an entirely new territory beyond our habitual dualistic way of thinking and being.

> " By separating from linkage and non-linkage sides and developing an Aware Ego in relation to them, we are able to claim and use both our mental and feeling capacities with balance and choice."

Almost everyone you facilitate will feel a real difference when in the Aware Ego place – if not in the first session, then probably soon after. First of all, they will recognize that being in the Aware Ego is *not* like the energy of the self that was just being facilitated – a recognition that will become more clear as you work on enhancing the separation from the self. The next realization is that their relationship *to you* feels different. All of a sudden the room will come into a different focus, you will look and feel different to them, and in the Aware Ego they will become open to a new way of relating that is outside of the realm of the primary self(ves). If they have been identified with a very linkage-oriented personal self, it will be a revelation to be able to feel connected to you as their facilitator and still be able to have breathing room, *boundaries.* If they have been identified with a very energetically disconnected power self or a mental energy, then they will have the unusual sensation of feeling your presence, of actually feeling connected. This happens simply because once they separate from a particular primary self and come back to the Aware Ego, *the Aware Ego is automatically in touch with the opposites, the linkage and non-linkage sides.* Separating from the side I've been identified with instantaneously opens up the door to a world beyond the borders of the reality in which I've been living.

Practicing linkage through the Aware Ego gives us access to a new kind of conscious intimacy. What a treat to be able to connect deeply with another person without that awful feeling of "losing yourself," losing your boundaries. And, for those who have had the problem of always feeling disconnected and separate from people, coming into the Aware Ego for the first time and experiencing energetic linkage with another person can feel like a kind of magic, as if the world suddenly went from black and white to color! As a Voice Dialogue facilitator you have the honor of initiating the people you work with into this new energetic awareness, and it's really quite easy to do. In order to train the people you facilitate to link consciously through the Aware Ego, you need to:

> *"As a Voice Dialogue facilitator you have the honor of initiating people into a new energetic awareness, training them to link consciously through the Aware Ego."*

☆ **teach the person you facilitate** to recognize when they are energetically connected with you and when they aren't.

☆ **take time in the Aware Ego place for the subject to feel the linkage** between you. You want them to get used to the sense of connection and also enjoy the ability to maintain boundaries.

☆ **show the subject both how to deepen the connection** and how to disconnect according to their conscious choice.

☆ **give the subject feedback on their energetic expression** so they know when you can feel their energy. Encourage them to tell you when they can feel yours.

Remember from our last chapter what it was like for Joan coming into the Aware Ego after being in her quiet self and in her opposite active self. She commented that she felt "not speeded up or slowed down, just kind of… here." (We last worked with Joan on p. 180.) As her facilitator, what might you do next to help Joan settle in to this new place and intensify the experience of the Aware Ego? How would you support the process so that Joan goes beyond what she feels inside herself and begins to link with you? Here is one possibility:

Facilitator: *(breathing easily and extending warm, relaxed energy toward Joan)* I can feel what you're talking about – I can feel you very even and balanced between those fast and slow selves… Let's stay here for a bit… *(speaking slowly and allowing his energetic outreach to fill the spaces between words)* Take a moment just to notice the room and see how you feel being here in the Aware Ego place… Does anything feel different to you?

Joan in the Aware Ego: *(looking around and then opening her eyes wider, looking at the facilitator as if she just saw him there for the first time – they both stay silent and relaxed for a bit)* Well, this sort of sounds funny… *you* feel different to me… or maybe it's that I can actually *feel* you at all. *(Joan speaks slowly too)* I think I'm finally getting what you were talking about last time, about feeling a connection… *(more silence – the facilitator strengthens the linkage from his end and Joan naturally follows suit without anything being said)* You know, I'm just realizing that even though I see people all day, I never really connect with any of them… *(she sighs and her eyes seem to darken)* Some part of me feels sad about that.

Facilitator: *(he is still linked energetically with Joan so he could feel when the sadness came in and noticed that it didn't pull Joan out of the Aware Ego into a self)* It does feel sad, but we have to remember that your primary selves are doing the best they know how to make your life work. The active part is so busy it doesn't have time to be with anyone, and the quiet one is so exhausted it just wants to go home and hide… *(just as he says this, Joan looks at her watch and he can feel her energy shift ever so slightly – the feeling of warmth between them cooling down just a degree)* See? All I have to do is mention the active self and it starts to come in again. Can you feel it?

Joan in the Aware Ego: *(taking a breath and nodding)* I did feel it. I tighten up when that part comes in… *(frowning and shaking her shoulders)* I can feel it grab my shoulders.

Facilitator: *(relaxing his shoulders and breath)* Now that you can notice it, see if you can just let it go again and reconnect with me… *(he extends his energy toward Joan by imagining that's what he's doing, and she responds, relaxing her energy and coming back into linkage, like a picture coming back into focus)* That's it, you're doing really well… Just feel our connection again – let my energy support you being in the Aware Ego… How does that feel?

Joan in the Aware Ego: *(smiling)* It feels good, comfortable. I feel like I have some space from all the pressure I've been feeling… *(pauses, resting into the connection with the facilitator)* and I sort of feel more "real," if that makes any sense.

Facilitator: I think I know what you mean. Everything is more "real" in the Aware Ego because you get to enjoy *more* of your reality here – you don't have to be in just one part of yourself at a time. Imagine that you can reach out and put an arm around that active part over there and then put your other arm around the quiet one on the other side – you get to stay here in Aware Ego, in the middle.

Joan in the Aware Ego: *(looking thoughtful and then smiling again)* I'm starting to like these guys… *(nodding to each side)* as long as I don't have be stuck in an elevator with them! *(Joan laughs)*

Questions

Can you imagine one or two entirely different ways the conversation with Joan in the Aware Ego could have gone?

What does the facilitator do to create and maintain energetic linkage with Joan?

Would you follow up with the sad energy? How?

What helps the Aware Ego become more real, become stronger?

The facilitator and Joan could choose to talk about any number of things and as long as the linkage remains strong between them, Joan will get to practice using her Aware Ego. So many people are unsure about energy at first because even though they really can feel it, they aren't used to acknowledging it out loud. It definitely helps to ask the subject how they feel and let them know that it's okay when they talk about energy to use their imagination or feel as if they're making it all up.

The more you focus on linkage in the Aware Ego with the people you facilitate, the more you will support them in learning to successfully negotiate the world of energetic communication. Now that we've created a separation from at least one primary self and have initiated an Aware Ego process, there is room for something new to happen. This is the place in the session where the subject can begin to really notice energetic changes. Separating from a primary self and coming into the Aware Ego can be like coming out of an enclosed stuffy room into the fresh air. All of a sudden you're not boxed into that one small reality. You begin to see people and things that the primary self didn't notice, and you can feel energy the primary self wasn't interested in. Some people will feel this very physically, as if the room got bigger or their body expanded or just that their breathing opened up. Some people describe their mind clearing, being able to notice more of what is around them. On their own they might take a long time to reach the level of awareness where they can easily put these feelings into words or consciously reach out and connect, but with your help they can become practiced and familiar with this new kind of linkage through the Aware Ego. (Remember this experience of linkage through the Aware Ego is very different from an unconscious linkage or non-linkage that comes directly through the subpersonalities). You'll know you're succeeding by what the subject reports back to you. If they feel balanced in themselves and can feel their energy linked with yours, you know you're on the right track.

"You'll know you're succeeding by what the subject reports back to you. If they feel balanced in themselves and can feel their energy linked with yours, you know you're on the right track."

④ *Learning to adjust the intensity of the linkage with the facilitator*

Once you get used to noticing the energy exchange between yourself and your subject and it's clear that they can feel it too, then the next step is to help them become aware of and in control of their energy. One of the best ways to learn this is for the subject to practice regulating the amount of energetic linkage they have with you. *A great advantage of working with linkage through the Aware Ego is being able to have choice about how much to connect – and the freedom to disconnect when you want to.*

Let's return to Kelly from our facilitations-in-progress. (We last worked with Kelly on p. 179.) Kelly's "mother bear" self is on the power side of her personality, concerned with protection and control. This self doesn't really have time for relationship, and though it might carefully monitor other people in Kelly's life to gauge the safety of a situation, it's not at all a "warm fuzzy" part that enjoys linking with others. No wonder when Kelly comes back to the

Aware Ego, she's surprised to suddenly have energy free to focus on the facilitator. The facilitator suggested that they "stay here a moment and enjoy the connection." The facilitator could also suggest that Kelly:

- ♦ **make the connection with the facilitator stronger** just by imagining it. (Images such as turning up an energy dial or opening an energy valve really help some people to do this. Others just go straight to imagining the result.)

- ♦ **intentionally withdraw her energy,** "turn down" the connection, so she gets used to being in control of it. (This really can be as simple as just thinking to pull back energetically and it happens.)

- ♦ **hang out with the facilitator for a little while,** talking or being silent, noticing when the linkage between them is strong and bringing it back when it fades.

In each of these instances it's very helpful for the facilitator to give feedback, to let the subject know that a real change has occurred which can be clearly felt on the receiving end. After all, most people aren't used to getting direct feedback on their energetic communication, so it's easy for them to doubt themselves without some sort of confirmation. It is also very important for the subject to begin to see what forms of communication, which ways of expressing energy, *break* the linkage with the facilitator. Paying attention to this in the Aware Ego will also give subject and facilitator some good ideas about which selves it might be useful to explore next in this or subsequent sessions.

The facilitator has to have a sense of how much work with linkage is appropriate for each subject. Of course, the facilitator will always be working with *her own* energy, but not all of the people she facilitates will be ready to do a lot of energetic exercises. There's no rule about how much to focus on energy in each session, and it can really vary from one person and one session to the next. It is essential, though, to stop before exploring the energy becomes work, i.e. becomes tiring, too challenging, or confusing. You want to help your subject stay in the Aware Ego and link with you from the Aware Ego. As soon as there is any feeling of overwhelm or confusion, the linkage will disappear and you'll be back to a primary self.

What about our session with Glen? Do you think his "hesitant self" is more on the linkage or non-linkage side? What do you think would happen if the facilitator tried to talk with Glen at this point about linkage and energy? (We last worked with Glen on p. 182.) My guess is, given that doing something like Voice Dialogue is so new to him, talking too much about unfamiliar concepts might make him uncomfortable. On the other hand, the facilitator could get some of these ideas across indirectly. One possibility is that after Glen says he can feel a difference in the Aware Ego, that he feels lighter and clearer here, the facilitator can confirm that this is what separation from the self is all about. At this point the facilitator could just continue the conversation a little longer to give Glen the opportunity to relax into his new experience.

Facilitator: That's exactly it. And actually, now that you mention it, *you* feel lighter and clearer to me too… That self we were talking to was so worried about a lot of things – you just feel more relaxed to me now.

Glen in the Aware Ego: *(taking a deeper breath and smiling a little bit)* That's true, I am more relaxed. I guess I got it over with and I did okay! *(laughs)* It's odd, but I sort of feel like I just arrived here.

Facilitator: *(talking slowly and making sure that she stays conscious of her linkage to Glen in the Aware Ego)* Now you're beginning to get more of a sense of what Voice Dialogue work is all about... When you're in one particular self, then you can't help but be completely caught up in that self's concerns... When you separate from it and come back to the Aware Ego, it really *is* like arriving at a new place because you can be *aware* of the part that has all the hesitations and still be able to focus on other things too.

Glen in the Aware Ego: *(looking interested and making eye contact with the facilitator)* Yeah.

Facilitator: We have more time and I'd be curious to meet the part of you that said "I did okay!" – the one who's concerned with performance and really wants you to excel. Do you feel up for doing a little more?

Glen in the Aware Ego: *(the facilitator can quite clearly see thoughts passing across Glen's face as he sorts out the different energies, probably who wants to keep going and who doesn't)* I think that would be okay as long as it doesn't take too long.

Facilitator: *(again relaxing her breath and her body, keeping her energy connection to Glen)* Well, tell you what, let's just start with the part that's concerned about it taking too long. We can always get to the performance self another time. In Voice Dialogue we try to go the easiest route and work with the part that's most concerned first.

Glen in the Aware Ego: *(taking a breath too, again the shoulders go down)* That feels okay. You certainly do make it easy for me. I appreciate that.

The facilitator and Glen are beginning to make a real connection with each other. Glen is more present, able to listen to what she's saying instead of just voicing his primary self concerns. He smiles (even laughs once), and makes eye contact. His hesitant self that was out earlier in the session is very sensitive to other people's energy but doesn't *enjoy* connecting with them. This self mostly experiences relationship as painful and embarrassing, so being able to relax with the facilitator is contrary to Glen's expectations – it's a new experience. The facilitator wisely refrains from going into too much detail about her observations of Glen, feeling it might overwhelm him – after all it's only his first session. *Her first objective is to create an energetic shift in Glen that will help him to deepen his new experience.* And, she realizes this is a tentative beginning – she doesn't want to overpower it with too much analyzing or discussion.

The facilitator seems so relaxed with Glen – is the process really that easy? Sometimes it is very easy and sometimes it isn't. The Stones explain that there are times when the facilitator doesn't get any linkage the first time around with a subject because there is a "very strong primary self that continues to lock up the linkage." This could easily have been the case with Glen, and the facilitator might have had to help him separate from *several* primary selves before there was any opening for linkage through the Aware Ego.

Every facilitator, no matter how experienced she is, encounters some challenging sessions where it seems really hard to connect with a subject. In general, however, being able to recognize when a subject is connecting with you (or not) is really quite simple. Glen's facilitator can feel energy coming back at her, can feel it when Glen relaxes, can feel it when he connects. Doing this isn't at all a big mystery. *When you stop to think about it, as long as you are in touch with your own linkage side, with your own feelings, then you can tell if someone else is linked with you or not.* You can also feel when the connection disappears as surely as you would if you were trying to talk with someone close to you and they were preoccupied or became distracted in the middle of your conversation. In daily life, functioning as we do from the operating ego, there is a tendency for feelings to be hurt when someone pulls their energy away, even though we may not be able to articulate what happened or why it doesn't feel good. Mostly this occurs because we're not conscious of energy and haven't yet developed good "energy manners." The Voice Dialogue session is an ideal place to begin practicing energetic awareness, and as a facilitator it is part of your job to teach the people you facilitate how to extend and withdraw energy. As the facilitator, you are always encouraging the subject to link more through the Aware Ego than through the selves, teaching them to return to center and manage their energy consciously.

> *"As long as you are in touch with your own linkage side, you can tell if someone else is linked with you or not."*

The facilitator supports the subject in becoming more familiar with and strengthening the Aware Ego process. Each time the subject returns to the Aware Ego there is an opportunity to practice using energy and energetic linkage consciously.

The awareness level

If separation from the selves is one key ingredient in the development of the Aware Ego, then the other essential ingredient is accessing awareness. Awareness, you will *also* remember, is one of the three parts of our model of consciousness.* We have already focused in detail on the other two aspects of consciousness, the selves and the Aware Ego, and now it's time to turn our attention to awareness. It is through awareness that we are able to be conscious of our selves, and it is the ability to tap into and use awareness that distinguishes an *"Aware"* Ego from an "operating" ego. The operating ego, as we have noted before, runs on automatic and is based on a lifetime of conditioning and reaction to experience, while the Aware Ego is able to take independent action from a position of real choice. The primary selves which comprise the operating ego tend to be locked into one view of reality at a time. The primary selves are also polarized against disowned selves, most often unconsciously projecting these disowned energies onto other people. In contrast, when the Aware Ego is able to be present, it is aware of both sides of the story in any inner or outer conflict, and it can balance and utilize the different energies of the selves in new and innovative ways. The Aware Ego is able to live life in a new way, making choices to shift direction or stay solidly on course, *because* of its ability to separate from the charge (either attraction or repulsion) that the selves always carry. *This unique ability of the Aware Ego is directly supported by accessing pure awareness and integrating it into the decision-making process.*

Pure awareness is imperturbable and exists apart from everything else in our psyches. This is what gives it its extraordinary range of perception and also what limits its applicability in our lives. As the Stones point out, "Awareness is ignited easily, but it is not designed to make decisions and choices or to take action." Remember in our picture of Andie reading her book on personal growth, there is a (proverbial) light bulb shining above her head as she gains new insights about her inner selves.** That really is the purpose of awareness, to bring to light what we otherwise might not see about

> *"It is through awareness that we are able to be conscious of our selves, and it is the ability to tap into and use awareness that distinguishes an 'Aware' Ego from an 'operating' ego."*

ourselves. Another way to think about this is in relation to our three-part model of consciousness: the selves act out the story of our lives, the Aware Ego is the director of the play, and awareness functions as an audience, a witness, an outside perspective.

Awareness is a common experience that occurs frequently in our lives. We all have realizations about ourselves when we read books, take time for reflection, go to see art or theater or film, talk with friends, meditate, listen to teachers, remember dreams, and so on. It's also a common experience for many (if not most) of us to encounter *the same realizations* again and again over time, often without making any real change in ourselves. This is quite understandable when we remember that *pure awareness doesn't really have anything to do with change.* It's the

*Refer back to p. 8 in our first chapter for the Voice Dialogue model of consciousness.
**See Andie on p. 17.

job of awareness to witness, to see. Change is the job of the Aware Ego, and without an Aware Ego process, awareness *is most often appropriated by the primary selves* for their own purposes. It is only when we combine our capacity to witness our inner selves with the Aware Ego's ability to separate from those selves and manage their energies, that we begin to access and use awareness in a very new and productive way. We could say that the initiation of an Aware Ego helps to bring awareness "down out of the sky" and plant it in the ground of our being where we can actually integrate and use what we are able to perceive through the awareness state.

Immediately after starting Voice Dialogue work, a subject will begin to become aware of the different selves, start to catch sight of them at home, at work, in relationship, etc. For example, you may facilitate a woman who has a very strong inner controller, a part that tries to micro-manage everything and everyone in her life. You spend most of the session talking with this self and then have her witness the self from awareness and feel the separation from it in the Aware Ego. The woman goes home, and all through the week there are times when she notices that the controller self is out and running things. *Nothing has changed in her outward behavior, but now she's aware of what energy is present and it actually helps the Aware Ego to separate from this self further.* When she comes back for her next session, the work of separating from this and other primary selves is likely to be a little easier. This is what we, as facilitators, want to foster and encourage in the people we facilitate – we want subjects to start tapping into awareness in this *very ordinary and practical* way. I often tell people I facilitate, "Just try to notice when the self we worked with comes around this week. You don't have to do anything about it, just *notice* that it's there." The ability to stand back and witness the selves is pure gold in the evolution of consciousness, *if* it is accompanied by the initiation and development of an Aware Ego process.

> *"It is only when we combine our capacity to witness our inner selves with the Aware Ego's ability to separate from those selves and manage their energies, that we begin to access and use awareness in a very new and productive way."*

Facilitating the awareness level

Moving to the awareness level strengthens the Aware Ego process. While it's true that some awareness becomes available through the movement out to the selves and back to the Aware Ego, there is more that we as facilitators can do to help the subject reach what has been called the "witness state" or a place of pure awareness. The Stones point out that *"Voice Dialogue presents us with a tangible way of expanding the awareness level and clearly differentiating it from other components of consciousness – it is given a space all its own."** By having the subject physically move to a place that is purely for witnessing – for awareness, we give them a tool for stepping outside the entire map of the psyche. This creates a perspective that supports the separation from the selves and brings in new energetic information that the Aware Ego can use.

To facilitate the awareness position effectively, you need to be able to report information simply and clearly, model the detachment of the witness state, *and* stay energetically connected with the subject. If this seems like a lot to hold in your consciousness all at once, it is! So it's all the more important to take your time with the awareness position, allow for silent pauses,

*Stone & Stone, *Embracing Our Selves*, p. 69.

and make sure that *you* are actually observing everything you ask your subject to witness. Like most things, the more you practice, the more familiar and easy this process becomes, and the more valuable it will be for the people you facilitate.

Awareness, precisely because of its detachment from the selves, offers an opportunity for a multidimensional, energetic observance of the psyche – it has the potential to go far beyond an emotional response or a mental review. *One thing that is essential in the awareness position is that both the facilitator and subject go to a neutral place of observation or witness and do not engage in any judgment or analysis of the selves.* If you encounter any kind of judgment or analysis from the subject in the awareness position, either because they start to comment or have an emotional reaction, then you know you have one of the selves and not the actual pure awareness state that you are looking for. Of course, it can be much harder for a facilitator to spot her own unconscious

> *"One thing that is essential in the awareness position is that both the facilitator and subject go to a neutral place of observation or witness and do not engage in any judgment or analysis of the selves."*

judgment, or the presence of *her* analytical mind, than it is for her to recognize when the subject is having difficulty holding neutrality in the awareness position. While most facilitators are fairly good at steering clear of negative statements, it can take some attention and discipline to avoid positive judgments. It can be very easy to unconsciously say something like, "I was very interested when we went over here to the part that wants to change careers," or "this creative part over here was really engaging." What is important for the subject in the awareness position is to simply observe and perceive the energy of the self, and not be distracted by what the facilitator may have considered to be attractive or interesting. To support the subject in doing this, the facilitator has to be *an unprejudiced, objective reporter.*

Let's look now at the basic steps for facilitating the awareness position. Having already said that the awareness position may be quite challenging for the facilitator, be reassured to know that the process of working with this part of the session is actually very straightforward. After coming back to the Aware Ego, the facilitator:

☆ **asks the subject to move to a place that is separate from the Aware Ego and from all the selves** – usually the most logical and practical place is right next to the facilitator so the subject can share in the facilitator's perspective which is clearly outside the subject's psychic map.

☆ **orients the subject to the awareness position** by explaining what the awareness position is and what it isn't. The facilitator makes sure that the subject actually leaves the selves behind and *energetically* moves into a place of witness from which they can survey the landscape of the psyche without judgment or attachment. (Just as a facilitator can't *assume* a self is present or that the subject has arrived at the Aware Ego, he also cannot assume the subject has actually moved into the awareness level. *It is essential to check and see if the person you are facilitating is in awareness by sensing their energy and by asking them if they feel themselves to be in a place of awareness and ready to continue.*)

☆ **points out the different selves one at a time,** indicating where they were located, and then recapitulates some of what they had to say (how much may vary greatly from one session to the next and from one person being facilitated to another).

☆ **encourages the subject in the awareness position to use all of their skills of observation** – seeing, sensing, feeling – so that working with the awareness level becomes more of an energetic and intuitive process than a mental exercise. The Stones comment that it is "the observing mind that often comes in and gets you thinking that it's awareness." Focusing on these other kinds of perception can actually help to keep the analytical mind and rational observer from coming in. (To help the subject stay in a place of awareness and avoid getting caught up in a lot of thinking, it's best that the subject observes silently for the most part while they are in the awareness position, and the facilitator does the talking.)

☆ **checks to make sure the subject has a sense of each self** before moving on to the next one, and a sense of all of the selves being reviewed before going back to the Aware Ego. (This can be as simple as pointing to a self and asking, "Do you have a sense of what that self is like?" and the subject nodding a reply.)

☆ **guides the subject back to the Aware Ego** when their observation from the awareness position is complete.

As with all the different parts of a Voice Dialogue session, there is a lot of flexibility and variation on how to work with the awareness level. Beyond the basic requirements, the facilitator has choice about where the subject positions themselves physically and about how much to talk about the selves and what they had to say. The facilitator also has choice about when to go to the awareness level or even whether to go there in a particular session at all. There is also a lot of variation from one person to the next as to how well they "take to" the awareness position, with some people finding it initially uncomfortable and a struggle and others feeling very much at home in this place. In order to learn more about how to work with the awareness position, let's take a closer look at some of these variables.

There is no hard and fast rule about where the subject should stand or sit in the awareness position, though they need to be away from the selves and away from the Aware Ego position – some place where they can see the whole "stage" on which the drama of their selves has been playing. One optimal place is standing next to the facilitator, who has, after all, been holding a position of neutral observation in the room. The facilitator might say, "Why don't you come stand near me so you can have the same view that I've had while we've been talking with the selves." There is no reason the subject can't sit down if they want to, and sometimes in a larger space they may move clear across the room to some place that was not used in the work.

♦ **Standing** in the awareness position has the advantage of both placing the subject in a new physical position which definitely shifts the energy and gives the subject a clear view over the landscape of their psyche.

♦ **Sitting** is easier for some people, and it has the advantage of being physically lower down, of being more "humble." Since certain subjects have difficulty in reaching a simple place of awareness without the "above it all" selves crowding in, having the subject *sit* in the awareness position may avoid attracting "higher consciousness" or judgmental selves which like to stand up high and look down over everything. If you facilitate this kind of person, you may want to experiment with having them sit near you and apart from the selves for the awareness level work.

CAUTION: Years ago the Stones discovered that having the subject stand up behind their chair (behind the ego place) is *not* a good place for awareness because it has a lot of negative connotations in many cultures – people had flashbacks of being made to stand up behind their chair in school to recite information or receive reprimands. In addition, standing this close makes it difficult to reach an effective emotional distance or to get the kind of perspective on the selves that awareness can offer.

The facilitator decides in each session how much information to recapitulate for the subject in the awareness position. Sometimes when the facilitation has involved very non-mental dream or being states, the subject in the awareness state might not remember much of anything that has happened in the facilitation without the facilitator's recapitulating most of the details. In this case, when you are talking to the subject in the awareness position, you might want to repeat more of what each self had to say and probably remind the Aware Ego later about a lot of it as well. However, if the session up to this point has focused primarily on critical, analytical, or control selves, doing a great deal of talking about these selves can sometimes make it quite difficult for the subject to stay connected to awareness. A lot of talking may pull these strong primary selves right into the awareness position. In this situation it might be appropriate to only say a sentence or two about each self and encourage the person in awareness to get an *energetic* sense of the selves using a broader spectrum of perception – perhaps just taking time to look at where the self was sitting and get a feeling or image or energetic sense of what was there. In many ways working with the awareness position is no different from the rest of the Voice Dialogue process. The facilitator simply has to remember to *stay tuned in to the needs of each particular situation, pay attention to the energy, and stay in touch with his intuition.*

The facilitator needs to be intuitive and flexible in finding the best approach to the awareness position for each subject. Some people very easily perceive the non-physical, and immediately all kinds of energetic awareness comes to them. Other people either have a really hard time looking at something that "isn't there" or lack the confidence to believe what they perceive. With the latter it may be necessary to encourage and reassure them that they are doing just fine with awareness, even if they think/feel they can't "see" anything.

It is particularly helpful if you as facilitator make working in the awareness position a very low-pressure situation, assuring the person you are facilitating that ANY perception they have will be useful (and it will!). Let them know that all they need to do is look over at the place a certain self was sitting and observe whatever they can notice about the energy of that self from an objective distance. Whatever response you get from a particular subject, it's definitely very worthwhile coming back to the awareness position consistently, but without any expectations.

Most subjects will understand the value of this part of the work and will get a lot out of it right away. Some others may continue for several months before they suddenly one day say, "You know, I really had a very clear sense of the energy this time. I think I finally got it!" When this happens, it usually accompanies a big opening to a new level of consciousness (beginning to feel and understand energy) that is definitely supported by simple and consistent work with the awareness level.

The energetics of the awareness position

Facilitating a person in the awareness position requires imagination and presence. Let's talk first about "presence." The facilitator has to have a real live connection to awareness. *You can't be tentative about guiding a subject in the awareness position because you are the only one talking – the impact of the whole exercise depends on how you lead it.* As facilitator you induct selves by matching their energy, you anchor the Aware Ego by modeling it, *and* you also support your subject in realizing the awareness position by yourself holding a dispassionate level of witness. How familiar *you* are with the impartial observing place of awareness will have a lot to do with how well the people you facilitate understand what you mean when you direct them to "go to awareness," and how much they are able to open to the experience of being in the awareness position.

Imagination is what makes working with the awareness position exciting and real, and without the use of imagination the exercise can be unproductive or confusing. Keep in mind that you'll be asking the person you are working with to look at the self or selves that have been out during the session – i.e. asking them to look at an "empty space" and imagine that the energy of the selves is still perceptible. To make this work well, the facilitator himself has to be comfortable with this imaginative reality. He also has to stay energetically connected to both the subject and the selves that were facilitated in order to ground the experience and support the subject's use of their own imagination in this new and unfamiliar way. The facilitator who can do this successfully "holds a door open" for the subject to have a multidimensional experience of the work that has been done in the session. This experience can be similar to the deep witnessing of oneself that occurs in many meditative practices. It can also be dreamlike in that the person receives information through images and other non-verbal perceptions while in this place.

"The facilitator who can work comfortably and well with the awareness position 'holds a door open' for the subject to have a multidimensional experience of the work that has been done in the session."

Creating energetic depth for the subject in the awareness position often comes through the facilitator encouraging the subject to use all of their perceptual abilities. The facilitator may suggest that the subject:

➡ **notice the kind of energy the self has** – dense, expanded, heavy, light, moving, still, quiet, loud, etc.

➡ **feel how much space the self takes up** in the room and how it moves in that space.

Finding ways to make the invisible visible...

As you gain more experience facilitating the awareness position, you can try experimenting with a variety of images, suggestions, and analogies to make looking at the selves from awareness more alive and real to the people you facilitate. Remember that you *don't* want to start the subject analyzing the selves, trying to figure things out, but you *do* want them to use all their senses and to be open to "aha's," to new ways of perceiving the energies. Here are a few ideas that have worked for other facilitators – you may want to add many more of your own to the list over time.

Concretize – suggest that the subject get a sense of how big a particular self is, of how much space it takes up in the room. Or, perhaps there is a color, sensation, movement, or even a taste or smell that is connected to a particular self.

Quote the selves – the subject is likely to recall a particular subpersonality more easily and completely if you repeat actual phrases the self had to say or "quote" gestures and sounds the self made.

Imagine the selves as actual people – have the subject look at the selves as if they are real people they can see sitting in a room. As facilitator you need to make sure that you are holding the neutral energy of the awareness position, and then perhaps you can say something like, "Imagine that you just entered this room and that self *(pointing in the direction of the self)* is an actual person sitting over there. Notice what this person's energy is like. Do they have a strong presence and take up a lot of room, or could you walk right by them and not even notice anyone is there? Do they look and feel different from that other self over there *(pointing again)*?" For some subjects, imagining the selves as actual people in the room really makes the experience of looking at the selves from awareness "click in." The facilitator has to take care, though, that talking about the selves in this way doesn't trigger evaluation and judgment in the awareness position. The idea is to *sense into and feel* what it's like to be with the person/self, not come up with emotional or mental reactions to it.

Think of going through a photo album – this can be an effective image to use with people who are having trouble comprehending what it is exactly that they are supposed to do in the awareness position. Snapshots preserve memories, but by the time we look at them, we usually have some distance from the people and events that are captured there. Imagining the different selves around the room as a series of pictures in a photo album can make the experience of the awareness more tangible and visual, and at the same time can give many people a clearer understanding of how to separate from their selves and witness them.

➡ **remember certain things the self had to say,** what it was concerned about, advice that it gave or requests it had.

➡ **sense the self's presence and tone,** the way it seems to vibrate or resonate.

➡ **recall particular gestures or sounds the self made,** or the way it felt in the body.

➡ **see if the subject notices anything else** while they are in this position.

Part of the magic of the awareness position is that the person in awareness can sometimes see beyond what is evident to the Aware Ego, the facilitator, or to the selves. Awareness has a panoramic view of the whole map of the psyche, and as facilitator you can ask the subject in awareness to look for selves that were only alluded to or ones that haven't appeared yet. However, it's important *not* to put the subject on the spot. *Make it clear that they may or may not be*

"Just looking around from the awareness position and being open to insight can open up a whole new area of exploration for the work."

able to perceive anything and either way is okay. There is a potential for the subject in awareness to see energetic dynamics going on between the different selves or catch sight of other subpersonalities that weren't facilitated in the session, so it's definitely worthwhile for the subject to take a look around just to see if anything else comes to them in awareness. Often if you simply tell the person you are facilitating that it's possible to see more, they will! Then when the person is back in the Aware Ego and you ask what awareness they brought back with them, the results can often be quite startling and revelatory. Just looking around from the awareness position and being open to insight can reveal a whole new area of exploration for the work.

To get a clearer sense of how new direction might emerge from working with the awareness level, let's listen in on a session with a young man named Josh. Here the facilitator is concluding work with Josh in the awareness position. They've already taken a look at the selves that were facilitated – one that pushes for focus and efficiency and one that worries all the time.

Facilitator: Before we go back to Josh, look around and see if there are any other selves that you notice. There was an artist self that was mentioned… Maybe you can get a sense of that self somewhere here… You might notice some other parts as well.

Josh in the awareness position: *(nodding and looking around at different parts of the room)* I see that artist… I see some other parts too.

Facilitator: Take your time… And then when you're ready, we'll go back to Josh, back to the Aware Ego… *(Josh takes a little more time, actually quite absorbed in the act of perception, then he sits back down in the Aware Ego place)* Come back to yourself now, back to the Aware Ego… *(the facilitator shifts his energy too)* How are you doing?

Josh in the Aware Ego: Good… I feel good. That was very interesting… there are a lot of different me's running around out there!

Facilitator: *(feeling the linkage with Josh as he comes back into the Aware Ego place and reaching out energetically to strengthen that)* What stands out for you?

Josh in the Aware Ego: *(turning around in his chair so he can look behind and to either side)* I'm intrigued by a part that seems to be way back there in the corner, really quiet and kind of removed from everything else… I can feel the artist part too, much closer to me.

Facilitator: We have time to go to one more self. Which of those two would you most want to explore right now?

Josh in the Aware Ego: You know I really want to find out about the quiet one back there – there's something about it.

Facilitating this quiet self opens up a whole area of wisdom for Josh. The quiet self suggests how Josh can create some distance from all the pressure in his life. This self brings in an energy of stability and nurturance that the worrying part really felt was lacking. When Josh returns to the Aware Ego at the end of the session, he comments that he was completely surprised by this distant quiet part.

Josh in the Aware Ego: You know that quiet part of me is actually around quite a bit, but it didn't register before now… I mean when I came in here today, I would never have thought to go to that part of myself.

Facilitator: Now that you're more aware of it, you'll have a much easier time recognizing it when it's there and you'll be able to use its gifts to good advantage.

Josh in the Aware Ego: I'm looking forward to that!

When is it optimal to go to awareness?

Most typically, the awareness position is used toward the end of the session when the facilitation of the selves is completed. At this time in the session awareness can help to give an overview of the work. However, this is not a hard and fast rule. The facilitator needs to stay alert to when he can use the awareness position most effectively. For example, you might work with a couple of selves and sense (like Josh's facilitator above) that you have reached a natural point of completion, even though there may still be a lot of time left in the session. It can work very well to take the person you're facilitating to the awareness position right then, so they can look at the completed piece before moving

> *"It isn't necessary to go to the awareness position in every session, but it is essential to access the awareness or witness state in some way as part of the development of the Aware Ego process."*

on. This supports the Aware Ego in becoming more aware of the selves and trains the subject to separate from the selves and witness them right in the moment. And, in doing this, the subject may very well see something from awareness that gives them a new direction for where to go next in the session. If you do decide to facilitate another self, you may or may not want to go back to the awareness position again at the end of the session. It is your creative and intuitive choice as the facilitator.

It isn't necessary to go to the awareness position in every session, but it is essential to access the awareness or witness state in some way as part of the development of the Aware Ego process. For example, there are times when simply feeling the different selves from the Aware Ego, feeling the separation, is more organic than going to the awareness level. This can work quite well *if the subject is already familiar with what awareness is and how to get in touch with it.* Facilitating the subject in awareness is often the hardest part of Voice Dialogue work to master, perhaps just because it looks "so easy on paper." For this reason, you want to make sure that *you* also take all the time you need to develop a familiarity with facilitating the awareness position so you can really use it to its best advantage. That way, if you choose not to "go to awareness" it will be because that particular session calls for another approach and *not* because you're unsure about how to work with the awareness position or because you're not yet comfortable with it. I

A few tips on facilitating the awareness level...

If you have the opportunity to observe experienced facilitators demonstrate Voice Dialogue, you may come away *both inspired and confused* about facilitating the awareness level. The inspiration is in watching the facilitator so "effortlessly" recall what the selves had to say. "It's like magic," and "How can anyone remember all that?" are comments I've heard from student facilitators. The confusion comes in seeing how frequently advanced trainers leave out the awareness position altogether, making students wonder if awareness was a phase in facilitating that is now out of style.

It's easy to explain the "magic" of facilitating the awareness position. The more a facilitator separates from her own selves, the more free attention she has for the people she facilitates. Without a lot of internal distraction it becomes easier and easier to recall what happened in the session. Understanding this helps to clarify the "magic" that is so inspiring in the work of many of our senior Voice Dialogue teachers.

To understand why the awareness position is occasionally omitted in teaching situations, it helps to remember that the subjects in demonstration sessions are often already trained in the work and very familiar with how to access awareness. With this kind of subject, a higher level trainer can opt to bypass the awareness position and use the limited amount of time available in a demonstration session to show new developments in the work. Most of us, however, facilitate people who are unfamiliar with the Psychology of the Aware Ego and have little or no experience with Voice Dialogue. We need to get them grounded in all three aspects of consciousness – we need to take them to awareness as well as facilitate the selves and work with the Aware Ego. Once we have established this groundwork, then we may find that it's not *always* necessary to "go to awareness" in each session.

personally feel that it is very important to use the awareness position when I'm *first* working with someone so that the experience of witnessing from a place outside the system of the selves becomes a familiar one to them. Certainly using the awareness position can almost always be helpful – even after years of being facilitated I still appreciate the opportunity to stand and get an overall energetic view of the work that I've just done.

SUMMARY

Taking the subject to the awareness position gives them direct access to the awareness level of consciousness and helps them to strengthen the separation from the selves. Working with the awareness position requires active imagination and energetic presence – the facilitator guides the subject in energetically perceiving rather than mentally evaluating the selves.

Here are a few tips to help you facilitate the awareness position with finesse:

☆ **Less is more** – you don't have to remember everything the selves had to say! There's usually no need to repeat the entire facilitation to the subject in the awareness position – focus on supporting *their energetic experience of the selves* instead. If talking to the subject is overused in the awareness position, it can readily induct the subject's rational mind or analytical observer and then the energetic experience of awareness can be lost.

☆ **Keep the focus on the selves** – and not on you as the facilitator. It helps if you *avoid the word "I" when you are talking to a person in the awareness position.* "I" involves you in the process and draws the attention of the subject away from the selves and onto you. (It also helps to avoid addressing the subject by name when they're in the awareness position, so they're not pulled to identify with the operating ego.)

☆ **Look at the selves, not at the subject** – this may seem awkward at first because you're probably used to looking *at* a person when you speak to them. In facilitating the awareness position, however, you want the subject to look out over the "landscape" of the psyche, you want them to see the energetic dynamic of the selves. If you turn to look at them while you are talking, they will naturally turn to look back at you, and *you* will become the focus instead of the selves. As facilitator you want to point out the view and not compete with it.

☆ **Spontaneity and intuition are a key to success** – if at any point along the way you feel spontaneity has gone out of the process or that you've lost touch with your intuition, check to see if you have been trying to follow too many rules or to make the work meet certain expectations. If facilitation starts to feel lifeless, the "culprit" may be your obligation to the form of the session, when what is really called for is a response to the needs of the moment.

Working with Joan, Glen, and Kelly in the awareness position

Keeping in mind all that we have discussed about facilitating the awareness position, we can now take what we've learned and begin to apply it to our continuing sessions with Kelly, Glen, and Joan. You may have already had an opportunity to observe skilled facilitators work with the awareness position, or these sample sessions may be your first experience of this part of the process (outside of being facilitated yourself). Either way, please realize that what we have here are *only a few* possibilities for how a facilitator might work with the awareness level. Even more important, the most telling part of the awareness work is in the energy – between the lines

"When we learn from others, our inclination is to model what we do on the visible and more external part of facilitation, and we may miss much of the invisible, energetic part of the work."

and in the silences. When we learn from others working with the awareness position, the inclination is to model what we do on the visible and more external part of the facilitation, i.e. listening to the facilitator talk (or reading what the facilitator says here on the page). This makes it possible to get caught up in the words and miss much of the invisible, energetic part of the work. To help you deepen your understanding of how to work with awareness, take the time to observe as many sessions as you can and experiment with different approaches of your own. Practice going beyond your initial impressions and see if you can begin to get a sense of which ways of working make the awareness position effective and why. With this in mind, let's return to our three subjects and see how their sessions continue in the awareness position.

Joan

In the last chapter Joan's facilitator spent time with her in the Aware Ego place, focusing on the linkage between them (Joan's last facilitation was on p. 189).

> *Could Joan's facilitator have taken her to the awareness position first?*
>
> *Would it work to go there now?*
>
> *Would it be okay if they didn't go to the awareness position at all?*

Yes, yes, and yes. It would work well to go to the awareness position before working with linkage in the Aware Ego, and it can work fine to go there after being in the Aware Ego for a bit. The facilitator really has to "tune in" to what is needed in each session.* If a quiet thought comes, "let's do awareness next," it's probably wise to listen to that internal hint. That kind of thought feels quite different from worrying about what to do or checking off a mental list of tasks to accomplish. The facilitator may also feel that it's not necessary to go to awareness in this particular session at all. In this case he would probably choose to continue working with the Aware Ego in ways that would bring more awareness into the Aware Ego place.** In Joan's facilitation today, her facilitator did ask her to go to the awareness position. Let's see how that unfolds.

---

*See p. 66 in the chapter on "Energy, our hidden language" for an explanation of "tuning in."
**We'll explore more ways of doing this in "Learning to access the selves through the Aware Ego," p. 265.

Facilitator: Joan, why don't we take a moment to look at these two opposite parts of you from the awareness position.

Joan in the Aware Ego: *(half starting to move, with a quizzical look)* Come stand next to you, right?

Facilitator: *(nodding)* Sure, next to me works fine, then you can look at the selves from this perspective. *(Joan gets up and stands next to the facilitator and looks at him, waiting for what's happening next)* I know you've done this before, but let me just give you a little reminder to help you come into awareness... Take a breath or two and put yourself in a place of awareness... a neutral place that's outside of Joan and all her selves where you can look at everything from an objective distance... *(as he says this, the facilitator is also accessing his own awareness level – he takes a couple of deep breaths himself)* Are you beginning to find this place?

Joan in the awareness position: Well, I think so. I'm never sure I'm doing it right, but I can imagine looking at the quicksand part and the busy part.

Facilitator: *(still reaching out with his energy to support Joan as he was doing earlier)* That's fine. That's all you have to do in awareness – just be willing to look and "see" whatever you can... It's important to look without needing to judge or analyze what you see.

Joan in the awareness position: *(nodding and relaxing her energy so it feels as if she's standing more solidly in the awareness place)* Okay.

Facilitator: So take a moment first to look at Joan *(the facilitator is pointing at the chair where Joan was sitting)* who came in to the session with two very different energies – one part really excited about work and people and the other part just wanting to stay at home and not see anyone or do anything... We thought we were going to go to the more active part first, but when Joan moved over there *(pointing to the place where the first self was sitting)*, it was actually the quiet, tired part that came out... *(pausing while Joan looks over at this part from awareness)*

Take a moment to look at the quiet part from awareness, from this witness place... This is the part that said it felt like an anchor trying to hold Joan back from taking off too fast... It's really worried about the consequences of taking on too much responsibility, afraid Joan might experience the kind of setback that her father did, that she could be "tempting fate" by taking on something too big... *(the facilitator pays close attention to Joan in awareness, checking to see that she isn't getting pulled into the energy of this self)* Make sure to keep your distance and observe this self from the outside, and not get pulled into its energy... *(slow with lots of pauses to allow time for Joan to follow what he's suggesting)* Notice how much space this quiet self takes up... or if it moves at all... Just get a feel for what it's like... *(pausing again for a while)* Any sense you have of this part will help the Aware Ego become more aware of it... Do you have a sense now of that part? *(looking at Joan – she nods her head)* One thing this part really wanted was to be able to have some quiet time during the work day and not only when Joan gets home... *(pausing to let the last piece of information be received before moving on)*

Well, let's look over at the other side too. *(the facilitator points again, this time to the second self and turns his attention toward the place where the self was sitting)* We came back to the Aware Ego and there was an opposite part that popped out, one that just couldn't stand all that quiet... Again, take a look at this part without trying to figure it out at all, just perceiving what it's like... This is the part of Joan that wants to be up and moving, that feels that other self is like quicksand. *(the facilitator talks a little about what this self had to say and asks Joan to get a sense of this part as well – his voice remains calm and relaxed)*

Remember that there are no good selves or bad selves, no negatives or positives from the point of view of awareness. Your job in awareness is to simply notice the energies... Take another moment to look at both of these parts now and just feel the energetic difference between them.

Joan in the awareness position: *(looking back and forth between the two, suddenly laughs)* It really is a big difference!

Facilitator: Good... Your seeing differences and similarities from awareness is a big help to Joan's Aware Ego... When you feel complete... when you feel like you've seen all you can see right now, come back to the Aware Ego... *(Joan takes a moment more and then sits back down in the Aware Ego position)* Come back to yourself now, back to Joan in the Aware Ego place... How do you feel?

Joan in the Aware Ego: Okay. *(smiles)* Lighter than when I came in today... for sure.

Glen

What can you say to Glen or to any of your own first-time subjects that will help make the awareness position more real for them? What descriptions or images have you used in the past that were most effective? It's good to find something that makes sense to you and to have more than one way of talking about the awareness position just in case your favorite metaphor (such as getting an aerial view from a helicopter, looking out over the landscape from a look-out point, watching actors on a stage, etc.) doesn't make sense to the person you're working with today. What's important is that the facilitator describes the awareness position in such a way that it opens the door for the subject to step outside the world of the selves and view it without any judgment or attachment.

Of course, people are very different. Some of the people you will facilitate may not have any sense of what the awareness position is, and it may take them a while to feel comfortable working with it. Others will be totally at home with imaginative work and the minute they move to awareness, they'll look around the room and "see" colors and shapes and images where the selves were sitting, or they'll feel a strong vibrational difference between two different parts of the room. Glen falls more into the category of people who are hesitant about the work, not sure what it is they're being asked to do, easily embarrassed by not doing it right, and quick to give up on the unfamiliar. *Fortunately the process itself will accomplish a great deal even if a subject like Glen can't tell if much of anything is happening.* As the facilitator, trust that simply having your subject get up and move into a place of awareness, just their making the effort to look around and listening to you talk about the selves from this place, will support the Aware Ego process. It may not feel like much is happening in the moment, but it does start things rolling and establishes awareness as a resource which the Aware Ego can continue to access.

Let's pick up with Glen again. (If you want to check back, we last talked with Glen on p. 192.) The facilitator talked with the second self, the one that was concerned about taking too much time, which actually turned out to be a part that wanted to protect Glen from getting involved in anything too personal or revealing. Now Glen has come back to the Aware Ego for the second time.

Facilitator: Once again, bring yourself back to center, back to the Aware Ego, and get a sense of separating from the protective part we were just talking to… *(the facilitator senses Glen coming back into connection with her – when the protective self was present, there wasn't any linkage)* Just leave the protective part over there *(pointing)* and come back to yourself, come back to the Aware Ego… How do you feel?

Glen in the Aware Ego: *(nodding his head, smiling a little, and adjusting to a more relaxed position in his chair)* It's kind of startling, but I think I'm starting to get the hang of this. I'm kind of amazed to see how protected I am. I'm actually glad to know I have these guys working for me. *(nodding toward the two selves that were facilitated and smiling)*

Facilitator: *(she laughs warmly)* That's a great way to think about it! Especially the idea of them working *for* you rather than against you. *(Glen nods with a rueful smile)* There's one more thing we can do in our session to help you become more aware of these parts of you, and that's to give you the opportunity to take a look at them from a place of awareness. It's real simple – want to give it a try?

Glen in the Aware Ego: *(looking and feeling open, much different from his hesitancy and suspicion at the beginning of the session)* I guess so – what do I have to do?

Facilitator: All you need to do is move to a place where you have a good view of the selves we worked with… so if you just come stand next to me that would work fine. Then you can see the selves we've been talking with from this perspective.

Glen in the Aware Ego: *(starts to get up and then looks around)* Could I just go over there? *(pointing to a spot behind and off to one side of the facilitator, farther away from her)*

Facilitator: Sure, that'll work fine. *(Glen moves to his chosen spot and looks to the facilitator for direction – she speaks slowly, allowing time for what she is communicating to land and settle in)* Good. Now that you're there, just imagine that you're in a *place* of awareness… kind of like one of those spots where you pull over to the side of the road and park to see the view… You're separate from Glen and you're not one of Glen's selves… you're just in a neutral, non-judgmental place outside Glen's whole personality where you can get a detached and objective view… Can you imagine that?

Glen in the awareness position: *(a bit of a quizzical look on his face, but nodding yes)* I'll do my best.

Facilitator: *(still staying conscious of her own energy and Glen's so she can feel if the energy shifts and he starts to go off into a self instead of staying in awareness)* Good. This won't be difficult. In awareness, your job is just to take a look at the selves that were talking before… You don't have to say anything about what you see or feel. *(points at where the hesitant self was sitting and turns her attention toward this place, knowing that if she looks at it, in all probability Glen will also turn his attention to the place where the self was sitting)* First notice the hesitant part over there – imagine it's still sitting there and just get a sense of what that "person" feels like to you…

I'll remind you a little about what was important to him. He definitely doesn't want Glen to make a fool of himself and feels uncomfortable in situations where other people can watch him and judge him. He's conservative and private, and always tries to protect Glen from embarrassment… Relationships are really hard for this part because they can make Glen too vulnerable… *(the facilitator has been speaking slowly, pausing to give Glen in the awareness position time to remember and to sense the energetic reality of this self)* Those were some of the things this self is most concerned about. Take a moment just to get a sense of him…

Glen in the awareness position: *(shifting on his feet a little)* I'm not very good at imagining things, so I don't know if I'm doing what you want…

Facilitator: *(keeping her energetic connection strong so that even if Glen has doubts, he'll still feel comfortable with her and trust the process)* That's okay. Just *intending* to be in a place of awareness and taking a few minutes to look at the selves is enough to be really helpful to Glen in the Aware Ego… You don't have to imagine anything except to just remember how that part of Glen felt… *(Glen in the awareness position now feels more relaxed to her, so the facilitator moves on)* Let's take a look at that other protective self too *(pointing at where it was sitting)* It was kind of on the same team with the hesitant part, but maybe more of a tough guy and more internal – this self said it was more likely to keep watch on the inside and not ever come out and say anything to other people… See what this self feels like to you and if you notice any difference between these two… *(Glen nods and has a kind of surprised look on his face)* Do you feel like you have a sense of these parts of Glen?

Glen in the awareness position: *(still looking surprised, nods again)* I… do actually. I'm kind of amazed…

Facilitator: Well, let's go back to the Aware Ego, back to Glen, and then you can tell me about it… *(she gestures for Glen to move back to the Aware Ego place, which he does)* Do you feel you're back to yourself, back to the Aware Ego? *(Glen nods)* You look as if you definitely reached some new awareness – what was surprising for you?

Glen in the Aware Ego: That was strange because I really did have a sense of those two parts and how different they are from each other… I don't know… they… *felt* different to me, even though they didn't sound all that different. I mean the first one is how I am a lot, cautious and conservative, but that other one actually felt kind of tough and protective, like a big brother… *(laughs)* This is *not* the way I usually talk about anything!

How would you compare Glen's and Joan's facilitations? What is similar and what is different in the way Joan's and Glen's facilitators chose to work with the awareness position?

How do Joan's and Glen's facilitators support them energetically?

Were there any surprises for you in these examples? Would you have taken another direction or worked with awareness differently?

Discussion

Glen's facilitator very appropriately keeps this part of the session as simple as she can, giving him the opportunity to go to awareness without making it any more complicated than need be. Joan's facilitator doesn't assume Joan will remember what to do just because she's done it before — he makes it easy for her too. Both facilitators make sure that the subject doesn't feel they are doing anything wrong, and that makes it possible for them to relax and see more. Watching (i.e. keeping your energetic "feelers" out) to make sure the subject doesn't get pulled back into one of the selves is a very important way to energetically support them in the awareness position.

Kelly

Now that we've looked at a few examples of working with the awareness position, it's your turn to try your hand at it by facilitating Kelly. Pick a time and place where you can be relaxed and uninterrupted. It's a good idea to go back and read over Kelly's session (we last worked with Kelly on p. 179), or you may also want to look over the alternative ways of facilitating Kelly that we talked about back on pp. 126-127. Once you have Kelly clearly in mind, try doing a facilitation for her in the awareness position. Simply imagine Kelly is standing by your side and guide her into and through the awareness process. Since the subject remains mostly silent in the awareness position, you don't need to imagine Kelly's comments, but you do need to imagine her energy and notice if she is getting pulled out of awareness and into a self. If you like, try recording yourself on a cassette, so you can listen to yourself later and learn from the way you work with this part of facilitation. You may want to try a couple of ways of facilitating awareness, maybe something different from what you're used to. Feel free to be inventive and allow for the possibility of fun.

Returning to the Aware Ego at the end of the session

After observing the selves from the awareness position, it will be even easier to feel a clear separation in the Aware Ego place. The facilitator asks the subject to come back to the Aware Ego and once again *makes sure that they arrive there* – that it's truly the Aware Ego and not a self who sits back down in the central place. Facilitator and subject may then:

♦ **talk about the session,** taking note of what feels significant to the subject from the Aware Ego place.

♦ **focus on linkage through the Aware Ego.**

♦ **bring the energy of the selves in and out of the Aware Ego.** (See the chapter on "Learning to access the selves through the Aware Ego," p. 265.)

♦ **work with energy exercises,** helping the subject to practice managing their energy while in the Aware Ego place.

All the different ways of working with the Aware Ego that we discussed in our earlier chapter on "Returning to the Aware Ego" (p. 169) can be used appropriately at the end of the session as well. The only difference is that now the focus is on concluding the work, consolidating the movement that has occurred, and helping the person you've just facilitated get ready to shift back to meet the demands of the world. The facilitator plays a key role in enabling the subject to make the most of this transition.

It's important that the facilitator resist the temptation to jump in with an analysis of the process the subject has just been through. As in talking with someone about a dream they have had (and a Voice Dialogue session does take a person into an altered energy state that is in some ways like a dream), it is more supportive of the subject's process to first leave space for their own observations and interpretation so that they are able to feel into what happened before there is any overlay from the facilitator's commentary and ideas. The facilitator can help by orienting the subject to the Aware Ego place and encouraging them to talk about their experience:

"Now that you are back in the Aware Ego place, how do you feel?"

"As you come back to the Aware Ego now, what do you notice about the process you've just experienced?"

"What stands out for you? Were there any surprises?"

In listening to the subject at the end of the session, the facilitator may remind them of their new response-ability in the Aware Ego place, reinforcing the subject's capacity to be aware of energy and to be conscious of the different selves and their concerns. Often at the end of the session, in the Aware Ego, the subject has a kind of "got it!" experience that only results from having achieved a broader perspective, an overview, and not being attached to any part of the picture. To get a better idea of how this works, let's observe a facilitation with a woman named, Ruthann. We are listening in on the part of her session where she is completing the awareness position and returning to the Aware Ego.

Facilitator: Now that you've got a sense of the selves from the awareness position, let's go back to the Aware Ego, back to Ruthann. *(Ruthann takes another moment and then moves back to the Aware Ego place)* Bring yourself all the way back to the Aware Ego now… Can you feel yourself here in the center separate from the two selves we talked with earlier?

Ruthann in the Aware Ego: Yes, I feel them really clearly. It's almost like I was too close to see them before, they were out of focus. Now that they're at a distance, I have a better sense of both of them.

Facilitator: Now that you're in the Aware Ego and you've had the experience of being in those two selves and also seeing them from awareness, is there anything that really stands out for you, any new insights?

Ruthann in the Aware Ego: You know, just as you were saying that, this thought popped into my head that I did a lot of bouncing back and forth between those two parts of me growing up… one moment I'd be defiant and then the next I'd feel isolated and depressed. I know that those two parts of me we worked with aren't kids and the issue *now* is about my job, but I can just see myself as a kid doing the exact same thing… It really gives me a new perspective on what's going on.

Facilitator: *(feeling a new softness in Ruthann's energy – the linkage between them much stronger than it was before)* You know… as you made that observation, it felt like something relaxed in you… and relaxed between us. Can you feel a change in the energy too?

Ruthann in the Aware Ego: *(nodding and taking a deep breath)* Now that you mention it, I do feel different. Something just feels peaceful to me, like I'm not being pulled the way I was before.

It's unlikely any interpretation the facilitator could offer would be as meaningful to Ruthann as what she discovers for herself. Only Ruthann has access to her memory, her childhood, etc. Plus, waiting for the person you are facilitating to collect their own thoughts first, gives you time as the facilitator to allow your own deeper understanding about the work to come to the surface. Not rushing in with your commentary allows you to rest and organically acquire more information from your intuition as well as from the person you are facilitating. You may also find over time that your feedback to the people you facilitate is as much or more about energy as it is about thought. After all, analysis and ideas are readily available in the world, but it's relatively hard to get real feedback on what is happening with one's energy and linkage. The Voice Dialogue facilitator is a particularly precious resource to the people he facilitates because he is able to work with them in the feeling, mental, *and* energetic aspects of their lives. In our example above, the facilitator is not invested in interjecting his own ideas about Ruthann's selves. Instead he allows her the space to open up to her own realizations and at the same time remains very alert to the energy so that he is able to provide an energetic context and perspective that she isn't yet ready to have on her own. Together they make a really good team.

The more you work with Voice Dialogue facilitation, the more you'll come to see working with the Aware Ego (whether in the middle or at the end of the session) as the most powerful part of the work and an opportunity to anchor all the movement that has occurred in the session. Every time the person you are facilitating returns to the Aware Ego place, they strengthen the Aware Ego and further the process of separating from the selves. When you direct someone to "move back to yourself and come back to the Aware Ego," *you are quite literally bringing them back to center from the polarized reality of the selves.* Through their experience of relating to *you* from this new place, the subject will build a base from which they can begin to relate from an Aware Ego place in daily life. You may or may not have time to continue working with energetics in the Aware Ego at the end of a particular session, but your continued focus on linkage, on alerting the subject to shifts and changes that have occurred during your work together, will make a big difference in how well the new energetic experience and awareness take root in the ground of the subject's life.

> *"When you direct someone to move back to the Aware Ego, you are quite literally bringing them back to center from the polarized reality of the selves."*

It cannot be overemphasized that *the* most important part of the work is helping the Aware Ego become more and more present in each person's life. Talking with the Aware Ego at the end of the session is not just a short conversation to finish off work for the day. Rather, it is a crucial time for solidifying the separation that has been accomplished and helping the Aware Ego to become part of this person's daily reality. The time facilitator and subject spend at the end of the session also provides an important transition between the session and reentry into the business of living life.

The facilitator makes sure that the subject returns to the Aware Ego. Talking with the Aware Ego and working with it energetically at the end of the session helps the Aware Ego to be more available in daily life.

Concluding our sessions with Kelly, Glen, and Joan

Kelly

How was your facilitation of Kelly in the awareness position? Did you review the session with the "mother bear" self or did you decide to work with one of the alternative directions for facilitating Kelly? (You worked with Kelly in the awareness position on p. 211, and our last facilitation of Kelly was on p. 179) Now that we're at the end of Kelly's session, what do you think might be most helpful to her in integrating the work she has done so far? Kelly's facilitator was thinking to keep it simple and help Kelly ground in the new sense of balance and connection she found the first time she returned to the Aware Ego. However, as we will see, new selves can pop up at any time, including right at the end of the session.

Facilitator: *(Kelly has just moved back to the Aware Ego place)* Take a moment to come back to yourself, back to the Aware Ego… How do you feel?

Kelly in the Aware Ego position: I think I feel okay, though some part of me feels a bit nervous.

Facilitator: *(can feel contraction in her own shoulders and stomach and realizes she's picking up on Kelly's nervous energy in herself)* Well, we know that's *not* the Aware Ego that feels that way. Why don't we take a moment for you to move over and see who that is… do you have a sense of where in the room that part might be?

Kelly in the Aware Ego position: I think it's right behind me. *(she scoots her chair back a few inches)*

The facilitator talks with a self that is anxious about Kelly getting everything done, both for her family and at work. Whatever Kelly is doing and wherever she goes, this self is already on to the next thing, worrying that there isn't enough time. Right now this part wants to know that Voice Dialogue is going to work, that it's going to improve Kelly and make her a better person. This self is not at all sure that talking with a "mother bear" will really help. How would you respond to this part of Kelly?

> **CAUTION:** Feeling obligated to justify Voice Dialogue to a self that questions the usefulness or validity of the work can be very tempting and can be a real trap. As a facilitator you need to keep the perspective of an Aware Ego and not get hooked in to the anxieties a particular self may hold (even about Voice Dialogue). Instead of taking the self's comments personally, you would want to investigate this self's concerns about the Voice Dialogue session in the same way that you would follow other selves' misgivings about any aspect of the subject's life. Once the self realizes that it's okay to express negative as well as positive feelings about the work, it will be much easier for it to open up and reveal what it finds most troubling.

Facilitator: *(conscious of sinking her own energy more solidly into the ground, providing a kind of energetic stability)* It sounds as if you really worry a lot about Kelly – what is your biggest concern about her?

Nervous self: *(her whole body seems tense and pulled up as if she were a puppet on invisible strings)* That she won't make it… that there are things she's supposed to do, expectations she has to fulfill, and it won't happen… or it won't happen on time.

Facilitator: *(letting herself feel the same kind of upper body energy, but not to the point where she feels strung out or stressed – just an alertness to match but not exaggerate the energy of this self)* What happens if she's not on time?

Nervous self: Then she fails... there's a cut off point for everything.

Facilitator: So you're really under the gun all the time.

Nervous self: I am, and I don't like it. I wish I could take a break.

Facilitator: Well, if there were just one thing you could have Kelly do differently on a consistent basis that would make *your* life easier, what do you think that would be?

Nervous self: *(looking a bit surprised)* Nobody ever thinks about making *my* life easier! I know it sounds strange, but I'd like her not to take on so much, not to commit to so many things. Everything she commits to is another possibility of failure, one more thing that keeps me freaked out all the time.

Facilitator: *(it feels with this last remark that the nervous self released something and calmed down)* That's a clear request. I will make sure that Kelly gets to hear about that in the Aware Ego. Is there anything else you need to say before we go back to Kelly? *(the nervous self shakes its head, "no")* Well, thank you for being here. Let's go back now... *(Kelly moves back to the Aware Ego place, closes her eyes for a moment, wriggles her shoulders, and opens her eyes, smiling)* It feels as if you're back this time – how does it feel to you?

Kelly in the Aware Ego: Much better! I can really feel the difference from when that nervous part of me was here – it feels so different to have some space from that!

Facilitator: If you think of it during this week, when you feel that nervous energy coming in, you may want to try separating from it again, maybe even getting up and moving to a different place to see if you can start to sort out these parts on your own... plus I promised to remind you in the Aware Ego that the nervous worried part very much wanted you to make fewer commitments so it wouldn't have so much to worry about.

Kelly in the Aware Ego: I'll do that as long as it's not another commitment! *(laughs)* I do feel like I just peeled another layer off, like an onion. That self is a big part of me.

Facilitator: It is a big part of you and we'll probably want to come back to that self again another time. It takes a while and a lot of repetition to unhook from our strongest primary selves. Right now, before we go, let's take a moment to feel the energy in the Aware Ego again... feel what it's like just being here together in the Aware Ego place. *(as she says this, the facilitator can feel Kelly focusing in on their connection – it's almost tangible)*

Kelly in the Aware Ego: *(as they sit in silence for a moment or two, feeling the energy between them, Kelly seems to both expand and relax with several deep breaths)* I like this energy stuff. I didn't realize how cut off from people I feel a lot of the time.

Glen

When we last left Glen, he had already returned to the Aware Ego and was commenting on how amazing it was for him to get such a clear sense of the selves that had been facilitated. (We last worked with Glen in the awareness position on p. 208.) The facilitator, wanting to avoid overloading Glen with too much input in his first session, simply concludes the session with a short conversation.

Facilitator: *(paying as close attention to her energy and to connecting with Glen as she has through the whole session)* I think you had an easier time working with the different parts of yourself than you thought you would. You did great.

Glen in the Aware Ego: *(still in his new relaxed mode)* Yeah, I'm definitely intrigued now. I mean, I can understand there are these parts of me, but I guess I couldn't really see them before.

Facilitator: Well, moving to the selves and back really does help you separate from them, and when you have some distance, it's much easier to see clearly... How about now, can you still feel that hesitant self over there? *(pointing)*

Glen in the Aware Ego: Yes... I can feel it. *(looking to either side of him)* Actually, I can feel them both... I really like knowing I have that protective one around.

Facilitator: It seems you feel more relaxed knowing he's around and it also seems to me that you're not so caught up right now in the worries the hesitant self has. *(Glen is nodding his head in agreement and looking more directly at the facilitator than he has throughout the whole session – they simply sit in silence for just a short moment, linking energetically, even though Glen doesn't yet have a cognitive understanding of what that means)* Do you have any questions before we stop for today?

Glen in the Aware Ego: *(taking a deep breath)* No... no, you know I think I just want to leave it here and think about it a little bit. I'm not sure what happened, but something feels different, and I'm glad I came. Thank you.

Questions

How do you see both Kelly's and Glen's facilitators supporting the Aware Ego process – what do you see as their key questions or comments?

How would you work with Kelly if you were at the end of her session and had no time to facilitate the new self that appeared?

Would you talk more with Glen about the Aware Ego and about learning to take care of his hesitant primary self?

Discussion

It's not an unusual occurrence to have a self appear at the end of the session, so it's a good idea to allow room for that if you can. With Kelly, time pressure is what actually brings out this part, but sometimes there are selves that are allowed to make a quick cameo appearance at the end just because the primary selves think there won't be time for them. The facilitator has to stay tuned in so she can make an intuitive decision about what to do in this kind of situation. It's good to remember that if a primary self shows up suddenly, even a brief separation from and acknowledgment of the self can accomplish a lot. If it's a disowned self that starts breaking through, however, then observing it from the Aware Ego place and consciously containing the energy can bring in new awareness without shaking up the primary selves (especially right before the person walks out the door).

Joan

If you like, you can take the opportunity now to use what you've learned about working with the Aware Ego and try completing Joan's session on your own. (We last worked with Joan on p. 206.) You can run through your facilitation of Joan in your mind or perhaps take the time to tape yourself doing it out loud. You may even want to write your facilitation on paper or computer. After the experience of writing out Joan's and Kelly's and Glen's facilitations, I can definitely recommend writing as a powerful way of deepening your own understanding and relationship to the facilitation process. I also found it to be a lot of fun because, like characters in a novel, these subjects seem to come to life on the page. Whatever method you choose, take the time to sense into Joan as you've grown to know her through the sample facilitations and leave enough room for your imagination to do what it does best as well. The process of working with Joan will take on a life of its own as you allow the energy between you (as facilitator) and Joan (as subject) to unfold. You'll find that you really can learn a lot from the sessions you invent, and you may enjoy the creative aspect of working (with Joan) in this way.

Becoming ever more conscious of our energy...

One of the easiest ways for the facilitator to model and teach mastery of one's personal energy field is by making sure to disconnect the energetic linkage created throughout the session. If people really welcomed each other's energies when they met, and clearly and cleanly disconnected their energies from each other when they parted ways, relationships would be deeper and more conscious. And, it would be much easier to let go without feeling either pulled on or abandoned. Essentially, when we manage our energy in this way, we are relating to each other more from the Aware Ego than from the primary selves. Intentionally disconnecting linkage is a simple and powerful way for each of us (facilitator and/or subject) to reinforce the Aware Ego and take care of our *selves*. In bringing our energy back to center we let the selves know *we're* going to be responsible for them now and they don't need to hang on to (or push off from) the person we've been with.

The ability to connect and disconnect energetically at will is the basis for creating autonomy and it helps us to both access and protect our vulnerability. This is equally true for both subject and facilitator. Without the simple step of disconnecting linkage, facilitator and subject could leave the session feeling incomplete and uncomfortably interdependent (which in actuality is the way many of our social interactions regrettably wind up). Fortunately, disconnecting linkage is not at all hard to master with a little practice.

Disengaging the linkage at the end of the session requires just a moment's time and your clear intention. We learned in the chapter on energetics that "energy follows thought,"* so what is needed in order to disconnect our energy from each other is to *intend* to disconnect and to *imagine* doing so. The facilitator can suggest this in any number of ways depending on the subject's experience with the work and their level of understanding. At the beginning, it may be enough to simply say,

> *Before we end our session, let's take a moment to disconnect our energy from each other*
> *– that way we're free to go without feeling like we're leaving any part of ourselves behind.*
> *If you'd like, you can imagine that your energetic connection to me is controlled by some-*
> *thing like a dial, like a volume dial on a radio, and if you turn it down, the energy be-*
> *tween us will turn down. Let's both try that now.*

Other images work equally well: a valve that closes the flow of energy, a thermostat that regulates the amount of energy, or just picturing pulling your energy back from the person you're

*See p. 59 in "Energy, our hidden language."

221

with and into the center of your own being. Look for an image(s) that works well for you, and the people you facilitate may come up with some excellent ones also.

The natural result of turning down your end of an energetic connection is that the other person's energy will disengage as well. An analogy would be when you meet someone and shake their hand, you will only want to hold on to their hand as long as they hold on to yours. If they let their hand go limp, you'll naturally want to let go. It's a similar feeling with

"Pulling our energy back when we say good-bye means we're really free to leave and go about our own lives."

linkage. We respond to changes in energy automatically without thinking about it, but teaching your subject to disconnect *intentionally* will help them to become conscious of and in charge of their own energy. At first the facilitator will want to make this a short and easy process, disconnecting her own energy at the same time the subject is disconnecting theirs. Once the subject is used to the idea, it's empowering to have them disconnect on their own so that they can experience how this affects the facilitator.

Disconnecting linkage supports the primary selves too. If you're working with someone for whom connecting energetically is a brand new experience, then disconnecting the linkage at the end of the session reassures their primary selves that the doors that have been opened can be closed again and they don't have to be overwhelmed by this new way of being. After all, it's the primary selves that are going to need to regroup and get ready to take care of business – an "infant" Aware Ego isn't going to be able to come in and take over running this person's life. And, for the people who have difficulty creating boundaries – who have never had any ability to pull their own energy back into themselves – the simple act of intentionally and freely disconnecting linkage can be empowering and life-changing in a very positive way.

The act of disconnecting linkage is accomplished from an Aware Ego place and is not the same as withdrawing into a non-linkage self – it's the Aware Ego that can access both linkage and non-linkage sides of the personality and the Aware Ego that has the choice to link energetically or to disconnect. *Pulling our energy back when we say good-bye means we're really free to leave and go about our own lives.* Once people understand and learn to use this principle in their

"Teaching the people you facilitate to disconnect their linkage with you gives them a solid practical experience of functioning in the Aware Ego."

daily lives, it can eliminate a great deal of stress. Knowing how to disentangle our energy from each other makes it possible to gracefully and unobtrusively extricate ourselves from social involvement without resorting to avoiding people, pushing them away, tolerating energetic invasion, or any of those things that are likely to happen when we don't have conscious control of our energy.

At the end of the session, the natural tendency for the subject will be to move back into a familiar primary self(ves). The primary selves come back into their accustomed role of managing our lives as we begin to think about where we're going next, what responsibilities we have to meet, who we're going to see, etc. – we (literally) "pull ourselves together" and get ready to go back into the outside world. In contrast, teaching the people you facilitate to disconnect their linkage with you gives them a solid practical experience of functioning in the Aware Ego right before they walk out the door. Of course, if you're just beginning to work with a person and you feel it's too soon to be talking with them about energy or linkage, it obviously won't

222

make any sense to instruct them to pull their energy back into themselves and disconnect. Even in this case, though, *the facilitator* still needs to be conscious of the energetic connection and pull *her* energy back at the end of the session. This is both for the protection of the subject's and your own vulnerable selves; and because it's your role as facilitator to model the process, whether it's appropriate to talk about it yet it or not.

The more you work with Voice Dialogue, both being facilitated and facilitating others, the more adept you will become at sensing when the energy is or isn't connected. When you instruct your subject to pull their energy back, you will be able to accurately tell them when they have or haven't done this successfully. When two people disconnect linkage, the space between them usually feels emptier and each may have a sense of being more self-contained. This tends to be true for facilitator and subject alike. If you're not sure you can tell clearly when the energy has shifted, ask the person who facilitates you to work on connecting and disconnecting linkage with you, or practice with a colleague or partner. Like all the aspects of working with energy, repetition and familiarity will quickly build your confidence and skill.

SUMMARY *At the end of the session, facilitator and subject intentionally disconnect the energetic linkage between them. Even if it's too soon to talk with a particular subject about energy, the facilitator takes care to disconnect his own energy from the person he is facilitating — this can be done without comment.*

Saying good-bye to Kelly, Joan, and Glen...

Kelly

At the end of her session, Kelly was relaxed and enjoying the linkage with the facilitator. (See our last facilitation with Kelly on p. 215.) Her last remark was, "I like this energy stuff. I didn't realize how cut off from people I felt a lot of the time."

Facilitator: *(still relaxed and focused on the linkage with Kelly even though it's time to go)* It seems to be getting much easier for you to feel energy now.

Kelly in the Aware Ego: Well, it's like I have a lot more room to feel what's going on inside myself, and somehow that gives me more room to feel *outside* myself too.

Facilitator: Excellent. This is a perfect place to stop. Before we go, though, let's take a moment to disconnect our energy from each other so we'll both be free and clear to go on to the next thing in our day. Just imagine you can pull your energy in or turn it down and I'll do the same. *(the facilitator adjusts her own energetic field and senses the space between herself and Kelly, waiting for an impression of disconnection, perhaps a feeling that the* *space between them is emptier or cooler)* There… that feels much more separate to me. Can you notice the change too?

Kelly in the Aware Ego: It feels peaceful actually… like it's okay to go.

Joan

If you recall, it was your role to be facilitator for the last part of Joan's session. Go back to your mental or written notes and review your facilitation. (You worked with Joan on p. 219, and our last sample facilitation with Joan was on p. 206.) With Joan, as with Kelly, there is already a certain familiarity with energy, so it won't be confusing to her if you ask her to disconnect energetically. If you already started to guide Joan in increasing and decreasing linkage with you as her facilitator earlier in the session, then you might suggest that she be the one to initiate the energetic separation at the end.

Facilitator: *(not trying to do anything different with his own energy field)* Why don't you try one more time turning down your energy, turning down your imaginary dial that regulates how much energy you have connecting with me… *(he waits to feel a change in Joan's energy and in his own)* There… I can feel a change… what do you feel?

Joan in the Aware Ego: I know you didn't move, but I feel sort of… farther away.

Facilitator: When you turn down your end of the connection, it definitely affects me… I pull back on my end too.

Joan in the Aware Ego: That's really cool… I like that. I could use this when I'm dating!

Facilitator: It's very useful in a lot of situations where you just don't have the time or desire to connect with people and you need a graceful way to separate and go back into your own space. And for us, now, it means we can leave the session free of each other's energy and be ready to go our separate ways.

Glen

Doing Voice Dialogue work is very new to Glen and we have already come to a natural conclusion for today's session. How would you accomplish the task of disconnecting the linkage with Glen at the end of the session? (We last worked with Glen on p. 218.) Would you say anything about it to him? Would you try to explain linkage, or would you simply turn your own energy down and leave the explanations for another time?

Glen really stretched himself to try Voice Dialogue in the first place, and he has clearly stated that he's had enough for today. If his facilitator were to start in explaining energy and linkage, it would really be disrespectful of Glen's boundaries. Since the facilitator wants to honor Glen's sovereignty *(an important ground rule)*, she ends the session by gently disconnecting linkage on her end without saying anything to Glen about energy or linkage at all. The facilitator is experienced enough with doing this that she can sense when disconnection has occurred, and she knows there will be time enough to talk about this with Glen, if and when they do more Voice Dialogue work together. The last thing she wants is for him to walk out the door overwhelmed from taking on more than his primary selves are willing to do.

Facilitation evaluation sheet

The following questions are designed to help the facilitator reflect on his own progress and learn from each of the sessions he facilitates. If you would like to try this evaluation tool in your own Voice Dialogue work, photocopy the questionnaire so that you can use it as many times as you want and still have the original. It's probably impractical to go over all these questions for any one facilitation, so you may want to focus on one particular area at a time – perhaps a part of facilitating that is of particular interest to you or that you find to be especially challenging. You may choose to glance over the questions right after a session while everything is fresh in your mind, or you may want to think about the answers to these questions at the end of the day or the end of the week in relation to a number of facilitations. Over time you may start to see where your strengths are and also what aspects of facilitation could use strengthening. If you come up with additional questions, please feel free to share them with us for possible inclusion in future printings of *The Handbook* (see p. 312, "How to contribute to *The Handbook*").

General questions about the session:

What part of the session did I feel/think was most supportive of the subject's Aware Ego process?

Overall, what did I like best about my facilitation?

Did I try anything new or different? How did it work out?

What do I notice in my facilitations that seems to consistently work well over time?

How was the linkage between me and the subject? Was there any time in the session where we lost the linkage? Is there anything I would like to do differently?

Did I enjoy the session? Was I relaxed? Did it seem to flow or was it "a lot of work?" If the latter, what made it difficult and how can I change that?

At the start of the session:

Did I find the time and space to center before the session began? Did I take time to connect energetically?

What worked best about the first part of our session?

Were there any problems or confusion? Did I get distracted by what was being said or lose track of "who" was saying it? What might I do differently another time?

Did I need to talk more with this person more before moving on to facilitating the selves?

If this was a person I've worked with before, did their energy seem different from usual? What kinds of changes have they been experiencing in their life?

Facilitating the selves:

Did the subject and I choose a direction for the facilitation together?

Was I readily able to match the energy of the selves? Which ones were easy? Which were a challenge? Are there hints here about what I need to work on in my own process?

Did I follow the self's lead? How was I as an interviewer?

Did I allow enough space for silence? Was I comfortable with it?

Did anything unexpected occur? How did I respond to it? How did the subject/selves respond?

Did any of the selves seem to be a "combination self," several different characters all rolled into one? Did we need to separate those more clearly in this session or was it fine to wait for another time?

Did we go deep enough and get to the bottom line of what is important to each self? What were its greatest concerns? When does it come out and why? How does it function in this person's life?

Was I fully present with the self and did I stay with it long enough? Or, in retrospect, was I in a hurry to move on? Did I work with the primary self long enough to really understand it and create a good rapport with it?

Were the selves fully present energetically? Did any of them fade out? What did I do to bring the self back? Did I have the subject go back to the Aware Ego and/or to another self? What did I learn from this process?

Did we locate the self in the body?* Did the subpersonality give itself a name or identify itself with a place or time or activity or a feeling – something that could help the Aware Ego to find it again?

Was it difficult to get a particular self to stop talking and leave? Are there ways I could manage this kind of situation better – what would I do differently if this happens again?

Working with the awareness position and the Aware Ego:

Could the person I facilitated feel a clear separation from the self(ves)?

Was there a difference in the connection between *us* when the subject came back to the Aware Ego? Could I feel it? Did they feel it?

Did I allow enough time in the session to work with energy in the Aware Ego? Did I need to communicate more about energetics and linkage? Did I communicate too much too quickly?

*See "Locating the self in the body," p. 231.

Did I choose to work with channeling any of the selves through the Aware Ego?*   Am I satisfied with how that worked out? Did the subject understand this process and begin to gain facility in moving from one energy to another?

Did we use the awareness position effectively? How did going to awareness add to the session? Did I tailor my directions and review to the needs of this particular subject and what their energy was like today?

Did I keep energetic linkage with the subject while they were in the awareness position?

Did I keep energetic linkage with the subject while they were in the Aware Ego?

Concluding the session:

Was there enough time for the subject to get grounded in the Aware Ego/operating ego before we brought the session to a close? Or, did we get too deeply involved in working with the selves so that we ran out of time at the end?

Did I manage to steer clear of offering advice and interpretations? Was it difficult to do?

Was there an opportunity for the subject to talk about the session from an Aware Ego place? Did they really get time to function in the Aware Ego either through talking, learning to shift energy in and out of the Aware Ego, or enjoying linkage through the Aware Ego? Or all three?

What clues were there about where to go next in the work, what selves might we want to explore next time?

Did we take time to disconnect linkage at the end of the session?

*See "Learning to access the selves through the Aware Ego," p. 265.

Introduction to Section Four

In this final section of *The Handbook* we look at ways to deepen the facilitation process and broaden the scope of our facilitation skills. Now that we are familiar with the basic components of a Voice Dialogue session from beginning to end, we can start to do more focused work with the Aware Ego and pay attention to the subject's guidance from the Unconscious through dreams. In addition, there are chapters on locating the self in the physical body and working with silence – two very important ways for the facilitator to expand her understanding of the selves and her capacity to link with the people she facilitates.

Every self uses the body differently...

Locating the self in the body

Locating the self in the body

Everyone has innumerable selves but they all must express through one physical body, so it makes sense that noticing how each self relates to the physical body and how it inhabits the body, tells a great deal about the nature of that self. One could think of it as many different people staying in the same house – some barely leave a trace, some blast through like a storm, some only hang out in the attic, some never come up out of the basement. *Discovering the nature of a self and how it expresses physically is one of the most fascinating aspects of Voice Dialogue work and one of the most useful to the Aware Ego because it provides tangible, physical "data" on the self being facilitated.* If I know how one of my selves moves, breathes, or feels in the body, then I have physical clues I can look for to help me recognize when that self is out and active. If my responsible self, for example, has tight shoulders or the advent of my worrier is heralded by a sinking feeling in the pit of my stomach, then the presence of those physical feelings will alert me that these selves have come to the fore. Sometimes other people may point out the shift in my energy as when an excited child self shows up in quick, or even hyper, movements and a high breathy voice. The body is always changing depending on "who" is using it, so the body can also be an indicator of which self(ves) is present. And, once the subject learns to recognize the different selves by their physical characteristics, the body can provide a way to call in or access a particular self or energy when it is needed. If, for example, my spiritual or wisdom self is facilitated in a Voice Dialogue session and I learn that this part breathes deeply and holds a calm feeling throughout my body, then I can actually bring that part out again by sitting calmly and deepening my breath. The body has given me a pathway to the self.

> *"Noticing how each self relates to the physical body and how it inhabits the body tells a great deal about the nature of that self."*

Many selves communicate directly through the body, while others have very little relationship to physical reality. By paying attention to each self's relationship to the body, both facilitator and subject can learn much about that self. This in turn will help the Aware Ego to access the self and utilize its energy appropriately. Here is a list of some of the ways in which observing the body can help both facilitator and subject learn more about the self:

♦ **The self may tell you directly that it has a different experience of physical reality than any of the other parts.** It may be quite obvious that the body feels very different to this self than what is experienced by the subject in the ego place – this self may have physical sensations that other subpersonalities don't have. The subpersonality may feel itself to be bigger or smaller, more grounded or less so, or it may have more or less physical energy available to it, etc.

231

♦ **Each self expresses through the body in a particular way** – perhaps by making gestures, kicking its feet, falling asleep, speeding up or slowing down the breath.

♦ **The self may be connected to physical movement** either by moving around the room during the session, or by coming out in the subject's life when they are involved in physical activities.

It can be quite amazing to see how physically different our selves can be from each other, nearly startling at times! A person may sit down at the beginning of the session with a headache, a stomachache, even a cold, and then when they* move into a particular self, *the symptoms go away.* Perhaps this particular self just doesn't have a headache or a cold, or perhaps this self doesn't use the part of the body that's been suffering. Sometimes the reverse happens. The person walks in feeling fine, but when they move into a self, physical symptoms suddenly appear. Physical differences between selves that you are likely to observe in a Voice Dialogue session are not usually of the extreme nature found in people with multiple personality disorder, but you may still encounter remarkable differences in the selves' experience of physical reality.

By identifying the physical nature of a self, the facilitator supports the Aware Ego in separating from and being aware of that self. One of the most powerful ways you can enable a person to become aware of their selves is to help them find where each self "lives" in the body. Some selves are so exuberantly physical in their expression that they sprawl on the floor,

> *"One of the most powerful ways you can enable a person to become aware of their selves is to help them find where each self 'lives' in the body."*

stand up and walk or dance around, huddle in a corner, or make great sweeping gestures; and you, as the facilitator, can simply point out these characteristics both to the self and to the Aware Ego. For example, a facilitator might say, "It looks as if you're a part that really likes to use your hands and arms…" The self may agree and feel acknowledged. Or, the self might correct the facilitator and say, "I *use* the arms, but I really feel my energy centered in the shoulders, the arms are swinging around because of me – I'm the power behind them." The facilitator could then go on to ask this self if it "shoulders" responsibilities or other questions that would reveal more about its nature. However the self responds, the body language and physical associations help facilitator and subject learn a lot more about that self.

How a self moves the body will tell you a lot about the nature of its particular energy. In the following example, the facilitator is talking with Farrell's political activist self, a long-standing primary energy for Farrell, who works for an environmental agency.

Facilitator: *(getting physically into the same energy he perceives in Farrell's activist self)* I notice that you really planted your feet firmly on the ground as if you were about to take a solid stand.

Activist self: *(bringing even more energy through the legs as if for emphasis)* That's what I'm all about, taking a stand.

When the facilitator helps a self become aware of its physical posture or gesture, he reinforces the self, and the subpersonality may suddenly realize more about itself than it knew be-

*See "A word about grammar," on p. xix, for an explanation of why plural pronouns are used here to refer to singular subjects.

fore and its energy often comes out more strongly. The facilitator can then build on this response by asking other questions that may expand the awareness of what this self is all about.

Facilitator: It feels to me that you really enjoy using the body, that you *like* having strong legs. Do you also come out during any physical activity in Farrell's life?

Activist self: *(looking surprised and pleased)* Well, yes… you're right. I really like it when we get out in the woods or when we meet people… I *don't* like sitting behind a desk at all! *(suddenly his expression changes, clearly a thought is moving through)* There's another part coming in… well actually, it's sort of like Aware Ego – I just realized something.

Facilitator: That's okay, go ahead and say what you're thinking…

Observing self: Well, I just got why I don't have much energy, much fire, when I'm involved in the office part of my work – my activist is really physical and he doesn't like it there… the "fire goes out."

Facilitator: That is a very important observation… *(he pauses to make sure that the energetic communication lands along with his words, so this simple statement is not at all a perfunctory comment)* I'll make sure we come back to that again when we return to the Aware Ego. If it's okay with you I'd like to continue with the activist for a little longer, in case it has something more to tell us. (Farrell nods agreement) See if you can bring yourself back to that strong energy in the legs… *(as he says this, the facilitator brings his focus back into his own legs, getting back into the feeling of an energy similar to the activist self in his own body – when he can sense that Farrell is back in the energy, he begins to talk to the activist again)* It seems you really are an "activist" – that you like to be *active* in all senses of the word.

By making some simple associations through watching Farrell's physical body and feeling the connection in his own body, Farrell's facilitator has already taken the work deeper than it would go if he had followed a straight mental line of questioning. Because the body is so straightforward and "says" things we might not want to think or say in words, following body language and bringing its message to awareness is an almost guaranteed way to bring out the self more fully and understand more of its nature. As long as you ask questions respectfully, you'll find that the selves are quite willing to talk about their physical experience, and then a whole world of information opens up through paying attention to how each self moves and utilizes the body.

> *"Because the body is so straightforward, following body language and bringing its message to awareness is an almost guaranteed way to bring out the self more fully."*

Your skill in recognizing the specific physical nature of each self will grow as you become more conscious of your own selves and the distinctive ways in which each expresses, both energetically and physically. If a self doesn't give overt clues to its physical whereabouts, don't hesitate to come right out and ask:

> *"Do you have a sense of where you live in the body?*
>
> *"Is there a part of the body that feels like home to you?"*

"What part of the body contains your energy?"

"Do you have a sense of what happens in the body when you're around?"

You can also ask the self how the Aware Ego can find it again – for example:

☆ **A wisdom self** that has a strong, calm feeling in the center of the torso and a deep breath might tell you that the person can find them by sitting quietly and breathing deeply into their center.

☆ **An impersonal part** usually draws energy in closely around itself, pulling in all the "psychic feelers," and it may have a strong, centered body posture as well. A person who is new to impersonal energy may have difficulty maintaining it – if other primary selves such as a pleaser or nurturer come rushing in. You might have them practice calling in the impersonal *just by adopting its posture* and imagining they are pulling their energy in close to the body.

☆ **An adventurer or a warrior energy** may be rooted in the pelvis, legs, and back, and may have a much wider range of movement. Talking with this kind of part, you may find that it used to come out when the person was more physically active, and that physical work or exercise might be a way to bring this energy out more in daily life.

When a self has a message for the person being facilitated, it is essential that the facilitator take care to deliver the self's message to the subject when they are in the Aware Ego place. Receiving a message from an inner self helps the Aware Ego to both separate from and become aware of that self. When the message from the self reveals something about its physical nature, this gives the Aware Ego a concrete and reliable way to access the energy of that self, even if the self is relatively new and unfamiliar. Remember that being in a self is an altered state of consciousness and your help is needed to ground in the information and make it available to the person in their daily life. You may even want to repeat the message, mentioning it first to the subject in the awareness position and again when they return to the Aware Ego.

> *"When the message from the self reveals something about its physical nature, this gives the Aware Ego a concrete and reliable way to access the energy of that self."*

The Aware Ego also lives in the body

Many people not only feel different emotionally in the Aware Ego place, they feel different *physically* as well. When a subject returns to the Aware Ego after being facilitated in a self, one of the most common responses to the facilitator's, "How do you feel?" is an expression of spaciousness and expansion. Once a person has separated from even one self and the Aware Ego process has begun, there is a new openness at the center of their being – the self(ves) is no longer crowding in on them in quite the same way.

Remembering how it feels physically and energetically to be in the Aware Ego place can help the subject return to the Aware Ego. For example, a subject may report that they have more breathing room, can relax more, and that they feel more open in the Aware Ego. In contrast, the selves may have more extreme physical sensations – they may feel constricted, tired, extremely energized, etc. As facilitator you can remind the subject of how they felt in the Aware Ego to help them recenter themselves. If a subject comes up with a particularly strong description of how it feels to them to be in the Aware Ego place, this is a teaching gift. Make a point of remembering their description and referring to it again in their sessions because their own image/association will be stronger for them than any example you could think of.*

As the subject becomes more familiar with what it feels like to be in an Aware Ego, they will also begin to recognize when they are experiencing body sensations that definitely do *not* belong to the Aware Ego. With some guidance from the facilitator, it often does not take long before a subject begins to actually physically feel when one of the selves comes crowding in on the center space of the Aware Ego and starts to take over. The more the subject notices these changes, then the easier it will be for them to develop a facility in shifting their energy intentionally. Part of the work of developing an Aware Ego process is making the Aware Ego place more physically (as well as mentally and emotionally) familiar. *When the subject can identify the feeling of being in an Aware Ego, it will be easier for them to recenter themselves and find their way back to the Aware Ego on their own.*

> *"With some guidance from the facilitator, it often does not take long before a subject begins to actually physically feel when one of the selves comes crowding in on the center space of the Aware Ego and starts to take over."*

Keep your Voice Dialogue "body workout" low pressure and low impact

---

Every facilitation is different and it won't always be appropriate to ask questions about what the self does physically – some sessions won't organically go in that direction. Certain selves are very disconnected from the body and from physical experience. For example, the rational mind, an analyst, or higher consciousness may simply be disinterested, confused, or annoyed if you ask them how they relate to the physical body. Rather than forcing the issue or trying to find a physical/body connection for every energy that emerges, start with the easy and the obvious. With a person who comes in very hyper and short of breath, it's possible to simply ask to speak with the "hyper, short-of-breath" part without having to know any more about who that self is. If another subject moves over into an energy that stretches out sensuously and contentedly on the floor, it's safe to observe that "you seem to really enjoy the body," and ask it about its physical experience. In these and many other facilitating situations, it will feel quite natural and organic to talk about how the self experiences the body. In each of these instances, finding out some specifics about the physical nature and expression of the self will help the Aware Ego to remember and learn.

What should I do if a self doesn't seem to have any physical expression? Some selves really don't have much connection to the physical body, and it's important to discover this about them. This may be especially true of selves that evolved to take a person *out of the body* in traumatic situations. As the person begins to separate from this kind of protective energy and

---

*See p. 185 in "Teaching the Aware Ego to work with energy" for an excellent example of a subject's description of the Aware Ego place.

Your body can help you to "match the energy" of a self...

Your body can be as valuable as your mind in facilitating the selves! At the same time that you are having a verbal conversation with your subject, your body is communicating in an energetic and physical language we commonly call "body language." The body, which is an animal part of ourselves, relaxes or tenses, is comfortable or uncomfortable, based on whether it recognizes someone else's physical communication to be friendly or hostile, supportive or aggressive. Each time a different self is present, the body's response will change. When the facilitator is talking with a businessperson self, he uses body language – posture, focus, rate of talking, etc. – that would put a corporate businessperson at ease. That same body language might be disconcerting for a soft feminine self. In Voice Dialogue work, the facilitator wants all the selves to feel "at home" with him, so that they are relaxed and present and easy about revealing themselves. In order to make this connection, the facilitator has to keep adjusting his own energy to match the energy of each self being facilitated, *and often the easiest way to create this energy match is through developing an awareness of your own body.*

The ability to *feel* in his own body the physical reality of the self he is facilitating helps the facilitator to find and meet the energy of that self. Energy is invisible, but gestures, posture, breathing patterns, movement, tension, relaxation and physical symptoms all give tangible evidence of what kind of subpersonality is present. If you're in touch with your body, pay attention to the movements it makes, follow how it's feeling – it will lead you right where you want to go, automatically, without having to figure it out on a mental level. Start by making sure you are centered and in touch with your own body – feel your body resting on the chair, your feet on the floor, make sure you are grounded. Once you have a clear sense of your own physical being, you can:

➡ **feel where the self is in the subject's body** and direct your inner attention into that part of your own body.

➡ **bring your breathing into rhythm with the self** you're facilitating.

➡ **change your voice tone and rhythm** to be in harmony with theirs.

➡ **shift your body posture** to complement theirs.

➡ **feel which chakra is "home base" for this self** and focus your own energy there.

➡ **extend or withdraw your energy field** to support the self being more present.

A facilitator who can sense the physical and energetic presence of a self can match its energy with his own. The next step after simply noticing physical changes and the shifts in energy that they indicate, is to *intentionally send out a similar energy through both physical expression and the*

236

power of imagination. With a young and vulnerable self, for example, you may drop your attention and energy right down into your belly (your second chakra) or feel a lot of tenderness in the heart area (the fourth chakra). If you intend and imagine sending energy out from these areas, your presence will automatically feel supportive to the vulnerable self – you will both induct and resonate with it. You may also find that you naturally slow down your breathing, and when you talk with the self, your voice will be soft – not "baby talk," but a tone that holds a soft energy. You may automatically change your posture too, not slumping but softening your body language so that it looks and feels safe and supportive. In fact these are probably the normal ways you have always adjusted your body and your energy when being with vulnerable real life children, probably without ever even thinking about it.

Communicating with the power selves can call for a different range of energy and expression. If the facilitator's body language communicates respect (sitting up straight, looking attentive), a power self such as an inner patriarch or critic or protector will feel acknowledged. The facilitator probably wants to keep her voice tone and line of questioning deferential but straightforward, with her energy field extended to match the self so that the respect will be mutual (not too weak and not trying to overpower them either). When you stop to think about it, this is exactly what makes for good relationships with outer patriarchs and protectors in the world. What works with judges, traditional fathers, policemen, corporate heads, etc. will also work with those kind of selves in a Voice Dialogue session. The people who are successful in dealing with these folks are usually other people like them, guys who are part of the same club, *who match their energy.*

By matching the energy of the self, you both welcome and honor it. Working in this way makes it much easier for the self to become fully present because it feels at home, safe, and understood. Remember that Voice Dialogue is a tool for communication and that linkage – staying energetically connected – is what makes this communication alive and rich and intimate. But, before you worry too much about how to go about getting your energy to match each self you facilitate, consider that your body may be way ahead of your thoughts. *Your body may have already sensed the changes in the energy and may start to feel and move in response to the new self you're facilitating before you even have time to plan or strategize.* This is a natural thing for our bodies to do if we let them, if we step out of the way. Our bodies are naturally receptive to energy, and it's important to remember that we've all had a lifetime of experience in reading other people's energy in order to survive and function in the world. Matching energies with a self is not nearly as much of a challenge as it may at first appear. By paying attention to changes and responses in your own body, you may find that you are able to access the kind of energy you want as easily as your mind thinks of the next question to ask, and you'll find your skill in facilitation growing organically without a great deal of conscious effort.

develop an Aware Ego process in relation to it, the way will be opened to reconnect more positively with the body again while still honoring the primary self that has been protecting the person's vulnerability from a lifetime of negative physical experiences.

The subject's energy also resonates in the facilitator's body

Besides listening to the person you are facilitating you can also pay attention inside yourself to see what shows up in *your* body, what changes in *your* feelings (emotional and physical) while you are with them. Just as you observe and sense the subject's body language, check your own physical reality as well – how does your body respond to this person's energy? What do you notice in your body when the subject first sits down to talk, and is there a change later when you facilitate a self? When the subject moves through an energetic shift, can you perceive a matching shift in your own energy? Or, if you think you are speaking with one self but your physical feeling seems contrary to what you would expect of that subpersonality, your body may be telling you that another energy is coming in.

How can I be sure that I'm perceiving these physical sensations through my Aware Ego? What if I'm really feeling one of my own selves reacting to the subject's energy? These are important questions because as facilitators we always want to center ourselves and work from the Aware Ego as much as possible. And, of course, the facilitator has to be aware of pre-existing physical feelings and take those into account as well. However, we're not talking here about taking *action* based on your physical sensations – we're just recommending that you add *paying attention* to physical feelings to the ways that you usually observe what is going on in a session. As you

"Your own body can be an amazingly accurate instrument of energetic perception. Sensing your body's responses to the subject's change in energy can significantly deepen and simplify the work of facilitation."

separate more and more from your own inner selves and as you practice facilitating others, you will naturally become more aware of when you are *responding* to a subject's energy versus when one of your selves has come out in reaction to it. Working with your physical awareness is well worth some attention and effort because your own body can be an amazingly accurate instrument of energetic perception. When you can sense your own body responses to the subject's change in energy, you can significantly deepen and simplify the work of facilitation. See if you notice any of the following (or similar) changes in yourself when you are facilitating – each of these observations can be a guide to help direct the work.

☆ Does the space between you and the person you are facilitating feel empty or full? Can your body feel a change in the energy between you?

☆ Are you suddenly tired? Energized?

☆ Do your shoulders tighten or relax?

☆ Is there pain anywhere in your body? Headache? Stomachache?

☆ Do you feel compelled to sit up straighter or to slump?

✮ Do you feel tense all of a sudden? Irritated? Anxious? Sad?

✮ How about the opposite? Feeling light? Easy? Laughing? Relaxed?

✮ Is there a sensual and/or sexual vibration that you feel with this self?

Your own body awareness is a key to enhancing your energetic understanding of the selves that you are facilitating, so it's important to start with an inventory of your own energy before beginning facilitation. When the facilitator notices her own shifts in physical and emotional feeling, she will be more open to the selves, more able to match their energy and will very likely ask more intuitive questions. The facilitator needs to notice if she is coming in to the session with "pre-existing conditions" such as a headache, or feeling anxious, or being turned on (or turned off), or feeling giddy, etc. *Only by being aware of her energetic starting point, will the facilitator be able to evaluate whether her own physical reactions during the session are revealing anything about the energies being facilitated.*

When you open yourself to feeling the subject's energetic changes in your own body (and through your Aware Ego), there is a natural empathy and the linkage deepens. Now the energy is affecting both of you, and it may be startling to notice how accurately you can pinpoint the physical location of a self just by feeling its reverberation in your body. In a very real sense the facilitator now has physical "evidence" within herself that may indicate even more about the subpersonality than it knows about itself.   The facilitator may say something quite simple like "I can tell you must really be tired – I can *feel* it!" Or, with a self that is feeling sad, the sense of the self's location in the body might be quite precise:

Facilitator: Where do you feel yourself to be in the body?

Sad self: *(pointing to the throat where there is probably grief lumped up inside)*

Facilitator: *(already feeling the energy of this self deeper down in the heart area as well as the throat)* I have a sense of you down in the heart area too… *(patting the center of her chest)* It feels kind of achy in there to me.

Remarkably, many subpersonalities don't seem to be puzzled or disturbed to hear a facilitator say to them that she can feel something in her own body that is connected to what they are feeling. If a self tells you that it can feel its energy in the subject's shoulders, check to see what you're feeling in your own body. You may report back that you can feel an energy like that in *your* shoulders too. In fact, you may be able to feel the energy all the way down the arms and in the upper back as well. When you are able to simply report this kind of observation from a neutral Aware Ego place, it is unlikely that the self you are working with will be confused or taken aback by your being able to feel something similar to what it is feeling. In-stead, the self will probably check it out. If it's true that this energy is in more of the upper body than it noticed at first, then you have helped it to become more fully present, more filled out in its own territory, than it was at first. This not only enhances awareness of the particular self, but also *for many people this may be the first time that they become aware of their own energetic expression*

"For many people this may be the first time that they become aware of their own energetic expression and how it is received by another person – quite a revelation!"

239

and how it is received by another person – quite a revelation! And, there is no need for you to worry about making a "mistake." If you are off the mark in your observations, all that is likely to happen is that the self comes back and says something like "No, I really don't feel that," and then you can excuse yourself, let it go, and move on.

If you are a person who is used to being physically sensitive, observations about the body may come very easily to you. Almost as an afterthought, you'll realize you've been feeling things like this all along and just never stopped to think about it. For others, especially people who usually take a more mental, analytical approach, it may feel overwhelming at first to pay attention to so many unfamiliar details. Try working with this *a little bit at a time,* so that you pace the learning process (perhaps giving yourself a single assignment for a session or a day or a week). Here are some sample assignments to work with and you may want to come up with some of your own as well.

➥ **Practice observing yourself before the session starts,** before the person you are going to facilitate arrives. How are you feeling physically? emotionally? Have you been more in your mind and not feeling at all? What is your breathing like? How fast? How slow? Notice any tension you may feel and where it's located – does the tension belong to a particular self in you? Now, when the person you are going to facilitate walks in the door, you'll be "warmed up and ready to go," and since you're more aware of how you're feeling at the start of the session, you'll be able to notice when the way you feel changes.

➥ **Try making it a habit for a while to actively notice how your body feels** each time a person you are facilitating moves from the ego to a self and back again. *Maybe there will be a change, maybe there won't, and paying attention will make you more aware.* When you talk with someone's perfectionist, does the energy seem to move into their upper body? Do they hunch their shoulders a bit and do you feel a tension in your shoulders? Is there a tightness in your breathing at the same time? And later in the session, when they move into a self that doesn't want to work so hard and doesn't care what the boss thinks, do you feel an expansion in your chest or is there a feeling of energy moving in your solar plexus? How does their posture, breathing, and body language create change in you?

➥ **When it's natural and appropriate, utilize gestures similar to those the self makes** – not to mimic, but to confirm your understanding of the self and to reflect to it what part of the personality it is. For example, you might comment, "You're the part that sighed so deeply when you talked about missing the place you used to live," and then quietly sigh and move in a way that reflects the way that self gestured. The self will know that you've really aligned with its energy, and *you'll feel that energy in your own body.* With a different type of subpersonality, say an inner patriarch, you might very naturally use body language that both matches and shows respect toward the self – sitting up straight and proper (and perhaps female facilitators not crossing their legs!). In this instance, you probably wouldn't make a comment to an inner patriarch about gesture or posture, but your body language would communicate respect.

The more you work with facilitation, the easier it becomes to recognize the energetic nature of each individual self. *The process of learning to facilitate is one of becoming conscious of energy shifts,* and then, once we get good at facilitation, we're able to work with energetic, non-verbal communication naturally and without having to think about it. Think of learning to drive a car. When you first start to drive, you have to pay attention to every little detail, your feet on the pedals, hands on the wheel, turning signals on and off – driving seems almost overwhelmingly complex. Once you are adept at driving, your focus becomes automatic and you are able to just concentrate on the "road," on the world out there, on the conversation with your passengers. Learning to drive the "vehicle" of Voice Dialogue facilitation is very similar. Expanding your attention to include body language as well as verbal language and creating new habits of awareness are simply some of the new skills you have to integrate in order to be free to enjoy the journey.

The most important way to support your development as a facilitator is to take the opportunity to be facilitated as much as possible – i.e. follow the first ground rule for facilitators. As we have noted before, being facilitated is essential in order to internalize the Voice Dialogue process and to truly understand the living dynamics of the selves and the development of the Aware Ego. At the end of *The Handbook,* there is a "Work list for the facilitator" which suggests some of the primary selves and pairs of opposites you might want to work with in your own sessions in order to become more adept at facilitating others. The more you develop your own Aware Ego process, the easier, more natural, and more enjoyable you'll find facilitating others. So definitely indulge in as much Voice Dialogue facilitation for yourself as possible! It's a gift to yourself and to the people you facilitate.

"I discovered the courage to pause." Paul Eddington, British actor

Silence —
a key to getting good at energetics

If you are tuned in energetically there really aren't any silences. This is one of the most amazing realizations in doing Voice Dialogue work. It touches on the mystery of all intimacy. If you are energetically linked with another person, you can be together for hours in silence and experience a great deal of "communication," or perhaps it would be better called "communion." The absence of verbal communication removes one layer, but it does not leave an empty space. In fact, sometimes you can feel the energy all the more strongly in silence in the same way that you might hear music better with your eyes closed.

In Voice Dialogue facilitation, silence can truly be golden. Western culture doesn't really allow for much silence – it's considered rude to just sit there and not say anything. It's perfectly acceptable, though, to talk for hours and never give a conscious thought to the energetic exchange that occurs along with the verbal conversation. Voice Dialogue work is completely the opposite of this. In facilitation, what does not work is to stop paying attention to the non-verbal exchange. Silence, however, *within a context of energetic connection*, is not only okay but often very helpful, providing an opportunity for the self being facilitated to emerge more strongly. *Allowing yourself silent pauses as a facilitator gives you a chance to feel more deeply into the energy and provides a space for the subpersonality to fill with more information about itself.*

There are a number of ways in which silence can enhance Voice Dialogue work. It's a relief as a facilitator to realize that you don't have to fill every space that opens up in the conversation with an insightful thought or brilliant new direction. Your job is to *follow* the subject's energy, watch their body language, observe how each self opens up naturally. As long as you keep the *energetic* communication going, you will find appropriate places to relax in silence. You can actually wait and see what happens next because it's not your job to *make* it happen. *Developing a working relationship with silence not only gives the selves you're facilitating more room, it makes the job of facilitation easier, opening further access to intuition and guidance.* It's easier to pay attention to your gut reaction and intuition (that "still small voice"), and to your own physical responses, if you allow yourself time in silence to listen inside for these cues. Here are just a few of the possible results of consciously allowing for silence while maintaining energetic connection:

> *"Allowing yourself silent pauses as a facilitator gives you a chance to feel more deeply into the energy and provides a space for the subpersonality to fill with more information about itself."*

- ♦ **The energy of the self may solidify and become stronger** – some of the more vulnerable, more "being" selves are less verbal and need energetic space. They may have a hard time coming in fully if there is a lot of talking.

- ♦ **An opening will be created** for the subpersonality to express itself on a deeper level – memories surface, realizations click into place.

- **Linkage between facilitator and subject can often deepen** when they remain in silence in the Aware Ego place. (As long as the primary selves are comfortable, it may even work to sit a few moments in silence before beginning the session so that you have time to settle into the energetic linkage right from the start.)

- **The facilitator has the additional time and space to slow down and be receptive** to her own intuition and tune in to the subject. Sometimes, in that fertile silence, the facilitator may get a "hit" or hunch to ask about dreams, to follow an image, to pick up on a phrase that a self said – something she might miss if she were too involved in talking or in trying to figure out where to go next.

- **It becomes easier for both subject and facilitator to separate from the mind,** since the mind tends to be very verbal.

- **Both facilitator and subject learn "energetic manners,"** refraining from interrupting the energetic "conversation."

- **The facilitator models the Aware Ego's ability** to hold an energetically open space, allowing information to emerge from a new source.

The "art" of facilitation often develops in the creative emptiness of silence. As we have indicated above, sometimes just being still and allowing silence offers the self you are facilitating an opportunity to emerge more fully, the way a deer or a rabbit might come close to you if you sit peacefully and wait. Suddenly the self will say something more than what you asked or expected – a hidden part of the person you're facilitating will reveal itself, a memory will surface, a realization will have time to form. This is a "magical" aspect to the Voice Dialogue process that a facilitator can allow for but not intentionally create. The feeling is very much like working in any artistic medium – watercolor, stone, etc. – where part of what happens is the result of what you do and part is the nature of the medium you are working with. The magic is the "happy accident," the creative interface where intention and mystery meet.

Working with silence – examples and discussion

Let's look first at facilitating Andrea. The facilitator is talking with a self in Andrea that is her "female intuition self," the one who knew right away that Andrea's last boyfriend "would be a loser." Try reading these two different approaches *out loud* to yourself and note how each one feels to you energetically.

Andrea – first example:

Female intuition: I can *smell* them when they're up to no good. I get the vibe right away. I could save her a lot of time! I'd cross most of them off the list before they ever got on it.

Facilitator: So you really can tell right away when a man Andrea meets isn't going to be a worthwhile prospect.

Female intuition: Absolutely.

244

Andrea – second example:

Female intuition: I can *smell* them when they're up to no good. I get the vibe right away. I could save her a lot of time! I'd cross most of them off the list before they ever got on it.

Facilitator: *(doesn't speak – just sits quietly observing and matching the energy of this self)*

Female intuition: *(after a few moments of silence, starts talking some more)* I really want to help Andrea find somebody wonderful instead of just protecting her from making the wrong choices over and over again.

Facilitator: How would you help her?

Female intuition: She needs to relax more, be more magnetic, allow someone to come to her.

Facilitator: Are you a part of her who could help her do that?

Female Intuition: I can help her when she's not hyper – she's so frantic about having a relationship.

Facilitator: There must be another part of Andrea who feels really desperate.

Questions

How did these two facilitations feel energetically different to you?

What would it take to get the conversation going again at the end of the first example? What emerges out of the silence in the second example?

How do the questions in these two facilitations feel different from each other and do they yield different information?

Which of these two approaches feels more appealing to you? More familiar?

Discussion

The first facilitator painted herself into a corner by asking questions that led to yes or no answers rather than to expanding the conversation. To continue, she will have to restart the conversation and think of more things to ask, and this makes the process more work for the facilitator and more difficult for the subject to go deeper into the energy of the self. And, even though the facilitator may be very intuitive, she might not think to ask questions that would elicit the kind of important personal information that emerges so easily and organically from the self in the second example. By remaining silent and waiting, the facilitator in the second example leaves an opening for the self to talk. There's no guarantee that the self will say anything significant, but there's also nothing to be lost by allowing the space for it to open up and talk more (as long as the facilitator keeps the energetic connection).

The facilitator's questions in the second example express ordinary curiosity about the female intuitive self and a desire to know it better. This is a more comfortable conversational approach in contrast to the first facilitator's use of a therapeutic method in which she paraphrases what the self said and reflects it back. For those of us who have been trained in various therapeutic approaches, it's easy to forget that a subpersonality <u>is not a person who has agreed to do therapy.</u> Methods that may work great for therapy can fall really flat in talking with selves, and a good rule to go by is "If it doesn't work well in a conversation with friends, it probably won't go very far in a dialogue with a self." It isn't necessary for the facilitator to second guess the self or keep figuring out really great questions to ask. Instead the facilitator's job is to connect with the self energetically and let it lead the conversation. Following the self's lead naturally takes you to the deepest part of the story.

Let's look at another example of working with silence. Bert is a consultant to large organizations and corporations, and the facilitator is talking with the part of Bert that jumps in (for better or worse) to try and resolve interpersonal difficulties in the groups he leads. In the last program he led, this part (called "Bert's fixer") intervened inappropriately... with embarrassing results:

Facilitator: Sounds as if you really feel compelled to jump in and resolve things.

Bert's fixer: That's true, I really do. I can't stand to sit and watch people in conflict with each other when I have all the tools to help them work it out.

Facilitator: What tools do you use?

Bert's fixer: Oh, I've done tons of training and read all the literature. I understand the dynamics, and if I can get people to do the work, then it goes along really well. Sometimes it works better than others... *(sighing and slumping a bit)* The other day didn't work out so great.

Facilitator: What do you feel went wrong?

Bert's fixer: I'm not really sure what went wrong. It's not the first time somebody's gotten upset and left a group Bert was leading. I don't really know how to do anything different from what I've learned, and in this case it didn't work.

Facilitator: Sounds as if Bert might need some other part of himself to come in and help you out.

Bert's fixer: *(energy brightening a bit)* That would be great... if there is one. I feel like I'm always on my own.

There's nothing "wrong" with any of the facilitator's questions – they are all good and very useful questions that will lead to an understanding of how this self operates. When Bert comes back to the Aware Ego, he will be able to separate from this self with probably some new awareness about how the self functions in his life. Plus, the facilitator and Bert will most likely find another self to facilitate that will give insight and support for Bert's work in the future. However, even though this certainly is a viable facilitation, it may feel a little flat because a dimension of depth in communication is missing. Here's a different facilitator working with Bert:

Facilitator: Sounds as if you really feel compelled to jump in and resolve things.

Bert's fixer: That's true, I really do. I can't stand to sit and watch people in conflict with each other when I have all the tools to help them work it out.

Facilitator: *(doesn't say anything, but instead listens to Bert's fixer, getting a sense of this self's energy... the facilitator notices a tension from his own solar plexus up to the center of his chest and he thinks to himself, "there's something off here, something that doesn't figure about this self")*

Bert's fixer: *(kind of folding his body forward in the chair)* I could see everybody in the whole room being so uncomfortable with this one person in the group...

Facilitator: *(the facilitator is still listening silently – he has been asking inside his own head, "Where does this need to go?" and he hears a really clear response, "Ask this part how old it is." – making sure his energy stays connected to Bert's fixer self, he speaks gently and directly with an open tone of pure curiosity)* How old are you?

Bert's fixer: *(looking startled but not offended, and then reflective)* Seven.

Facilitator: I had a feeling you weren't very old – you've got a huge job for such a young person!

Bert's fixer: *(looking relieved to be recognized)* Yeah, I guess I do.

Facilitator: *(extending energy from his heart center, speaking softly)* Have you been trying to jump in and fix things between people since Bert was seven?

Bert's fixer: *(somehow seeming smaller with the far off look of remembering)* I guess I have... That's when his parents got divorced... *(his eyes half fill with tears)* It didn't really work then either.

Facilitator: It's a lot for a seven-year-old kid to have to do. Maybe now that Bert is more aware of you, he can learn to take care of *you* more and not have you out there doing such a big job.

Questions

How does the energy in each of these facilitations feel to you? What's your sense of the linkage between Bert and his facilitator?

Have you had moments like this facilitating where you just asked inside what to do next? How did that work out?

Facilitating isn't a ping pong match, so you don't have to always bat the ball back to the other side. This leaves room for a great deal of internal listening. Try experimenting with simply asking questions inside yourself such as "What's going on here?" "What am I missing?" "Where would be the best place to go next?" "What does this self most need to be asked?" See what kind of response comes and how it helps or hinders the work.

Some further guidelines on working with silence

Silence is most effective in facilitation when we use it appropriately and organically, and it can backfire if the facilitator tries to impose it in the session. Here are some examples of when trying to work with silence might *not* be desirable in a Voice Dialogue session.

- ◆ **It isn't wise to try to get a self to be silent if that's not its nature.** The facilitator never wants to make a subpersonality feel that it's talking too much.

- ◆ **If you are facilitating a mental/intellectual self,** expect to be engaged in a fast-paced and/or idea-rich conversation and be ready to match that energy.

- ◆ **Some selves are very uncomfortable if the facilitator remains silent for very long** – the pleaser, for example, is very concerned about "getting it right" or being judged, and it thrives on responsiveness from others.

- ◆ **If the facilitator is not comfortable with his own silenc**e and/ or not yet familiar with how to access the rich non-verbal communication that occurs in that silence.

- ◆ **If there is no energetic linkage between facilitator and subject,** silence, whether the subject is in a self or in the Aware Ego, will feel like a big blank space rather than a rich matrix out of which new awareness can emerge.

- ◆ **If the facilitator tries to use silence as a facilitation *strategy*** (rather than just being silent when it feels natural), many feeling selves will feel manipulated by and distrustful of this approach. This is a clear indication to the facilitator that he is "in voice" rather than in his own Aware Ego, and that the linkage with the subject has been broken.

What is most important is to learn to use silence effectively on *your* end of the facilitation rather than attempting to change a subject's relationship to silence. Probably the most useful guideline is to realize that *if you are facilitating from your Aware Ego, you will be equally*

> *"If you are facilitating from your Aware Ego, you will be equally comfortable with talking and with silence because the Aware Ego can hold these opposites in balance."*

comfortable with talking and with silence because the Aware Ego can hold these opposites in balance. If you find yourself feeling uncomfortable with silence, you may very well be experiencing a primary self of your own that worries you are not doing enough to move the facilitation forward and get the "right" results. Your best strategy is to "know your selves." If you've always been identified with very verbal parts of yourself, then you want to be particu-

Silence in the awareness position...

If you think of silence as a way to allow "breathing space" and to make room for energetic perception, you'll immediately understand how it can be very useful in working with the awareness position. Remember that even though the facilitator may go over some of what each self had to say, the awareness position is not a mental review of the facilitation. Rather, the facilitator wants to encourage the subject to feel/sense the different energies of the selves that have been facilitated during the session. If the facilitator keeps on talking because she is not at ease with silence, it can be difficult for the subject to get in touch with other more subtle levels of perception – hearing the facilitator's voice without any silent space to absorb and assimilate information may draw the subject out of the awareness state and put them right back into a verbal/thinking place.

As you work with the awareness position, experiment with leaving room for silence right after you first instruct the subject to look at a particular self. If you have told your subject to spend time perceiving the energy of a self, you may want to try following your own instructions, feeling into the energy along with the subject, getting a sense of the self's tone, how much space it takes up, whether it's expansive, contracted, light, dark, etc. Chances are by the time you're done, the subject will be finished too, and you can move on before they can drift into analysis or other distractions. At this point you can turn to the person in the awareness position and say something like, "Do you have a sense of this self?" or "Do you have a feeling for this energy now?" Usually people are pretty good about saying, "No, I'm not done yet," or "Yes, I have a sense of it." This question is also good because it creates an opening. If the person is having trouble with the awareness position they will indicate it to you at this point – for example, "I'm not really clear about what I'm looking at..." "I feel confused about this self, I'm not sure I can sense anything about it..."

larly careful when you "match" the energy of a very talkative self, that you do this *by bringing in that energy through your own Aware Ego.* This way you won't get caught up in a very talkative subpersonality. And, the opposite is true as well. If the part you are facilitating is very non-verbal, *you want to hold that being energy through your own Aware Ego* and not drift off into a super relaxed state with it. The Aware Ego can evaluate the whole picture, so that when you work with the energies of the selves through the Aware Ego, you will have a much clearer sense of when to speak and when to allow for silence.*

Often it really pays to just hang out with a self *after* **most of the information you were expecting has already spilled out.** If you allow a little silent, "empty" space at the end, the self may surprise you with an additional comment that either takes the work much deeper or indicates the next direction to go. *You may find that some of the most revealing comments, even with an intellectual self, will be expressed spontaneously when you hold the energy and wait in silence for whatever the self will say or do next.* And, if a talkative self you have been listening to suddenly falls uncharacteristically silent and there is no comment forthcoming, it may be a strong indication that another part has come in, that you're dealing with a new energy. It's so much easier to

*See the chapter on "Learning to access the selves through the Aware Ego" on p. 265 for an in-depth discussion of bringing different energies in through the Aware Ego.

notice that kind of shift when you don't have to be really busy thinking of how to immediately fill each natural silence with some question or remark.

Silence doesn't have to be long to be effective. The ability to stop and hold stillness for even just a moment can give the facilitator the leverage she needs to guide the flow of words and take the work deeper. This can be especially important in working with a very verbal sub-personality where lots of rapid talking may actually be a long-time protective device, a way to steer clear of conflict and emotions. (Remember that the mind, for example, works much more quickly than the rest of our faculties – the mind can come up with a whole conversation while our feelings are still struggling to reach the surface.) As facilitator, you don't want to *stop* a mental energy from talking or make it feel unacceptable, but it's certainly okay to *create a moment's pause*, even right in the middle of an outpouring of information from the self, and guide the conversation in a direction that may yield a more significant level of revelation that the Aware Ego can use in separating from the self. Here is a facilitator talking with Warren's very active mind:

"You may find that some of the most revealing comments will be expressed spontaneously when you hold the energy and wait in silence for whatever the self will say or do next."

> **Warren's mind:** I keep going all the time, all the time. I read books, I read magazines, I keep him awake at night going over information from the office – sometimes he wakes up in the middle of the night and I start going again, say from 3 to 4 am. *(This part is obviously very pleased with itself and speaks very rapidly with a voice that seems to be coming from high up in the body – the facilitator feels almost out of breath just listening to this self)* I write his e-mail, I just love e-mail. It's so quick!
>
> **Facilitator:** Well, you certainly have a lot of energy… *(the facilitator's tone is enthusiastic but also firm and peaceful – if Warren's mind feels energetically like it's spinning out on the rim of a wheel, the facilitator is holding the same energy at the hub of the wheel where there is stillness and nothing is moving)* Let me stop you there for just a moment. I think I'm getting a very good sense of the kind of things you do and enjoy, and I'm wondering how long you've played such an important role in Warren's life? What do you remember doing when he was younger?

The facilitator takes the conversation in a direction that will yield more in-depth information about the self. She can interrupt the self without upsetting it because she is appreciative of what it does in Warren's life and she is energetically in sync with it. As the facilitator learns more about this self's history, there will be more of a chance to find out how and why the mind became so active. As facilitators we need to constantly assess the value and depth of the information coming through and *ask questions that will disclose not only the self's opinions but the motivation behind those opinions and the way each self uses its information and skills in the subject's life.*

Both facilitator and subject may be amazed by the answers that come out of a willingness to stop and listen, even for just a moment. The facilitator who settles in, waits a bit, doesn't push with too many questions, allows moments of silence while keeping an energetic connection with the subject, will find that she has a tremendous amount of support coming from intuition and the Unconscious. It will seem that the self opens up easily, and just the right questions come to mind. In fact, it often feels as if the whole session has its own natural flow, like moving gently with the currents down a river. The facilitator not only receives inner support for herself, but also demonstrates clearly and powerfully for the subject what it is like to function from the Aware Ego place and not be constantly pushed and pulled around by the ongoing needs and concerns of the primary selves.

When the facilitator pauses in silence and waits for information in a session, this models an important way in which an evolved Aware Ego process functions in our lives. When you wait and listen inwardly for direction, you not only access a wider range of information, you teach the people you facilitate to wait and listen inwardly as well. As you balance *doing* facilitation with an ability to *be* with the subject and *be* with the process, both you and the subject will find that it becomes easier to access an Aware Ego – an Aware Ego that is separate from, but connected to, the opposite energies of doing and being, of talking and silence. This can lead to quite far-reaching results in the subject's life because the Aware Ego not only develops between opposites but is able, as the Stones say, to "stay with the tension of those opposites until the solution comes from another place."

> *"The facilitator who allows moments of silence while keeping an energetic connection with the subject, will find that she has a tremendous amount of support coming from intuition and the Unconscious."*

An Aware Ego can act in ways that the primary selves would not be able to imagine, as the subject begins to move into a freer and more balanced Aware Ego consciousness. It's important to remember, however, that for most of us the Aware Ego is still just beginning to develop and we do the greatest part of our living out of the operating ego. It is wonderful if we actually have an Aware Ego that can step in when a business deal is threatened or a child is in danger or when we get lost traveling in the Amazon – the Aware Ego can make some very innovative and effective choices in situations like these. But, if we're in an intense situation and our Aware Ego process isn't *already in place,* we're quite grateful to have the primary selves kick in and take action to help us and our loved ones survive. There is time enough to worry about separating from those primary selves and balancing between opposites when we're not in crisis.

The primary selves, however, tend to live *all* of life as if it were a crisis! The primary selves usually want to resolve any tension as quickly as possible and will settle for familiar answers and safe decisions just to get disturbing questions out of the way. *In contrast, the Aware Ego recognizes the needs of all the selves but is able to hold steady and outwait their "clamoring" for quick solutions.* The Aware Ego can act on the spot when this is appropriate, and it can also make time to sleep/dream on a question before taking action, even in situations where the primary selves would see no possibility of doing that. The Aware Ego listens to both intuition and logic, examines what the Unconscious brings, and reads when "the energy feels right." In this way the evolution of an Aware Ego in a person's life brings new wisdom

> *"The primary selves will settle for familiar answers and safe decisions just to get disturbing questions out of the way. In contrast, the Aware Ego recognizes the needs of all the selves but is able to hold steady and outwait their 'clamoring' for quick solutions."*

and balance into their decision-making process. In doing Voice Dialogue facilitation with people, your ability to pause and to hold even a moment's silence, models an Aware Ego approach to life and helps to train the subject in this new, centered way of acting and being.

"When working with dreams, what you are looking for is the dance of the selves," the Stones

Beginning to work with dreams in Voice Dialogue

Many facilitators find working with dreams one of the most exciting aspects of Voice Dialogue. As a person starts to separate from the primary selves and opens up to new energies in their life, the Unconscious often sends remarkable dreams that both guide and confirm the process. One of the ways that we know the Aware Ego is unfolding in a person's life is by energetic shifts in the dream landscape, the exploration of new territory and the appearance of new personae in their dreams. For the facilitator who has developed a basic familiarity with the symbolic language of dreams, looking at dreams in relation to the Voice Dialogue work can add inspiration, imagination and depth while actually making the job of facilitating easier.

Dreams also indicate a person's inner readiness to approach specific issues in their life – they let us know where it's safe to go next in the work. For example, one of the ways you might be able to tell it's the right time to begin focusing on vulnerability would be when the subject's dreams show images of babies or children that have been forgotten or are needing to be nurtured, cared for, or unearthed. Dreams tell us in symbolic language the "soul's agenda," the direction the Unconscious feels we need to focus our attention. Because of this, dreams can be deeply helpful to the facilitation and the ongoing development of the Aware Ego. Though not everyone you facilitate will remember dreams or want to work with them (and it's important not to make anyone feel that they *should* work with dreams), those who do will find that looking at their dreams, connecting with the energy of dream elements, and facilitating dream selves, can be both revelatory and open a direct

"As a person starts to separate from the primary selves and opens up to new energies in their life, the Unconscious often sends remarkable dreams that both guide and confirm the process."

path into current "hot" issues in their lives. And, as a facilitator, you can rely on the "dream maker" (one name for the aspect of the Unconscious that creates our dreams) as an ancient and wise mentor – you can follow its lead and let it guide the work.

There are some facilitators who use dream facilitation as the core of their work with the selves. Many other facilitators do very successful Voice Dialogue work without incorporating very many dreams at all and tend to attract clients who do not dream very much or are not as interested in working with the dream material. Between these two ends of a spectrum lies a full range of possibilities for working with the energies, images, and people of the dream world. As with most aspects of Voice Dialogue facilitation, you will probably attract active dreamers to work with you *if you yourself are involved in understanding your own dream process and are interested in expanding your comprehension of dreams.*

Doing Voice Dialogue work often stimulates the dream process, so it is important for every facilitator to develop *some* level of fluency in the language of dreams. Facilitation "stirs the pot" of the Unconscious, and sometimes people who rarely remember dreaming have

"Because dreams are multi-dimensional, even different and contradictory interpretations can be equally valid."

quite vivid and significant dreams after beginning facilitation. So even though you don't need to specialize in dreams, it's a great help if you are ready and able to do at least some basic work with them when the occasion calls for it. With that in mind, we'll look at some of the fundamentals in approaching dream material through the Voice Dialogue method. Please remember, however, that it isn't within the scope of *The Handbook* to engage in an in-depth discussion of all the different kinds of dreams people have and what their dream images may mean. To be most successful in working with dreams in the Voice Dialogue process, it is best that the facilitator begin by looking at his own dreams and have his own dream selves facilitated. If you are attracted to working with dreams, there is a lot of fascinating literature for further study. You may also want to honor and study your dreams by keeping a dream journal, and you may be drawn to work with dreamlike therapeutic tools such as guided imagery and sand tray. In addition there are many opportunities worldwide to attend workshops led by teachers who are skilled at working with the dream process.

A Voice Dialogue approach to dreams

Around the world and through the ages peoples of all cultures and beliefs have honored dreams and used their understanding of dreams for everything from prophecy to spiritual guidance to political decision-making to personal growth. Dreams are rooted so profoundly in our human consciousness that they easily touch all the layers of our lives and accommodate themselves to multiple usage. Looking at a dream from one perspective doesn't rule out looking at it from any other perspective. Because dreams are multidimensional, *even different and contradictory interpretations can be equally valid.* The more one explores the territory of dreams, the more one comes to understand the advantages and disadvantages of different ways of working with the dream material. Using Voice Dialogue facilitation with dream energies is a very effective way of retrieving the gifts that a dream brings, especially in helping us to see more clearly what we are over-identified with and/or what we have disowned.

The first step in listening to dreams from a Voice Dialogue perspective is to look for the opposites – opposite primary selves as well as opposite disowned and primary selves.

"The Unconscious, through the dream, lays out a challenge to the dreamer to begin to separate from their own primary selves and to learn to embrace the selves they have disowned."

Dreams often clearly show the interplay of opposites in a person's life. This may be very simple and direct. Perhaps a family member the dreamer doesn't get along with or someone else they don't like shows up in the dream, and through the appearance of this disowned self it becomes very clear where the dreamer is identified and which primary self is upset by the appearance of its opposite. Then the focus of the Voice Dialogue session is to begin working with *the primary self* as it relates to both dreaming and waking life. In essence, the Unconscious, through the dream, lays out a challenge to the dreamer

254

to begin to separate from their own primary selves and to learn to embrace the selves they have disowned. The dreams encourage us to find balance. *Our purpose in working with dream selves is the same as it is with waking selves – to consistently and creatively enhance the Aware Ego process.* In looking for the opposites in a dream you'll want to pay attention to:

♦ **any explicitly polarized elements** – people, courses of action, choices to make, etc. that seem to be in obvious opposition to each other.

♦ **problems, adversaries, threats** that may indicate disowned energies.

♦ **contrasting personalities** such as people in the dream who are very different from each other or different from the dreamer. Just as in waking life, knowing what kind of people the subject dislikes in a dream will tell you a lot about their primary and disowned selves.

♦ **odd juxtapositions and incongruities,** in everything from people to places to vehicles to behavior, can be indications that the Unconscious is pointing out opposites inside the personality.

♦ **anything that upsets the dreamer,** that causes fear, embarrassment, anger, discomfort, will give you clues about where they are identified and what they have disowned.

♦ **whether the subject appears in their own dream,** what they do in the dream, and how they feel about what happens in the dream. When a person appears in their own dream, the self they are in the dream is called the "dream ego." The nature of this dream ego shows the dreamer's relationship to the story of the dream, and it also indicates where the dreamer is identified in waking life in relation to the issues that the dream brings to light. For example, if I dream that a desperately poor family moves in next door to me and I try to help take care of them, one interpretation of my dream ego might be that I'm identified with the caretaking part of myself. Given that caretakers often look out for others at the expense of their own needs, the needy family might represent parts of myself that are not getting any nurturance. Or, since I disown being needy and receiving help, another interpretation might say that a whole family of these disowned selves is moving in next door in my dream to help me see the opposites in myself.

To work with the dream material, the facilitator can actually ask the subject to move over into one of the dream selves, or he can simply take a hint from the dream and focus on the same issue without actually working directly with any dream characters. If you decide to do "dream dialogue" and facilitate a self from the dream, the same rules apply that you would follow for facilitating any other selves. Make sure that you respect the concerns and limitations of the primary selves and don't begin by facilitating parts of the dream that are frightening or threatening to them. You may find that some dream selves seem to be messengers from the subject's unconscious and are confined to the context of the dream. Other energies spill out over the edges of the dream story and begin to talk about the subject's waking life as well. These

> *"If you decide to do 'dream dialogue' and facilitate a self from the dream, the same rules apply that you would follow for facilitating any other selves."*

selves that bridge both waking and dreaming reality often have very interesting perspectives on what is going on in the subject's life and process. You may find, too, that the dreams bring up issues that might be difficult to approach directly in waking life. Even if some of the disowned energies in the dream are too uncomfortable for the primary selves to deal with head on, you can talk about the different parts of the dream when the subject is in the Aware Ego and use the information to build a more detailed and accurate map of the selves.

Dreams serve as an excellent guide for both facilitator and subject, telling us what the inner priorities are and where to focus the work. Paying attention to issues as they arise in the dream life can prevent the necessity of acting out those issues at a considerable cost

"Paying attention to issues as they arise in the dream life can prevent the necessity of acting out those issues at a considerable cost in waking life."

in waking life. For example, Sharon, a high-powered, workaholic businesswoman has a dream about being angry at her lazy younger brother for sitting around doing nothing. She takes a hint from the dream and decides to work on separating from her pusher, a very strong primary self, and begins to integrate her "being" nature, which has been deeply disowned. This is much less painful in the long run than ignoring the message of her dream and continuing to push herself until she collapses from cumulative stress. In this way Sharon can receive the gift of her opposite, her disowned brother in the dream, and she is able to gain awareness and grow in a much easier way. It's not unusual, too, for this sort of dream to return every once in a while in the dreamer's life as a warning signal if the workaholic pusher self starts to take up too much space again. Sharon might learn that when she occasionally dreams about her brother in this way, it is a timely message to slow down, and that paying attention to her Unconscious through the dream will save her a lot of stress and grief. It may also, incidentally, improve her relationship with her brother as he stops having to carry the energy of "not-doing" for her.

It's easier to work with a disowned dream self than a disowned waking self. It might be too threatening to facilitate the part of Sharon that wants to quit working and hang around all day doing nothing – her primary controlling and pushing selves might be

When working with dreams, don't miss the obvious!

Not all dreams are symbolic, and if someone you are facilitating reports a dream about circumstances that might threaten their own well being or that of others, it is wise to be cautious and suggest that they do a safety check in waking life. For example, if a subject dreams that they have cancer, it would be a good idea to take the hint and have a physical check up. Dreams about car accidents, plane crashes, injuries to family members, etc. also fall into this category. The more you know about this person and how their primary self system operates, the more you will be able to sense "who in them is dreaming," and whether to interpret the dream literally or symbolically. There is never any harm in checking to see if a dream is telling you something practical or prophetic about waking life.

uncomfortable admitting even to the possible existence of such a self in Sharon. Asking to speak to her little brother in the dream, however, is another matter. *Sharon doesn't have to take responsibility for him, doesn't have to admit he's a part of herself, in order to let him speak.* After first talking with the primary self in the dream and separating from it, the facilitator may find it's okay to invite the brother to speak too and ask him questions such as, what he observes about Sharon, what he has to say to her, and what would happen if some of his energy were present in Sharon's life.

Dreams delineate the work that needs to be done with humor and imagination. They can lay out the focus of the session for you and contribute clear and powerful images to anchor the meaning of the work.

➡ **Dreams say things to the subject that they might not be ready or willing to hear from you or anyone else.** Of course, there are many possible ways to understand a dream, but if a dream opens such subjects as an estranged brother, a sexual attraction, an abandoned baby, or a violent confrontation, there's really no way to avoid it or argue with it. A primary self will often reluctantly admit the need for change based on a dream.

➡ **Following the dream makes the work safe.** The dream shows us what the Unconscious is ready and willing to deal with – it gives us the organic timing for approaching key issues in a person's life.

➡ **If the subject keeps dreaming the same dream,** this may be an indication that they need to "unhook" from a particular primary self and begin to embrace a disowned energy that is its opposite. A recurring dream can be a clear indication of the priorities the Unconscious holds for the dreamer – i.e. the Unconscious keeps bringing up the same images and story until the subject makes real changes in relation to this issue in waking life. The wise facilitator will follow the lead of the subject's Unconscious and make its "message" his priority too.

➡ **The dream can be an ally and guide for the facilitator,** giving him symbolic tools to take the work deeper and make it more relevant, specific, and personal to each subject he facilitates.

Dream facilitation – some good places to start

We've already talked about looking for opposite primary and disowned selves in dreams. Now let's add some guidelines for approaching the dream energies and integrating the process of working with dreams into the rest of a Voice Dialogue session.

☆ **Working with dreams follows the same rules as all of Voice Dialogue work.** The central focus in dream facilitation is still on the development of the Aware Ego, and it is also essential to respect the primary selves, pay attention to energy and linkage, and make sure the subject remains in charge of the process.

☆ **Ask the person you are facilitating what they think about their dream** *before* **you offer your interpretation.** In this way, they will develop their own relationship with their dreams and begin from an Aware Ego to be able to hear what the dream maker is trying to tell them. The connection to the Unconscious is often tenuous at first, and we can all use support and encouragement in looking at our own dreams– it's so much easier to understand someone else's! Sometimes if you speak your mind about someone's dream before they get to say their own thoughts, they will actually forget what they were thinking. Remember how slippery dreams are and how difficult it can be sometimes to hold on to them – you want the Voice Dialogue work to help "land those dream fish" and not let them get away!

☆ **Let the dream self(ves) make the first tracks on the dream territory** – once you've decided to facilitate a self or selves from a particular dream, don't step in to comment on the dream until after you see what that self has to say in the facilitation. *As with all selves that you facilitate, you want to go into the facilitation with an open mind and no preconceived ideas of what the dream selves are like.* This way you won't color the energetic field with your own energy or pull in an analyst self. There's always time to talk more about the dream later.

☆ **Certain dream symbols seem to be universal:**

Vehicles represent how we are moving through our lives and who is at the wheel (i.e. in control).

Houses/rooms show where we live (or have lived or are moving to) in ourselves. In dreams we may go back to old houses we lived in, discover rooms we never knew were there, or move into an entirely new home.

The ocean or large bodies of water most often represent the Unconscious.

Water also represents the emotions.

Animals are symbols for the instinctual part(s) of ourselves.

Men and boys represent the masculine part(s) of ourselves.

Women and girls represent the feminine part(s) of ourselves.

Babies and children often indicate new energy being born in the psyche, some new aspect coming into our lives, or perhaps a new aspect that came in when the baby was born (e.g. dreaming about a 3-month-old baby might indicate something that came into the subject's life 3 months ago).

☆ **Dream symbols can also have vastly different significance depending on what they mean to the individual and what they signify in that person's culture.** Owls, for example, are a symbol of wisdom to some people and of death to others. An image of Christ will have much different significance to someone brought up Catholic than to a person with a Hindu background – it's essential to know the dreamer in order to know what the dream might mean for them. *This is why it is important that the facilitator not offer interpretations based on her personal life assumptions, beliefs, or gender and cultural expectations.*

☆ **Dreams can have opposite messages depending on where the person is in their life** – a journey for example could reflect in one person's dream that they are really moving in their process, but for a different person the dream might be telling them that they're stuck and need to move.

☆ **Even though dreams are symbolic, the easiest and most accurate way to interpret them is usually quite literal.** For example, we already mentioned above that dreaming about men indicates something about the masculine side of the personality and dreaming about women indicates the feminine. It's quite typical, however, for a dreamer to begin searching for obscure meanings for a dream and overlook some of the most basic facts such as the gender of the dream characters or that a house is something that contains our selves or that vehicles are a way of getting through life.

You don't really have to dig to find elaborate meanings for dreams. For example, if something is chasing you or attacking you in a dream, usually the energy this person or creature carries is an energy you have disowned in your waking life – there is no need to look for a mysterious motivation. It also helps to think literally about the qualities of people, places, and things in dreams. A kitchen is a place where food is cooked, a place that supplies nourishment – a dream that takes place in a kitchen has a different meaning from one in a classroom or a hotel lobby. A toilet is where we eliminate what we no longer need, so people in the process of emotional release often dream about using the toilet. If you practice looking for the obvious simple facts about people, places, animals, objects, etc. in dreams, you will soon find that understanding dreams may be a lot easier than you imagined.

☆ **When you talk to a dream self you can ask the same kind of matter-of-fact questions that you ask other selves:** "What are you feeling?" "What do you want?" "What do you do?" "Do you have a message for (the person dreaming the dream)?" "What do you think of (the person dreaming the dream)?" *Don't assume that the awareness of the dream self is limited to the dream.* Go right ahead and ask questions like, "What would it be like if some of your energy were around in (the dreamer's) waking life?" If the dream self doesn't know, it will say so, but you may get some surprising and helpful answers.

☆ **Pay special attention to the dream ego, the role of the subject in their own dream.** Is the dream ego participating, observing, not there at all, acting upon others, being acted upon, going forward, running away, fearful, brave, etc.? How the dreamer acts or doesn't act in their own dream is a strong indication of where they are in their life process. It is often very helpful to facilitate the dream ego, and you can talk with it as you would any other self: "You're Sally in the dream – can you tell me something about what's going on in this dream." "How does it feel to you?" "How are you different from Sally in waking life?" "How are you like her?" "What would you like her to understand from this dream?"

"What not's" – things to avoid in facilitating dreams

If you suggest facilitating a part of a dream and meet with hesitation/resistance/ fear, step back and go to the primary self (or selves) that has the discomfort and work with that energy instead. Of course, you want to see if there actually *is* any discomfort before doing this. Don't let your own primary selves sneak in and make assumptions about another person's dream – what would be a nightmare for you might not feel that way at all to the person you are facilitating. Find out *their* reaction first.

Guiding your subject into the dream time...

With many people who are quite accustomed to their dream life, it is just as easy to say "why don't you move over and be the man driving the car in your dream" as it is to suggest that they move into the part of them that is responsible or the self who wants to please people. The person simply moves with the intention of becoming a particular character in their dream, and the "dream self" easily appears.

With other people who are not as familiar or comfortable with dreams, it may be useful to help the subject reconnect with the energy of their dream and help bridge them into the dream reality. If you are comfortable making up your own guided meditation in the moment, this is always best because it will be tailored to the needs of the person you are working with and adapted to your own style of facilitation. What is important here is that you help the person you are facilitating to relax into a deeper state of being where they can access the dream material. The idea is to give them a vehicle through which they can easily reach a dream self and experience it on more than a conceptual level – help them feel it in their body, feel its aliveness.

What follows is *only one* of many ways to help a subject relax and return to the energy of the dream. The facilitator is working with a subject who had a dream about an old woman. Try using this example as a model to stimulate your own creative ideas for accessing dream selves and guiding people into the dream time.

Facilitator: Before we talk with the voice of the old woman in your dream, how about if you move over anywhere that feels like a good spot for that energy... *(the subject moves over and settles in)* and just close your eyes for a few moments... close your eyes and take a few deep breaths... breathe in... and breathe out... let yourself relax...

(As facilitator, your guided meditation will be easier for the subject to follow if you breathe deeply and relax too. Pace the meditation with your body and your breath rather than with your mind, and then both the subject's body and mind will be able to follow you comfortably. Remember that the ellipses indicate pauses, silences, space for the subject to absorb and relax.)

Develop your own natural style and don't feel compelled to work with dreams.
The Voice Dialogue process is most effective when you allow it to move organically. Everyone dreams, but while some people dream intensely and bring dreams to their sessions as a matter of course, others recall their dreams sporadically and some not at all. Ask about dreams in such a way that the person feels it's fine if they have dreams and fine if they don't. You certainly don't want people apologizing to you for not dreaming!

Not all dreams are good Voice Dialogue facilitation material. Some are intensely spiritual and need to be absorbed – allowed to change the life through the Unconscious – rather

…and just let go of everything we've been talking about… each time you breathe out, let that outbreath release all the selves we've been talking to… whatever you've been thinking, feeling, breathe it out…

Now begin slowly to drift back into the dream time, back into the dream Mary had a few nights ago about an old woman… let yourself float easily back in time, back into the dream… and as you enter the dream, look for the old woman… and let yourself easily come into the consciousness of the old woman… let yourself become the voice of the old woman in the dream.

Start to feel what it is like to be the old woman in the dream… *feel* it in your body… *(the facilitator leaves some silent space for the subject to begin to feel the dream self)* let me know when you feel you are fully present as the old woman in the dream.

(The facilitator has been following Mary energetically, feeling in his own energy field and body a series of subtle shifts as Mary first relaxes, then remembers, and finally begins to take on the persona of the old woman in the dream. The facilitator feels that he can literally "see" Mary remember, and even before she opens her eyes he can sense that a different "person" has entered the room. While the facilitator waits for Mary to settle into this new self and be ready to speak from that place, he gets ready to meet the dream self by matching what he perceives to be its energy with his own.)

When you are ready, you can open your eyes… are you the old woman in Mary's dream?

Take note: Most dreams come when we are sleeping, so of course our eyes are closed. However, this doesn't mean that a dream self can't open its eyes while it talks with you in the session. As a facilitator you can follow your sense of what is appropriate in terms of a subject having their eyes open or closed when they are in a dream self, but keep in mind that *it really helps us bring in awareness when we have our eyes open.* If the dream self is difficult to access, deeply symbolic, or strongly disowned, it might be better to follow the Stones' suggestion (on p. 263) and approach it from the Aware Ego place. This way the subject can receive its energy and message without venturing too far into the dream territory.

261

than being disturbed or explored by any other process. There is no rule about which dreams are too numinous or spiritually vibrant to facilitate, so use your intuition, listen inwardly and see if it feels appropriate to facilitate this particular dream. For example, a dream of a luminous angel coming to give someone a message might be better *appreciated* than facilitated. (If they have already received a strong message from the angel, either verbal or energetic, they don't need to become the voice of the angel to hear what it has to say.) Such dreams often bring the energy of initiation into the person's life and once that process is underway, there will be plenty of other material to work with while the whole system of selves adjusts to the new input from the dream maker.

> *"Working to separate from the primary self that disowns the instinctual will often do more toward reconciling with these energies than approaching them directly."*

Don't venture into the jungle – observe powerful, wild dream animals and dangerous violent dream people from a safe distance. The primary selves are counting on you as the facilitator to keep everyone on the "dream safari" safe in the protected vehicle of working through the Aware Ego. The fact that the dream maker is bringing a disowned energy into a person's dreams *does* indicate a basic readiness to deal with their own personal "lions and tigers and bears," but *working to separate from the primary self that disowns the instinctual will often do more toward reconciling with these energies than approaching them directly.* Once you have begun separating from the primary self and have some Aware Ego functioning in relation to these opposites, there are a number of ways to approach scary dream creatures without inducting their energy full force into the session.

Important things to keep in mind when working with dreams

When someone brings you a dream, it is important to honor it, but you do not necessarily need to work with it in the session. The dream weighs in with everything else the person is saying to you about themselves, and as the facilitator you need to follow your own intuition about what direction to guide the work. Often I'll hear a dream and say, "Let's leave that for now and keep our focus on the things you were talking about in your waking life." Then at the end of the session there may be an obvious way to tie the dream imagery in with what has been revealed in the facilitation. As always, what is most important is to take the work in the direction where you sense the energy is opening and the Aware Ego is ready to grow.

Follow dream themes. In addition to looking at individual dreams, it can be very helpful to pay attention to the themes that extend through several dreams over a period of time. Notice if there are certain images that repeat. For example, someone who is going through a lot of reorganization in their personality, relationships, and work might dream a whole series of dreams about houses. As you look at the dreams, there may seem to be a progression, a meta-story, where the person moves from being locked out of their old house in the first dream, then moves into a new house in another dream, and finally discovers a whole part of the house they never knew about before in a later dream. Houses are the structures that hold our many selves and moving and expanding can be one indication from the Unconscious that the dreamer is going into new territory in the psyche.

Especially look to see how the dream ego changes over time. The dream ego, where the person is identified in the dream, will tell a great deal about how the subject is doing in the process of separating from the primary selves and developing an Aware Ego. The meaning, though, will be entirely individual. Pat, for example, has never developed his power side and in his dreams he was always watching nervously from a distance or from a hiding place while thugs carried out various aggressive acts. It was revolutionary when he had a dream where he was just one of the guys at a football game, something he would never ordinarily do in waking life. Jackson, on the other hand, had dreams where he was always trying to run the show and coming up against all sorts of obstacles. After separating from his primary controlling selves and beginning to allow for a new kind of relaxation, he had a dream where he was just observing while someone he had known a long time ago from school struggled to organize a business presentation. Having the dream ego be an observer meant the opposite for Jackson than it did for Pat.

The Stones suggest working on the symbolic level when the dream contains intense symbolic images that may be overwhelming or threatening to the primary selves. They recommend having the subject *remain in the Aware Ego* and then energetically link to the powerful dream energy by picturing it clearly and then being present with it. "Honor it. Let it know you're afraid of it, but willing to hang out with it from a distance. This is a part of you, it lives inside of you, but you haven't been on good terms with it. Now, by hanging out with it, you are building a temple for it." Working in this way with strong symbolic images both helps preserve the energetic intensity of the dream, and helps the dreamer keep a safe distance from aspects of the dream that feel threatening. The Stones go on to say that "building a temple" to a dream image doesn't mean that you "act stupidly or put your head in its mouth," rather this is a way for the person *to begin to create an energetic bridge with a part of themselves they have pushed away for so long that it has begun to turn against them.* Simply being present with the dream energy, without a lot of talk or analysis, allows healing to begin to take place. Change will be evident in the dreams that follow and/or in energy shifts in the person's life.

Look for dreams that give direct feedback on the progress of the Voice Dialogue work. Being facilitated takes the subject on an inner exploration, and a dream about a journey (with or without a guide) may tell you something about how the subject is progressing in their new venture of doing Voice Dialogue work. Separating from the selves and initiating an Aware Ego process will create shifts in the emotions and in the Unconscious. The dreams may show images such as something emerging from the ocean, a bridge over a waterway, or someone diving for treasure, because water often represents our emotions, and the ocean

"When the subject has a positive dream about the facilitator, it often indicates that the Unconscious has accepted the facilitator as a support for the subject's growth."

our Unconscious. Disowned selves (perhaps in the form of people the dreamer doesn't like or animals they are afraid of) may show up, indicating that the Unconscious knows that there is now enough support available to work with these energies.

When the subject has a positive dream about the facilitator, it often indicates that the Unconscious has accepted the facilitator as a support for the subject's growth. For example, one woman after her first session with me dreamed that I took her to a party in a big house where she met a lot of people. In the dream I took her to the kitchen to show her where the food was and then left her to explore on her own. This dream is a very literal representation of the Voice Dialogue process where the facilitator guides the subject to meet their many selves, makes sure they are nourished/supported and honors their ability to explore on their own. Right before deciding to try Voice Dialogue, this same woman left a counseling situation after she dreamt that she and the counselor were in a car together with the counselor driving and had come to a place where the road was blocked, in fact the road itself was crumbling beyond the barricade. The counselor had been very helpful in many ways, but the Unconscious was obviously indicating that it was time for the subject to move on to new work.

Be on the lookout for when dreams give clear messages about what is *not* working in the facilitation or indicate that it's time to let go of working with you and move on. If someone dreamed they had come to a road block with *me*, I would have to seriously look at whether our work together had reached its natural conclusion or whether we needed to change direction entirely in the facilitation – I wouldn't dismiss the dream as being only about the subject's personal growth. The Stones say that they, "never assume that a dream is just subjective – that's not fair to people." This also means that if a person you are facilitating has a dream about you, it's quite possible that there is a real message for *you* in the dream, that it's not only about them and their projection onto you. You will need to use your intuition and good judgment to decide whether it's appropriate and empowering to share with the subject what the dream meant to you personally.

In conclusion let's re-emphasize that the dream maker is your partner and will give you enormous support as a facilitator. Once you assist someone in the initial separation from their primary selves and begin the journey of developing an Aware Ego, the Unconscious, for many people, will guide the continuation of the Voice Dialogue process through the dreams. The Stones have often said that the "Unconscious has thousands of years of experience" and can therefore come up with answers we can, literally, only dream of. The Unconscious pushes us toward more awareness. If there is something important it wants us to know, we will receive recurring dreams until we "get the point," and then it will move on and bring in new dream material, new "assignments" for the continuing facilitation process.

"The dreams bring safety to the work because the facilitator can rely on the subject's Unconscious to introduce material that is appropriate for this person at this time."

In fact, once we move through the initial separation from the primary selves, the dream maker is released from its "chore" of having to repeat "the same old message" about balancing the opposites and is free to channel more and more concise and brilliant guidance into our lives.

As a facilitator you will also find that working with your own dreams enhances the Voice Dialogue process as a whole. After all, Voice Dialogue facilitation *is* a bit like a dream – it has a similar intensity of energy and the feeling of an altered state of consciousness. Looking at dreams can make the work more exciting – it expands the scope of life experience and can bring in tremendous creativity. And *the dreams bring safety to the work because the facilitator can rely on the subject's Unconscious to introduce material that is appropriate for this person at this time.* In short, dreams, though sometimes confusing and always containing a certain amount of the unexplainable, *of mystery*, truly support the facilitation process. It is not at all unusual for a facilitator to find that as she grows in her understanding and enjoyment of dreams, her imaginativeness, intuition, and skill in facilitation increase as well.

Learning to access the selves through the Aware Ego

At the beginning of Voice Dialogue work, the facilitator is the midwife for the birth of the Aware Ego. The next step is to help the person you are facilitating "take the baby home" and train it to take steps on its own. This is a very appropriate analogy because many of our primary selves are indeed parts of us that learned from our parents (and other influential people in our formative years) how to protect us and how to manage our lives. Most often it is these powerful inner parents that we separate from first in the process of developing an Aware Ego. As we do this, we begin to have conscious choice about how to manage our selves, rather than being unconsciously overtaken and run by them.

One of the most effective ways to teach a person how to manage their energy is to have them invite the selves *in* to center and express them *through* the Aware Ego. The facilitation process of moving *out* to experience a self is very helpful in creating initial separation from, and awareness of, that self. However, in most real-life situations, the person is going to have to reverse this process and call the needed energy *in.* If I'm in a business meeting, I can't excuse myself and begin moving around to different chairs to access the parts of myself that would be useful for doing business. I need to have *internally available* the energy of my businessperson self. It would also be useful if I could access some of my impersonal energy (which is probably closely related to the businessperson) and some part of me that has some social graces as well. I have to be able to call in these parts of myself and count on them to appear and function appropriately (inside of me) if I am going to be successful – indeed one can see that the most successful people are usually the ones who are quite skillful at "putting themselves together" internally as well as externally.

Learning to channel the selves through the Aware Ego creates a major shift in the way we live, proactive rather than reactive, *creating* a personality instead of struggling with the long history of our conditioning. Through this process we learn to develop a new and enhanced capacity for choice. The Stones comment that "the Aware Ego is the choice maker, making choices between competing self systems," and that "really there is no choice until we are in touch with both sides." *One of the most basic and important choices a person can make is which aspects of their personality to express in each of life's situations.* Ironically, this is a choice that most of us are not even aware we have, until we start to separate from our primary selves and begin to approach at least a small part of our reality through an Aware Ego process.

"One of the most basic and important choices a person can make is which aspects of their personality to express in each of life's situations."

The experience of consciously choosing to bring a self in to the Aware Ego place is the complete opposite of being unconsciously pulled out to that self in the course of one's daily life. The Stones say that "As long as we are functioning out of the operating ego, identified

265

with only one side of our personality, then someone else will 'handle' the disowned side for us if we aren't in touch with it."   In contrast, when we can stand between opposites and honor both sides from within the Aware Ego, we no longer have the unconscious need to try to find balance by pulling in a friend or colleague or family member to express the energy of our disowned self or selves. More of who we are becomes accessible to us. We are also free to relate – or not to relate – to others, and can sense more clearly who *they* truly are.

We have already learned how to work with the basic Voice Dialogue method – to separate out from the selves and embark on the journey of the Aware Ego process – in the context of a Voice Dialogue session. As a facilitator, you need to take the process further by teaching the people you facilitate how to work with energetics in a very practical way in order to help them carry this shift in consciousness into everyday life. In this chapter our work with facilitation examples will help us to:

♦ **guide the subject** in consciously bringing the selves in through the Aware Ego.

♦ **teach the subject how to manage and balance** the strength of the energetic presence of those selves while in the Aware Ego.

Let's review the functions of the Aware Ego...

Now that we are going deeper into working with the Aware Ego process – inviting the selves into the Aware Ego place and learning to regulate their energy – it's a good time to review the functions and capabilities of the Aware Ego itself. The following list by no means covers all aspects of an Aware Ego, but you can use it to refresh your memory about the *basic* nature of the Aware Ego process:

♦ **The Aware Ego accesses the awareness level** and uses it to be aware of the selves, aware of the opposites in us.

♦ **The Aware Ego experiences the selves in action in our live**s (and, of course, in the process of a Voice Dialogue session). The Aware Ego is aware of both the vulnerable and power sides of the personality and does not close itself off to the feelings or thoughts that any of the selves experience.

♦ **The Aware Ego develops an ever greater ability to make choices** about how to use energy. In one situation the Aware Ego might invite a self *in* and direct the self's abilities appropriately. In a different situation, the Aware Ego might send that same self *out* and/or decide to tone down its energy – this is not to censor or repress that self, but simply to hold off on using its energy until the time is right.

♦ **The Aware Ego learns to regulate the energy of the self system,** to "turn the volume up and down." This means, for example, that a self such as a "judge" that has been overbearing in the past and that has always come in full blast, flattening everyone with

♦ **show the subject how to combine** *the energies* **of previously incompatible opposites** in the Aware Ego to create new levels of internal harmony and empowerment.

Step One: Channeling the energies of the selves through the Aware Ego

Most facilitators find that moving out into the selves and inducting their energy is a powerful beginning, but in and of itself, this is not enough to get the Aware Ego up and running in daily life. Bringing the energies of the selves *in* through the Aware Ego, on the other hand, is one of the best exercises for solidifying the process and making the Aware Ego more reliably present and functional.

The process of inviting a self into the Aware Ego is not at all complicated or difficult to do. Once you have had the subject move out to a particular self so that they are familiar with its energy, it is then very easy when you have returned to the Aware Ego place to invite the

its judgments, can now be turned way down by the Aware Ego so it can begin to function, at a much lower volume, as discernment.

♦ **The Aware Ego makes choices based on the whole picture.** This is very different from having one self or set of selves win out (temporarily) over another, which is the way we normally live most of the time. The Aware Ego is always taking action, but it is not *compelled* to act in a particular way nor is it bound by the parameters of any specific inner conflict. It is not invested in wanting or not wanting – rather, it can be in touch with the part that wants and the part that doesn't, and it is able to combine information from these opposites as well as from other sources to make decisions that are beyond what the selves can provide.

♦ **The Aware Ego has the capacity to handle judgments** both from the outside and from the inside with ease. The more the Aware Ego is present in our lives, the less we are at the effect of attacks coming from our inner critics or from outer critics.

♦ **It's the Aware Ego's job to embrace the opposites inside of us,** and to make room on an energetic level for all of our selves. As the Aware Ego develops and is able to embrace more opposites over time, we find that we take more responsibility for the totality of our nature and gradually no longer need to project the energies our primary selves don't like onto others. Another way to think about this is to say that the presence of the Aware Ego takes us out of duality, out of the either/or reality of the selves, and gives a third point of reference. The Stones say that when the Aware Ego is able to be present, "we move from duality to trinity." This means in that moment, with that particular pair of opposites, we are no longer trapped in conflict.

energy of that self in. It does help many people to suggest that they imagine this as a physical reality. Saying something like "invite that energy in, take it right into your body," will help to make the concept of "bringing the energy in" feel real and alive. Also suggest that people use their imagination: "Just imagine you can invite your creative self into you, imagine you can bring that energy right into you." As soon as you say the word "imagine," the subject enters the world of make-believe, where it's okay not to be absolutely sure that the energy is there – you're no longer in the realm of fact and having to do it exactly right. After all, everyone's imagination is different. This ability to invite the energies of the selves in or send them out the Stones call "channeling the selves through the Aware Ego." It teaches the person you are facilitating to employ their Aware Ego in the conscious management of their energies/selves.

"The ability to invite the energies of the selves in or send them out is called 'channeling the selves through the Aware Ego.' It teaches the subject to employ their Aware Ego in the conscious management of their energies/selves."

Make your first attempts at bringing energies into the Aware Ego straightforward and easy. Although a facilitator with a lot of experience can use this tool in a great variety of facilitation situations and with all kinds of energies, it's best to *begin* using this technique in a situation where:

☆ **The selves you have been working with are clear *energetic* opposites** – the selves need to be energetically accessible and it has to be easy to feel the difference between them. Two very mental selves wouldn't be very good to start with because even if they held contrasting opinions, *energetically they would feel confusingly similar.* In fact, since mental selves, are often "up in their heads," it can be hard to feel their energy in the body at all. Especially when you are first learning to facilitate this part of Voice Dialogue work, it's important to pick clear, easy-to-feel opposites with which to work.

☆ **Both the opposing selves are primary selves** – this avoids upsetting the primary self system and/or triggering a lot of vulnerability, which might happen in working with a primary/disowned pair of opposites. It is useful to choose an issue that is simple, clear, and central in the subject's life, but not something too emotionally charged or too threatening. Stick with the primary selves while you are still building your skill in teaching people to bring energy in through the Aware Ego.

☆ **Bringing the opposite selves into the Aware Ego will be really useful** – make sure the opportunity to practice working with energy in the Aware Ego makes sense to the subject. The work will go farther and be more meaningful if, for example, the person you are facilitating experiences real relief in being able to turn down the energy of a hyper-vigilant self or delights in being able to invite a relaxed energy in. If the selves you have facilitated in a particular session seem less central to the subject's life and are less well-defined, trying to bring the energy of these selves into the Aware Ego may feel somewhat frustrating or pointless. Wait for another time when the selves you are facilitating are more appropriate for this exercise.

With these guidelines in mind, let's start to get a sense of how to work with channeling the energies of the selves through the Aware Ego. We'll begin by looking at the example of Gertrud, who is going on a business trip representing her company's product at a trade fair. Gertrud tends to be completely serious and focused at work, cramming facts and figures. Her job rarely calls for much social interaction or having to interface with the public. As a result, she came to her Voice Dialogue session really nervous about the upcoming trade fair, afraid that her businesswoman primary self would be professional but too constricting and she wouldn't be much good at being personable with potential customers.

Talking with the primary self:

When the facilitator talked with Gertrud's businesswoman, this part confessed that it was afraid if Gertrud were to be too friendly with people, she would become an "airhead socialite" like her mother and lose all her hard-won professionalism and intellectual acumen. This self took after Gertrud's father and really worried it would take very little for Gertrud to lose everything she had gained (a very typical fear for a primary self) and slip back into being a brainless female like so many in her family – it felt she should keep business strictly business and segregate her social life completely.

Returning to the Aware Ego:

After listening to the concerns of the primary self, the facilitator had Gertrud come back to the Aware Ego and get a clear sense of separating from her professional businesswoman. Gertrud in the Aware Ego felt as if she had more breathing room. She also felt less nervous than she had been at the beginning of the session now that she had created some distance from the anxiety of that primary self.

Going to the opposite primary self:

Talking with Gertrud in the Aware Ego, the facilitator asked her if she also had a self that liked to socialize outside the context of her work. It turned out this part wasn't really disowned, rather it was another primary part of Gertrud that took after her mother instead of her father and that appeared in parts of Gertrud's life that had nothing to do with her work. This self knew how to be charming at parties with her husband and very sociable on vacations. This sociable self had no interest in Gertrud's work at all and said if it only were around a bit more in her life, Gertrud wouldn't be so serious about everything and would learn to relax.

Bringing opposite energies into the Aware Ego:

These two opposite primary selves are quite used to being mutually exclusive. It's always been that when one appears the other leaves, *but it would be really useful for Gertrud to be able to have both these valuable parts of herself available to her not only on this particular business trip but in her life in general.* Back in the Aware Ego place, the facilitator suggests that they do some energetic work to help Gertrud call in these parts of herself when she wants and needs them.

Facilitator: Earlier you moved over so each of these two opposite selves could be present and talk. Now let's try moving the energy in the opposite direction by learning how to bring each of these selves in to the Aware Ego. The idea is for you to be able to access these parts of yourself when you need them, rather than one or the other coming in unexpectedly and pulling you off balance.

Gertrud in the Aware Ego: That sounds good – what do I do?

Facilitator: Just stay where you are, relaxed and connected to me… *(the facilitator pauses for a moment to feel that the linkage is indeed there – eye contact isn't always essential, but it feels very natural for two people who are linked in the Aware Ego to make eye contact with each other)* and very easily now… as Aware Ego… invite the professional self, the businesswoman, to come in. Just ask that part to come in from over there… *(the facilitator points toward the place where that self was sitting and the facilitator also brings in some of her own professional, businesswoman so her energy matches and supports Gertrud's)* That's right… I could see your professional self come right in, your back straightened and your face began to have the serious focused expression I know that part of you has. See if you can make room for some of that energy inside yourself and at the same time stay connected to me… How does that feel?

Gertrud in the Aware Ego: *(looks slightly amused and bemused, shakes her head a little – the businesswoman energy is definitely present, but Gertrud's talking more slowly than that self would on its own)* Well, it's funny… I can feel that part of me, it's definitely here, but I guess I'm not used to feeling it and being connected with anybody… *(laughs)* That's almost embarrassing… I mean I guess I don't really connect with anyone very much when I'm in work mode. Plus I'm not used to being aware of this part of myself…

Facilitator: *(monitoring the energy from inside herself)* You're doing a great job of holding that energy and staying connected with me… *(they stay in silence for a moment, just connecting and feeling the energy)* Now try letting that part go again, just invite it to leave and go back over there to where the self was seated. *(the facilitator waves the energy away with her hand to indicate the motion of it leaving, of letting it go – at the same time she lets her own version of that energy go while staying in the Aware Ego. She watches and senses what is happening with Gertrud so she can tell whether Gertrud has truly let the energy of the businesswoman go back to its place)* Does it feel as if that part has gone back now?

Gertrud in the Aware Ego: *(kind of shaking herself a little bit, and then it suddenly feels to the facilitator as if Gertrud has come more into focus, the linkage with her feels stronger)* I think so… it feels easy for that part to come in but much harder to get it to go.

Facilitator: Well, that part of you is used to being fully present and it doesn't usually leave until work is over. *(Gertrud smiles, nods, seems to relax into herself more and the linkage with the facilitator feels as if it solidified in some way)* How about inviting the opposite self in now, asking the social part of you to come into the Aware Ego? Are you ready to try that?

(Let's stop for a moment in the middle of our session with Gertrud to ask some questions about how the facilitation is going.)

When the facilitator brings in her own "businesswoman" energy to support Gertrud, how does this help the facilitation process?

What different clues would you use to help you recognize when Gertrud has succeeded in bringing in her businesswoman energy?

Discussion

"Takes one to know one" the old saying goes – if the facilitator can feel her own businesswoman (or if it were a male facilitator, a businessman), she'll be much more likely to recognize the same energy when it comes into Gertrud's Aware Ego. And, because the facilitator was observant of this self's way of being earlier in the session, it's quite easy to recognize its mannerisms, the way it affects Gertrud's body, and the way it feels energetically when Gertrud channels it in the Aware Ego.

Gertrud in the Aware Ego: Sure, I'm ready.

Facilitator: Good, then simply invite your social self to come in… *(gesturing toward the place where this part was sitting)* Bring some of the social energy into yourself here in the Aware Ego. *(the facilitator can immediately feel a change, as if the space between herself and Gertrud just warmed up several degrees)* That's right, that part came in very easily.

Gertrud in the Aware Ego: *(smiling, her shoulders more relaxed)* This is a good feeling… I can feel it relaxes me when this part is present.

Facilitator: I can feel it too, and you and I feel more connected when you bring this energy in. This is a part of you that knows how to link energetically with people. *(the facilitator has also brought a similar energy into her Aware Ego and can feel a strong connection between herself and Gertrud)*

Gertrud in the Aware Ego: It's funny, but I don't feel any of that anxiety now that the professional self usually feels about this social part… everything feels okay when I "invite" it in this way. It feels manageable.

Facilitator: That's exactly the idea. When the Aware Ego can *choose* to bring in the social part and adjust how much of it is present, then the Aware Ego effectively manages and contains this energy. Then the other side doesn't get so worried about the possibility of the social part taking over… Why don't you let it go again now… *(the facilitator waves the self back toward the place it came from and lets her own similar energy go at the same time)* Just imagine that you can send this part of you out, that you can just let it go.

Gertrud in the Aware Ego: *(laughing again)* This one isn't so easy to let go of either… I'm surprised.

Some tips for channeling the energies of the selves through the Aware Ego...

Remember that channeling the energies of the selves through the Aware Ego is a more subtle process than facilitating those same selves. This is because you are most often intentionally working with only a modest percentage of the "full blown" energy that the self would express if it came out directly. In this situation, the facilitator has to have a heightened level of energetic sensitivity in order to recognize when the subject has succeeded in bringing the energy of the self into the Aware Ego. The facilitator also has to learn to perceive when the subject turns the energy up, when they turn it down, and if they have actually sent it back out of the Aware Ego again. The following are some tips to help you achieve more ease and skill in this aspect of Voice Dialogue facilitation:

➡ **Ground the process in physical reality.** Physically pointing to the different energies/ selves, where they are located in the room, really helps to orient the person being facilitated. This also helps you as the facilitator to stay connected to the physical and energetic reality of the selves. Bringing the energies of the selves in through the Aware Ego is an energetic rather than a mental exercise, so it is essential that the facilitator stay energetically present and make sure that the person they are facilitating moves through the experience on all levels, physical and emotional as well as mental. You can do this best by observing the physical changes and feeling the energetic shifts along with the verbal exchange.

➡ **Don't go it alone – invite the subject to work with you.** If you're not sure your perceptions of the energy are accurate, remember that it's fine to ask the person you are facilitating to help in the process. Ask them what it feels like to them. Can they sense the self coming into the Aware Ego place? If the energy seems too vague to *both of you*, encourage the subject to invite it in more fully.

➡ **Use the body to help bring in an energy.** For example, the facilitator might suggest that the subject bring in *"the part that was so expansive."* To remind the subject in the Aware Ego what that part was like, the facilitator could throw her arms out wide in a gesture that this expansive self made earlier in the session. Certain movements and other physical body cues may often help the self to come in. Keep experimenting with this exercise and pretty soon you will find that you can "see" a self come in without even thinking about it. Or, you'll clearly know when the self isn't present and can adjust your own energy level to help it come in more.

➡ **Anchor the experience of the Aware Ego.** Voice Dialogue sessions are often the only place where a subject is really sure that they are "in the Aware Ego" and are conscious of it while it's happening. Bringing energies in through the Aware Ego is an excellent exercise for making the reality of the Aware Ego more secure and familiar, something the subject can begin to count on in "real life." The more you sit and talk with someone in the Aware Ego, bring energies in and out through the Aware Ego, connect energetically with the Aware

Ego, discuss Voice Dialogue with the subject in the Aware Ego, etc., then the more the Aware Ego will become a solid reference point for them rather than just a fleeting experience. For the person who is very at ease with energy, you may want to suggest exercises they can do on their own, perhaps taking some time to practice bringing a particular self into and out of the Aware ego or "turning the volume up and down." You may come up with other ideas tailored to an individual subject's needs.

➨ **Work with the disowned selves indirectly through the Aware Ego.** So far we have been talking about bringing in the energies of selves *that have already been facilitated*. It's also possible to bring in an energy that has *not* been facilitated. This can be particularly useful when a disowned or vulnerable self is energetically present, but it would be too soon in the process to ask the subject to move over into that disowned part because they have not yet done the basic work of separating from the related primary selves. Instead, the facilitator can suggest that the subject, *while in the Aware Ego*, invite a small amount of the disowned energy in: "How do you feel about inviting just a little bit of that angry part into the Aware Ego? Just enough so you can feel its energy, but not so much that it comes out and takes over." If that feels safe to the subject, then bringing in the angry part, perhaps turning its energy up and down *a little*, gives them a way to approach this self – feel it and honor it – without the primary selves being threatened by it. And, of course, in the process of doing this the Aware Ego becomes stronger and more present, and the primary selves begin to trust the Aware Ego's ability to manage energy.

➨ **Practice moving your own selves in and out of the Aware Ego.** This is an excellent exercise because as facilitator you have to be able to call in a matching energy for each of the selves you ask your subject to bring in. The more the facilitator practices this, the more adept he is at pulling in energies and adjusting his own internal energetic levels, the better he will be able to model the process and the easier it will be for the subject to follow his directions.

The more you work with channeling the energy of the selves through the Aware Ego, the more comfortable you will become with energetics and the more easily you will recognize important shifts in the people you facilitate. You may want to keep some notes on this more subtle part of your sessions for a while to help you identify the challenges and notice the changes. If you discover new ways of working that are particularly effective, you may also want to consider sharing them with other facilitators through *The Handbook* and website (see "How you can contribute to *The Handbook*" on p. 312).

Facilitator: Usually when your social self comes in, it's for a well-earned "vacation." It's probably hard to let go of that energy so soon, but we'll come back to this part again… for now just send it out… (*feeling her own energy as well as Gertrud's and waiting to sense a shift that indicates the social self is gone*) There it goes now… can you feel the difference? (*Gertrud nods affirmatively and looks relaxed – the facilitator allows some time for silence and strengthening the energetic linkage in the Aware Ego before going on with the exercise*) How about bringing the business self back in for a moment, but just a little bit of it… Let's not invite it in full force this time – just invite it to come in at a small percentage… (*the facilitator waits for the energy to reappear and then begins talking with Gertrud, who is now channeling her business self through the Aware Ego*) How does it feel to have the business self back again?

Gertrud in the Aware Ego: It feels fine… normal. I really have a sense of being bigger than these parts of me… I'm not sure I know how to explain it.

Facilitator: It doesn't seem like your business self was upset or worried about the social self being invited in too.

Gertrud in the Aware Ego: No, it felt okay… I really don't feel worried about it when we're doing this and you're here. I guess what I don't want is for either part to take over at the wrong time.

Facilitator: That's exactly what we're trying to avoid. By bringing a little bit of a self into the Aware Ego, you can use its energy to your advantage without completely dropping into that part. (*the facilitator can feel the business self and it's definitely more relaxed than before*) Now let's send the business self out again… just let the energy go… (*waiting to feel it leave*) and now just stay in neutral in the Aware Ego for a moment and focus on the energetic connection between us.

Questions

How would you proceed from here? How many times would you want to bring these selves in and out of the Aware Ego?

What stands out to you as the most important information the facilitator offers Gertrud in the Aware Ego?

What could you suggest to Gertrud to do on her own that might help her with the upcoming trade show?

Discussion

Gertrud is having an easy time bringing the selves into the Aware Ego and she's beginning to understand what a difference it makes to be working consciously with these energies. It is probably very important that in addition to the energetic experience of separating from the selves, the facilitator tells Gertrud that the Aware Ego's ability to bring in an energy and manage it makes it easier for the business self to relax and not worry so much about the social self taking over. Given that she really needs to develop some aware-ness in relation to these opposites and the ability to work with both of them at the trade show, it would probably be a good idea to bring these selves in and out several times until it becomes familiar and fluid to do so. The more comfortable Gertrud is doing this in her Voice Dialogue session with the help of the facilitator, the easier it will be to practice this on her own at home, particularly as preparation for the trade show. In the next examples, we'll continue to work with bringing energies into the Aware Ego and start to focus on regulating their intensity. We'll also experiment with inviting in two opposite selves and having the Aware Ego hold them simultaneously. These exercises could work very well as part of Gertrud's session too.

Step Two: Regulating the energies of the selves while in the Aware Ego

Once we learn to bring a self into the Aware Ego, the next step is to be able to regulate its energy. Though it is a simple exercise to "turn the volume" of a particular self up or down, learning to do this can have very powerful results. *Regulating the amount of a self's energy that is present changes our experience of that self.* If a part that is used to coming in full force and taking over can be modulated to a small percentage of its usual expression, then the likelihood is that it will be both more useful and more enjoyable to have

"If a part that is used to coming in full force can be modulated to a small percentage of its usual expression, then it will be both more useful and more enjoyable to have around."

around. At a *small percentage,* a judgmental self can become discerning, a compulsive caretaker may be simply warm and caring, and an oppressive energy like the inner patriarch can evolve into a protective, rational male presence that supports a woman rather than undermines her. Managing our energy in this way also changes others' experience of us, and we are able to balance our linkage and non-linkage sides to create intimate connection and still maintain boundaries.

Once the person you are facilitating can bring the energy of a self in through the Aware Ego, then they can also practice turning the volume of that energy up or down. In the chapter on "Teaching the Aware Ego to work with energy" (p. 185), we already experienced increasing and decreasing the linkage between facilitator and subject just by imagining doing so. The same ability is what you use to increase or decrease the presence of a particular self in the Aware Ego. Let's listen in on two new sessions, one with Nolan, who has been very identified with his rational side and one with Laurel, whose primary selves are very personal, warm and feeling and who has a hard time accessing any impersonal energy. We'll quickly review what occurred in the first part of each of these facilitations so we can move on to working with the opposite energies in the Aware Ego at the end of Nolan's and Laurel's sessions.

Nolan's session:

At the start of Nolan's session, the facilitator asked to speak with Nolan's mind, and it had a *lot* to say! It was quite a surprise for Nolan to come back to the Aware Ego and feel the linkage with the facilitator – this wasn't what he was used to at all, but at the same time he really enjoyed it. Nolan in the Aware Ego commented that everything seemed very vibrant and fresh all of a sudden. They sat in silence together for a few minutes just feeling this new reality. Nolan's mind had mentioned that it wasn't always around, that sometimes Nolan just listened to music and relaxed, so the facilitator asked to speak with the music-lover as well. This was definitely a more feeling part that Nolan cultivates actively on vacations and occasionally in his spare time. Back in the Aware Ego, Nolan was able to invite the mind in, but found that as soon as he tried to talk about anything with the facilitator, the mind would start to take over and the energetic

Beginning to exercise choice by learning to regulate the energies of the selves...

As the subject in the Aware Ego place practices regulating the level of energy of the selves they have brought in, they will gradually get better at noticing energetic shifts on their own. They will be able to tell when a strong primary self has taken over and in time they will be able to naturally and easily adjust the volume of a particular self in real life as they do with the help of a facilitator during a Voice Dialogue session. They may even be able to modulate the energy before a take-over occurs. Here are a few suggestions to support the people you facilitate in learning to regulate and manage their energy through the Aware Ego:

➡ **Talk to the subject in the Aware Ego,** *remind them that the Aware Ego stays while the selves come and go.* This is very effective in helping the subject to distinguish between "being in voice" and calling an energy into the Aware Ego. *The act of inviting in the energy of a self helps define the Aware Ego as the center point of balance and of a more conscious form of power.* For one thing, this makes it perfectly clear that the self is separate, out there, to be invited in. Reversing the pull of the primary self, bringing it *in* instead of letting it pull you out, really feels as radical as reversing the pull of gravity in the physical world! Even *intentionally* inviting the self *in* at a very high percentage is quite different from having the same self appear uninvited at 100%, which inevitably takes the subject unconsciously *out* of their center and "into voice."

➡ **Take note of how forcefully an energy comes in** when you ask the Aware Ego to bring in a particular self. Many selves are what one could call "all-or-nothing" energies – they either come in at 100% and take over, or they're not there at all. Other parts may be difficult to access at first and it will take more energetic support from you as the facilitator for the subject to be able to call them in.

➡ **Experiment with bringing the self in at different levels.** With the kind of self that's used to being very fully present, it can be helpful to have the subject intentionally bring in the energy *at a "low volume."* This way they can practice modulating the amount of connection would be lost. Nolan's facilitator is relaxed about working with this energy and not at all easily discouraged. He has just had Nolan send the rational side out again and allowed time for them to rest back into the linkage.

Facilitator: *(bringing in some of his own rational side and focusing at the same time on his energetic connection to Nolan)* Let's try bringing in some of that rational, mental side of you again, but this time without talking at first… Why don't you just nod to me when

energy from the very beginning rather than letting it blast in full force and then attempting to turn it down. It's fine for the subject (in the Aware Ego) to invite certain primary selves to come in fully within the context of the session, as in this case the Aware Ego is doing the inviting and is therefore (with the support of the facilitator) much more in control. It is, however, very important for the facilitator to realize that working with energy in this way is a *real experience* and not merely an exercise. For example, inviting a *disowned* energy to come in at a high percentage (even through the Aware Ego) could be very threatening to the primary self system and consequently quite overwhelming for the subject.

Note: **Having a subject turn the "volume" of a self up or down is only acceptable in the Aware Ego place.** It is very empowering for the subject in the Aware Ego to begin to have choice as to how much of a self's energy they want to allow in at any one time. *However, when you are directly facilitating a subpersonality, you don't want to ask it to change itself, to tone down or come on more strongly. You can't ask an energy to be anything other than what it is – it cannot be either less or more of itself!* For example, say you are facilitating a person who has a very strong "doing part" that comes over them like a steamroller and works up to a fever pitch, making lists, running a million errands, always doing at least 4 or 5 things at one time (like listening to self-improvement tapes on a headset while jogging, wheeling the baby and walking the dog). Once this person achieves some separation from their "doing self" it can be wonderful to bring just a small amount of this energy into the Aware Ego. At a low level this self becomes stimulating and energizing in contrast to the usual 300% overwhelm it brings in at full-strength. *However, it's one thing to ask the Aware Ego to bring in a small amount of a particular energy – it's quite different and unacceptable to ask the "doing" energy itself to become small.* If you ask a subpersonality to diminish itself, it will not only feel insulted and/or rejected, but it really won't be able to comply. If you ask a part that is small to make itself bigger, it will most likely feel (once again) that it isn't big enough. In either case, you as facilitator will have broken one of the ground rules – that the facilitator must always be willing to accept the selves as they are without judgment. A self can only be itself, and we cannot predict or control when and how changes in the person will lead to an evolution in the subpersonality. *The place for choice, for consciously mixing and matching energies at different levels, is exclusively the domain of the Aware Ego.*

you feel that part coming in. *(the facilitator can both see and feel the energy come in because it enters and really changes the upper part of the body, as if Nolan got bigger from the shoulders up – this feeling echoes in the facilitator's body too)*

Nolan in the Aware Ego: *(nods his head)*

Facilitator: *(nodding back)* I can feel it too… That part really seems to fill up the shoulders and neck and head. I can still feel our connection, though… how about you?

Nolan in the Aware Ego: *(nods his head again)* I do feel it… I'm afraid if I talk, though, that I'll lose it.

Facilitator: *(focusing on connecting with Nolan from the lower body, the lower chakras, so as to balance all the energy that's going up)* Let's try something to help with that. Just imagine you have a valve that you can use to control how much of the rational mind is present. Can you picture that? *(Nolan nods his head)* Okay, so just imagine turning that valve down a bit… *(watching and feeling to see if the energy really does seem to be decreasing)* That's right… maybe a little bit more… How does that feel now?

Nolan in the Aware Ego: *(taking a deep breath – always a good clue that the energy has shifted)* That feels… different. I feel more… on the ground.

Facilitator: Try talking with me a bit… keeping your connection with the ground… and the connection with me. It's okay if you have to talk slowly… we're not in a hurry.

Nolan in the Aware Ego: *(a bit of a bemused smile)* It does feel really different to talk with you like this. I don't feel like I've "lost" my mind… it's here… but I'm not so speeded up.

Facilitator: Tell me a little more about the project you're working on… See if you can do that and stay connected.

Nolan in the Aware Ego: *(laughs)* Thinking about the project makes me feel tongue-tied! I'll try… Well, we're starting work on the second phase next week. My partner is flying in from Chicago and we'll meet with the president of the company on Friday… *(by the end of the sentence his speed has picked up and the energy has picked up)*

Facilitator: Okay, stop for a moment and feel where the energy has gone.

Nolan in the Aware Ego: *(laughs again and takes a breath)* This isn't easy! As soon as I start to think, I go up, up and away… like a balloon.

Facilitator: *(smiling encouragingly)* It takes some practice to get to a point where you can use your mind through the Aware Ego and still stay in what we call "linkage" with another person. Try imagining that valve again and just turn the energy back down… *(sensing the energy coming down and the linkage getting stronger again)* That's good… How does that feel now?

What do you think works best in this facilitator's approach? Would you have done anything differently?

Have you facilitated anyone who reminds you of Nolan? What challenges have you encountered in working with the rational side?

What exercise(s) could you do to help yourself become more aware of energetic shifts, and be more readily able to recognize when a self comes into your subject's Aware Ego and when it leaves?

Discussion

It works particularly well that Nolan's facilitator is relaxed and patient. The facilitator follows Nolan's lead all the way through the session, picking up information he reveals about the opposite parts of himself. For example, rather than choosing some arbitrary counterpart to the rational side, the facilitator hears Nolan's comments about loving music and follows this lead in order to explore the more sensitive, feeling side. Following these kinds of cues keeps the facilitation organic and makes the job of facilitation easier because there's no need to speculate or make something up in order to find an opposite and work with it.

The more you work with bringing the energies of the selves in through the Aware Ego, the easier and more obvious it will be to perceive when the energy is present and when it leaves. A useful exercise (and you may think of others) is to partner with another facilitator and have one of you bring in a specified energy while the other indicates when they feel it. If you switch roles and give each other feedback about when you each feel the energy come in and when you feel it leave, you'll find that you can quickly become more sensitive to energetic shifts.

The facilitator and Nolan can continue this exercise for quite a while – they can invite the mental self in and send it back out several times, practice turning it up as well as down, or hang out with it so that Nolan experiences using his mind through the Aware Ego. All of these exercises will help Nolan become more adept at working with his very powerful mental primary self with intention and choice, rather than having it just run away with him. It would also work well for Nolan to:

♦ **alternate between inviting in his rational mind and his music-loving self** which is on the feeling side.

♦ **practice connecting energetically with the facilitator with each of these energies present** so that he can begin to learn how each of these selves affects his ability to link with other people.

Dr. Martha Lou Wolff's exercise for working with the Aware Ego:

As a facilitator I like to complete a session with an energetic exercise. After the subject has returned to the Aware Ego at the end of the session, I bring each of the selves facilitated into the Aware Ego in the following way:

Facilitator: Pull in the energy of this first one *(pointing to the self that was facilitated first in the session),* but bring it in at about 10%... You can feel that with only 10% of this self present, there is still a lot of you here – there is a great deal of Aware Ego process available. At this small percentage other people might not even notice this part of you, but you can check in with it internally and listen to it.

After the subject has settled into this energetic dynamic...

Facilitator: Now pull the same self in about 50%... With it taking up half the space there is still a lot of room for the Aware Ego process. *(the facilitator stays alert to the energy, watching and feeling to see that the subject really is bringing in more of this particular self)* This is where you can wrestle with this part of yourself, where you can have an active relationship with it. You can remain present in the Aware Ego while at the same time being deeply aware of the partial truth the self holds. There is still lots and lots of you present.

Once the subject has a solid sense of the energy being present at 50%...

Facilitator: Now bring in more energy of that same self, perhaps 80% to 90%... *(the facilitator again senses the change in the subject, not assuming the energy will shift until it's evident that it has)* This is for when you want this energy to be *the* one you are carrying, but you still want to have some Aware Ego present. This could be very helpful when you want to use this energy in a specific situation... 80-90% feels like the whole truth, but not quite – there is still a 10% to 20% Aware Ego process which allows choice about when to let this self out again... The self has a very strong presence, but it's not the same as being taken over by this self – it's not the same as you being 100% *in* it... When you are 100% in the self there is no awareness of the limitations of the self or the need to return to center. *(the facilitator keeps holding and monitoring the energy while she is explaining these concepts to the subject – in this way talking allows time for the subject to have a deeper energetic experience of the self that they are channeling through the Aware Ego)*

To conclude the exercise…

Facilitator: When you are ready, release the self completely at your own pace… You may want to thank the self for it's gifts or set an intention to check in with this part of you again soon. *(the facilitator watches to see that the subject has indeed let go of the self and is now sitting in the Aware Ego without that energy present)* When you let go of the self and are simply sitting in the Aware Ego place, it often seems a bit empty. We are accustomed to feeling the "charge" of one self or another. As you increase your ability to sit with this ambiguity, this tension between opposites, the Aware Ego will seem less empty and more like liberation.

As facilitator, you may want to do this exercise with two or three selves that were facilitated in a particular session. What you tell the subject about experiencing the self at different levels can change depending on the kind of energy the self has and the role it plays in the subject's life. For example, with a part that is vulnerable, 10% might be the level where the subject can begin to feel the vulnerable energy and to get used to it. Bringing the self in at the 50% level allows for really *being* with it, comforting it. Bringing this self in at 80-90% really honors it. You could suggest to the subject, "You may want to thank this self and tell it you are committed to helping it."

Another example might be a creative self. Bringing it in at 10% would give the subject an energetic "buzz," a feeling for its energy. As the subject brings in more and more of this energy, the experience becomes more powerful and more complete, and the skills this self has to offer become more accessible.

It is important to acknowledge the linkage that occurs between myself and the subject when only the Aware Ego is present, after separation from the selves. This linkage differs from the energetic connection when a self is present. I remind the subject that we don't live in just the Aware Ego without any of our selves present, but the Aware Ego is an effective place to review a situation and choose the self we wish to use.

(Dr. Martha Lou Wolff is a clinical psychologist who has been teaching Voice Dialogue facilitation since 1984. She travels worldwide offering workshops on all levels as well as individual and relationship sessions. Dr. Wolff can be reached in California at 888-726-8575 or through e-mail at <marthalou@compuserve.com>.

♦ **bring some of one energy into the Aware Ego and, keeping it there at a comfortable level, also bring some of the other opposite energy in with it** so that he holds them both in the Aware Ego together – then the Aware Ego can find a livable balance between these energies. (See the second part of our next session with Laurel for ideas on how to do this.)

The facilitator, for his part, needs to stay very alert to the changes that occur and not make assumptions about what the energy of a particular self will be like. For instance, even though the music-lover is more *feeling,* it may also be an introverted or very *internal* energy and may not necessarily have learned how to link with others. The more practice Nolan gets in regulating these selves, the more conscious he will become of where his energy is and of whether he is connecting to other people or not.

Laurel's session

Laurel is a "therapist" for all her friends, always ready to listen, always attentive and involved in everyone's problems. It doesn't seem, though, that her relationships really nurture *her* and she comes away from it all feeling exhausted and taken for granted. Laurel's husband tells her that she needs better boundaries, but he's the first person to take advantage of her lack of them. The facilitator spends quite a lot of time talking with the part of Laurel that is so energetically open to all the people in her life (strangers included). When she comes back to the Aware Ego, it's like coming up for air. For the first time Laurel has a sense of being connected with another human being without feeling compelled to take care of them.

Before moving on to any other selves, the facilitator has Laurel practice inviting in this first self that was facilitated. It's fine to go right ahead and work with bringing the energy of just one self through the Aware Ego – there's no rule that says you have to facilitate an opposite (or any other) self before working with energy in the Aware Ego place. You can structure this part of the session in whatever way seems most suited to each subject. In Laurel's session, the facilitator wanted to build on Laurel's wonderful new sense of "having her cake and eating it too," of being able to feel a real connection and not having to be so enmeshed, so energetically entwined, in order to make the connection happen. Laurel in the Aware Ego is amazed to feel that a real warmth between herself and the facilitator still exists even when she partially turns the volume of her very attentive and involved self *down.*

In the next part of the session, Laurel tells the facilitator that there is a part of her that will finally come in and shut everything down "if Laurel's really really *really* on overload." "That's when I'm like one of those little windows that come up on the computer with a little picture of a bomb on it." They talk with the withdrawn self, which is an opposite primary self to Laurel's involved and attentive part. The withdrawn self says that it comes out every time that Laurel is on overwhelm (which is fairly often), but nobody in Laurel's life likes this part of her very much and Laurel tries to swing back into her friendly, involved self just as soon as she can. There certainly doesn't seem to be any graceful way for her to withdraw from overextension and overcommitment. When they move back to the Aware Ego after facilitating this self, Laurel shakes herself as if she were trying to get rid of something that was stuck to her.

Facilitator: Come back to yourself again, to the Aware Ego… really get a sense of separating from the "withdrawn" part that was just out over there… *(pointing to its place)* and also feel yourself separate from the first self we talked with over there, the one that gets really involved with people… *(pointing to that one too)* How are you doing?

Laurel in the Aware Ego: *(shaking herself a little again and coming into a more focused connection with the facilitator)* I can feel how much the outgoing part really doesn't like it when that withdrawn part is around… I mean, it's a relief for sure to have that part come in and shut everything down because everything just gets to be too much sometimes, but then when I pull out of it, I feel so awful and embarrassed… like I broke all the rules.

Facilitator: That withdrawn self *does* break the rules that you follow most of the time, and it's usually only allowed to come out and break those rules when you've been in complete overwhelm. *(Laurel sighs and the facilitator takes a deep breath too – the linkage between them still seems strong)* We can also work with your withdrawn self in the Aware Ego – just like you did with the self that's very involved with everyone. Then you'll learn to create a balance between these parts of yourself.

Laurel in the Aware Ego: *(taking a big breath)* That would be really different... I've always felt I had to be all one way or the other.

Facilitator: Let's start with the really involved one again – only this time, see if you can begin by bringing in just a little bit, a really small percentage, of that self. Go ahead and do that now... *(the facilitator invites her own similar energy in, and though she's trying to sense a shift in Laurel, this is more subtle than the first time because Laurel is bringing in just a small percentage of the energy and the facilitator is not totally sure if she's picking up on it)* How does that feel? Can you feel that part coming in?

Laurel in the Aware Ego: I think so… it's really hard to put into words… it's like my attention is open to you but I don't feel pulled. I guess this is what people try to tell me about boundaries.

Facilitator: Being aware of this energy and being able to turn it down when you don't want so much of it, will certainly help you to stay in balance and not feel so pulled off center by other people's needs. Try turning it up some… *not so much that it takes over totally,* but enough so you really feel its presence. *(Laurel adjusts her body posture ever so slightly, coming a little more forward toward the facilitator and all of a sudden the facilitator can really feel a warmth coming from this self through Laurel's Aware Ego)* There, I can definitely feel that part now… Do you notice how easy it is for you to regulate this part? *(Laurel nods, she's smiling)* Try turning it down again now… *(the facilitator waits to sense the shift)* How does that feel?

Laurel in the Aware Ego: Easier… I like being able to turn it down and still feel it's okay being with you. I mean, it's kind of a relief… I don't have to be so "on."

Facilitator: *(the facilitator finds that her own energy tends to shift automatically when Laurel turns hers up or down)* Definitely! That very involved part of you takes a lot of energy a lot of the time, so when you turn it down, it's much less demanding on you and probably on other people around you... And, you can still have as much of it as you want... Try turning it up again... experiment with it and see if you can feel where it starts to be too much. *(Laurel makes a funny face, indicating that it's starting to feel disturbing, and nods her head)* Okay, so now turn it down to a point where it's comfortable again... *(the facilitator takes plenty of time to let the changes happen and waits for Laurel in the Aware Ego to settle into them)* And now just send that part back over there... *(pointing again to where the self had been sitting)* and let's keep our connection with each other. How does that feel?

Laurel in the Aware Ego: It feels good. I'm still amazed that I can just ask that part to leave... of course it's easy to do here! I mean, that part of me usually *never* leaves until I'm just about dead from exhaustion.

Facilitator: Well, the way to learn is to start in a situation like this one where it's easy, and then later you'll be able to do more on your own. You're really starting to move energy in and out of the Aware Ego very smoothly. How about bringing in some of the other side, the part that withdraws when you're exhausted. See if you can invite in a *comfortable* amount of that energy... *(the facilitator shifts too, bringing in a small amount of an energy comparable to the one she sensed in Laurel's withdrawn self when it was being facilitated)*

Laurel in the Aware Ego: *(Laurel's shoulders square off and her energy recedes)* Yes.

Facilitator: That changed very quickly – you feel very different to me, almost as if you moved away.

Laurel in the Aware Ego: I do feel like I have more... space around me... This withdrawn part feels really different too.

Facilitator: What do you notice?

Laurel in the Aware Ego: Well, this is usually an all-or-nothing part of me too... I mean when it comes in, I just shut down completely and there really isn't any connection with anyone 'til I get out of it. Right now I still feel like I'm here... in fact in a funny way, I feel more like myself.

Questions

Why do you think the facilitator started with the attentive self again before bringing in the energy of the withdrawn self?

Would you work differently with the withdrawn self?

What is the advantage for Laurel to bring both these energies into the Aware Ego rather than just working with the first one?

Even though these are both primary selves, the involved one is predominant in Laurel's life and the withdrawn one only appears under pretty extreme circumstances. After Laurel made the comment about how having the withdrawn side present felt like "breaking the rules," the facilitator wanted to honor the seniority of the first self by calling in its energy again for balance before bringing in the withdrawn part.

These two energies are mirror opposites of each other – one pulls away from people and the other is pulled toward them. Bringing them in through the Aware Ego, Laurel gets to experience being in balance in the middle, able to contain her own energy and still able to connect.

Step Three: Holding two energies together in the Aware Ego

As we grow up and struggle with the opposites inside of us, we learn to trade off one part of ourselves against another. We learn that we "can't be in two places at once," and that if we're going to get anywhere in life, we have to give up those selves that are not directly involved in our survival or in our push toward success. What one is expected to give up varies from country to country, culture to culture, family to family, but the concept of having to give up part of our selves in order to succeed, to be accepted, to get through life is so prevalent around the world that few people ever question its validity. Often, as in Laurel's case, it is only when a person is completely worn out by striving in one direction that an opposite energy comes in to handle the resulting stress.

Only the Aware Ego can hold and express opposite energies simultaneously. It is true that we can't physically be in two opposite selves at the same time, *but we can energetically hold both of those selves together in the Aware Ego* with very liberating results. By channeling and balancing the energies of our selves, the Aware Ego gives us back our birthright of being fully human and whole. It frees us from having to trade off one part of ourselves against another, from having to live our lives feeling compromised and fragmented. When appropriate, one of the most exciting parts of a session can be the moment when a subject brings two opposite energies together into the Aware Ego and experiences the Aware Ego's ability to hold, balance and utilize these opposites. The Aware Ego (as we shall see with Laurel) literally combines opposites into an altogether new way of being. This is the moment when the subject realizes that the rules are different in the realm of energetics. In everyday life we may have to give up one course of action over another or decide to be in one location instead of another, but when it comes to energy we really can "have all of ourselves" if we channel those energies through an Aware Ego.

When is it optimal to bring two opposite energies together in the Aware Ego? In working with Laurel, the facilitator can see that Laurel has already started to get a really good feel for what it's like to bring her selves into the Aware Ego and she is becoming adept at turning those energies up and down. It also seems to the facilitator that it would be very empowering for Laurel if she could access both of these sides of herself together and not have to live in one

Helping the subject learn to link through the Aware Ego is key to making Voice Dialogue facilitation a transformative experience...

Perhaps the most life-changing skill you can teach the people you facilitate is to be in linkage with another person *through the Aware Ego*. We already know that it's very important for the subject to learn to invite a self *in* through the Aware Ego and be able to send it *out* again when they choose. This puts the subject in charge of their own energy from an Aware Ego place and makes it possible for them to have choice about how they express themselves. You take the process further when you encourage the subject to bring in the energy of a self *and at the same time* remain energetically connected with you. When the subject is able to do this successfully, then they can both regulate and enjoy the energy of the self they are channeling *and* share linkage with another person at the same time.

The Aware Ego does not have to obey a subpersonality's desire to connect too much (blend energies with another person) or to disconnect completely. The Aware Ego is not limited by the nature of any particular self or selves that it channels – it can maintain linkage with the facilitator *even if the self being channeled doesn't normally link at all.* A rational mind, for example, may have no ability to link with you, but *the Aware Ego can bring in the rational mind and still stay energetically connected with the facilitator.* The converse is also true. There are selves that connect very intensely with other people, and when this kind of very personal self takes over, the subject loses their ability to disengage from others and to create energetic boundaries. *An Aware Ego, however, can increase or decrease the level of linkage by choice.* The Aware Ego can bring in the personal energy, channel it's warmth, and also enjoy a level of containment by turning down the amount of linkage. The more you work to strengthen the subject's ability to link with other people through the Aware Ego, the more you help them find a livable balance between linkage and non-linkage opposites.

The Voice Dialogue session is an ideal training ground for the subject's Aware Ego. Facilitation gives us the space to practice working with energy without the challenges and destabilizing influences that can distract us in everyday life. Here are some suggestions and ideas to keep in mind as you work with teaching people how to link with you as they channel the energies of the selves through the Aware Ego:

- **Encourage the subject to stay connected with you** even if it's a bit awkward or uncomfortable. When you direct the person you are facilitating to bring an energy in through the Aware Ego, it's important to make sure that they stay in the Aware Ego and the self they are channeling doesn't take over. You may want to say something like, "See if you can talk with me in the Aware Ego with this energy present and not lose the energetic contact between us." The person being facilitated may resist doing this – "It's a lot easier to have this energy here if I don't look at you." Encourage them to try, though, (without being coercive!) because this is the skill they are going to need in order to make it possible to successfully manage these energies in "real life." Being able to stay linked with the facilitator in the Aware Ego is probably the most supportive way for the subject to practice working with this, but if the process is too effortful, it may be a clear indication that you've moved too far too fast. Try taking more time to facilitate and separate from the selves before attempting this exercise.

➡ **Exercises for creating balance:** The Stones spend a lot of time with people in the Aware Ego, having them bring in the side they have been identified with and teaching them to use it in a new way through the Aware Ego. With a person who has been very identified with the rational mind, a favorite exercise is to establish separation from the rational mind and then have the subject channel the mind through the Aware Ego. The facilitator and subject link energetically through the Aware Ego, and then the facilitator invites the subject to talk about any idea or project that involves the mind. The challenge for the subject is to *maintain linkage while thinking and talking*, to utilize the energy of the mind without "going off into their head."

With someone whose feeling/linkage selves are predominant, you can use an opposite exercise, one that helps the subject link through the Aware Ego *and still maintain boundaries*. The facilitator can begin by (1) making a strong energetic connection with the primary self and asking the subject if they can feel the linkage. The next step is to (2) see if they can feel a shift in energy when you have them go back to the Aware Ego place. Once the subject can perceive a clear differentiation, the next task of this exercise is to (3) bring that same feeling/linkage self into the Aware Ego and link with the facilitator without "losing themselves." In the Aware Ego they can also turn the energy up and down until they find a comfortable setting where they can feel both the warmth of the connection *and* a clear sense of boundaries. Later, the facilitator also needs to make sure that the subject releases the energy of the feeling/linkage self and returns to the neutral place of the Aware Ego. In this last part, it's important that the subject notices what it's like to be in the Aware Ego *without* the added energy of their feeling/linkage self, and that they also notice how it feels to connect with the facilitator with just the Aware Ego present.

extreme or the other, flipping back and forth and exhausting herself in the process. There are no rules (or guarantees) about when bringing more than one energy into the Aware Ego will work well, but the following three criteria may be helpful in deciding when to try using this approach in your own sessions:

♦ **The subject is able to separate well from the selves.** The facilitator can tell from Laurel's responses so far in the exercise – "my attention is open to you but I don't feel pulled," "I feel like I have more space around me," "somehow I feel more like myself" – that Laurel is definitely in the Aware Ego and *is experiencing the energetic quality of the selves without being taken over by them.*

♦ **The subject is able to regulate the energies with ease.** Laurel is not having any trouble in adjusting the amount of each self in the Aware Ego – it's pretty easy for her to turn a dial up and down (or open and close an imaginary valve) to allow more or less of a self's energy to be present.

♦ **There is good reason for wanting to use these opposites together.** The nature of Laurel's opposites is such that it really would work well for the Aware Ego to use them both at the same time – the involved one to keep connection with people and the withdrawn one to maintain boundaries.

Laurel's session continues...

Feeling that it's practical, timely, and worthwhile to continue working with Laurel's opposites, the facilitator asks her to bring the involved self into the Aware Ego one more time.

Facilitator: This is getting easy for you now... just invite in some of the very involved energy again... bring it in again at a comfortable level... (*the facilitator stays energetically alert, feeling for the shift as the involved self comes in, not assuming that it will appear just because it has before*) How does that feel?*

Laurel in the Aware Ego: It feels fine.

Facilitator: I'm going to ask you to do something a little different with it this time... Try holding that energy right there, just like you have it, and now bring in some of the opposite energy at the same time... just invite in a small amount of the withdrawn energy too... (*the facilitator brings in a little of each of her own comparable energies so she can be more sensitive to a shift in Laurel, and at the same time she watches Laurel's facial expressions and body language closely to see what changes*) That really looks different... what are you feeling?

*Note: Subtle changes in the way you express yourself as a facilitator can affect the subject's energy and how well they are able to stay in the Aware Ego and channel the energies of the selves. If Laurel's facilitator asked "How do *you* feel?" instead of "How does *that* feel?" Laurel might have a very different answer. Asking "How do *you* feel?" might be perceived as a question for the self rather than for the Aware Ego because the self has a lot more feeling than the Aware Ego. And then there would be the chance that the self, having been invited to share its feelings, would start to take over. When the facilitator asks "How does *that* feel?" there can be no mistaking that the question is for the Aware Ego alone and refers to the *process* of bringing in the self. Fortunately, it's quite natural for most facilitators to make this kind of distinction, so rather than worrying about "doing it right," you can simply notice and appreciate the effect of what you are probably already doing.

This is a magical moment!

Our illustrator, Suzanne Perot, spent quite a few challenging days trying to capture the elusive qualities in Laurel's changing expressions and energy. The result is a "snapshot" of Aware Ego consciousness right as it comes into being, and it gives us a rare opportunity to study this moment of growth, to look at it and learn from it outside the context of facilitating a session. Take your time feeling into the differences between the first two illustrations where Laurel is channeling the opposite selves one at a time through the Aware Ego.

Then, in the third illustration, feel the shift in her energy where both of the selves come together. It's extraordinary to see how balanced and powerful Laurel's energy is while holding those two opposite selves simultaneously from an Aware Ego place.

Very often when a person experiences two energies simultaneously — energies which up to that time have been mutually exclusive — their whole face and body language change. As facilitator you can actually "see" a new energy that hasn't been there before, and it's important to feed back to the subject in the Aware Ego what it is you perceive in order to encourage them to express what they are experiencing.

Laurel bringing the energy of her "involved self" in through the Aware Ego

Laurel bringing the energy of her "withdrawn self" in through the Aware Ego

Laurel has brought the energies of both her opposite primary selves, involved and withdrawn, in through the Aware Ego. This creates a balance of these opposite energies that is only available to Laurel through her Aware Ego.

Laurel in the Aware Ego: I... feel different. I mean this feels a bit strange, but it feels kind of good too. I think my body understands it better than my mind does... It feels good in my body. *(Laurel definitely has a stronger presence than she did with either the withdrawn self or the involved self separately – the facilitator can feel her coming together in a new way that feels more complete.)* I could get used to this! It feels powerful.

Facilitator: It *is* powerful to be able to use both sides of yourself and not have to trade one part off against the other. That's really the idea of doing this work, making it possible for you to have all of yourself. This way, you have the part of you that really connects with people and gets involved with them *and at the same time* you have the part of you that knows how to pull back when that connection is overwhelming... *(the facilitator is careful to keep her focus on her linkage with Laurel while she talks because she knows how easily talking about the theory of Voice Dialogue can bring in her own mental energy and disrupt her connection with her subject)* Notice what the connection feels like between us when you have both of these energies present at the same time.

Laurel in the Aware Ego: *(a kind of quizzical expression appears on her face as she settles more deeply into her body)* I don't know if I can really describe what I feel... but it's definitely different. I feel sort of separate from you and really connected at the same time... Does that make any sense?

Facilitator: It makes a lot of sense. I don't know that I could describe it better. It's really new for people to be able to access all of themselves and not always have to switch back and forth between opposite parts, so I don't think we have really good language for it yet... Take a moment to enjoy being this way... to enjoy having both these important energies available to you at the same time... From this place you'd be able to relate to another person without having to be too involved or too withdrawn... *(the facilitator and Laurel just sit for a few moments in silence, an energetically full silence)* Both of these selves belong to you and you're entitled to both of them when you need them, not just one or the other... What do you think it would be like if you were able use a little of each of these energies together in your daily life?

Laurel in the Aware Ego: God, I think it would be great! If I felt like this at home, I think I'd get more done with less effort and less distraction. Do you really think I can do that?

Facilitator: Maybe not right away, but I do think you'll be able to. It's definitely easier to hold these energies together here where there are no distractions and where you're getting some support, but with practice, you can do this more and more on your own... I know sometimes you sit and meditate... maybe once in a while you can sit and play with these energies, just inviting them in and sending them out like we did here today, so you can get some practice during a "no-stress" time.

Laurel in the Aware Ego: I could do that.

Facilitator: For now, send the withdrawn one out again... *(the facilitator uses her hand to wave that part back in the direction from which it came)* That's right... and now let the involved one go too... *(waving that one too)* and simply return to the Aware Ego... just let those energies go… And now notice how it feels in the Aware Ego place without them.

Laurel in the Aware Ego: It feels kind of empty… but okay.

Facilitator: It *is* emptier – it's like being between acts in a play where the actors have left the stage and the Aware Ego is the director, sitting alone. Remember that it's our selves that are full of energy and really live life. The Aware Ego is aware of all the parts and can redirect the script, but it may feel a little empty to be in the Aware Ego until the selves come back on stage.

Laurel in the Aware Ego: *(laughs)* Knowing that involved part of myself, I don't think intermission will last very long!

Facilitator: You're right – we don't really have to worry that the primary selves will disappear. It's exciting, though, to have a really new experience of holding both of these energies in the Aware Ego at the same time. Now you have a key to accessing them when you want to, and we can practice bringing in these opposite energies another time as well.

Questions

What do you feel were the most significant choices the facilitator made in working with Laurel in the Aware Ego?

What do you see as the key to Laurel's overwhelm and how will bringing both her involved and withdrawn selves together in the Aware Ego help her find balance?

Can you think of additional or alternative suggestions for Laurel to continue working with these opposites on her own?

Discussion

The more you explore the Voice Dialogue process, the more rich will be the range of possibilities for the work. It can feel as if the facilitator is at the center point of a network of paths – each line of questioning, each way of working, leading to more exciting changes and discoveries. Certainly there isn't time for it all in one session, so perhaps the most significant "choice" is to focus on and maintain the linkage between facilitator and subject as the foundation for any and all approaches you might decide to use. In Laurel's session, the facilitator's modeling the process she is attempting to teach (bringing her own opposite energies into the Aware Ego and relating to Laurel from that place of inner balance), also plays a big part in making her work with Laurel effective. Demonstrating how to hold and move energy while maintaining linkage creates a container in which growth and learning can occur – in fact, this is what makes the work we do in a session into a real life event rather than just an interesting exercise. Without linkage, no amount of explanation by the facilitator, no matter how brilliant or perceptive, will effect change in such a deep and organic way.

In the past Laurel tended to think it was other people who were overwhelming her and the only escape was to shut down, but her real source of overwhelm is (and has been) her own overinvolved energy spilling over – with no functioning boundaries to keep her from wearing herself out. When she can modulate that hyper-attentive part of herself, turn its energy down, then there is the possibility of being around a lot of people without becoming so drained or having to push them away. People usually push away something external when in actuality it is their own internal imbalance – their own inability to regulate and balance the opposing energies in themselves – that is causing the exhaustion.

☆ Suggested Exercise ☆

Take the time to return to Gertrud's session and Nolan's session and continue working with them on your own, imagining bringing their opposite selves simultaneously into the Aware Ego.

See if you can locate similar energies in yourself and practice inviting those energies in and out, try turning their "volume" up and down, or holding them together in your own Aware Ego. You may find this will enable you to better support your actual subjects and the ones you practice with in these exercises.

The facilitator as a teacher of energetics

Voice Dialogue sessions provide an ideal context in which the people you facilitate can develop skill and ease in using energy consciously and managing it from the Aware Ego. Once you have laid the groundwork of separation from the major primary selves, working with the Aware Ego is where you really begin to empower people to use energetics in their lives – on their own. You may find that moving selves in and out of the Aware Ego and adjusting their intensity is simpler to do than you expected, but don't underestimate its impact and effectiveness. Stick with it, and with a little practice, both you and your subjects may be amazed at the positive results. It may take a while, but you'll begin to get reports from people you facilitate that they were able to recognize a particular self coming out at work or at home and actually managed to turn its energy down to a more comfortable level. *That new dimension of empowerment is directly related to the Aware Ego starting to take charge in a way that comforts rather than challenges the primary selves.* You'll see people exploring new ways of interacting with their partners, families, colleagues and finding that formerly stressful situations have begun to shift. These changes may often be small, slow, and subtle, but they add up; and your role as the facilitator is of key importance in supporting the subject's growth.

The facilitator plays an essential role in helping the subject learn to gracefully hold the tension between opposites and avoid the stress of first being in one self and then finding themselves landing suddenly in its opposite. In having the person you facilitate learn to channel the energies of the selves through the Aware Ego, you are coaching them in how to find their own center. With two opposite primary selves (or with a primary self and its disowned opposite), and no Aware Ego available, a person often has a real "ping pong" experience of being batted back and forth from one side of their personality to the other. Finally finding some centeredness can be a huge relief.

When the two opposites you are facilitating are primary and disowned, accessing the long-repressed disowned self can bring a more serious challenge.* We have already talked about how threatening the disowned selves can be to the primary self system, but it also happens that disowned selves can be very seductive. Certain energies that have long been repressed can seem so liberating and exhilarating for the subject that they flip over 180° and begin living in the opposite extreme. Suddenly a very conservative person starts to take risks they never took before; a formerly very rational, intellectual person discovers the body and the emotions and has a wild affair; a business person leaves their career and moves to the country, etc. – you get the picture. This is exactly what happens to many people when they enter a "mid-life crisis" where the primary self system is abandoned and the formerly disowned energy becomes the new primary self. Because flipping from one self to its opposite can be enormously disruptive and *merely substitutes one unconscious reality for another,* this is exactly the kind of "change" we try to avoid in Voice Dialogue work.

"Teaching the subject to channel the energies of the selves through the Aware Ego trains them to develop mastery over their own energy, making their communication with the world more effective, subtle, and graceful."

From a Voice Dialogue perspective the only real liberation we experience comes when we can consciously choose how to live, and this conscious choice is actualized through an Aware Ego process. When we live unconsciously through the selves, it makes no difference if a self is intellectual or feeling, conservative or radical, primary or disowned – if we're identified with the self and have no Aware Ego in relation to it, then we're still living without choice. The whole idea of helping the people you facilitate to separate from the selves and develop an Aware Ego process is to cultivate consciousness and choice. Teaching them to channel the energies of the selves through the Aware Ego takes this one step further and trains the subject to develop mastery over their own energy, making their communication with the world more effective, subtle, and graceful. The facilitator can't control the direction his subjects take in their lives, but by teaching *the people he facilitates how to be in touch with and experience their selves energetically (without being compelled to act those energies out), the facilitator can open the doorway to a much more centered and fulfilling way of life.* In order to empower others in this way, the facilitator needs to:

> ☆ **stay centered in his own Aware Ego and not become invested in any of the selves he facilitates.** It is so easy to be tempted by a very exciting disowned energy, to think "ah yes, what this person really needs is to loosen up, take a break, stop being stuck in their old patterns (i.e. primary selves)." It's also possible, for example, that a facilitator who hasn't yet done the work to separate from his own very conservative primary selves might actually be frightened by a subject's emerging risk-taker and unintentionally react to it. Neither of these approaches, either being attracted or repelled by the selves you facilitate, will work. As facilitators, we have to do enough

*An in-depth discussion of facilitating disowned selves is reserved for The Handbook, Part II.

Troubleshooting...

Most of the time you can expect the people you facilitate to have an easy time channeling the energies of the selves through the Aware Ego. As long as you've done the work to separate from those selves in the first part of the session and you've picked appropriate energies for this exercise, it's likely that bringing the selves into and out of the Aware Ego will be both enlightening and rewarding. *Remember that nothing in Voice Dialogue, however, is pre-planned or totally predictable*, so let's take a moment here to discuss some additional things to keep in mind and approaches to try when working with this process:

➡ **Once in a while you may meet some resistance.** Even people who have done Voice Dialogue for years may be sometimes quite reluctant to invite a strong primary self into the Aware Ego. *"God, that part of me is around all the time and I'm so relieved to separate from it. I don't want to invite it back in — I just want a break from it!"* You may have activated a self that is afraid inviting the dominant self into the Aware Ego place will only make it stronger. Depending on how much of a reaction you encounter, you may either need to do more work with the resistant selves before the subject is ready to channel their energies through the Aware Ego, or you may simply need to reassure the person that inviting a powerful primary self into the Aware Ego doesn't mean that the self will take over. In fact, taking over is what the self *usually* does. The purpose of inviting the self in is exactly the opposite – *it offers additional control and choice to the Aware Ego.*

➡ **Be sure the primary selves don't feel you're trying to push them out of the system.** The facilitator needs to remain respectful of the primary selves and not conduct the exercise in such a way that a strong primary self imagines you are criticizing it or, even worse, trying to get rid of it. This really depends on the tone and feeling of the connection the facilitator has with the subject. It's just as important to be non-judgmental and energetically welcoming toward the selves when the subject is channeling them through the Aware Ego as it is when you are facilitating those individual selves directly. *As a facilitator you must remain energetically "on" and not drop the ball.*

The more adept you become at working with energetics, the easier the process of channeling selves through the Aware Ego will become for the people you facilitate. You may find that you naturally go right to doing this exercise in a first session if the subject seems ready to work in this way. However, if you're still building confidence with facilitation, take your time and don't feel at all that you *should* be bringing energies into the Aware Ego immediately. Some of the most awkward Voice Dialogue work occurs when a facilitator's strong pusher and perfectionist try to do every technique they can think of that they've seen other more experienced facilitators do. A little work done well is much more helpful and significant than trying to do a great many things too soon and thereby getting confused and disconnected energetically in the process.

Voice Dialogue work of our own so that we can function from an Aware Ego during a session and not have positive or negative judgments about the energies we facilitate. *Every self is fundamentally only energy and will be equally useful or equally destructive depending on the person's ability to separate from it and manage its energy through their Aware Ego.*

☆ **practice in his own life what he is asking the subject to do.** Let's use the example of an adventurer self. If you, the facilitator, are beginning to integrate the adventurer energy in your own life, you need to know how to access the energy of the adventurer without letting it take over. As a facilitator, you would want to be experienced in bringing the adventurer energy in to the Aware Ego just enough to let it energize you, but not so much that it becomes disruptive and takes over the energy of the session – in other words you want to *practice* (frequently) working with your own adventurer energy. When you can personally live this difference rather than only understanding it intellectually, you will be able to communicate it quite easily to the people you facilitate.

☆ **embody what he is attempting to teach,** not so much to create an example in the old-fashioned sense, but to *hold an energetic* that the subject can use as a sort of "starter culture" for their own personal life recipe. This is an apt analogy because in a very real way, the facilitator is holding something alive inside himself that can be picked up by the subject through *practice* and *linkage* with the facilitator more easily than it can be analyzed or explained.

How do you know when the process is working? An overall relaxation and *lack of backlash from the primary self system* is an indication that the Aware Ego is balancing between opposite selves and successfully managing energy. You will know that the people you facilitate are achieving a new level of mastery in working with energy through the Aware Ego when they can either stop following the old pattern of behavior and/or try out something new without upsetting the primary self system. For example, let's look again at our session with Gertrud. It would not work very well at all if Gertrud were suddenly to bring her social butterfly persona into her work environment. She might charm a lot of people at the trade show, but it's pretty much a guarantee that when she came home from her business trip, her opposite and more predominate primary self would be truly mortified by what she had done and would probably lie awake half the night

> *"Every self is fundamentally only energy and will be equally useful or equally destructive depending on the person's ability to separate from it and manage its energy through their Aware Ego."*

agonizing about everything from casual remarks Gertrud made to strangers at the show, to imagining the possibility that she might lose her job. The Stones call this "getting slapped" by the primary self, and it is a sure indication that we've gone too far too fast from one end of an internal energetic continuum to the other. If, on the other hand, Gertrud can manage through the Aware Ego to bring an appropriate balance of her conservative business self and some of her more personal social energy to the show, she will probably experience success in her work without any backlash from the primary self system when she returns home.

298

As we evaluate our progress, it's good to remember that we are all, facilitator and subject, just beginning to develop an Aware Ego. The excitement (and sometimes challenge) of working with Voice Dialogue and the Psychology of the Aware Ego is that our work often takes place on uncharted territory. We may find ourselves barely a few steps ahead of the people we facilitate (if that!). Perhaps the best way to monitor your progress and measure success is to notice whether you and the people you facilitate are enjoying the process, having fun with it. Not having a good time is usually an indication that the facilitator's pusher or the inner critic (or both) have taken over and underneath these two "go-getters" is probably discomfort and vulnerability about being good enough as a facilitator. As you separate more and more from these primary selves, the pressure will ease up and Voice Dialogue and working with energetics may become one of the most enjoyable and rewarding things you do.

A Voice Dialogue work list for the facilitator

The facilitator is no different from the people she facilitates. She has her own unfolding consciousness process, guided by dreams, motivated by life issues and events, intensified by the interaction of her own primary and disowned selves in relationship. However, in addition to this already complex "curriculum for transformation," the facilitator has to also focus on what parts of herself are involved in being a facilitator and what she can do to enable herself to work with her subjects in a more relaxed and skillful way. The following list of selves/energies suggests useful areas of focus for when *you* are being facilitated. Chances are you have already worked with a number of these selves because many of them naturally emerge as topics of focus in the course of learning the work. It stands to reason that when you are learning to facilitate, you will want to have more impersonal energy available, more energetic awareness, and fewer "velcro patches" waiting to get hooked by the people you facilitate. You may want to use the following suggestions as a helpful reminder of what work has already been done and what still may need attention. If or when you find that your progress slows and you encounter (inner or outer) obstacles on your path, this list may offer some helpful direction.

> *Take the time to think about how working with, and separating from, each of the following selves or pairs of opposites will change (or has already changed) your ability to do Voice Dialogue facilitation.*
>
> *Think of specific examples from your own experience.*

Sooner or later every Voice Dialogue facilitator will encounter these inner selves. Taking the time to separate from these selves and to begin to develop an Aware Ego process in relation to them, will make learning to be a facilitator smoother and easier by far. There is no uniform order of appearance for these subpersonalities – each facilitator is different – so they are simply listed alphabetically rather than in any order of importance. Some of them are listed singly, but most are joined as pairs of opposites.

Controlling/Easygoing:
Separating from this pair of opposites can help you to relax around the open-ended nature of Voice Dialogue work and to allow space for the new and unexpected. Being identified with the controlling side can lead a facilitator to unconsciously push with too many questions or to be uncomfortable with silence. If, on the other hand, the facilitator is overly identified with her easygoing side, she might allow the work to drift and become un-grounded. Being able to balance between easygoing and controlling is also very helpful when

you encounter truly unfamiliar energies in yourself and in the people you facilitate, making it easy for you to venture into new territory without having to figure out everything that's going on or know all the answers ahead of time.

Doing/Being: Most of us need to slow down. At least in Western culture, we tend to be over identified with doing, especially in relation to our professional lives. Ironically, many of us think of being as something that we *do* on vacation. Practicing something new, such as learning to facilitate, also activates our doing side. This makes it all the more important that as a Voice Dialogue facilitator you separate from both *doing* and *being* energies and thereby learn to balance your energy appropriately between them. Then you will be much more likely to have a clear sense of when to move the session along and when to just *be* with the energy that is present. So much of facilitation involves *being* with the selves and *being* with the subject in the operating ego/Aware Ego – "hanging out" and "feeling in" can be more important than preparing, planning, directing. In addition, the power parts of ourselves that push to get things done are rarely interested in or capable of linkage – we need to be able to bring in our being side through the Aware Ego in order to create energetic connection and genuine communication with the people we facilitate.

Facilitator/Therapist: There are two aspects to working with the facilitator and/or therapist self (or consultant self, or teacher self, etc.). One is to separate from a subpersonality that may have been handling your role as a facilitator, so that you can work with people more consciously and from an Aware Ego place. Many of us already have a well-developed "therapist self" that may have a tendency to take over Voice Dialogue facilitation and shape it according to past training and expectations. Once we separate from this part, it becomes possible for our Aware Ego to utilize the skills of our therapist self without letting it take over. The other aspect of working with the facilitator self is accessing a part that loves to facilitate and is relaxed and happy and creative doing it. *The Aware Ego will be able to employ the skills of the "therapist self" and the skills of many other selves in your work as a facilitator, opening up a much broader range of creative possibilities while freeing you from the limitations of trying to do most of your Voice Dialogue work from just one or two primary selves.*

Inner Critic & Perfectionist: Even if you have only just begun to do Voice Dialogue work with people, you have probably already discovered how powerful the inner critic and perfectionist can be in many people's lives. A strong inner critic and/or perfectionist can effectively cripple a person, making it impossible for them to take action or do anything creative, i.e. anything that might incur criticism or risk imperfection. You may not experience your own inner critic or perfectionist to be as overbearing as some of the ones you facilitate in others, *yet even a mild "critic attack" can really cramp your style as a facilitator.* As you begin to separate more and more from the critic and the perfectionist, you'll find that you have more "breathing space" as a facilitator, more room to learn and grow. You'll find too that it becomes easier to keep your attention free for focusing on your subject rather than concentrating on your own "problems" and supposed shortcomings as a facilitator.

Personal/Impersonal: I'm not sure it's possible to do much Voice Dialogue facilitation without learning to balance personal and impersonal energies *and to channel both of them through the Aware Ego.* If you are identified with your personal side, you will be too vulnerable to what the people you work with think of you, and you'll end up with your attention on how *you* are doing instead of on the session and how it is going. And, though the personal side of you would be able to link with your subjects, you wouldn't be able to regulate personal energy through the Aware Ego or teach them how to have boundaries and connection at the same time. Being too rooted in the impersonal side can also be problematic. You might come across as cold to your subjects and even lose interest, not caring enough about their selves to talk with them in depth. With too much impersonal, you wouldn't be able to model and teach energetic linkage. However, with an Aware Ego in relation to these opposites, you can bring through both the warmth of your personal side and the detachment of the impersonal in a way that will bring harmony and integration to the work.

Psychological Parent: The psychological parent is a primary self that appropriates all the knowledge we gain about psychology and personal growth and uses it as a vehicle for power and control in relationship. Like other powerful primary selves, the psychological parent's ultimate concern is protecting our own vulnerability and it does that by making other people's vulnerability the focus of analysis and attention. Separating from the psychological parent helps you as a facilitator to release your investment in how your subjects' process is going and to disengage from any parent/child bonding patterns with the people you facilitate. The psychological parent, though extremely interested in other people, keeps an energetic distance from them, so it is pretty near impossible to achieve or teach linkage if you are trying to facilitate out of this self as the psychological parent will not allow for your own vulnerability. (Bonus – separating from the psychological parent will be very beneficial for your relationships too!)

Responsible/Irresponsible: Not separating from this set of opposites can also easily lead to parent child bonding patterns with the people we facilitate. The responsible parts of us tend to see themselves as responsible for the subject, responsible for the facilitation, even responsible for how well the subject understands explanations or how clear their dreams are! If we unconsciously work out of a responsible parent self instead of bringing an appropriate amount of responsibility in through the Aware Ego, *then there won't be much room for the subject to learn to take responsibility for themselves.* And, in such a situation it's not uncommon for the subject to carry the energy of *irresponsibility* for both themselves and the facilitator (just like a child who is unconsciously encouraged into the role of irresponsibility by an overly responsible parent). Separating from your responsible primary self(ves) will not only help to empower the people you facilitate, but it can also be very useful in keeping your own boundaries clear. Separating from the opposite energy of irresponsibility may keep you from "unintentionally" missing appointments or experiencing other sudden outcroppings of irresponsibility. Working with this pair of opposites and other related selves may also be very advantageous in organizing the business part of your Voice Dialogue practice.

Special/Ordinary: Sooner or later just about everyone has some important work to do with the energies of special and ordinary. In the United States there is an enormous expectation that each and every person "should" be special. To fail to stand out from the crowd in some significant way implies a much larger failure at life in general. For many of us, caught up in the energy of having to be special, it is not enough to do a good job; our inner critics and perfectionists compare us unmercifully with others, fearing that we're not special enough to achieve any real and lasting success. There is quite the contrary experience in many other cultures where standing out in the crowd is judged as arrogance or seen as setting oneself above others. In these cultures, the primary selves will try to hide our gifts for fear of rejection and judgment. As a facilitator, it's tremendously important to be able to access the energies of both special and ordinary without being identified with either one of them. You want to be free to use your imagination, your intuition, and your gifts as a facilitator, *and* at the same time not be caught up in feeling that every session has to be special – some kind of major "breakthrough." When you have separated from special and ordinary, then you won't be imposing your need to be a great facilitator on someone else's process. You can simply relax, stay present, and do your best in the moment.

Vulnerable Child: We've talked a great deal in this *Handbook* about how important it is to create a solid foundation of separating from the primary selves before approaching the disowned energies and/or buried vulnerability. Because our essential goal is to initiate and develop an Aware Ego process, it is recommended that vulnerability be expressed at first in the safety of the Aware Ego/operating ego place, rather than having the subject move into a vulnerable child self. In this way the subject develops an ability to access the vulnerable feeling part of their personality without being taken over by it and without threatening the primary selves that have been the lifelong guardians of this energy. With many people (though not necessarily with all) a time does come when it is natural, organic, and important to their process to have the vulnerable selves facilitated. We will be discussing in detail in *The Facilitator's Handbook, Part II,* how to go about facilitating the vulnerable child and related energies; and for those of you who are just starting to work with Voice Dialogue facilitation, *the place to begin preparing for this aspect of the work is with yourself.*

Facilitating a vulnerable inner child is a delicate process because this self is exquisitely sensitive and highly susceptible to emotional injury. As the facilitator you have to, of course, be able to match the energy of that very sensitive self, and this is really only possible if you have a conscious relationship with your own vulnerability. So when it comes to working with vulnerability, begin by exploring your own inner child(ren) and build a background of first-hand experience with your own vulnerability before approaching this energy in the people you facilitate. The ground rules of Voice Dialogue work encourage you to keep the work focused on the primary selves and on developing an Aware Ego process. Ultimately the goal is for the subject to be able to take care of these vulnerable selves from an Aware Ego place, and you need to at least *begin* an exploration of your own vulnerability before you attempt to guide someone else's journey. You'll also find that it is very useful to know where your own vulnerability is so you can (1) make it available when appropriate and (2) protect yourself in a difficult facilitation situation where you might feel personally at risk.

One of the ongoing challenges and concerns for all of us in the teaching, consulting, therapeutic, healing, or any other helping professions is the issue of self-care. It's so easy to become deeply involved in other people's needs and process to the point where we neglect our own. Fortunately, the Voice Dialogue method really has a built-in protection against the kind of self-neglect that can readily lead to burnout. In order to be effective facilitators, it is essential that we pay attention to ourselves, our process, our evolution – not merely while we are in training but throughout our careers – i.e. the entire time that we do this work. As we said in the beginning of this *Handbook*, the heart of any training program to become a facilitator is *being facilitated*. This means that whatever gifts you bring to the people you facilitate, *those gifts are for you as well*. Through coaching others in managing their energy, you will become more masterful at managing your own. As you help others to separate from primary selves, you will model what you are teaching through your own growth and transformation. By teaching the Psychology of the Aware Ego through Voice Dialogue facilitation, you invite the people you work with on a journey of self discovery, imagination, and evolving consciousness – a journey in which you are both seeker and guide.

Reading & Resources

Books

Hal & Sidra Stone

Embracing Our Selves: The Voice Dialogue Training Manual. Nataraj Publishing/New World Library, Novato, CA, 1989. The foundational text on the Psychology of the Aware Ego and the Voice Dialogue method. Every facilitator needs to read and reread this book.

Embracing Each Other: Relationship as Teacher, Healer & Guide. Nataraj Publishing/New World Library, Novato, CA, 1989. A revolutionary understanding of how relationships work (also applicable to the facilitator/subject relationship).

Embracing Your Inner Critic: Turning Self Criticism into a Creative Asset. Harper San Francisco, 1993. Topics include how to avoid or minimize critic attacks, and how the Inner Critic can become a supportive partner in life. The examples and exercises are particularly helpful for the facilitator in developing a personal approach to facilitating selves.

Hal Stone

Embracing Heaven and Earth: A Personal Odyssey. DeVorss & Company, Marina del Rey, CA, 1985. Reading Hal Stone's recounting of his own personal process gives the facilitator an understanding of the roots of Voice Dialogue work and an inspirational insight into one person's evolution along a transformational path.

Sidra Stone

The Shadow King: The Invisible Force That Holds Women Back. Nataraj Publishing/New World Library, Novato, CA, 1997. A very liberating and enlightening book for women (and for men), this work is also valuable for the facilitator because it includes many of the more recent developments in understanding and working with energetics and the Aware Ego.

Robert Stamboliev

The Energetics of Voice Dialogue. Mendocino, California: Life Rhythm Publishing, 1992. Building on the Voice Dialogue model of consciousness, this book utilizes selected material from the esoteric healing traditions and Tai Chi Ch'uan to give a larger understanding of the basic principles operating in facilitation. Includes excellent facilitation examples.

Shakti Gawain

Living in the Light: A Guide to Personal and Planetary Transformation, with Laurel King. Nataraj Publishing/New World Library, Novato, CA, 1986. A recognized classic on developing intuition, includes exercises that can be useful for both facilitators and their subjects.

Joy Drake and Kathy Tyler

Intuitive Solutions: A Tool for Inspired Action. InnerLinks Associates, 1996. An excellent tool for learning to work with your intuition and recognize its guidance. Based on the Insight, Setback, and Angel Cards from The Transformation Game®. Order from InnerLinks, Asheville, NC; Phone: 828-665-9937; Website: <http://innerlinks.com>.

Audio and Video Tapes

Stone, Hal and Sidra

Introducing Voice Dialogue and *Voice Dialogue Demonstrations* are two audiocasette teaching tapes that clearly present the Voice Dialogue method and demonstrate facilitation.

The Aware Ego – the definitive four-tape series on the Psychology of The Aware Ego is the next step in the work of Drs. Hal and Sidra Stone – an essential training tool for the facilitator.

The Mendocino Series is a set of 12 audiocassettes covering the Stones' basic approach to transformation, psychological development, and relationship. Of particular interest for facilitator: "Meeting Your Selves," "The Dance of the Selves in Relationship," "The Child Within," "The Voice of Responsibility," "Meet the Pusher," "Meet Your Inner Critic, I & II."

The Total Self is a 90 minute, two-part interview on video with Dr. Jeffrey Mishlove, host of the Thinking Allowed television series. Hal Stone both introduces the theory of the Psychology of Selves and demonstrates the technique of Voice Dialogue.

The Inner Critic in Action is Hal and Sidra Stone's first training videotape. It consists of five brief Voice Dialogue sessions and includes a written commentary which accompanies the tape and acts as a training guide.

All the above tapes are available from Delos, Inc., P.O. Box 604, Albion, CA 95410. Video tapes are available in VHS or PAL format.

Workshops and Trainings

There are a great variety of training opportunities in Voice Dialogue facilitation worldwide. I have listed a *few* of the people and institutions which offer classes or workshops in facilitation and have limited my selection to those that offer trainings in English. Many more facilitators are available for private sessions and/or to travel and teach, and there are many programs available in other languages. A more complete listing can be found on the world wide web at <www.delos-inc.com>, and we welcome listings of your classes on our website at <www.life-energy.net>. Please note also that each person and organization listed here may offer programs other than facilitator trainings. All of the following teachers have trained with Drs. Hal and Sidra Stone.

Centers/Organizations/Institutes

Delos, Inc., offers one week training intensives with Hal Stone, Ph.D. and Sidra Stone, Ph.D., in Northern California. Intensives include teaching sessions, discussion groups, demonstrations, exercises, and individual experience of the work. Level II is for people already familiar with Voice Dialogue, Level III is for facilitators with 3-5 years experience. P.O. Box 604, Albion, California 95410 (707) 937-2424; E-mail: <delos@mcn.org>; Website: <http://www.delos-inc.com>.

Institute for Transformational Psychology (ITP), The Netherlands, Bergen – Training programs for individuals, health care professionals, trainers, and managers in Voice Dialogue, dream work, energetics, psychodrama, group work. A multidisciplinary team led by Robert Stamboliev, trainings in English, French, German and Dutch. Phone: 31-72-581-8008, E-mail: <info@itp-psychology.nl>; Website: <http://archi.nl/it/>.

Latona Consulting, Australia – Foundation Training and Advanced Level Training in Voice Dialogue facilitation – one-year program includes 3 foundation and 2 advanced modules, 30 hrs of individual Voice Dialogue work and 30 hrs of group or individual supervision. Paul Gale-Baker, Robin Gale-Baker, Diana Scambler, trainers/facilitators. Melbourne, 61 (0)3-9459-2927 or 1-800-350-530; E-mail: <latona@ozemail.com.au>; Website: <http://www.ozemail.com.au./~latona>.

Voice Dialogue Connection International, Pacific Palisades, CA. Judith Tamar Stone, Executive Director and developer of Body Dialogue™ offers Level I weeklong intensives and a yearlong on-going training in Voice Dialogue (6 weekends per year) – either of these trainings serves as a prerequisite for Delos Level II. Phone: 310-459-0429; E-mail: <judith@voicedialoguecnx.com>; Website: <http://www.voicedialoguecnx.com>.

Individual trainers

Dassie Hoffman, Voice Dialogue facilitator and teacher, Dance Therapist, MA, ADTR, AMHC, runs a year long training program for facilitators in New York City. Trainings are Level I and a combined Level 2 & 3. The Center For Experiential Psychotherapy; Phone: 212-980-1355; E-mail: <Dassieh@aol.com>.

Francine Pinto, Voice Dialogue teacher and facilitator, B.A., J.D., offers a 12-week facilitation skills training – participants practice facilitating with the support of a supervising staff. Washington, D.C. area; Phone: 703-841-1517; E-mail: <fpinto@bellatlantic.net>

J'aime ona Pangaia, Delos senior staff member, teaches "Level I" week long Voice Dialogue training and leads on-going monthly training groups in Portland Oregon. Teaching since 1985 and travels by request. Phone: 503-788-8060; E-mail: <jonapangai@aol.com>

Judith Hendin, Senior Voice Dialogue facilitator, Somatic (body) Therapist, offers Voice Dialogue facilitation trainings and "Self Behind The Symptom" trainings for health care professionals and therapists. Pennsylvania, phone: 610-330-9778 , E-mail: <JHendin909@aol.com>.

Larry Novick, Ph.D. in Clinical Psychology, offers all levels trainings in Voice Dialogue facilitation, energetics, and the Psychology of the Aware Ego in Los Angeles, CA, and Boulder, CO. Trainings are both short- and long-term, will also travel to teach. Phone: 310-477-0141; E-mail: <Aiki1@earthlink.net>; Website: <http://home.earthlink.net/~aiki1/psyopen.html>.

Martha Lou Wolff, Ph.D., has been teaching Voice Dialogue since 1984 and travels worldwide offering workshops on all levels. Dr. Wolff is based in Southern California and can be reached at 888-726-8575 or E-mail: <marthalou@compuserve.com>.

Miriam Dyak, Delos senior staff member and author of *The Voice Dialogue Facilitator's Handbook*, teaches intermediate and advanced Voice Dialogue facilitation for clinicians and consultants. L.I.F.E. Energy Counseling, Seattle, WA; Phone: 206-932-1151 E-mail: <mdyak@life-energy.net>.

Shakti Gawain, author and workshop leader, conducts weeklong intensives which provide Level I training in Voice Dialogue and a 2-year Steppingstone program which includes Voice Dialogue facilitator training. Trainings are held on Kauai, Hawaii; Phone: 415-388-7195; E-mail: <sg@shaktigawain.com>; Website: <http://www.shaktigawain.com>.

Sindona Casteel, MA Clinical Psychology, MFCC, Delos senior staff member, offers training on all levels, consultations for therapists using Voice Dialogue, and teaches workshops worldwide. Director, Mountains and Rivers Voice Dialogue Center, CA; Phone: 530-265-3766; E-mail: <sindona@oro.net>

The Team

Miriam Dyak is a senior staff instructor at Delos, Inc., the Stones' training center in California. She has been a Voice Dialogue facilitator since 1983. Miriam is also a certified Transformation Game® facilitator and the author of three books of poetry. She has a private practice as a Voice Dialogue facilitator in Seattle, WA, and is available to travel and teach on request.

Suzanne Perot, free-lance artist and architect of Personia, facilitates individuals and groups in "finding a personal language of images that goes beyond words." You can reach her in Sonoma, CA at 1 01-938-3465 or E-mail: zanna@vom.com

Richard Berger and Jamie Streichler, editors extraordinaire. Jamie has set out on an adventure of creating a new life in North Carolina. Richard, who has been working with Voice Dialogue since 1983, is an entrepreneur and an energy work explorer.

Karl Bettinger, our computer wizard, is a Macintosh devotee, Pagemaker/Photoshop wrangler, web designer and hair farmer in Seattle.
karl88@pobox.com

"Richard, really, just one more short chapter to proofread..."

311

How you can contribute to The Handbook

The motivation for writing this Handbook is to support you in meeting the questions and challenges you face as a facilitator. Your feedback, ideas, and suggestions are most welcome, so please feel free to contact us at the address listed below. In addition, for *The Handbook, Part II*, we are actively looking for contributions in the following areas:

♦ Your experiences with and suggestions for using Voice Dialogue on one's own in "self-facilitation."

♦ Your experience using Voice Dialogue with groups.

♦ Your insights about working with Voice Dialogue in fields other than therapy, such as corporate consulting, conflict resolution, the creative arts, etc.

♦ Your success in combining Voice Dialogue with other theoretical systems, personal growth work, healing arts, etc.

♦ What you have discovered about how to present Voice Dialogue work to the public.

♦ What structure, style, and time frame of working has brought you the best results? What advice do you have for someone just starting to facilitate?

Contributions and comments may be sent to:

Miriam Dyak
L.I.F.E. Energy Press
6523 California Avenue SW #193, Seattle, WA 98136
E-mail: <handbook@life-energy.net>
Website: <http://www.life-energy.net>

How to order teaching kits and full color maps of Personia:

Two sections of *The Handbook* are designed for you to use as teaching tools for your clients and/or students – "Picturing the Process: Understanding the selves, awareness, and the Aware Ego," (p. 11), and "The Island of Personia: Mapping your inner selves," (p. 111). You can order a teaching kit that includes a set of ready-to-photocopy text and illustrations from these two mini-chapters plus a full-color, 2 foot by 3 foot poster of The Island of Personia. Kits are $6.95 (US) and extra posters (many students and clients will want their own map) are $5.95 (US) each. You may order both kits and copies of *The Handbook* with a credit card by calling the GP Book Fulfillment Center toll free at 888-265-2732, open 8am to 5pm USA central time, or fax to 1-316-442-9544. To order using check or money order, please call L.I.F.E. Energy Press at 206-932-1151.